$14.95

# HEMP

## *What the World Needs Now*

## John McCabe

Author of
*Sunfood Living*
*Sunfood Traveler*
*Sunfood Diet Infusion*
And *Igniting Your Life*

**Carmania Books**
Santa Monica, California

John McCabe

**Hemp: What the World Needs Now** By John McCabe

## Disclaimer:

This book is meant for information purposes only. How you interpret and utilize the information in this book is your decision. Neither the author nor the publisher will be held accountable for the use or misuse of the information contained in this book. This book is not intended as medical advice because the author and publisher of this work do not recommend the use of chemical drugs or surgery to alleviate health challenges. It also does not stand as legal advice, or suggest that you break any laws. Because of the way people interpret what they read, and take actions based on their own intellect and life situations, which are not in the author's or publisher's and/or distributor's control, there is always some risk involved; therefore, the author, publisher, and/or distributors of this book are not responsible for any adverse effects or consequences from the use of any suggestions, foods, substances, products, procedures, or lifestyles described hereafter.

**ISBN:** 978-1-884702-00-6
**Library of Congress Control Number:** 2010920341
**Dewey CIP:** 677.12.    **OCLC:** 37001480
**First Edition:** 2010

## Books by John McCabe
*Igniting Your Life: Pathways to the Zenith of Health and Success*
*Hemp: What The World Needs Now*
*Sunfood Diet Infusion: Transforming Health Through Raw Food
    Veganism*
*Sunfood Traveler: Guide to Raw Food Culture*
*Sunfood Living: Resource Guide for Global Health*
*Surgery Electives: What to know before the doctor operates*

# Endorsements

"No time has passed when *Cannabis* has not been an integral part of the worldwide fabric of society. John McCabe has pointedly brought hemp's past into the eyes of the future. Understanding where the issues stem from that surround *Cannabis,* both industrial and medicinal, allows us to make the right decisions today for a better, more sustainable conscience tomorrow. It has been with much pride that I was able to share with John an American-Canadian hemp perceptive. Governmental recognition of this viable agricultural fiber and grain crop is plausible and necessary for the growth of the future fabric of today's worldwide society."
– Anndrea M. Hermann, Canadian Hemp Trade Alliance, HempTrade.ca

"In *Hemp: What the World Needs Now*, McCabe assembles a vast collection of source materials to document hemp cannabis' uses throughout history and frames the quotes with discourse on the economic and environmental issues affecting hemp's status as a modern crop.

Importantly, McCabe doesn't avoid the often violate issues of cannabis as a medicine or a recreational herb. Rather than tiptoeing around the tension, he acknowledges that hemp and marijuana are irrevocably intertwined despite the vastly different varietal characteristics of the cannabis plant.

In all, McCabe presents compelling evidence and then steps back – allowing the reader to personally consider the possible outcomes of re-introducing legal hemp agriculture in the United States as well as revising retributional drug policies worldwide."
– Dave Thorvald Olson, Communications Director, HempLobby.org; Author, *Hemp Culture in Japan*; Producer, *HempenRoad*

"John McCabe has written a contemporary and politically relevant book that helps dispel and debunk many of the modern, government-created myths about the cannabis plant."
– Allen St. Pierre, Executive Director, National Organization for the Reform of Marijuana Laws/NORML Foundation, Member, Board of Directors, Washington, DC; norml.org

"A thorough study of the myriad industrial uses for hemp. It raises the question, 'Why is the U.S. missing out?'"
– Oregon NORML

"A very thorough and comprehensive overview of this amazing food, fuel, and fiber plant. I was left with the distinct opinion that our own American hemp history precludes the need for any further research.

Prohibition has many negative facets, but eliminating hemp as an industrial crop for struggling American farmers is one of the most ridiculous. Withholding medical cannabis from patients one of the most sadistic, and imprisoning otherwise innocent citizens for personal cannabis use the most hypocritical, destructive and unfair. This book shines a bright light of truth, exposing the lie that is prohibition."
– Cher Ford-McCullough, President, Women's Organization for National Prohibition Reform; wonpr.org

## Topics

- The history of industrial hemp.
- Laws regulating hemp in the U.S.
- How corrupt politicians and corporate leaders worked together to outlaw hemp farming in the U.S.
- How American farmers are losing out as the U.S. continues to outlaw hemp farming while allowing the importation of hundreds of millions worth of hemp products, including hemp foods, fuel, paper, paints, sealants, building materials, plastics, and fabric.
- Environmental issues relating to forests being cut down to make paper when hemp is a better choice as the world's most sustainable crop.
- Uses of hemp, including for fuel, food, paper, clothing, body care, oil, building materials, fiber, and other products.
- The intertwined relationship between hemp and marijuana.
- The history and laws regarding marijuana, including medicinal marijuana.
- The drug war, the prison industry, and political corruption surrounding the drug trade.
- Marijuana use among various groups and societies throughout history, including artists, musicians, writers, hippies, and shamans.
- Why the U.S. needs to restart its industrial hemp farming industry, as many other countries have done, including Canada and Australia.

# Acknowledgments

I'd like to express my gratitude to the many people who have helped propel this book forward. Among them:

Anndrea Hermann of the Canadian Hemp Trade Alliance. She was graciously helpful with her knowledge and contacts.

Brenda Koplin who copyedited the manuscript.

Daniel Laub who provided detailed notes helpful in preparing the book for publication.

Jenice Gharib of the Southwest Literary Center for information about hippie history.

Alicia Williamson of Oregon NORML who read the manuscript, provided notes, and connected me with some of the people who I interviewed for the book.

Arthur Hanks of The Canadian Hemp Trade Alliance; Allen St. Pierre of NORML.org; Don Wirtshafter of Hempery.com; Dave Wilson of Uncle-Weed.net; and Ralph Bronner of Dr. Bronner's Magic Soaps who all read the manuscript and shared their insight on various aspects of matters relating to hemp.

Every hemp activist must acknowledge the work of Jack Herer who wrote the 1985 book that launched a thousand activists, *The Emperor Wears No Clothes*. He was the person who first made me aware of the hemp issue. See the documentary made about him, *The Emperor of Hemp*, and access his Web site: JackHerer.com.

I'd like to acknowledge all of those working to educate people about hemp and those working to get industrial hemp farming legalized in the U.S. It is only a matter of time before the world wakes up to the importance of the amazing hemp plant.

One day U.S. farmers will be able to grow hemp and our society will take one giant step toward sustainability, cleaner air and water, protecting and restoring the forests, fewer farming chemicals, better nutrition, and healing.

# Table of Contents

# Introduction

I started learning about hemp as a teenager when I met a man named Jack Herer who was promoting hemp at a table set up on the Venice Beach boardwalk.

Little by little as I considered the topic I realized that people knew very little about hemp, and much like marijuana, much of what people did know about hemp was often mythical or a distortion of the truth. Because of this, I figured there was a pretty good possibility that I could write a book about it that could be useful. But my writing of a book about hemp wasn't going to happen overnight.

For some years I very casually and randomly researched the topic of hemp. I took notes, wrote some things, and sometimes interviewed people involved in the hemp industry. At the same time, I learned a lot about marijuana. I sporadically worked on the hemp manuscript with no plan of when to finish the thing. Sometimes I wouldn't touch the manuscript for several months, or more than a year – until something about hemp sparked my interest. Then I would go into another phase of working on the manuscript. I had no plans of focusing on the issue of marijuana, but that is how things worked out.

Meanwhile, Jack Herer published a book about hemp that became a best-seller on the topic. That book is titled *The Emperor Wears No Clothes*.

In the summer of 2006 I realized that my manuscript for the hemp book was nearing a stage where it could be published. It wasn't so much that the book was finished. Because of changes that are being made in laws, the number of people involved with the hemp movement, and the growing worldwide hemp industry, a book on this topic could never be finished. But the manuscript was at a point where it contained enough information that it could serve its purpose, or at least the purpose I want it to have.

In a similar way, a book about marijuana could never be finished. There are so many laws surrounding marijuana being developed or changed, uses and affects of marijuana being discovered, and studies focusing on marijuana being conducted, that the topic is not something that could be completely covered in any one book.

My manuscript reached a point to where it had the capability of doing what I intended it to do: to help bring people out of the dark ages about hemp, clear up rumors, dispel myths, bring people up to speed with what hemp is about, and help propel actions to legalize industrial hemp farming and a self-sustaining hemp market in the U.S.

I also knew the book contained more information about marijuana than most people knew or considered.

I found out about marijuana as a teenager. Before I knew what it was, I knew its smell. I knew that the smell was something that happened when certain people who were older than me got together. But I didn't know what the smell was. One day I was riding around with my friend, Gary, and we smelled that smell. Gary mentioned that the people in the nearby woods were getting high. I didn't know what the term "high" meant, and I didn't know that the smell had to do with what he was speaking of. I mentioned that the smell we were smelling was something that I often smelled coming out of my brother's bedroom. Gary explained to me that what I was smelling was marijuana, and that my brothers were getting "stoned." This to me was far beyond my understanding. I was naïve and innocent and also full of curiosity.

In a matter of weeks after my conversation with Gary, I gained an understanding of the marijuana plant in a way that most teenagers get to understand it: I smoked it with some friends.

I didn't feel that marijuana was a big deal. It made me feel a little funny, made me laugh, and made me want to be active, such as by riding my bike, playing Frisbee, swimming, or simply running. I also learned that it was interesting to paint or draw after smoking it, and that it made sounds and visuals more interesting in ways I had not experienced. It also made me laugh, which wasn't something I did a lot of as a child. It made me talkative, which was also not something that was common for me. I also knew that I needed to keep it a secret from the adults. I also realized that at least one of my brothers, all of whom I barely communicated with, was selling it to other teenagers.

Even so, I didn't smoke much marijuana. While other children seemed to want it every weekend, and sometimes more often, I wasn't much interested in being a "stoner." Anything I could do stoned, I could do straight.

While marijuana seemed to heighten my creativity and senses, and made me more open and less introverted, it wasn't something that became a part of my everyday activity. I did do the typical teenage things common among teenagers in the U.S., such as smoking a little weed, drinking a little beer, and making out with girls, I also didn't have money to support any type of regular use of marijuana, or beer. Nor did I like beer, or any other type of alcohol (which is a blessing, considering I am from a family with a long history of alcoholism [but not drug abuse]).

As I write this sentence, citizens of the state of California are one-week away from voting on Proposition 19, which would decide whether or not to legalize the taxed sale of marijuana.

Proposition 19 was initiated by Richard Lee, founder of the Oakland-based marijuana-growers trade school, Oaksterdam University. Lee largely financed the signature drive to get the measure on the ballot. It initiative needed 433,971 signatures to make it onto the ballot. There were 694,248 people who signed the initiative.

Even if the state voters approve the taxed sale of marijuana on the open market, they will also have to deal with the federal laws. The federal government has not given any indication of wanting to legalize the open taxed sale of marijuana. Instead, the federal government has indicated that they will treat marijuana the same no matter how California votes, and that is: it will continue to be a substance that is illegal to grow, sell, own, transport, smoke, or share. Under the U.S. federal Controlled Substances Act, marijuana is listed as a Schedule 1 drug, meaning it is of no use and is illegal for any reason.

Now, it is two weeks after I wrote that past paragraph. California voters rejected the Proposition 19 ballot measure that would have allowed adults in the sate to grow small amounts of marijuana in up to a 25-square-foot garden plot, and they would be able to purchase marijuana as a taxed product in the municipalities that approved sales within their borders. California's 58 counties and over 478 towns and cities would have been able to ban the sale of marijuana within their borders, or permit and tax marijuana sales, and add additional fees as they saw fit – such as excise taxes on growers and retailers.

Proposition 19 was defeated by fifty-three percent. This was the second time California voters rejected the legalization of marijuana. In 1972 there was a similar measure named Proposition 19 on the California ballot. Two-thirds of voters rejected the earlier Proposition 19.

While Proposition 19 may have presented problems with taxation and how each county, town, and city could go about deciding whether or not to permit sales, and how to go about taxing sales, and so forth, it would have been a major step toward legalizing marijuana for personal recreational use just as the state had earlier approved marijuana use for medicinal use. What it wouldn't have done is automatically created a surge in taxable marijuana sales overnight. It would have at least taken many months, and likely several years to form some semblance of a workable sort of taxable marijuana market. The way the measure was written may have also been so problematic in execution of the law that a large amount of the tax revenue could have been consumed by all of the different rules and regulations and administrative procedures and paperwork taking place in each county, city and town. Certainly, there is a better way to manage the taxation of marijuana than what was contained in Proposition 19.

Largely, the older population voted against it. That is one sign that it is only a matter of time before voters will be approving such a measure. California voters approved medicinal marijuana by passing Proposition 215, the Compassionate Use Act of 1996, which permits residents with prescriptions to purchase or grow marijuana for health-related issues.

Eventually, it would likely take a bill written in a way that would streamline state-wide taxable sales of marijuana, and likely one that would allow marijuana businesses to be handled like those that serve and/or serve alcohol.

As I write this, there are billions of dollars being spent every year to keep people in jails and prisons because they have been arrested for possessing, growing, selling, smoking, and or sharing marijuana. This is so even though the laws have not slowed the marijuana market. In fact, anyone who really wants marijuana can get it. Marijuana is so easy to obtain in the U.S., and many people are so free with their use of it, that it should be very clear that the laws having to do with the control and use of it never worked, and can't work, and they result in the waste of billions of dollars every year – money that should go to other things that will truly benefit humanity, such as the protection of the environment, the development of a legal hemp farming industry, and better education of young people to live more sustainable lifestyles.

> "I think it's time for a debate. And I think that we ought to study very carefully what other countries are doing that have legalized marijuana and other drugs, what effect it had on those countries, and are they happy with that decision."
> – Arnold Schwarzenegger, May 2010

In 2010, California governor Arnold Schwarzenegger signed California SB 1449, which lowered the fine for under an ounce of marijuana to $100, similar to the cost of some traffic tickets. A week after Proposition 19 was defeated, in November 2010 Schwarzenegger was on the Jay Leno show. When asked about the marijuana issue, he said that nobody cares if you smoke a joint, but he added that the recently defeated measure to legalize the taxation of marijuana would have gone too far. I disagree.

One of the main issues of concern in California for many years has been the state budget. In November 2010, the California budget deficit for the following year was $25.4 billion. Legalizing the taxation and sale of marijuana to adults would both bring in money to the cash-strapped state, and decrease the amount of money the state spends on law enforcement trying to enforce the corrupt laws. It would also cut the cost of running jails, prisons, and the courts, which have to deal with all of the thousands of people arrested for breaking the crazy marijuana laws.

A Cato Institute study estimated that Proposition 19 would have saved the state $960 million in law enforcement expenses and would bring in $352 million in tax revenue. A state that is struggling with budget issues, and

13

especially one that spends more money on jails and prisons than on higher education, would greatly benefit by having an additional $1,312 billion. But, the state keeps cutting funding from childhood education, social services, infrastructure maintenance, and so forth.

The week after Proposition 19 was defeated, because of the state budget cuts, the California State University Board of Trustees approved a 15% tuition hike for undergraduate programs in the 23-campus Cal State university system. Protestors outside the meeting included students, staff, and faculty. It had only been a year since tuitions were increase 32% - the same year that, according to the California Department of Corrections and Rehabilitation, the state was imprisoning 1,639 people strictly for time sentenced after breaking marijuana laws. Many more people who were serving time for various crimes had at least part of their sentence related to breaking marijuana laws – including those who were sentenced for life.

> "Pursuing these cases is a burden on the system, people's lives are ruined. In some cases, California's third-strike rule has sent people to jail for life for felony possession of marijuana."
> – Bruce Margolin, attorney famous for representing those busted for breaking marijuana cases in California

The California State Board of Equalization estimated that earlier efforts by Assembly Member Tom Ammiano to legalize marijuana sales, bills that died in assembly, would have brought in $1.382 billion.

People have been critical that Proposition 19 would have cut the need for so many law enforcement and court personnel that it wouldn't be a good thing for the unemployment rates in a state that already has high unemployment. The Cato Institute study concluded that the passage of Proposition 19 would have resulted in job cuts to police officers, prosecutors, judges, prison guards, and office and police department, jail, and prison facility personnel. But, if so many otherwise employed and tax-paying citizens are being arrested, prosecuted, and jailed or imprisoned, and some are being killed, for breaking laws that should not exist, and the people serving time are having their lives ruined by these laws, often placing families on welfare, children in foster care, and so forth, why would we want to keep the laws in existence? What is right about spending billions of dollars on a corrupt system?

Even if the legalization of marijuana does not result in increased tax revenue, the laws should still change. And they should change simply because they are wrong, and they damage the lives of innocent citizens.

Is this controversial? Or, is it stuff that we should be discussing?

Publishers interested in the book wanted me to shorten it, to cut out the controversial parts, and to simply focus on the environmental benefits hemp can provide. However, I saw no need to keep people ignorant about the history of hemp and how it is tangled up in the drug war, nor did I feel the need to remove the parts of the manuscript that the publishers thought were controversial: the overview of the drug war and the political corruption that keeps creating it.

As the economic downturn of 2008 set in, then deepened in 2009, many publishing companies limited the number of books they were publishing, some stopped acquiring new titles, and others simply put all newly acquired manuscripts on hold while eliminating some of their staff positions. During 2009, bookstores were closing by the hundreds.

With the problems facing the publishing industry, I wasn't sure when the hemp book was going to be published. In early 2010, the printed hemp book became a reality. Unfortunately, it couldn't be printed on hemp paper, because the U.S. government makes that financially impossible for U.S. publishers.

Even as I write this there are changes happening in the world of hemp, and in relation to marijuana in ways that I can't read up on all of the information being published. However, it is clear that more and more people are able to see through the decades of lies told about both hemp and marijuana, and more people are ready to make changes to laws governing both hemp and marijuana – and especially in ways that aim for the legalization of industrial hemp farming and the taxable sale of marijuana to adult consumers.

A number of Web sites and magazines are reporting on both hemp and marijuana issues. VoteHemp.com, which is the largest organization working to legalize industrial hemp farming in the U.S. is sending out very informative enewesletters regarding the various issues relating to hemp, its uses, laws governing it, and advances in bringing it back into everyday industrial use to replace toxic materials.

A whole lot of magazines are covering the issues relating to marijuana. Many cities now have their own marijuana magazine, and some states have one or more locally published marijuana magazines. Also, the Oaksterdam school that teaches how to grow and sell marijuana for medicinal marijuana clubs continues to expand its curriculum, has opened a network of schools, and is accepting more and more students wanting to learn the business of marijuana. Also, there are a variety of stores that are selling supplies for those involved in growing marijuana. These stores operate in the open, and are often located in common shopping districts in large cities, and in some small towns.

It is very obvious that many millions of Americans are growing marijuana, and a whole lot more are smoking it. And the city, county, state, and federal law enforcement personnel keep arresting people for breaking

15

marijuana laws – even though the majority of Americans think it is a waste of tax dollars.

When people are arrested for breaking marijuana laws, it instantly puts into play a number of expensive processes, including booking the prisoner, preparing paperwork for the prosecution, dealing with what level of offense the person committed, and going through the process of deciding what needs to be done with the person: jail, prison, probation, drug rehab, or a variety of all of those. Their families may became financially strained in dealing with legal matters and with losing a working member of the family, and their children and other family members may become more reliant on the government, such as through welfare, food stamps, child protective services, social work, foster care programs, and other expensive government services that otherwise would have never been spending time and money on the arrested person's family. By factoring all of these things, it should be clear that the marijuana laws are more damaging to society than simply allowing an adult to purchase taxed marijuana whenever they wish to enjoy the substance in the privacy of their home.

In January 2007 the state of North Dakota began offering "hemp gro-wers license applications." In April 2007 the North Dakota legislature passed Hemp Bill 1020, deciding that state-licensed industrial hemp farmers would no longer be required to carry Drug Enforcement Administration lic-enses. But the state also acknowledged that it could not protect farmers who decide to grow hemp from being prosecuted under federal drug laws. In 2008, the state of Vermont legalized industrial hemp farming. And, so far, as of the writing of this marijuana book in 2010, no farmers in North Dakota, or anywhere else in the U.S., have begun to grow hemp.

> "With the broad authority that has been granted to them by Congress, the DEA could have easily approved the applications of the farmers in North Dakota. The DEA could have also easily negotiated industrial hemp farming rules with North Dakota Agriculture Commissioner Roger Johnson who has been talking to them about this for a year. Instead, they kept stalling until the time to plant had passed. North Dakota had nothing left to do but cut the DEA out of the picture."
> – Tom Murphy, National Outreach Coordinator for Vote Hemp, April 30, 2007

> "I applied for my North Dakota license in January and was hopeful the DEA would act quickly and affirm my right to plant industrial hemp this year. Unfortunately, the DEA has not responded in any way other than to state that it would take them a

lot more time than the window of time I have to import seed and plant the crop. It appears that DEA really doesn't want to work with anyone to resolve the issue."
– Farmer and North Dakota Republican state representative, David Monson, April 2007

The reason North Dakota has been trying to work with the Drug Enforcement Administration (DEA) on this issue of allowing farmers to grow industrial hemp (which, let me remind you, cannot get a person high if they smoke or eat it) is that, as I explain in detail later in the book, hemp has been classified as a drug since the Nixon administration, even though hemp can't get a person high.

The DEA has been granted authority by Congress to interpret the statutes of the United States Code, such as the Controlled Substance Act, including rescheduling controlled substances and determining the rules and regulations of the substances.

Under the Administrative Procedures Act (5USC 536), the DEA could negotiate industrial hemp farming rules with the states. But the DEA has been refusing to do so. Not only that, but those working for the DEA have made statements confusing the issue, either because they want it that way, or because they are ignorant as to the power the DEA holds (which is not likely).

When it is taken into consideration how much control certain industries have over U.S. legislation and governmental procedures, including those that rule over which substances are controlled by various laws and regulations, it is easy to understand how U.S. government workers may be working to keep both industrial hemp farming and the cultivation, control, and use of marijuana under the old laws – which benefit certain corporations and industries, such as the prison industry, the petroleum industry, the corn industry, the textile and paper industries, and other certain industries that perceive financial benefit in keeping both marijuana and hemp illegal. I write more about this government and corporate corruption in the following chapters.

When North Dakota was trying to negotiate with the DEA to allow farmers in that state to grow industrial hemp, a special agent with the DEA, Steve Robertson, was quoted in the *Grand Forks Herald* saying, "The DEA does not have the authority to change existing federal law… It's very simple for us: the law is there and we enforce the law… we are law enforcement, not lawmakers." The lobbying group, Vote Hemp, responded with a press release explaining that, yes, the DEA does have the authority over the laws regulating hemp. Vote Hemp's National Outreach Coordinator, Tom Murphy, was quoted as saying, "It's interesting that Special Agent Robertson pretends that the DEA is purely a law enforcement entity, as they are not."

"The legislative action is a direct response to the DEA's refusal to waive registration requirements, including $3,440 per farmer in nonrefundable yearly application fees, and the agency's inability to respond to the farmers' federal applications in time for spring planting.

The North Dakota legislature's bold action gives Vote Hemp the opportunity we've been working towards for nearly a decade. Now that there is a state with comprehensive hemp farming regulations that has explicitly eschewed DEA involvement, we can finally make the case that states have the legal ability to regulate industrial hemp farming within their borders without federal interference. And, because ND Agriculture Commissioner Roger Johnson actually did spend nearly a year trying to work out an agreement with the DEA, it's clear that DEA isn't going to act in a reasonable way and isn't ever to going to acknowledge the practical differences between industrial hemp and marijuana and accommodate ND's plan to commercialize hemp farming."
– Alexis Baden-Mayer, Vote Hemp's Legislative Director, April 2007

North Dakota is a major producer of flax oil, sunflower oil, and canola oil. Allowing hemp to be grown in that state would mean the local economy would benefit from producing hemp seed oil, hemp seed nutrition powders, and other hemp products, including hemp fiberboard, hemp fabric, hemp for insulation, and hemp pulp for paper mills. Allowing another crop to be grown would also help preserve farmland in that state, protect forests, make the communities more sustainable, protect the water sources, improve the environment, localize economies, and provide jobs.

North Dakota borders a region of Canada where hemp is legally growing on Canadian farms. Many of the hemp products imported from Canada into the U.S. are brought through North Dakota. It is frustrating for farmers in North Dakota to see this taking place: Canadian farmers profiting in the U.S. in ways that U.S. farmers can't.

What kind of government is it that suppresses the economic possibilities of its citizens, especially in a way in which the people's livelihood and environment would both improve if a simple crop were permitted to be grown on farms by hardworking people who can use the work, money, and materials?

"American farmers look across the border in Canada, which exports hemp fiber to the U.S., and ask, 'why can't we grow it?'"

– Jeffrey W. Gain, former CEO of both the National Corn Growers and American Soybean Association

In July 2007, Ruth's Hemp Foods, a Canadian company, began producing a nutritional food bar, the "red, white, and blueberry" Vote Hemp Bar, which is sold with the intent of helping to fund the legal costs of farmers Dave Monson and Wayne Hauge in their lawsuit filed on June 18, 2007, against the U.S. Drug Enforcement Administration.

"The United States government should get past all the drug association rhetoric and take a clear-eyed look at low-THC industrial hemp for its many valuable assets, including its being a healthy, nutrient-dense food. And, as a bonus, it is a very low-impact, environmentally-friendly crop… It's time to give U.S. farmers the freedom to choose a crop that, in Canada and elsewhere, has proven to be an environmentally-friendly and economically-viable crop."
– Ruth Shamai of Ruth's Hemp Foods, July 2007

In the last several decades the U.S. has lost thousands of square miles of farmland to "land development" in the form of suburbs, shopping centers, factories, office complexes, golf courses, entertainment complexes, parking lots, parking garages, malls, and roads and highways. Allowing farmers nationwide to grow a new crop would increase the income of farmers and raise the value of farmland nationwide. As I explain later in the book, it would also improve the environment, protect wildlife, preserve forests, improve the quality of water, soil, and air, and fully help transform communities to become more sustainable.

Because hemp could be used to make oil (from the hemp seeds) that is excellent for running diesel engines, growing hemp for seed in the U.S. would help to cut down on petroleum use, lower the amount of petroleum being imported from distant countries, decrease pollution, prevent damage to the planet from oil drilling, reduce the chances of massive petroleum disasters, such as what happened in the Gulf of Mexico in the spring, summer, and autumn of 2010 (a disaster that will keep playing out for many years), help the country to be self-reliant, and simply improve the conditions for humanity and wildlife.

Because hemp cellulose could be used to make ethanol, which runs gasoline engines, legalizing industrial hemp farming in the U.S. would benefit the country, people, and environment in the same ways that using hemp seed oil for diesel engines would do.

Because hemp fiber can be used for insulation, growing it to insulate buildings and homes would decrease energy use, save people money, improve the environment, and help the country to be more self-reliant.

Because hemp pulp can be used to make paper, growing hemp can help preserve and protect forests and the wildlife dependant on them. It would also improve air quality as an acre of hemp absorbs more air pollution and puts forth more oxygen than an acre of trees.

But, I am getting ahead of myself. I will cover all of these issues more thoroughly in the following chapters.

> "There are numerous environmental advantages to hemp. Hemp often requires less energy to manufacture into products. It is less toxic to process. And it is easier to recycle and more biodegradable than most competing crops and products. Unfortunately, we won't realize the full economic and environmental benefits of hemp until the crop is legal in the United States."
> – Skaidra Smith-Heisters, policy analyst, Reason Foundation; reason.org

On February 13, 2007, Republican Representative Dr. Ron Paul of Texas introduced the Industrial Hemp Farming Act of 2007 to Congress. In the first half of 2007 there were 11 states that had industrial hemp farming bills introduced. These included California, Hawaii, Idaho, Minnesota, New Hampshire, New Mexico, North Dakota, Oregon, South Carolina, Vermont, and Wisconsin. None of these resulted in getting industrial hemp farming legalized in the U.S. – because the federal government refuses to change.

The federal government's refusal to allow the free market of industrial hemp farming in the U.S. should be considered criminal. Especially when it is taken into consideration that there are great benefits to be had by allowing U.S. farmers to freely grow industrial hemp.

On March 5, 2007, New Mexico lawmakers voted 59 to 2 to study legalizing hemp farming in that state. The vote authorized an "in-depth economic analysis to address the benefits of a legal hemp industry in New Mexico and the long-term impacts of establishing proper permitting and licensing procedures." A goal of the study was "to determine the costs and benefits associated with encouraging economic development in various areas, including textiles, pulping products for paper, biocomposites and building materials, animal bedding, nutritional products for livestock, industries related to seed extraction and resins for potential biofuels, lubricants, paints and inks, cosmetics, body care products, and nutritional supplements." The vote encouraged the U.S. Congress "to recognize industrial hemp as a valuable agricultural commodity, to define industrial hemp in federal law as a nonpsychoactive and genetically identifiable species of the genus Cannabis, and acknowledge that allowing and encouraging farmers to produce industrial hemp will improve the balance of trade by promoting domestic sources of industrial hemp and [that hemp] can make a positive contribution to the issues of global climate change and carbon sequestration [through, among other things, producing ethanol from hemp to fuel gasoline engines, and oil from hemp seed to fuel diesel engines]."

"The legislature has spoken saying that New Mexico lawmakers are on-board in support of industrial hemp farming, and encouraging our scientists and educators to look at the subject without fear of retribution by law enforcement or negative conventional wisdom. All of the benefits of hemp can now be explored in a legal forum. This will give people all over the country the ability to approach the federal Drug Enforcement Authority to demand that industrial hemp be removed from their schedule of narcotic drugs and be allowed to once again become one of our major cash crops in the United States."
 – Attorney John McCall of Albuquerque, New Mexico, March 2007

What many people don't know is that both hemp and marijuana were once legal substances in the U.S. They also were used for many marketable materials, including fabric, paper, fuel, food, oil, and medicine. But, because certain industries wanted hemp and marijuana made illegal so that those industries, including the petroleum and pharmaceutical industries, could cash in.

The way the European and British people got to what we now call the American Continent was by sailing on ships that had sails and rope made out of hemp grown in Europe and Britain. The way the people living on what is now known as the American Continent became more independent from rulers on the other side of the Atlantic was because the land on the American continent is perfect for growing hemp. Once the American settlements developed their own hemp farms and began making their own hemp fabric, paper, fuel, and oil, it helped set the stage for the American residents to detach from British and European governments.

Then, as I explain in the following chapters, various industries began meddling in politics to make laws that would allow those industries to make more money. One industry that wanted hemp out of the picture was the petroleum industry, so that hemp seed oil would not be available for diesel engines, and hemp cellulose ethanol would not be available for gasoline engines. As I explain in the book, it was in the 1930s that hemp farming and marijuana became illegal in the U.S. And that helped to fuel the market for petroleum gasoline and diesel oil.

Outlawing hemp farming in the U.S. starting in the 1930s was one of the worst moves the U.S. government took, and the result is a world polluted with petroleum, forests being clear cut for paper and wood (hemp can be used to make fiber board that is four-times stronger than plywood made from trees), and the great expansion of the cotton industry (which is a very water and farming intensive crop that is damaging to the land and surrounding environment).

By keeping hemp farming illegal, it has also helped the dramatic expansion of the corn ethanol industry. Hemp provides a better quality ethanol than corn, and is only one plant that can be used to make cellulosic ethanol (another crop is common landscape and lawn clippings – lawns are the number one cultivated crop in North America, and most of it ends up in landfills when it would be better to use it for industrial uses, such as for making ethanol).

The U.S. hemp farming industry was briefly revived in the early 1940s, and then suddenly halted a few years later when the government ended its *Hemp for Victory* program to supply hemp fiber and oil to the U.S. military – which used the hemp fiber to make ropes, towels, uniforms, tents, parachutes, and shoes. The U.S. military also used hemp oil for machinery. That is one part of American history that many people do not know of, and do not understand: that the U.S. encouraged farmers to grow hemp during WWII to provide the military with hemp materials.

Because the U.S. government has stupidly classified hemp as a drug, it has been a fight to get the Drug Enforcement Administration to allow hemp farming to proceed. But if things work out, the approval for indus-trial hemp farming may be granted and fields of hemp may be growing within the U.S. within several years.

If the procession of changes to marijuana laws on local levels continues to allow the adult use o marijuana, it may only be a matter of a few years before marijuana will be treated like alcohol in the U.S., which is that it will be sold to adults, and taxed.

Or not.

Even so, as hemp farming remains illegal in its borders, the U.S. is the world's largest consumer of industrial hemp products – all of which are im-ported from countries where hemp farming is legal.

From 2005 to 2010 the imported hemp products industry in the U.S. has increased by more than 50 percent. With that in mind, it is clear to understand how much revenue U.S. farmers are missing out on – because the money is going to farmers in foreign countries – while U.S. farmers continue to struggle.

It is my hope that this book could play some role in bringing hemp into the modern age, and in changing marijuana laws to make them more realistic in ways that the billions of dollars currently used to control marijuana are freed up and either saved or used to improve society — such as by protecting and improving the environment.

# Your Tax Dollars at Work

> "American farmers are prohibited by law from growing a low-input
> sustainable crop common in Europe and Canada with tremendous
> economic potential: industrial hemp."
> – Hemp Industries Association, HIA.org

A lot of times marijuana and industrial hemp are treated as one and the same, although there are very many differences. It seems that an educated society would not allow the types of things that have been going on in relation to hemp to continue, especially in a country where the mistreatment of native peoples runs so deep that it continues to be an open wound.

In early May 2000, as permitted under Oglala Sioux Tribal Law, the White Plume family of the Pine Ridge Reservation in South Dakota planted a one-and-a-half-acre field of industrial hemp along the Wounded Knee Creek. The hemp was being grown for the purpose of making fabric and other products for the tribe.

On August 24, 2000 the U.S. Drug Enforcement Administration (DEA) raided the reservation using 25 federal agents wearing bulletproof vests and carrying semiautomatic rifles. The agents surrounded the field as one helicopter and two small-engine planes flew overhead. The field of hemp, which was nearing its harvest stage, was plowed under. The agents left. Nobody was arrested.

What good did that do? How much money did that raid cost? And, why would anyone rationalize doing such a thing?

In 2001 the White Plume Family planted another field of hemp crop. On July 30, 2001 armed federal agents once again raided the land and destroyed the crop. Nobody was arrested.

> "As I stood there and watched, a helicopter would hover above.
> And the hemp plants were so tall, they would wave back and forth and
> knock those agents around a little bit you know. I seen that, and I said
> alright, they're fighting."
> – Alex White Plume

Under the Fort Laramie Treaty of 1868 the tribe is allowed to engage in agriculture and retains the right to grow fiber and food crops.

Why did the DEA invade sovereign reservation land to destroy the industrial hemp crop of these hard-working people two years I a row? This question is explored in the 2007 documentary *Standing Silent Nation* that was broadcast on public television in the U.S. on July 3, 2007. Among the

24

people interviewed in the documentary is James Woolsey, former director of the Central Intelligence Agency (CIA). Woolsey believes industrial hemp farming needs to be legalized in the U.S. to help farmers and to protect the environment. DVD copies of the documentary are available through VoteHemp.com. (Access: StandingSilentNation.com.)

Today, like millions of other people in the U.S., you can go to your local natural foods store and purchase hemp chips, hemp food bars, dehulled hemp seeds, hemp bread, hemp salad dressing, hemp waffles, hemp tortillas, hemp shampoo, hemp conditioner, hemp lip balm, hemp body lotion, crunchy hempseed chocolate bars, hemp nutritional powder, hemp oil, and reusable hemp shopping bags.

Stopping by other stores, you can buy hemp fabric rugs, hemp furniture, hemp pillows, hemp shower curtains, hemp drapes, hemp mops, hemp dinner napkins, hemp tablecloths, hemp table runners, hemp shirts, hemp pants, hemp ties, hemp socks, hemp jackets, hemp hats, hemp yoga mats, hemp backpacks, hemp wallets, hemp purses, and hemp shoes.

At new-car lots you can purchase cars that have hemp fiber used in door panels, dashboards, insulation, and other parts. Some new cars have upholstery and carpeting that is a blend of hemp and other materials.

At artist supply stores you can purchase hemp canvas to paint on. Some of the oil paints you purchase may contain hemp oil. Hemp linen has been used for thousands of years as an artist's canvas. Rembrandt, Picasso, Gainsborough, and Van Gogh painted on hemp. Many painters are once again painting on hemp canvas as they have found that it is more durable than canvas made of cotton.

At office supply stores you can purchase paper and envelopes made with a percentage of hemp pulp.

Music bands and performers including The Red Hot Chili Peppers, Jackson Browne, and the Foo Fighters have used hemp-blend paper for CD inserts. The paper was supplied by the Living Tree Paper Co. of Eugene, Oregon.

All of the hemp products you can purchase in the U.S. contain hemp materials that have been imported from other countries. Even though there are millions of dollars of hemp products sold in the U.S. every year, none of it is grown by U.S. farmers – because they aren't permitted to grow it. The situation is absurd and tragic. I believe it is also criminal on the part of the government, which is acting out of the interests of corporations, and not working to help the people.

"The bark of the hemp stalk contains bast fibers which are among Earth's longest natural soft fibers and are also rich in cellulose; the cellulose and hemp-cellulose in its inner woody core are called hurds.

25

Hemp stalk is not psychoactive. Hemp fiber is longer, stronger, more absorbent, and more insulative than cotton fiber."
– Hemp Industries Association, 2006; TheHIA.org

In the future there likely will be cellulosic ethanol made from hemp as well as hemp oil diesel fuel. These fuels burn cleaner than petroleum gasoline and diesel. Using more environmentally safe fuels greatly reduces the amount of lung damaging particulates that result from burning fossil fuels. Hemp ethanol and biodiesel also do not emit the cancer-causing polycyclic aromatic hydrocarbons (PAHs) and benzene found in petroleum exhaust. Hemp fuels also don't contribute to acid rain.

The whole world has become the site of the largest oil spill and environmental disaster ever, but it is in the atmosphere and being absorbed into the landscape, rivers, lakes, and oceans. It is the result of burning hundreds of billions of gallons of petroleum, and using enormous amounts of coal, tar sands, oil shale, and natural gas every year to fuel cars, motorcycles, trucks, trains, planes, boats, ships, and equipment.

Hemp plants grow densely, absorb air pollution, and are an excellent source of oxygen. Cellulosic ethanol can meet the demands of ethanol where limited starch ethanol (corn) leaves off. The Energy Policy Act of 2005 provides the requirement that the U.S. should be deriving 7.5 billion gallons of ethanol by 2012 from any feedstock. This can and should include hemp, and it should include ethanol made with landscape clippings.

Another plant that can be used for cellulosic ethanol is arundo donax, which is grass that is also known as "giant reed." This plant grows as much as two feet per week and produces more biomass per acre than hemp, and more than any other crop. But, giant reed is considered an invasive weed that is overtaking land in the western states, and farmers would not welcome it being introduced into their region. Other crops that can create more biomass per acre include corn, kenaf, and sugar cane.

The benefit of hemp is that it provides a wide variety of uses. More products can be made using hemp and its various parts and extracts than any other plant.

The Energy Policy Pact also requires the production of 250 million gallons of cellulosic ethanol, which excludes corn, beets, sugar cane, etc. (starch or sugar ethanol). But this can include hemp ethanol as well as ethanol made from the number-one crop produced in North America: landscape clippings – which can be collected from neighborhoods, schools, sporting facilities, and other places that produce lawn clippings.

A friend asked me how we could go about collecting all of those landscape clippings. I told him that we are already collecting huge amounts of it, and we are doing it with trash trucks that treat it like it is worthless, and that haul it to landfills and other trash dumps. Instead of landfills, the landscape clippings could be taken to biorefineries to make cellulosic ethanol.

While current ethanol production is still a relatively small industry compared to petroleum, it continues to grow. As it grows, it is facing problems of its own, including how much water and fuel it takes to produce the ethanol. As alternative fuel technology continues to advance, it is likely that ethanol production will become less fuel intensive. But, there is the issue of how much water it uses, and that can be a problem.

Even if a hemp fuel industry never develops, it is clear that U.S. farmers are missing out on hundreds of millions of dollars that they could be making from industrial hemp farming. According to VoteHemp.com, over $350 million worth of hemp products were sold in the U.S. during 2007. Canadian hemp farmers are shipping hemp food products (oil, protein powder, milk, nutrition bars, cereal, chips, and even dairy-free hemp cheese) to over 15 countries. Manitoba Harvest, a Canadian company that makes hemp food products, has seen its three flavors of hemp milk (vanilla, chocolate, and plain), quickly become popular in natural foods stores across the U.S. Hemp milk now competes with sales of soy and other non-dairy milk products. Hemp Oil Canada, which makes other hemp food products, experienced a surge in sales of over 40% during 2007. Hemp companies are among the fastest growing companies in Canada.

As mentioned, U.S. farmers can't grow hemp. If they did they would risk arrest and ex-pensive legal battles. That is the reality still facing those who wish to start up a U.S. industrial hemp farming industry in 2010. It should not be reality.

In Canada, just north of the U.S. border, industrial hemp farming was legalized in 1998. Farmers there are legally growing thousands of acres of hemp. In 2010 Canadian farmers grew an estimated 25,000 acres of hemp.

The European Union has provided subsidies to industrial hemp farmers since the 1990s.

The U.S. not only doesn't allow hemp to be grown, it subsidizes crops that would compete with and that are environmentally inferior to hemp. These subsidized crops include corn, soy, cotton, and forestry (paper and plywood). The U.S. also provides tax subsidies to the petroleum industry. The U.S. even provides hundreds of millions of dollars in tax subsidies to the tobacco industry, which is clearly a crop that is ruinous to people's lives.

Why can't farmers in the U.S. grow hemp?

Keep reading, and decide for yourself.

"California farmers are missing out on a multimillion-dollar market that already exists in California.

Hundreds of hemp products are made right here in California, but manufacturers are forced to import hemp seed, oil, and fiber from other countries. This measure will allow California to lead the way in tapping into a $270 million industry that's growing by $26 million each year."

– California's Democratic Assemblyman Mark Leno, co-author of bill, AB1147, which would have been a step toward allowing California farmers to grow hemp, June 2006. Governor Arnold Schwarzenegger later vetoed it. It was reintroduced in 2007, and never made it into law.

For thousands of years hemp was the most common plant grown for industrial uses. It is believed that hemp was brought from Asia into Greece by the Scythians, who are also credited with bringing it into Russia and Europe. It is believed that Arabs brought hemp into the Mediterranean port towns. By the Middle Ages hemp farming was well established in Europe and the fiber and seed of the crop was used to make fabric, paper, food, fuel, and shelter.

But today, U.S. farmers can't legally grow hemp. Native Americans can't legally grow it on reservations. If you plant five seeds you are committing a felony. Some of the founders and first presidents of the U.S. grew hemp on their farms. Today they would be arrested.

On June 1, 1996, actor and hemp activist Woody Harrelson challenged the legislation keeping industrial hemp farming illegal in the U.S. It was the day he planted four hemp seeds on his property in Lee County, Kentucky. Arrested on a misdemeanor, Harrelson was entangled in legal issues that lasted four years. Harrelson and his legal counsel argued that it was unconstitutional to prohibit the growing of hemp. Harrelson's attorney was former judge and Republican Governor Louis B. Nunn. Harrelson rejected the prosecutor's plea bargain of a five-hundred-dollar fine and one month in jail. The day he appeared in court to hear the jury's decision Harrelson wore a suit made of hemp fabric. The jury ruled that Harrelson was not guilty. The money spent on prosecuting Harrelson was clearly a waste, and the case stands as another example of how pathetic the laws are that keep hemp farming illegal.

"Now it is time to start promoting the growth of hemp so we can have a great economic future in Kentucky. We need to educate people about the distinction between marijuana and hemp."
– Louis B. Nunn, attorney for Woody Harrelson

And so, today the U.S. federal law still prevents the growing of industrial hemp because hemp is considered to be a drug – even though it isn't. The laws are mixed up with laws governing a sister plant commonly known as *marijuana*.

28

# A Little Bit of History

Marijuana has been known by the name *marijuana* in the U.S. only since the 1920s. There are many ideas of where the name originated, but the story that a cannabis smoker in Pancho Villa's army was a female soldier named Mary seems as likely to be true as a number of other stories. Mexicans also called the plant *mota*. Before the 1920s marijuana was known as *cannabis* and sometimes as *hemp*. Although the hemp plant is a member of the cannabis family, the word *cannabis* is now typically associated with the variety of the plant with psychoactive properties: what we also call *marijuana, dank, reefer, bud, tea, chronic, pot, ganja, weed, indigo, sense, locoweed, Mary, Mary Jane, skunk, herb, jive, muggles,* and other names, including the ancient Chinese name for it, *ma*, and the African name for it, *dada*.

The name *hemp* is now most commonly used for the plant that contains only trace amounts of the psychoactive substance (tetrahydrocannabinol [THC]) and is grown for industrial uses (oil, fabric, paper, fiber, food, etc.).

As Martin Booth explains in his excellent book, *Cannabis: A History*, the plant was given the botanical name of *Cannabis sativa* by a Swedish botanist named Carolus Linnaeus in 1753. In 1783 a Frenchman named Jean-Baptiste Lamarck assigned the Indian variety of the plant the name *Cannabis indica*. In 1924 a botanist in Russia named Janischewski gave a third variety of the plant the name *Cannabis ruderalis*.

Cannabis I all its forms is one of the easiest plants to grow. The seeds germinate within days, develop into male and female, and sometimes both, and the plant thrives in a variety of climates and soil conditions.

Cannabis plants are *dioecious*, which means there are male and female plants. Those who grow it for the psychoactive properties (marijuana) often destroy plants displaying male characteristics. This is because female cannabis plants produce greatly stronger psychoactive resin than the male plant. The flowering tops of the seedless, unpollinated cannabis plants are called *sinsemilla* (Spanish for *without seed*), and are highly sought for psychoactive properties.

In his book, Booth explains that the different varieties of cannabis seem to be somewhat more of a singular plant than the names imply. This is because within a few seasons of growth, the plants grown from the seeds of one variety will adapt to the characteristics of the other variety when grown with or near those associated with that other variety.

Today we associate the name cannabis with marijuana, and hemp with the industrial plant that gets its modern name from *hanap*, an Old Saxon name, or *henap*, an Old English name.

While all varieties of the plant appear to have originated in some area of central Asia, the difference is that cannabis can get you "stoned" while hemp can get you fed, sheltered, cleaned, moisturized, clothed, and warmed, and the growing hemp plants will provide oxygen while absorbing air pollution and improving certain soil conditions, but hemp won't provide any psychoactive fun if you smoke or ingest it.

Ancient people living in various parts of the world grew hemp for many uses. Some people speculate that hemp was the first crop to be cultivated by humans. It is likely that the first plant-based fabrics were made out of hemp fiber, giving people an alternative to wearing animal skins. The ancient Chinese created woven fabrics from hemp fiber. Early humans also made food from crushed hemp seeds and used hemp stalks to build shelter.

> "It would be wryly interesting if in human history the cultivation of marijuana led generally to the invention of agriculture, and thereby to civilization."
> – Carl Sagan, in his book *The Dragons of Eden: Speculations on the Evolution of Human Intelligence.* Using the pseudonym *Mr. X,* Sagan wrote an essay for Harvard Medical School psychiatrist Lester Grinspoon's 1971 book *Marihuana Reconsidered*

Thousands of years ago the Chinese made fabric, food, rope, shoes, and utensils from hemp. Upon examining ancient Chinese paper, scientists have found it consisting of a combination of mulberry bark or other bark pulverized with hemp and dried under the sun. Ancient Chinese burial sites have been found containing various hemp materials as well as containers holding hemp seeds.

> "I must mention that hemp grows in Scythia, a plant resembling flax, but much coarser and taller. It grows wild as well as under cultivation, and the Thracians make clothes from it very like linen ones – indeed, one must have much experience in these matters to be able to distinguish between the two, and anyone who has ever seen a piece of cloth made from hemp, will suppose it to be of linen."
> – Herodotus, Dorian Greek historian, fifth-century BC. From *Herodotus, The Histories* B. 4: 71-76, trans. Aubrey de Sélincourt, ed. A. R. Burn; Viking Penguin, Inc.: New York, 1972; page 294

Hemp was a common material in other parts of the world as well. The ancient Arabs and Egyptians made hemp rope and paper. Hemp rope had been used in the construction of the ancient pyramids. The Romans and Greeks traded in hemp. Hemp materials have been found in the ruins of Pompeii. The Vikings made sails out of hemp. By the eighth-century the hemp papermaking techniques from China had spread to Arabia and Persia. In about 1150 the Moors started manufacturing hemp paper in Spain.

> "Without [hemp rope] how could water be drawn from the well? What would scribes, copyists, secretaries, and writers do without it [hemp paper]? Would not official documents and rent-rolls disappear? Would not the noble art of printing perish?"
> – Francois Rabelais (1495-1553), French humanist and satirist during the Renaissance; quote from *At the Edge of History*, by William Irwin Thompson, 1971; page 124

Before the Renaissance the Italians were cultivating large fields of hemp to make fabric, cordage, and sails. When the sails had served their purpose and been worn by the wind, rain, and sun, they were turned into clothing, tablecloths, bedding, painters' canvases, cleaning rags, hats, insulation, and paper.

In the 1400s Johan Gutenberg took the idea of the Chinese woodblock printing process and created his famed printing press, which he used to print the first printed Bible on paper made from a variety of materials, including flax and hemp rags. Over the next several hundred years hemp paper was also used to publish political statements, fueling the revolutions.

People in the Baltics use hemp seeds in their traditional foods. In Poland hemp seeds are tossed at weddings.

In modern times there have been more laws applied against hemp and cannabis cultivation and more money spent to control the plants than on any other plant throughout history. This is being done to a plant that is closest to the needs of humans than any plant.

Because it is illegal to grow hemp in the U.S., all hemp products that are sold in the U.S. are imported from other countries. As a result, the U.S. loses hundreds of millions of dollars by importing hemp products and raw hemp material to make hemp products. If hemp were legal to grow in the U.S., hundreds of thousands of jobs would be created to farm hemp, process raw hemp, and to manufacture and sell hemp products, including fuel, food, nutritional and lubricating oils; cosmetics, clothing, hats, rugs, linen, paper, candles, paint, insulation, fiberboard, and many other items.

In 1994, when a company called Hempstead got a federal license to grow one half-acre of hemp near the town of Brawley in California's Imperial Valley, they had many companies interested in what they were doing. Sponsors included the Ohio Hempery and the Save the Earth Foundation. Two beds of hemp were planted, one for seeds and one for fiber. As the plants grew and began to produce seeds flocks of birds showed up and began to feast. To prevent the birds from consuming the seed crops ceramic owls were placed on poles to scare away the birds. When the state attorney general's office heard about the hemp fields they sent officers from the Imperial Valley Narcotics Task Force to investigate. On July 29, a week before harvest, drug enforcement workers foolishly plowed under the 20,000 hemp plants. Your tax dollars at work.

> "This (hemp) is becoming a serious commodity. You have farmers
> in North Dakota dealing with depressed soy and corn prices. They see
> Canadians farming industrial hemp. Why are we cutting American
> farmers out of this rapidly emerging market?"
> – David Bronner of Dr. Bronner's Magic Soaps, Escondido,
> California; 2005. Since this statement was made, corn prices have
> risen in relation to the demand for ethanol production. However,
> hemp is a better crop to use for ethanol because it is used to make
> cellulosic ethanol, which creates less pollution, and provides better
> engine performance than starch ethanol made from corn.

China is the world's largest exporter of hemp products. China also imports hemp from Australia and Canada. The Chinese military produces hemp seed nutrition packs for its soldiers. The hemp food packs include hemp protein food bars, hemp chocolate, hemp milk, and hemp coffee. As is explained later in the book, hemp is rich in a variety of nutrients, including amino acids (from which our bodies make protein), and essential fatty acids (especially omega 3 fatty acids, which are lacking in the diets of most people living in industrialized countries, and those following diets lacking in fresh greens.)

The hemp industry is growing around the world. Korea and Thailand allow farmers to grow hemp. The imperial family of Japan owns a small hemp farm to make fabric for their clothing. Germany lifted its 1982 ban on industrial hemp in November 1995. There are hemp paper manufacturing plants in Slovenia. Poland grows hemp for a variety of reasons, including to decontaminate soil and to manufacture building materials. Russia maintains a hemp industry. Other European countries, such as France and Spain, are also growing hemp and manufacturing products with it. Switzerland hosts a hemp convention called Cannatrade. Great Britain lifted its prohibition on hemp in 1993. Canada has allowed hemp to be grown on a "research" basis since 1995, and now exports hundreds of millions of dollars worth of hemp in various forms, including food, oil, fabric, fiber, resin, and paper.

Australia has been developing a hemp market since the 1990s and farmers there are now cultivating many acres of hemp. New Zealand began growing hemp in 2001. However, while Australia and New Zealand allow hemp farming for industrial uses, as of 2008, their food regulations continue to disallow hemp from being used as a food source for humans, but do allow it for pet food and farm animal feed. Farmers in Australia and New Zealand are growing hemp for a number of reasons, including for seed oil, wood sealant, paint oil, animal feed, absorbent materials, insulation, fiber board (plywood), animal bedding, biodegradable plastics, fabric fiber, and paper pulp. At least one Australian company is producing hemp masonry, which are bricks consisting of compacted hemp fiber hardened with lime, for use in construction of low cost green housing.

> "Industrial hemp has the potential to provide farmers with a much-needed additional fast growing summer crop option that can be used in rotation with winter grain crops. It's a potentially lucrative industry due to the environmentally friendly nature of (hemp) and there is strong interest for hemp products in the market."
> – Ian Macdonald, Australia's NSW Minister for Primary Industries

In addition to Canada, the U.S. imports hemp materials and products from other countries such as Chile, China, England, Finland, Hungary, India, the Netherlands, and Romania.

I receive email from people involved in the industrial hemp industry of various countries, and the tone of the emails is always that of concern for how long it is going to take the U.S. to finally banish it's laws banning hemp farming so that the farmers here can start growing hemp, and the country can become more sustainable. Unfortunately, I can't change the laws of the U.S., but I can educate people about how they need to change. Apparently my book about hemp has been selling in other countries. While that is nice, I am hoping that more people in the U.S. read it, as it is the U.S. citizenry that needs to be educated about the environmental benefits of hemp, and to push the government to abolish the laws preventing U.S. farmers from growing the world's most useful crop.

Meanwhile, in the U.S., industrial hemp farming remains in a legal limbo.

Some blame the limbo on the hydrocarbon industry, some blame it on the paper industry, some blame it on the cotton industry, some blame crooked politicians or businesspeople, or some combination of all of these and others.

Keep reading, and decide for yourself.

Then do your part to help bring the hemp industry into the modern age.

# Hemp Will Not Get You High

By writing about this topic, some people may think I am advocating that people turn into potheads. But if that is what you get out of this, you are missing the point. People who think that also are likely to misunderstand the difference between hemp and marijuana.

Some may ask why I'm writing this when I'm not a pothead, I've never owned a bong, and the most intoxicating substance in my house is an old bottle of whisky someone left in the kitchen after a dinner party a few years back, which goes untouched because nobody here likes the taste of brewed alcohol. My experience with hard drugs is staying far away from them. Even when I had surgery to repair broken bones I didn't take the pain pills after the first couple of days because I found the pain to be more tolerable than being stoned on pain medication and the subsequent "downer" feeling the drugs induced.

Some of this confusion about the topic of my hemp book is due to the fact that people think hemp is the same thing as marijuana. It isn't. Now that I'm writing this marijuana book with large chunks of material that is contained in the hemp book, I am getting this feedback from people who think I'm doing it to advocate for marijuana use. My goal has to do with getting industrial hemp legalized, and it takes getting the drug laws to change, then I'm all for that.

Because hemp absorbs so much air pollution, puts for so much oxygen, improves the soil, ad provides so much material that can be used to make sustainable and biodegradable products, it is important that people learn about hemp. Hemp can do a lot for the world now. Clarifying its history helps people understand the issue, and hopefully will play a role in getting the laws changed. We need to do away with the misunderstanding that hemp should remain illegal based on the concept that it can get you high. It can't get you high. Industrial hemp is not marijuana.

It appears that a rather large majority of people knows little about what hemp is, what it can do, and what it *can't* do.

Throughout history various cultures on many parts of the planet have relied on hemp for paper, fuel, clothing, food, and building materials. As I explain later in the book, the U.S. relied on hemp to supply fiber and oil for the U.S. military. Other countries, including Germany, England, France, Spain, and China, have used hemp materials in their military outfits, ropes, tents, parachutes, and other troop and camp supplies. More recently, in the 1960s China relied on hemp seed and hemp oil for nutrition during Mao Zedong's reign. I know of women in Canada who make hemp seed mylk (spelled that way when made from seeds or nuts, and not cow milk) to feed to their babies and toddlers. In countries throughout the world hemp seed provides nutrition in the form of food oil, flour, and cereal dishes. Closer to home, many people in the U.S. unknowingly are using bird feed containing imported hemp seeds to fill the containers on bird feeders they keep in their yards. Many products sold in American natural foods stores contain hemp oil, hemp protein, and hemp flour – all made from hemp seeds. Because U.S. farmers aren't allowed to grow hemp, these food products are made from imported hemp seeds. Nutritional powders that muscle-bound body builders use often contain hemp protein, again made from imported hemp seeds. More and more fabrics sold in the U.S. contain hemp fiber, also from imported hemp material.

"Over 30 countries are currently developing a hemp industry to meet international fiber demands. The United States is not one of them.
… Industrial hemp is not a drug crop. The international standard is that hemp of cannabis with less than 1 percent THC is not marijuana. Strains that would likely be grown in the U.S. would be 0.3 percent, or less THC [content] as is the case with Canada and the European Union."
– North American Industrial Hemp Council, NAIHC.org; 2006

What I do advocate is the total legalization of hemp farming for any farmer who wants to grow it. Many farmers do want to grow it and some state governments have legalized it, but, foolishly, the U.S. federal government won't allow it.

"The THC levels in industrial hemp are so low that no one could ever get high from smoking it. Moreover, hemp contains a relatively high percentage of another cannabinoid, [cannabidiol] CBD, that actually blocks the marijuana high. Hemp, it turns out, is not only not marijuana; it could be called 'antimarijuana.' "
– David West, PhD; Hemp and Marijuana: Myths and Realities; Madison, WI: North American Industrial Hemp Council, 1998; page 3; DrugWarFacts.org/Hemp

"U.S. farmers want to grow hemp legally like their counterparts in Canada, Europe, and Asia. Many of hemp's uses such as in foods, animal bedding, biofuel and composites will become more viable if hemp is treated like other crops. How can a raw material that's legal to import, to sell, to eat, and to use in all kinds of everyday products not

be legal for farmers in America to grow? No other agricultural commodity is restricted to just importation."
– Eric Steenstra, president of VoteHemp.com; May 2006

"Unlike the U.S., other Western countries (such as Canada, Germany, and Australia) have adopted rational THC limits for foods, similar to those voluntarily observed by North American hemp food companies which protect consumers with a wide margin of safety from any psychoactive effects or workplace drug-testing interference [see hemp industry standards regarding trace THC at TestPledge.com]. The 14-year-old global hemp market is a thriving commercial success. Unfortunately, because [the] Drug Enforcement Administration's drug-war paranoia has confused nonpsychoactive industrial hemp varieties of cannabis with psychoactive 'marijuana' varieties, the U.S. is the only major industrialized nation to prohibit the growing and processing of industrial hemp."
– From *Organic Consumers Association and Natural Foods Industry Slam DEA on Ban on Hemp Foods*; VoteHemp.com; March 28, 2003

The reasons U.S. farmers can't grow hemp has nothing to do with people getting high. But the law outlawing hemp is tied to marijuana, and vice versa, as well as to corporate greed, crooked politicians, and corrupt government officials. Actually, the only reason industrial hemp farming is illegal I the U.S. is because corporations were able to form U.S. policy by manipulating lawmakers and other people in government, and especially people in Congress, in the FBI, and other high-level government offices.

Many people mistakenly believe the laws banning hemp were created to prohibit the use of marijuana because hemp appears so similar to the marijuana plant. But the differences in hemp and marijuana plants are easy to differentiate. Marijuana is short and bushy, and hemp is tall and lanky with a leafy top. The hemp plant typically grows from six to 18 feet tall within a three- to four-month period. The marijuana plant usually stays below six feet tall. There are some shorter varieties of hemp, such as those grown for fine fabrics, but these are also easily distinguishable from cannabis.

"Industrial hemp plants have long and strong stalks, have few branches, have been bred for maximum production of fiber and/or seed, and grow up to 16 feet in height. They are planted in high densities of 100 to 300 plants per square yard. On the other hand, the drug varieties of cannabis are shorter, are not allowed to go to seed, and have been bred to maximize branching and thus [have] leaves and flowers. They are planted much less densely to promote bushiness. The

drug and non-drug varieties are harvested at different times, and planting densities look very different from the air."
– Vote Hemp, February 28, 2007 press release: Vote Hemp Exposes White House Office of National Drug Control Policy and Drug Enforcement Administration Lies about Hemp Farming

"Hemp is grown for its stalk and seed, with plants grown closely together to maximize the crops' yield. Industrial hemp can grow up to 18 feet tall with plants only inches apart. Marijuana plants, grown to maximize the flowering buds, need at least one square yard per plant to grow effectively. Realistically, anyone who's ever seen a field of industrial hemp could easily tell the difference. Canadian law enforcement officials can. Why can't ours?
… The USA is the only industrialized country that does not allow commercial hemp farming because American law enforcement supposedly can't tell the difference between these remarkably different plants."
– Kentucky Hemp Museum, KentuckyHemp.com

Growing hemp and marijuana together would not do much good for those wanting to get stoned. Hemp pollinates the marijuana, lowering the THC level in the marijuana grown from the seeds. The claim by some people that if we legalize hemp the hemp farms will also become marijuana farms is nonsense. People who grow marijuana would want their plants as far away as possible from hemp farms – miles away.

"Planting marijuana anywhere near industrial hemp would be ill-conceived. When hemp pollinates marijuana it transfers the genes for low drug content to developing seeds of the marijuana. The drug potency in the new marijuana plants will be about half that of the original marijuana. When hemp repeatedly crosses with new marijuana plants obtained each year, the drug content is repeatedly reduced in the plants. Thus, the drug content will become so low and uncertain that the derived marijuana will be useless as a drug plant."
– Dr. Paul G. Mahlberg, professor, department of biology, Indiana University, who has held a Drug Enforcement Administration research license for cannabis research for over 30 years

Even though it is well established that marijuana growers would not want their plants growing near hemp farms, the U.S. government keeps spreading misinformation about why people want hemp legalized in the U.S. Not only do they make it sound as if the reason people want to legalize hemp is so that they can grow marijuana, they also make it sound as if the law enforcement officers are stupid. Or perhaps the person who said the following is displaying his own ignorance:

"You have legitimate farmers who want to experiment with a new crop. But you have another group, very enthusiastic, who want to allow cultivation of hemp because they believe it will lead to a de facto legalization of marijuana. The last thing law enforcement people need is for the cultivation of marijuana-looking plants to spread. Are we going to ask them to go through row by row, field by field, to distinguish between legal hemp and marijuana?"
– Tom Riley, White House Office on National Drug Control Policy, as quoted in the *Minneapolis Star Tribune*, January 28, 2007

"The ONDCP is wrong in its characterization of industrial hemp advocates, and there is no evidence that farmers who grow industrial hemp are hiding marijuana plants in their fields, whether in Canada or anywhere else. Because cross-pollination of low THC industrial hemp and high THC marijuana is inevitable, illicit marijuana growers avoid industrial hemp fields to protect the potency of their drug crop. It's simply illogical that a farmer's industrial hemp fields are ideal places to hide marijuana plants with all the extra scrutiny that comes with growing the crop. It's sad that, instead of a real policy debate on the issue of farming industrial hemp in the United States based on legislative intent and agronomic facts, the ONDCP and the Drug Enforcement Administration (DEA) resort to false hyperbole and character assassination. Tom Riley is welcome to join me in Canada this summer for the Hemp Industries Association annual meeting and see for himself how our neighbors in the north can easily tell the difference between industrial hemp and marijuana crops."
– Vote Hemp President Eric Steenstra, February 8, 2007

The point I want to make in this book is not about marijuana, but about hemp, which is not a drug. I think it is important for people to understand what the hemp plant can do for society, the environment, and the health of both humanity and wildlife today.

"Hemp cannot be commercially grown in the United States because it is erroneously confounded with marijuana. In fact, industrial hemp and marijuana are different breeds of *Cannabis sativa*, just as Chihuahuas and St. Bernards are different breeds of *Canis familiaris*. Smoking large quantities of hemp flowers can produce a headache, but not a high."
– HempIndustries.org

"Hemp is cannabis grown specifically for industrial use and thus contains very low levels of cannabinoids (THC). The use of hemp dates back many thousands of years. Properly grown hemp has virtually no psychoactive (intoxicating) effects when consumed. With a relatively short growth cycle of 120 days, hemp is an efficient and economical crop for farmers to grow."
– HempNation.com

# Hemp in World History

Perhaps one of the misconceptions stalling the legalization of hemp is that it is often portrayed as some sort of hippie thing that came about during the 1967 "Summer of Love." Maybe the misconception also is because some of those working at the forefront of the hemp legalization movement appear as if they haven't taken a shower since Woodstock. But hemp was not discovered during an acid trip in Golden Gate Park in the 1960s, or during any of the several decades before that.

"Archeologists report that cannabis was one of the first plants cultivated by humans – about 8000 BC [*Columbia University History of the World*, 1972]. Its fiber was used for rope, paper, sails, and garments. It was used as a medicine in China by 2700 BC [*U.S. Department of Agriculture Yearbook*, 1913, with studies by botanist Lyster H. Dewey]. It [the psychoactive version] was smoked in India by 1400 BC [*Atharaveda*]."
– Family Council on Drug Awareness, 2006; FCDA.org

"The earliest known woven fabric was apparently of hemp which began to be worked in the eighth millennium (8000-7000) B.C."
– *The Columbia History of the World*, 1981; page 54

"Hemp is among the oldest industries on the planet, going back more than 10,000 years to the beginning of pottery. The oldest relic of human industry is a bit of hemp fabric dating back to approximately 8,000 B.C."
– *Hemp: A True Gift from God(ess)*, by Dr. Heather Anne Harder, SeattleHempFest.com/Facts

Hemp has been around a long, long time as a plant that provides food, fabric, oil, paper, and shelter, and as a soil enhancer because it improves soil nutrients. Its roots also filter, decontaminate, and purify soil and water.

"A number of studies have identified industrial hemp as a top candidate in bioremediation, especially phytoextraction of heavy metals from industrially contaminated soils. Hemp has been used to process greywater in Australia, extensively tested in Europe for the removal of heavy metals from soil, including cadmium, lead, copper, zinc, and nickel often associated with mining, used for the cleanup of polycyclic aromatic hydrocarbons at a site in Hawaii, and cultivated on

radionuclide-contaminated soils at the Chernobyl nuclear reactor site. Although industrial hemp is not considered a 'hyperaccumulator' of heavy metals, many researchers believe it has strong potential for use in phytoremediation because it is highly adaptable to conditions throughout the world, even moderately polluted soils, and is comparable or better in phytoremediation applications than many plants of equal economic value."
– March 2008 Reason Foundation Study on Hemp, Illegally Green: Environmental Costs of Hemp Prohibition. Policy Study 367, by Skaidra Smith-Heisters

From the roots to the leaves at the crest of the hemp plant, all parts of the plant can be used for the benefit of humans. Only the absurdities spread by those who work against it, and who would have something to lose if it became legal, prevent it from being recognized as a plant that can greatly benefit modern society.

"Industrial hemp's history is rich in advancements of civilization and exploration. It was utilized for weaving in Greece centuries before the time of Christ, and was harvested in most of Europe during the Middle Ages.
Colonists brought hemp seed with them to America and it was extensively grown for 'homespun' cloth and for the ropes and 'caulk' (oakum) that kept Yankee bottoms [ships] plying the seas."
– EarthRunnings.com

Hemp has been grown and used throughout the world for centuries. Because hemp was needed for sails and rope, wars have been fought over hemp. Napoleon's alliance with the Russian czar resulted in Great Britain being cut off from its access to Russian hemp, which was one of the driving forces behind the War of 1812 (more about this later in the book).

Years before, Italy had a hemp industry in the 10th century that created many of the sails and much of the cordage used on ships that sailed the trade routes of Europe. At that time, an entire hemp fabric and rope industry was established in the Venetian Republic.

Triangular sails for boats had been created by Arabs. Venetian sail makers improved on this design, opening up the potential for boats to travel long distances. These hemp sails were used on boats that brought European explorers across the oceans. Hemp was so important that it was one of the first crops grown by European and British settlers in what became the U.S.

The Dutch built windmills that used hemp fabric. The mills processed hemp materials into various hemp products, including sails. At one point

41

the Dutch were processing and using more hemp than they could grow and they began importing hemp from other parts of Europe.

Under King Henry VIII, Britain built its first navy using boats featuring hemp sails and hemp rope. These materials had to be replaced every year or so, which meant a constant supply of hemp was needed. In 1533 Henry imposed a fine on farmers who refused to dedicate part of their land to growing hemp or flax.

As more countries built their navy fleets, developed trade routes using ships with hemp sales and rigging, and increased their need for paper and clothing, the need for hemp increased.

Russia became the European leader in hemp production. Russian also had the landmass available to grow abundant hemp crops. Britain and the Dutch were not so lucky with their landscape, and they largely relied on imported hemp. But the Dutch, Britain, and France were turning west for hemp, across the Atlantic to the New World where they had established colonies in what became the U.S. and Canada.

In the 1600s, the Dutch had established New Amsterdam.

By 1610, thousands of British citizens were migrating to the Jamestown colony.

How important was hemp to the British government? In 1663, England's Parliament created a law allowing hemp laborers escaping persecution in Europe to be granted the same rights as British-born citizens, if they were to live in England or Wales, and 1) took the oath of allegiance to become a subject of the monarchy, and 2) established a business in the hemp industry.

On December 21, 1620 the so-called "pilgrims" landed at Plymouth Rock. Less than half of them were seeking religious freedom, and the rest of them had other reasons for leaving England. None of them knew the term "pilgrim," which was a label they were given many years after they had died. And all of them were ill-equipped for a cold, wet winter in their new land. It appears that they survived by stealing from the local native communities, who may or may not have taught them how to grow their own food, which today has resulted in the mythological "Thanksgiving" holiday.

In 1663, the British had established their Carolina colony.

In 1665 King Charles II sent British troops into New Amsterdam and seized it from the Dutch. It was then named New York, in honor of the brother of the king, James, the Duge of York, who was to become the king. In 1673 the Dutch recaptured New York, but then ceded it back to Britain in 1674.

In 1681, England established a colony in Pennsylvania. In 1682, they established a colony in Delaware. These colonies mostly consisted of farmland, and they became sources of hemp that was exported to and needed by England.

So important was hemp to the colonial governments that the colonies in Maryland, Pennsylvania, and Maryland allowed farmers to pay one-fourth of their taxes in raw hemp, or course this brought them to increase their hemp cultivation.

England's reliance on American-grown hemp was so strong that the colonies were forbidden from creating their own products from it. The monarchy did not want America to become industrialized, which was one way of preventing America from becoming independent.

Shades of independence were already taking place. The colonists had access to plentiful amounts of everything they needed to become independent. With the hemp, they began to make their own fabric and rope. With the abundant forests, they were able to build their homes, and to manufacture furniture, cabinetry, and farm equipment. Horses and other farm animals were easy to breed. Land that could be farmed was also plentiful.

It was evident that America was becoming a continent less dependant on England and Europe. This especially became more evident in 1629. That was the year that the Massachusetts Bay Company in the Plymouth colony started the continent's first industrial shipbuilding dock, which used domestic lumber, and the labor of some of those "pilgrims" who landed at Plymouth in 1620. The ships needed sails, rope, and caulking, which were all made from hemp fiber and resin. The need for inexpensive clothing, rope, sails, and also for hemp seed oil for food, fuel, and wood preservative increseed the importance of a domestic hemp industry. Hemp stalks were also used for insulating the homes. It is clear that hemp became the most important American crop, and perhaps the easiest crop to grow. Much to England's chagrin, America's textile industry was growing, and it was happening with the use of hemp. America's shipbuilding industry was growing, and it was doing so with the use of hemp. America's newspaper industry was growing, and it was doing so on hemp paper. America's colonists were becoming more independent, and they were improving their living conditions to levels higher than those of many areas of England and Europe, and they were doing so with hemp.

In 1705, the British government passed the Trade Act. This Act established law that the American colonies could only export hemp to British ports. England needed the hemp for their expanding Naval ships. Britain was in a continual battle with French forces, until defeating them in 1763. In 1690, British forces took control Ireland, which necessitated constant naval patrols and government presence. Britain was also in nonstop military strategies against the Dutch, French, and Portuguese for control of India, which they finally took control of in 1760. The British trade ships needed mass quantities of hemp for their own sails, rope, and caulking, and hemp seed oil for fuel, food, and wood preservative. Hemp seeds were also used as food on the ships to make mush and bread, and alcohol was common because it could be kept in jugs longer than water, which tended to grow bacteria when it was kept in jugs (not that they understood bacteria back then – but they did know that dirty water made them sick).

Many of the British naval troops were from America, and many of the trade ships employed those who were American colonists. This was a double-edged situation. The American colonists in the British military services were learning how to run the military, and American colonists working on trade ships were learning how to do international business.

Word was spreading that America was a good place to live. America was free of war, had land, forests, farms, docks, and several different growing industries, including a hemp industry.

By 1720, the textile industry in America was growing more industrialized. By this time there had been a number of Irish immigrant textile workers setting up shops in Massachusetts, and they were turning out fabrics made from wool and hemp.

In 1733, when British established a colony in Georgia, the founder, James Oglethorp, wrote, "It is proposed the families there settled shall plant hemp and flax to be sent unmanufactured to England, whereby in time much ready money will be saves in this Kingdom, which now goes out to other countries for the purchase of these goods, and they will also be able to supply us with a great deal of good timber. Tis possible too they may raise white mulberry trees and send us good raw silk. But at the worst they will be able to live there, and defend that country from the insults of their neighbors, and London will be maintaining a number of families which being let out of jail have at present no visible way to subsist."

So, it is easy to understand that one way England relieved itself of a dependency on Russian hemp was that it established colonies in America that grew hemp that was sent to England.

Hemp grew so well in North America that it was considered to be of the best quality. The original colonies of what was to become the U.S. enacted laws requiring its citizens to grow a certain number of acres of hemp based on the population of each colony. This helped establish an export industry. As each country increased its navy fleets and trade routes, they required even more hemp for fabric and rope to provide a continual supply for ships needing to replace their aging sails and rigging.

"Used in sails, rigging, canvas, and ropes, hemp was so essential to industry and, in particular, the maintenance of the Navy and shipping fleet in 1776, that in 'Common Sense' Thomas Paine cited the fact that

44

'hemp flourishes even to rankness' first among the fledgling nation's assets in the fight for independence."
– March 2008 Reason Foundation Study on Hemp, Illegally Green: Environmental Costs of Hemp Prohibition. Policy Study 367, by Skaidra Smith-Heisters

Until the late eighteenth-century the hemp industry flourished in the U.S. It was once second to cotton as America's largest cash crop. While the use of cotton for fabric increased after Eli Whitney designed the first patented and workable cotton gin (engine) in 1793, cotton could not replace hemp as a stronger material for industrial uses, including sails, rope, and wagon covers. Hemp also produces more seed oil per acre than cotton, and it remained popular because it could be grown in all regions of North America, whereas cotton grows in warmer climates. In the northern states, cotton was imported and was cheaper than hemp. But, because of its many uses and durability, hemp was more desirable than cotton.

Cotton was the king crop of the south because slaves (cheap labor) were used to farm it. After the cotton gin became a popular tool, the cotton industry flourished, and so did the fortunes of the slave owners. The spread of the cotton industry in the South also resulted in the 1820 Indian Removal Act, which tragically gave permission to force five Indigenous nations from their lands, and made them move to unknown lands in the west – a trek that killed many of them.

The hemp industry was impacted after slavery ended. This is because many slaves were used to farm and process hemp. Since there had not been a machine invented to process hemp in a way that the cotton gin was used to process cotton, the hemp industry faltered while cotton grew in popularity.

The hemp industry basically ended after 1937, when confusing and controversial laws went into effect overtaxing both marijuana and hemp (more on this later in the book).

Some of the first airplanes included the use of hemp fabric stretched over their frames. The military used parachutes made of hemp. For the first decades of their use, military airplanes often were lubricated using hemp oil.

Fire hoses used on military ships and bases have been made with an encasement of woven hemp fabric. Hemp was also used for military uniforms, hats, boots, shoelaces, and tents.

"It will displace imports of raw material and manufactured products produced by underpaid coolie and peasant labor and it will provide thousands of jobs for American workers throughout the land.
… It is used to produce more than 5,000 textile products, ranging from rope to fine laces, and the woody 'hurds' remaining after the fiber

45

has been removed contain more than 77 percent cellulose, and can be used to produce more than 25,000 products, ranging from dynamite to cellophane."
– Billion Dollar Crop: *Popular Mechanics* magazine, February 1938. This article had been printed in 1937, but wasn't distributed until the next year, after the U.S. government had all but killed the hemp farming industry with the Marijuana Tax Act of 1937. In 1974 a writer named Jack Frazier wrote about this article in his Hemp Paper Reconsidered, published in the *Ecologist*. Jack Herer also brought this article to light in his 1985 book *The Emperor Wears No Clothes*. The article largely was based on information written in an October 12, 1937, letter from H.W. Bellrose, president of the World Fibre Corporation to Elizabeth Bass, district supervisor of the Federal Bureau of Narcotics.

"Hemp offers significant benefits for the economic and environmental sustainability of our planet. Hemp can be grown organically and aids in weed suppression and soil improvement. Hemp can replace problematic and rare resources. The fiber is strong and features absorption and insulation qualities. The seed and oil are highly nutritious for our health."
– HempIndustries.org

"Hemp fiber, blended with everything from tencel to organic cotton, can be used to create textiles as diverse as terrycloth, flannel, and luxurious satin brocades. Hemp fiber offers greater durability and breathability than cotton, which [cotton farming] accounts for 25 percent of the pesticides sprayed on the world's crops. Hemp-based textile products on the market include apparel and accessories such as T-shirts, pants, dresses, baby clothes, bathrobes, and shoes; housewares such as blankets, shower curtains, and rugs; and sundries such as hammocks and pet supplies."
– HempIndustries.org

"In 1989, a number of entrepreneurs took interest in hemp and began to manufacture products [out of hemp]. The growth rate has been so phenomenal that the newly re-emerging hemp industry has doubled in size every year since. The early hemp companies soon realized that they had a political and economical interest in joining forces. In late 1994, one hundred hemp importers, manufacturers, merchants and researchers met in Arizona. They formed the Hemp

Industries Association (HIA) to promote the use of and protect the integrity of hemp."
– HempIndustries.org

"The fast-developing interest in building with hemp-based materials, such as hemp-lime hempcrete and hemp fibre insulation matting, will have two very important effects.

First, it will provide those who wish to build houses using natural materials from the growing ecologically minded market a quantifiable and economic way to do so using what is becoming known as the 'hemp building system.'

Second, the potential for growth in the production of hemp as a result of hemp building being taken up in many countries around the world could be enormous. Certainly no other use is likely to produce such an increase in demand for hemp in the near future."
– Steve Allin, author of *Building with Hemp*, in correspondence with the author; September 2006

"Industrial hemp is not pot. There simply is no sensible argument that validates the long-held misidentification of *Cannabis sativa* (the plant that has produced hemp fiber for *thousands* of years) as marijuana (*Cannabis indica*).

Industrial hemp is not the profit-driven, behind-closed-doors-dealing, earth-polluting business that has long been cotton's, paper/pulp's and polyesters' method of production – a method that has produced more waste and irreversible environmental damage during the first-century of their mass production compared to millennia of hemp production."
– EarthRunnings.com

# Hemp Is an Excellent Source of Sustainable Fuel

"There is one farm crop that can fill all our energy needs. Hemp is the only biomass resource capable of making America energy efficient...

By the year 2000, America will have exhausted 80 percent of her petroleum reserves. Will we go to war with the Arabs for the privilege of driving our cars? Will we stripmine our land for coal, and poison our air so we can drive our autos an extra 100 years? Will we raze our forests to make fuel?"

– From an unfortunately prophetic 1980s-era flier, *Hemp for Clean Sustainable Fuel,* distributed by the Business Alliance for Commerce in Hemp. For the record, while hemp does hold amazing promise as a crop with energy benefits, it can't answer all of America's energy needs. But, it can make a large dent as part of the solution to the energy problems, especially in that it absorbs greenhouse gasses and puts forth oxygen, and it can be used to produce a variety of fuels – and structural insulation.

"Hemp could end our dependency on fossil fuels. Fossil fuels, such as natural gas, oil, and coal, are nonrenewable resources since they are the by-products of eons of natural decomposition of Earth's ancient biomass. Fossil fuel contains sulfur, which is the source of many of the aggravating environmental pollution problems threatening America. When burned the ancient [collections of] carbon dioxide trapped in these fossil fuels are released and increase the effects of global warming and the greenhouse effect.

... According to Environmental chemist Stanley E. Manahan, if we dedicated about 6 percent of continental U.S. land to hemp biomass, cultivation could supply all current demands for oil and gas. This production would not add any net carbon dioxide to the atmosphere. Pyrolysis is the process of converting organic biomass into fuel similar to the process currently used to create charcoal. Hemp 'charcoal' has the same heating value as coal, with virtually no sulfur to pollute the atmosphere. Hemp yields approximately ten tons per acre in four months, is drought-resistant and produces a heating value of 5,000-8,000 Btu/per pound of dried hemp. Hemp biomass can also be converted to methanol."

– *Hemp: A True Gift from God(ess)*, by Dr. Heather Anne Harder, SeattleHempFest.com/Facts. For the record, the figure given is an example of how much land might be needed. The claim that it could supply all of the current demands for energy and gas is a stretch. In combination with other crops, including landscape clippings, the U.S. can certainly become more energy efficient. Technological breakthroughs in fuel-efficient engines, public transportation, in producing fuels, and in household electronics, and the spread of the bike culture and the use of insulation, would also need to play a part. A change in the typical American lifestyle, including in what is considered to be food, how it is grown, and how it is prepared, also would play into the factor. Food growing, harvesting, production, shipping, packaging, marketing, and preparation, cleaning, and disposal use the majority of natural resources.

"According to the U.S. Department of Energy, hemp as a biomass fuel producer requires the least specialized growing and processing procedures of all hemp products. The hydrocarbons in hemp can be processed into a wide range of biomass energy sources, from fuel pellets to liquid fuels and gas. Development of biofuels could significantly reduce our consumption of fossil fuels and nuclear power."
– Hemp Industries Association, 2006; TheHIA.org

Hemp produces about 200 to 300 gallons of oil per acre from the seed of the plant, which has a 35 percent oil content. A crop that produces more oil per acre is canola, but the plant fiber of canola does not provide as many uses as hemp.

Because hemp grows to its full height in just a few months, hemp also produces an impressive biomass tonnage per acre.

Using hemp oil for fuel and hemp cellulose to create cellulosic ethanol, one acre of hemp provides as much energy as 18 to 25 barrels of petroleum oil. Hemp grown for seed takes about a month longer to mature, and is planted wider apart than hemp grown for fiber or pulp.

Extracting the oil from the hemp seeds and using the plant cellulose to make cellulosic ethanol, a revived modern-day domestic hemp industry can make an impressive reduction on U.S. dependence on foreign oil and help prevent the damage now created to the ecology by oil drilling, crude oil processing, and the heavily polluting worldwide shipping of petroleum. As mentioned elsewhere, using hemp as insulation can also reduce the use of other fossil fuels, coal and natural gas – and a reduction in the petroleum used by those industries.

Currently the most common crop being used for ethanol production in the U.S. is corn. Corn is not the best plant substance to use for ethanol.

Corn ethanol/petroleum gasoline blends reduce greenhouse tailpipe emissions by about 12 percent from regular petroleum gasoline. Soybean oil biodiesel reduces greenhouse tailpipe emissions by about 41 percent from regular petroleum diesel. According to Department of Energy studies conducted by the Argonne Laboratories at the University of Chicago, cellulosic ethanol made from plant fiber (such as hemp, landscape clippings, or switchgrass) reduces greenhouse gas emissions by a whopping 85 percent. Jatropha seed oil is also being used as a biofuel, and has been particularly of interest as a replacement for highly toxic jet fuel.

The leftover material from the creation of hemp ethanol can be used to make fiberboard, which would reduce cutting down trees for construction materials. As mentioned, using hemp for insulation can reduce the use of heating fuels, which would reduce the production of greenhouse gasses. It could also be composted back into the soil to help maintain soil health.

The leftover "seed cake" material from creating hemp oil can be used for nutritional powders for both humans and animals. The seed cake can also be used as compost.

"The potential for carbon neutral ethanol production is still a topic of intense research and debate. At the optimistic end of the debate, life-cycle assessments have suggested that cellulosic ethanol could reduce greenhouse gas emissions by more than 80 percent below those of gasoline, as compared to a 20 or 40 percent reduction in emissions (at best) derived from corn-based grain ethanol. (This is in large part due to the fact that, as in the paper pulping process, waste material in the cellulosic ethanol process can be gasified for energy to power the mill facilities.)"
– March 2008 Reason Foundation Study on Hemp, Illegally Green: Environmental Costs of Hemp Prohibition. Policy Study 367, by Skaidra Smith-Heisters

The most common irrigated and/or managed plant material in North America is landscape clippings. This material can be used to make cellulosic ethanol. Lawns already exist throughout towns and cities. The crop is already harvested by lawnmowers, weed eaters, and hedge trimmers. The lawn clippings are also already being collected, but with trash trucks that take the otherwise useful material to garbage landfills. Cities should be collecting lawn clippings and taking these to cellulosic ethanol refineries. This cellulose material can be gathered freely as a waste product from lawns surrounding homes, school campuses, office complexes, sports parks, and government buildings. This would be smarter than turning to the farming industry and paying them billions of dollars in government subsidies (corporate welfare) to grow more corn and soybeans to produce fuels that are not as environmentally safe as the cellulosic fuel that can be made from grass and from a rotation crop of hemp.

Currently the U.S. government is spending billions of dollars subsidizing the corn and soy industries to produce more crops to turn into fuel. This is in addition to the billions those farm crops already receive to provide animal feed. Even if 100 percent of American corn and soybean crops were used to make ethanol and biodiesel, the fuel would provide only 12 percent of gas and 6 percent of diesel. The starch ethanol would also not burn as cleanly as the ethanol made from cellulose. And the leftover material from growing the soy for oil would not be as useful as the leftover material from growing hemp for seed oil.

As detailed in the documentary, "King Corn," this surge in corn farming is increasing the practice of monocropping, which is planting thousands of acres of a single crop. Monocropping is not good for the soil, for groundwater, for rivers, lakes, or oceans, or for wildlife. On May 12, 2007, the U.N.-Energy consortium of 20 United Nations agencies and programs released a report warning: "Use of large-scale monocropping could lead to significant biodiversity loss, soil erosion, and nutrient leaching." Also problematic is that corn and soybean fields are commonly treated with farming chemicals such as the herbicide Atrazine, which is not good for the soil and is known to cause cancer, especially cancer of the breasts.

The growing use of corn for ethanol production has increased the price of corn on the world market. This is increasing food prices, especially in poorer countries like Mexico. A National Academy of Sciences study concluded that ethanol and biodiesel would have a major impact on the food supply if the world keeps turning to corn, soy, and other current farm crops to make biofuels. What people may not consider when they hear that statement is that most food grown in North America, and an increasing amount of food grown in other parts of the world, goes to feed farmed animals. Those of us who follow a vegan diet do not support this terrible waste of resources that consists of growing massive quantities of grain and other crops to feed billions of factory farmed animals that lead horrible lives in confinement while they eat unnatural diets and are treated with a variety of pharmaceutical drugs to keep them alive and growing.

Corporate single-crop farming is taking over family subsistence farming around the planet. This is displacing poor people from land their families have lived on for generations. Additionally, multinational corporations dump huge amounts of monofarmed crops into markets of poor countries, making it difficult to impossible for local farmers in those countries to make money from farming – thus the farmers leave their land and move into cities. They also risk their lives to get into richer countries to make money to survive.

This leads into the reasons why the 700-mile border wall the U.S. government wants to build along the Mexico border is a VERY bad idea. The wall would be a catastrophe for wildlife of all sorts – what is bad for wildlife is bad for all life. Building that wall is a far from helpful solution relating to the issue of "illegal immigrants" and "undocumented workers." Building walls and the practice of multinational mono-cropping does not help anyone, harms wildlife, damages human cultures, and does not help solve the problem of human suffering or of immigration issues.

Both corn and soy are grown using large amounts of pesticides, fungicides, insecticides, and fertilizers. Cotton uses even more of these chemicals, which are largely fossil fuel-based. Because cotton is such a water-intensive crop, using large amounts of chemicals on the cotton fields also means that those chemicals end up in the water. Nitrogen fertilizer made from natureal gas (a fossil fuel) accounts for nearly half of the energy used for corn farming in the U.S. Most of the nitrogen fertilizer used in the U.S. is imported. Hemp does not need any of these harmful chemicals. Hemp also produces up to 200 percent more fabric per acre than cotton.

"In western Germany between 1982 and 1995, hemp cultivation was illegal except for use as a barrier to cross-pollination in commercial beet breeding. Subsequent research has shown that hemp hedges don't completely block the spread of beet pollen, but this sort of detail helps to highlight the value of inter-crop relationships in general. Hemp might be an especially valuable option as a secondary crop for organic vegetable farmers, or as a value-added cover crop between either organic or conventionally grown crops, naturally reducing weeds and other pests in the process. Hemp is reportedly used in China as a barrier to repel insects from vegetable crops.

Researchers in Canada have reported that in rotation with soybeans, industrial hemp reduces cyst nematodes, a parasitic pest, by 80 percent. (Kenaf and corn, among other crops, produce similar benefits, though maybe not to the same extent.) Dutch research has suggested similar results through hemp rotation on nematodes that damage potato crops. In the Netherlands, rotation experiments with corn, hemp, winter barley, and winter rye indicated that hemp was the best crop for reducing infestations of Cyperus esculentus, a weedy nutgrass. Fiber hemp has also reportedly suppressed aggressive agricultural plant pests quackgrass (Agropyron repens) and Canadian thistle (Cirsium arvense). Complimentary crop rotations can boost the field productivity of both hemp and the subsequent rotational crop. One study reported that in the Netherlands a 10 percent increase in yield of winter wheat was observed following rotation with fiber hemp. Some of the benefits seen in crop rotations with hemp—in particular, the contrast between vegetable and fiber crops—illustrate the positive value of crop diversity as opposed to the regional dominance of any single crop.

– March 2008 Reason Foundation Study on Hemp, Illegally Green: Environmental Costs of Hemp Prohibition. Policy Study 367, by Skaidra Smith-Heisters

Hemp can be grown as a rotation crop on farms, and on the approximate one-sixth of U.S. cropland that is being left fallow to control food prices. Industrial hemp would not take away from the food industry. Instead, hemp would improve certain soil conditions to grow other crops because hemp both destroys invasive weeds while mining nutrients from deep below the soil.

As mentioned, the leftover material from creating hemp biofuels could be used to make fiberboard and food. It also can be returned to farm soil as compost to build soil base, prevent erosion, and provide nutrients for soil organisms.

Not allowing farmers to grow industrial hemp also presents another issue. Why should farmers have to purchase fuel made from petroleum, which is often shipped thousands of miles from other countries, and causes a tremendous amount of pollution to drill for, refine, and ship, when instead farmers could be growing hemp for fuel, or get hemp fuel from farmers' hemp fuel co-ops? Why? Because blatantly ridiculous taxation and drug laws that should never have been created now prevent it.

If U.S. farmers and businesses began using hemp fuel in their diesel engines rather than petroleum-based diesel fuel, the petroleum industry would lose tens of billions of dollars every year... Unless of course they instead got involved with the hemp fuel industry, which would be less expensive for them than drilling for, shipping, and refining petroleum.

*If* hemp farming were legal in the U.S., the air would be cleaner, the oceans would be less acidic, acid rain would be reduced, and the hemp plants grown for the production of the fuel would remove tons of global warming gasses from the atmosphere, emit oxygen, and improve the soil. If hemp farming were legal in the U.S., farmers would have more stable incomes and the economies of the small communities would improve.

Under the 2005 energy act approved under the George W. Bush administration the petroleum, shale, tar sand, natural gas, and coal industries are given $13.1 billion in tax incentives, loan guarantees, and other benefits at the expense of taxpayers, wildlife, and the environment. This is at a time when the petroleum industry is experiencing record profits amounting to billions of dollars each quarter – even when many people are loosing their homes, jobs, retirement funds, and other securities. The U.S. government also encourages energy gluttony by giving tax breaks to companies that purchase SUVs, and to people who build large houses. People who have second homes (read: The Wealthy) also get tax breaks on their homes, which is another way that government does not support a sustainable future. The government also falters on the great opportunity to build a renewable economy by way of its lack of requirements for automobile companies to improve their fuel efficiency standards. (As I write this, the Obama administration seems to be progressing on this front. But, time will tell if any significant changes are made.) At this stage it is deplorable that the government would be giving such tax benefits to highly polluting energy industries, especially those that derive fuel from oil sand, which produces more carbon dioxide than is produced by fuels from standard petroleum.

Perhaps the oil tragedy that is taking place in the Gulf of Mexico (and I mean all of the damage being done to the Gulf area in the present day, and the past several decades, and not just the "oil spill" of 2010) is finally raising the critical mass awareness of the damage that the petroleum industry and the use of many millions of petroleum-burning vehicles is doing to all areas of the planet. Maybe this awareness will result in the changes we really need to protect Earth.

In January 2007 the newly elected Democratic Congressional leaders announced plans to remove some of the tax subsidies from the petroleum industry and put that money to work developing and encouraging renewable energy sources, such as from wind, solar, water, and carbohydrates. They announced plans to double the budget of the National Renewable Energy Laboratory in Golden, Colorado, which was established under the Carter administration. Some of that is now happening in 2010, but not enough – and the petroleum industry is still being given access to drill on more public land and in the waters off the U.S. coasts. If the Congressional leaders are smart they will make sure money goes to developing industrial hemp farming inside the U.S. borders.

"In the 2004 and 2006 election cycles, the National Corn Growers Association [a nonprofit that represents more than 300,000 farmers], the Renewable Fuels Association [a trade group], and the handful of companies building ethanol refineries gave a combined $1.2 million to political candidates, according to the Center for Responsible Politics, a nonpartisan group that tracks political donations. Federal legislators from Illinois and Iowa received the most funds."
– Shuck and Jive: How industry and politicians are harvesting ethanol for all its worth, by Rebecca Clarren, *Utne* magazine, May-June 2007, utne.com; written in part with a grant from The Fund for Investigative Journalism, fij.org

Large farming corporations as well as the trade and business associations involved in ethanol production are doing a very good job at getting the government to fund corn ethanol production. They spend millions every year on funding lobbying firms that work to get politicians to pass bills that benefit the corn industry.

Currently the U.S. government is subsidizing the corn ethanol industry with well over five billion dollars per year in tax credits, exemptions, direct funding, and research grants. Multi-billion-dollar corporations in the farming industry, such as Archer Daniels Midland, often benefit from these tax breaks, grants, and other government corporate welfare – while family farmers struggle.

The corn and ethanol industry boasts that the subsidies and so forth create jobs and revive farming communities. But when a large amount of the money is going to large farming and ethanol plant corporations with headquarters in cities, and when the corn is not the best form of fuel that can be created from plants, one has to question who is really benefiting from this government assistance. As ethanol becomes more common, and profits grow, it is likely that large corporations will successfully put more and more effort into owning the industry.

People need to work to get that money flowing into producing more sustainable fuels, including into hemp ethanol, into hemp biodiesel, into cellulosic ethanol made from lawn trimmings, and into solar power.

Government and industry should also work to make the biofuels industry less reliant on fossil fuels for the production of biofuels. While many ethanol distillers use natural gas, which is a major contributor to global warming, currently some ethanol plants burn hundreds of tons of coal per day, which also results in a tremendous amount of air pollution. This is a financial windfall for the coal industry, but horrible for the environment, wildlife, and the health of all life on the planet, including in the oceans, where much of the pollution is settling – turning ocean waters more acidic, which is damaging to all sea life.

In his state of the union address at the beginning of 2007 George W. Bush spoke about funding switchgrass ethanol research and production. We don't need to be planting thousands of acres of switchgrass for fuel, which would take up even more wild and farm land. We already produce an enormous amount of grass in the form of lawn and landscape clippings, which are typically tossed into the trash and hauled to toxic landfills.

The National Renewable Energy Laboratory budget should be more than quadrupled, and a chunk of that budget should be allocated toward intensive development of renewable fuels that have a negative output of greenhouse gasses. Hemp is one that does this because the plant absorbs more pollution than it lets out in fuel use because not all of the plant can be used in energy, and it also grows easily, requiring lower energy output to create than the production and refining of many other types of fuel.

"Hemp could replace most oil and energy needs, and could revolutionize the textile industry and stop foreign dependency on oil imports. And it could significantly reduce or eliminate the negative ecological impacts of these polluting industries.

It is estimated that methane and methanol production *alone* from hemp grown as bio-mass could replace 90 percent of the world's energy needs."
– Hugh Downs, ABC News, 1991

"Hemp oil could be a major player in reducing the fuel crisis. Hemp oil could be a very successful replacement for diesel oil."
– William C. "Bill" Miller, President, Miller Consulting Group, Jackson, Mississippi; North American Industrial Hemp Council Director, NAIHC.org; 2006

"Methane and methanol fuels produced from hemp emit 50 percent less air pollution than its fossil fuel competitor. Co-fired biomass generating facilities can produce cheaper and cleaner electricity. We as a nation are importing more of our energy needs today than we did in 1974, before the OPEC oil embargo, over 50 percent."
– *Practical Guide to Hemp*, HempLobby.org

Hemp does not contain sulfur. Burning hemp fuel does not spew sulfuric acid into the air, and does not cause the acid rain that is the result of burning fossil fuels, such as coal. The increasing acidity of the oceans is a major problem facing the planet.

"We only have three percent of the world's oil, and the Middle East has 66 percent. Do the math. We can't drill our way to energy independence."
– Chuck Clusen, head of the Natural Resource Defense Council's Alaska Project (NRDC.org), as quoted by syndicated columnist Molly Ivins, February 9, 2006

"Seriously, we have a major addiction to petroleum and it has caused many an environmental catastrophe. The oil from hemp seed can fuel your car. It burns much cleaner than the gas you get at the filling station, and you don't have to go to the Middle East to get it. Presently you might have to go to Canada to get it, but that's beside the point. Just think about it… the gas you buy could be grown and processed in your own county!"
– Rob Moseley, Kentucky Hemp Outfitters, KentuckyHemp.com

"The hydrocarbons in hemp can be processed into a wide range of biomass energy sources, from fuel pellets to liquid fuels and gas. Development of biofuels could significantly reduce our consumption of fossil fuels and nuclear power."
– *Practical Guide to Hemp*, HempLobby.org

Some studies have concluded that cities reliant on ethanol and biodiesel will be dealing with more ground level ozone than if the cities remained dependent on petroleum gasoline. The studies I have read did not take into account some or all of the factors that contribute to the toxicity of relying on fossil fuels. They may not have considered the amount of pollution that growing thousands of acres of plants would remove from the atmosphere and how these plants would improve land and water quality. They also may not have considered the lung-damaging and cancer-causing heavy particulate-laden soot that results from burning fossil fuels, or the benzene and polycyclic aromatic hydrocarbons (PAHs) found in petroleum exhaust. They may not have considered the damage done to the land, air, and water of the planet by drilling for, shipping, refining, and then transferring the petroleum gasoline and diesel fuel. At least one of the studies only considered petroleum/ethanol blends as well as petroleum diesel/plant bio-diesel blends, and did not consider 100 percent plant-based fuels. The toxic benzene, hexene, touline, and zylene used in making petroleum fuels are not needed when making plant-based ethanol and biodiesel. 100 percent plant-based fuels would decrease many types of environmental damage while growing the plants would improve the environment.

It is important to note that removing all "plant waste matter" or "plant residues" (such as the "stover" that is the corn stock left over after the corn is harvested) from crop farms is not good for the soil, weakens plants, and propagates insect infestation. To maintain healthy soil there needs to be composting that returns plant matter to the soil. This is important in maintaining nutrient base, soil depth, and preventing erosion. Many of the organisms in the soil survive on rotting plant matter, which in turn feeds the plants that filter rainwater, clean the air, produce oxygen, and provide food for wildlife.

One way to improve and build up the soil base of farms is to return more plant matter to the soil in the form of compost. Currently the food scraps from kitchens, restaurants, cafeterias, and food processing plants mostly end up as trash that is taken to landfills. This is valuable matter that should not be treated as trash. Instead of taking this compostable and nutrient-rich material to landfills it should be taken to compost plants and then returned to the farms. This would help offset the plant matter nutrients that are being removed from the land when the crops are harvested

57

and used as food, oil, fabric, fiber, and fuel. This is even more important in a society that is increasing its reliance on plant-based fuels.

If a cellulosic ethanol industry is to be created, hemp and landscape clipping have many advantages over other forms of cellulosic materials. Problematic issues include the harvesting, shipment, and storage of materials needed for creating cellulosic ethanol.

No matter what, we are going to have to figure out a way to break from the highly polluting and massively destructive fossil fuels that create problems at every stage of their development and use.

Soy and corn are not the answer. Both corn and soy farming are leading to massive environmental damage, especially from the use of farming chemicals used to grow the crops, and from deforestation. One only has to look to Paraguay, Argentina, and Brazil to witness the damage being done by the spread of soy and corn farming, which now take up hundreds of millions of acres in South America. Soy and corn farming is largely controlled by transnational corporations, such as Archer Daniels Midland, Bunge, Du Pont, Monsanto, Pioneer, and Syngenta. Hundreds of thousands of small farmers have lost their land to operations run by these companies. Rivers are being poisoned with chemicals used to grow soy and corn. This has killed off fish, reptiles, crustaceans, and other waterlife, and contaminated sources of drinking water. Birth defects are increasing as women of childbearing age are exposed to the toxic chemicals used to grow mass quantities of corn and soy. Cancer rates are also on the rise among the people who live and work on or near the chemically treated corn and soy fields. Many hundreds of millions of acres of rainforest, wetlands, and swamplands have been destroyed to provide the land for the corn and soy mono-cropping farms. This has also destroyed many forms of wildlife.

When hemp is grown it not only provides oxygen, it also removes $CO_2$ from the air. When the oil is burned, some of the $CO_2$ is released back into the air. Because only part of the plant is used to create cellulosic ethanol and biodiesel, the plant removes more $CO_2$ than is released through burning of the fuel. In this way hemp takes in more $CO_2$ than it lets out, helping to reverse global warming.

"Industrial hemp is a non-drug, earth-friendly, industrial crop that can help reduce greenhouse gas emissions and achieve a greater level of U.S. energy independence."
– R. James Woolsey, Shea & Gardner, Washington, D.C.; Legal counsel to the North American Industrial Hemp Council and former Director of the Central Intelligence Agency, 1993-1996; as quoted by NAIHC.org; 2006

"Hemp is the world's champion photosynthesizer. It converts the sun's energy into biomass more efficiently than any other plant, with at least four times the biomass/cellulose economically as petroleum-based fuels.

Coal and petrochemicals got their energy from the sun, thousands of years ago, storing energy as the plants decayed. When they are burned, they release pollutants into the atmosphere. Biomass fuel releases fewer pollutants, and the fuel source spends the growing season removing carbon dioxide from the atmosphere through photosynthesis; biomass fuels contain no sulfur.

The environmental impact of hemp, then, has been the use of far more environmentally damaging alternatives. If hemp were legal, it could become an economically viable and low-polluting source of fuel, paints and varnishes, textiles and fabrics, paper, and even food. Hemp might replace trees as raw material for press-board or particleboard construction material. You could even make PVC pipe from hemp.

In 1988, the chief administrative law judge of the Drug Enforcement Administration wrote: 'There is no record in the extensive medical literature describing a proven, documented cannabis-induced fatality… In strict medical terms, marijuana is far safer than many foods we commonly consume.' The dangers of hemp are far from overwhelming.

Relegalizing hemp could be the single most important environmental reform we could undertake."

– *The Environmental Impact of the Laws Against Marijuana*, by Alan W. Bock, *The Orange County Register*, Thursday, May 3, 1990. For the record, certain types of grasses can produce more biomass per acre than hemp. This is one reason why landscape clippings are an excellent source for making cellulosic ethanol. In combination with hemp, the landscape clippings collected in towns and cities and brought to ethanol plants can greatly improve our domestic fuel production and use, and reduce our reliance on fossil fuels, including imported petroleum.

"In July 2005, Cornell University published a study saying that it is not economical to produce ethanol or biodiesel from corn and other crops. The study confirmed what other studies have shown in the past. The vegetable sources that are currently (legally) available are insufficient. Hemp is the only proven source for economical biomass fuels, a biomass source."

– Hemp4Fuel.com. For the record, hemp is one of several alternative biomass fuels. See above.

59

"The growing dominance of the petroleum industry had vocal critics at the turn of the century. Scientists Thomas Edison and George Washington Carver, engineer Rudolph Diesel, industrialist Henry Ford, chemist William Hale, and his father-in-law H.H. Dow (founder of Dow Chemical Company) were among those who championed bio-based fuels and plastics."
  – March 2008 Reason Foundation Study on Hemp, Illegally Green: Environmental Costs of Hemp Prohibition. Policy Study 367, by Skaidra Smith-Heisters

"August 13, 1941, Henry Ford first displayed his plastic car at Dearborn Days in Michigan. The car ran on fuels derived from hemp and other agricultural-based sources, and the [fiber and resin] fenders were made of hemp, wheat, straw, and synthetic plastics. Ford said his vision was 'to grow automobiles from the soil.'"
  – The Kentucky Hemp Museum and Library; KentuckyHemp.com. 1998 Historical Hemp Calendar, February. John Roulac. *Industrial Hemp Practical Products – Paper to Fabric to Cosmetics,* page 11; Hemptech.com

"When Henry Ford told a *New York Times* reporter that ethyl alcohol was 'the fuel of the future' in 1925, he was expressing an opinion that was widely shared in the automotive industry. 'The fuel of the future is going to come from fruit like that sumach out by the road, or from apples, weeds, sawdust – almost anything,' he said. 'There is fuel in every bit of vegetable matter that can be fermented. There's enough alcohol in one year's yield of an acre of potatoes to drive the machinery necessary to cultivate the fields for a hundred years.'
  … Ford knew that hemp could produce vast economic resources if widely cultivated.
  … Ford's first Model-T was built to run on hemp gasoline and the car itself was constructed [partially] from hemp. On his large estate, Ford was photographed among his hemp fields. The car, 'grown from the soil,' had hemp plastic panels whose impact strength was 10 times stronger than steel (source: *Popular Mechanics,* 1941).
  … Ethanol has been known as a fuel for many decades. Indeed, when Henry Ford designed the Model T, it was his expectation that ethanol, made from renewable biological materials, would be a major automobile fuel. However, gasoline emerged as the dominant transportation fuel in the early twentieth-century because of the ease of operation of gasoline engines with the materials then available for engine construction, a growing supply of cheaper petroleum from oil field discoveries, and intense lobbying by petroleum companies for the

federal government to maintain steep alcohol taxes. Many bills proposing a national energy program that made use of America's vast agricultural resources (for fuel production) were killed by smear campaigns launched by vested petroleum interests."
— From *Energy Crisis: Ford and Diesel Never Intended Cars to Use Gasoline*, Organic Consumers Association, OrganicConsumers.org

So involved was Henry Ford with developing uses for hemp that the Ford Motor Company ran an operation in Iron Mountain, Michigan, that created various forms of fuel from hemp, including hemp ethanol and hemp coal. Ford workers studied hemp-growing techniques on the Alberta, Canada farm of Albert Fraleigh. Ford wanted to make everything from hemp carbohydrates from fuel to plastics, paint, glues, resins, and fiber. These are also made from petroleum hydrocarbons,

Ford's company developed enamel out of soy. By the mid-1930s soy was also used to make plastics for the horn button and the knob on the gearshift of Ford vehicles. The Ford company also developed fabrics that were about 25 percent soy and used this in the upholstery. A marketing phrase was that Ford cars contained a "bushel of soy," and that Ford was "growing automobiles from the soil."

A photo of Ford is in the December 1941 issue of *Popular Mechanics* magazine. He is shown with a typical-looking car manufactured by his company. But the car wasn't typical. It was made using various plant materials, including hemp fiber and resin, and its engine ran on ethanol. To demonstrate the strength of the material the car is made of, Ford is shown hitting the back fender with a sledgehammer. The title of the article is "Auto Body Made of Plastics Resists Denting Under Hard Blows." The photo is subtitled, "Here is the auto Henry Ford 'grew from the soil.' Its plastic panels, with impact strength 10 times greater than steel, were made from flax, wheat, hemp, spruce pulp."

"After twelve years of research, the Ford Motor Company has completed an experimental automobile with a plastic body. Although its design takes advantage of the properties of plastics, the streamline car does not differ greatly in appearance from its steel counterpart. The only steel in the hand-made body is found in the tubular welded frame on which are mounted 14 plastic panels, 3/16 inch thick. Composed of a mixture of farm crops and synthetic chemicals, the plastic is reported to withstand a blow 10 times as great as steel without denting. Even the windows and windshield are of plastic. The total weight of the plastic car is about 2,000 pounds, compared with 3,000 pounds for a steel automobile of the same size. Although no hint has been given as to when plastic cars may go into production, the experimental model is pictured as a step toward materialization of Henry Ford's belief that some day he would 'grow automobiles from the soil.'"

– *Popular Mechanics* magazine, December 1941

While Ford's personal history of anti-Semitism defines him as a troubled individual, he could at least be credited with wanting to make his cars into what today we call "green vehicles" with ethanol-run engines and parts made from plant matter. He was not successful in these dreams. If Ford had been successful in his car design, we would have a different world. But he didn't succeed, and much of that can be attributed to the companies, investors, and politicians who worked against his ideas (chiefly, the petroleum industry and its network of puppets in the halls of lawmakers, including some of the lawmakers – such as the those owning petroleum wells). Now we have car bodies made of metal with interiors made of petroleum plastics. Engines running on petroleum gasoline became standard – as did roads made out of petroleum asphalt.

Ford was not the only major figure in the automobile industry who had ideas to run cars on plant-based fuel.

When Rudolph Diesel invented the diesel engine he meant it to be run on plant oils, not on petrofuel, which, like Ford, he considered to be a dirty fuel. At the 1900 World's Fair, Diesel demonstrated his engine using peanut oil. Hemp oil is a biofuel that can run diesel engines.

The grime and soot spewed from diesel engines would not exist if diesel engines ran on hemp fuel (or other seed fuels) rather than petroleum fuel. Smog would be reduced. Global warming would be slowed. Lung disease rates would drop. The rivers, lakes, and oceans would be cleaner and safer for wildlife. Growing hemp for fuel would create jobs and oxygen as well as improve the air, soil, and water.

"Ethanol – ethyl alcohol, currently produced by fermenting cornstarch from kernels – is gradually replacing toxic Methyl Tertiary Butyl Ether (MTBE) in the United States as a high-octane, pollution-reducing gasoline additive. As a source for ethanol, corn kernels are economically viable only because of high federal subsidies [corporate welfare]. In the next two to five years, the energy-efficient production of ethanol from cellulosic biomass such as wheat and rice straw, hemp, flax, and corn stalks will become commercially viable. This process also generates much lower overall emission of greenhouse gas $CO_2$, and because most automobile engines can run on 15:85 ethanol/gasoline blends without modification, ethanol will help nations worldwide meet their greenhouse gas reduction goals. Hemp grown for both seed and biomass has a stalk yield of up to 3.5 tons per acre, which would make it an economical source of cellulose for ethanol production. Farmers in

the Midwest could welcome hemp as a profitable addition to their marginally profitable soybean and corn rotations."
– Hemp Industries Association, TheHIA.org; 2004

Government subsidies of the corn ethanol industry plays a part in presidential politics because politicians continue to suck up to Iowa, which has both a huge corn industry and a strong voter pool. The company called Archer Daniels Midland and a few other multinational grain farming companies are making record profits because of the surge in money going toward building a corn ethanol industry. As mentioned, this corn is largely grown using fertilizers made from fossil fuel in the form of natural gas and is spread using farm equipment that uses more fossil fuel in the form of petroleum diesel. The massive monocropping of corn and soy for fuel is depleting nutrients from the thin layer of soil that we rely on for life; is damaging the soil organisms that support life; and is polluting the air, land, and water. The nitrogen fertilizers that leach from the farmland lead to eutrophication (nutrient-loading of water bodies), which reduces water oxygen levels, creating dead zones in streams, rivers, lakes, and the oceans. Massive corn and soy operations are damaging the biodiversity of the planet through the destruction of huge swaths of natural landscape. Continual corn cropping, where corn is the only plant grown season after season without a rotation crop, is particularly damaging to the soil.

As the corn prices rise, farmers in the U.S. are increasing the acreage of corn farming, including on fragile Conservation Reserve Program land that has been identified as environmentally sensitive and that farmers have been under USDA contract to keep uncultivated. Also, because millions of acres of farmland in North America have been turned into subdivisions, stores, offices, and roads, the farmers and large multinational farming companies are looking to produce more corn and soybeans on land that is covered with forest. This is one of the key situations leading to the destruction of the South American rain forests.

As mentioned earlier, people need to work to get money and research invested in more sustainable fuels, including hemp ethanol, and hemp biodiesel, and also cellulosic ethanol made from lawn and landscape trimmings.

However, this is not the answer to the world's problems. The construction of an ethanol industry requires enormous resources in all areas, including land, cement, steel, transportation, delivery, production, and use of machinery to use the end product. Retooling or replacing the 200,000 or so gas stations and the millions of engines that exist in North America alone would be a huge undertaking using multitudes of resources.

I'm not advocating a culture that remains at the same level of relying on the combustion engine and on burning mass quantities of fuels of any kind.

An ethanol-based society is not all rosy and perfect. Especially with the way the ethanol is currently being produced.

The amount of fossil fuels, such as coal, being burned to produce the corn ethanol produces huge amounts of global warming gasses.

Ethanol plants also cause water pollution, which cannot be ignored.

Ethanol also uses water, and each region of each continent has a different water situation, with some regions not as suited for producing large amounts of ethanol. Because ethanol requires huge amounts of water, drought can also severely impact the production of ethanol. Relying on the aquifers is not a solution as they have been greatly depleted (In North American the chief culprit in damaging the aquifers has been the grain industry – which largely exists to produce food for millions of massively overbred farmed animals, to supply meat to restaurants and stores).

I am for reducing use; for rethinking and remodeling our cultures; for changing the way we lead our daily lives; and for massively improving the way we treat Earth. We should all be involved in doing what we can to re-store and protect the environment and all nonhuman forms of life.

To reduce pollution and protect the environment and the soil base that we rely on for survival, people need to rely less on the combustion engine. Living locally, purchasing less, living more frugally, growing some of your own food; composting all food scraps; recycling; reducing electricity use; insulating our homes with natural materials; planting trees and protecting forests; eating a plant-based, organic diet that is mostly raw and locally grown; using cloth shopping bags instead of paper or plastic; and riding a bike or walking instead of using a car are ways that will reduce our use of fuel, and reduce our footprint on Earth more than any advancement that can be made in the alternative fuel industry.

The choices people make in their daily lives that are in tune with "green living" collectively have an impact on what industry is doing. This is be-cause industry reflects culture and/or the demands of the buyers. If you want the world to change, you should change. If you are at all paying attention to the environmental condition of the planet, and how that is rapidly degrading because of human activity and use of resources, it should be very clear to you that human culture needs to make extensive and radical changes to the way it is treating Earth and the life on her.

"We are desperate to preserve our access to Middle East oil because that is the only way we can keep running our society the way we're used to running it. Mostly, we don't want to face the tragic misinvestments we've made in the infrastructure of happy motoring, and we don't want to face the inconvenient truth that there really isn't any combination of alt fuels that will permit us to keep running all the cars the way we like to run them. Either we keep getting the oil or say goodbye to the American Dream Version 2.K.

... Every time somebody blames the politicians for this predicament, I'm reminded that the politicians are actually doing a fine job of representing what their constituents want. What they want is to not change their behavior. Not even the science and technology folks want to think about changing our behavior. They just want to find new ways to continue the old behavior. They've invested in the triumphal effort to come up with a happy motoring rescue remedy.

... It seems to me the answer to all this is clear: the first thing the U.S. has to do is reach a different consensus about our behavior here at home, starting with the proposition that the happy motoring era must end."

– Jim Kunstler, author of *The Long Emergency;* Kunstler.com

Stop driving. Walk or bike. Use less plastic. Become a vegetarian. Grow some of your own food. Compost all food scraps. Disconnect from fossil fuels. Work for a more sustainable economy on a local level. Support organizations working to restore, protect, and preserve forests, meadows, wetlands, swamps, rivers, lakes, and oceans. Donate money and/or time to organizations working to protect wildlife and its habitat. Doing these things will improve our health.

# The Palm Oil Debacle

Another oil that is being used for fuel is palm oil.

Palm oil is the most widely produced food oil. It is an extract of the fruit of the oil palm tree. Palm kernel oil is extracted from the seeds of the fruit.

The sprawl of oil palm plantations is wiping out thousands of species in Malaysia and Indonesia. That is where more than 25,000 square miles of hardwood rainforest have been cleared and are being used to grow palm oil. In 2006 Malaysia was the world's leading producer of palm oil. Their palm oil industry brings in about $6 billion, and is second only to their electronics industry.

One of the chief reasons why orangutans on Borneo and Sumatra are facing extinction is that vast expanses of the forests where they have lived have been cleared by fire to expand oil palm and tropical wood plantations. Included in the list of species that are facing extinction because of these plantations are the Sumatran rhinoceros, Asian elephant, and Sumatran tiger. Several hundred people have also died in recent years defending their land against the expansion of the palm oil industry.

Oil palm plantations and production of palm oil damages the environment by reducing the soil base, poisoning the rivers, and polluting the air. Because peat swamps of Southeast Asia are also being drained to grow oil palm plantations, this increases environmental damage as the carbon escaping from the drying peat contributes to global warming. Roads created to manage the plantations cut through waterways, destroy more wildlife habitat, and provide ways for hunters of exotic animals to gain easy access to endangered wildlife.

Palm oil, which is high in saturated fat and low in polyunsaturated fat, is often cited as unhealthful oil that promotes heart disease. It is especially harmful to health after it has been heated.

It is often cited that raw palm oil is beneficial to health because it contains carotenoids, co-enzyme Q-10, magnesium, vitamin K, omega fatty acids, and tocotrienols. Because of its betacarotene content, raw palm oil has an orange tint, but when it is heated the carotenoids and other nutrients are destroyed and the oil becomes white and very unhealthful to consume.

There are many fruits and vegetables that are excellent sources of the nutrients found in palm oil, and that do not cause damage to the environment and wildlife.

Often palm oil is labeled as "vegetable oil" in everything from chocolate to bread, cookies, margarine, shortening, and microwave popcorn. It is also used in makeup, lotions, soaps, shampoos and conditioners, in toothpaste, and in detergents. It has been used as an industrial lubricant for

66

machinery.

More recently palm oil is being used as an ingredient in biodiesel. As demand increases for biodiesel, the governments of Southeast Asia have been seeking out every possibility of taking advantage of this market and are promoting the export of palm oil.

A more environmentally safe and sustainable oil to use for combustible engines is hemp oil, and preferably grown in the regions where it is being used.

# Alcohol and Petroleum

"In 1859, near the peak of domestic industrial hemp production, another event occurred that would soon change both the politics and economics of U.S. industry: the drilling of the first oil well. Three years later, a federal tax was levied on alcohol to help pay for the Civil War. Though the target of the tax was purportedly beverage alcohol, it made fuel and industrial uses of alcohol prohibitively expensive—a condition which persisted, despite the repeal of the tax in 1906, through alcohol Prohibition from 1920 to 1933. The result was exceptionally fast growth in the use of petroleum feedstocks in first fuel and then plastics. Petroleum-derived textiles diminished the market for domestic hemp even further."
  – March 2008 Reason Foundation Study on Hemp, Illegally Green: Environmental Costs of Hemp Prohibition. Policy Study 367, by Skaidra Smith-Heisters

"Last year Royal Dutch Shell alone spilled a record 14,000 tons of crude oil in the Niger Delta. That's more than 4 million gallons. The Exxon Valdez spilled 11 million gallons in Alaska in 1989. The Niger Delta is the largest wetland in Africa, spanning 20,000 square miles, and is inhabited by some 150 species, all now endangered thanks to oil spills."
  – Shell Game, *Earth Island Journal*, Autumn 2010. EarthIslandJournal.org

"Each day, an area the size of a football field goes under water. In the last half-century, Louisiana's coastal wetlands have vanished at an average rate of 34 square miles a year. One of the main drivers of this loss is the oil and gas industry, which, since the 1990s has dug some 8,000 miles of canals and pipelines through the marshes, allowing seawater to intrude inland and destroy fragile coastal grasses. Before the (2010 Gulf of Mexico) oil disaster made Louisiana's wetlands a national emergency, the place was already suffering from chronic distress."
  – We are All Louisianans, by Jason Mark, *Earth Island Journal*, Autumn 2010. EarthIslandJournal.org

It is interesting to note that the reason biofuels aren't as common today as they should be has to do with a combination of events that began in the 1859. At the time of the Civil War the government placed a tax on liquor to help pay for the war. Because ethanol, which is made from plants, contains alcohol, it too was taxed. At the same time the first petroleum wells were being drilled. A common petroleum fuel of the day, kerosene, was free from alcohol, and couldn't get people drunk. So kerosene escaped this alcohol taxation, and its popularity increased, even though kerosene smells horrible, and is not a clean-burning fuel like hemp oil or ethanol.

The alcohol tax was finally eliminated in 1906, but by this time petroleum fuels had taken over the market, and the electric light bulb was replacing the use of kerosene lamps. When ethanol use began to increase for motors, the government just happened to impose Prohibition on alcohol with the Eighteenth Amendment to the Constitution, which was passed on December 18, 1917, ratified on January 16, 1919, and was set into law on January 16, 1920, once again killing the ethanol/biofuel industry. The enforcement of this law led to a whole underground culture in which a crime element flourished as they made loads of money by providing booze to those who wanted it. This, of course, was not what some people had expected. When prohibition became law, some municipalities thought it would be the end of most crime, and some sold their jails.

For several decades those in the temperance movement had been manipulating the government into passing laws against alcohol. This was only a continuation of various movements to outlaw alcohol based on the belief that alcohol was against God's will. Throughout American history such laws were backed by strict religious groups, such as the Puritans, Amish, Quakers, Shakers, Calvinists, and Baptists, and, after they were established in the 1800s, the Mormons.

In 1784 a prominent doctor in Pennsylvania named Benjamin Rush gave the opinion that excessive alcohol consumption lead to physical and psychological ruin. His opinion was in response to the problems alcohol consumption was causing in society, and especially among those in poverty or who were committing crimes. Using his opinion, in 1789 a group of Connecticut farmers formed a group in support of reducing the use of alcohol.

Another doctor, this one named Billy J. Clark, started a small group in New York in 1808 to support their own struggles with alcohol. Other abstinence or temperance groups formed in various parts of the country, with some being based on mutual support to help the local community members, and others being based on religious beliefs, and some a mix of the two. Those that were stringently religious in nature became the most aggressive, preaching against alcohol with religious zeal and using terminology that related alcohol with ungodliness.

A scowling Presbyterian minister by the name of Lyman Beecher became well known for preaching against the use of alcohol from his pulpit in New England. After Beecher graduated from Yale Divinity School in 1797, he became a pastor in East Hampton, Long Island, where he spoke out against alcohol use and labeled the Jeffersonian Democracy political movement as ungodly. In 1810, Beecher moved to Litchfield, Connecticut, where he preached Calvinism, a strict and conservative religion that was opposed to alcohol consumption. In 1813, he helped to organize the Connecticut Society for the Reformation of Morals, which worked to rid the society of gambling, prostitution, alcohol sales, and drunkenness. Upon moving to Boston, where he was minister of the Hanover Church, Beecher preached against the spread of Unitarianism. In 1825 he helped found the American Society for the Promotion of Temperance, which was backed by a flourishing network of conservative churches with the goal of ridding society of everything they considered to be immoral, and especially alcohol consumption, gambling, and prostitution. Apparently Beecher wasn't against all fun things. He was the father of Harriet Beecher Stowe and 12 other children. The first 8 were from his first marriage. After being widowed, he married again and had four more children. After that wife died, he married a third time. Upon moving to Ohio in 1832, he became pastor of the Second Presbyterian Church of Cincinnati. Also in Ohio, Beecher was a founder of the Lane Theological Seminary, which was involved in turning out ministers who would move west to spread Protestantism. Beecher's ministers carried his religious booklet, "A Plea for the West." It was at the Lane Theological Seminary in 1834 that debates were held to discuss the issue of slavery. After 18 nights of discussions, some joined the abolitionist movement. However, Beecher was against abolitionism and refused to allow Black students into his seminary. He was also against Catholicism. A talk he gave against Catholicism in Boston in 1834 lead to the burning of the convent of the Catholic Ursuline Sisters. Back in Ohio, Beecher was accused of heresy for his evangelistic tactics. After being exonerated by the Presbyterian Church, he spent his last years with his family in Brooklyn, New York, where he died in 1850.

While Beecher had used the pulpit and network of churches in New England to organize temperance groups throughout New England, there were plenty of other preachers and societies at the forefront of the temperance movement, both in New England, and in other states.

In 1934, the American Society for the Promotion of Temperance changed its name to the American Temperance Society and continued its moral righteousness crusade, complete with pamphlets and public gatherings, to rid the country of alcohol consumption. In the following decade the membership of the American Temperance Society grew to what they claimed to be hundreds of thousands throughout the states. Throughout the 1800s, a number of other anti-alcohol groups had formed. Among them were the Anti-Saloon League, the Sons of Temperance, and the Independent Order of Good Templars.

The temperance movement in Britain had also been organized since about the 1830s. The Band of Hope was founded there in 1847. The temperance movement also spread to other countries, including to Australia and New Zealand. Basically, wherever the religious fervor of radical Christianity spread, and wherever they organized to profess their shame and guilt and their so-called high moral standards onto others, so too did the temperance movement. Apparently people were really into the theatrics of having scornful preachers preach hellfire and brimstone, and paid to attend the meetings. As today, in the 1800s, preachers projecting the right level of shame and damnation to guilt-ridden churchgoers could make a good living at it.

Among the rumors the temperance movement spread in the U.S. was that those who drank too much could be engulfed in flames, a result of spontaneous combustion. Another rumor was that alcoholics could set themselves on fire when they lit a cigarette or pipe. Another was that alcohol turned blood into water, which filled the lungs and caused people to drown. Still another was that many types of alcoholic drinks were made of fermented insects, which gave the alcohol its color and smell.

The temperance movement in the state of Maine was lead by Neal S. Dow, who was elected mayor of Portland in April 1851. The product of a Quaker home, Dow founded the Maine Temperance Society in 1827. After failing in earlier attempts, Dow was successful in getting the Maine legislature to pass a bill against the sale of alcohol in 1851, and got the governor, John Hubbard, to sign it into law on June 2nd. The law stated that alcohol was illegal to manufacture and sell in the state of Maine, with the exceptions being that it could be used for "medicinal, mechanical, or manufacturing purposes." By 1855, twelve other states had passed alcohol Prohibition laws. Dow became known as "The Napoleon of Temperance." Two months after the bill was signed into law, Dow was the lead speaker at the National Temperance Convention. He had lost his reelection bid for mayor. With the backing of the Republican Party, he won the mayor's seat again by a slim margin in 1855. It was during his second stint as mayor that the Portland Rum Riots broke out on June 2, 1855. This happened after it was revealed that Dow had authorized the purchase of alcohol that was to be used for "medicinal or mechanical" purposes. Although he claimed that the alcohol was for distribution to doctors and pharmacists, a protest occurred outside of the building where the alcohol was being stored. As night set in, fights broke out and Dow called for the militia, which fired on the crowd, killing a man named John Robbins, and injuring several other protestors. Dow was tried and acquitted of improperly acquiring alcohol. Maine repealed its Prohibition law in 1856. In the 1860s, Dow co-founded the National Temperance Society and Publishing House.

The laws of course didn't stop the sale or consumption of alcohol in any of the "dry" states. Personal distilleries became common, as did trips to purchase alcohol from bordering states. Homemade "bathtub gin," became popular, and also lead to many people becoming poisoned, and some dying. Making wine at home was as easy as could be. The Catholic Church was allowed to keep using it in their ceremonies, which gave winemakers an excuse to label their wine as "sacramental" or "communion" wine, even though it was meant for consumption by anyone who wanted it. Despite the laws, some saloons never stopped selling the stuff.

The anti-alcohol movement gained steam as the National Prohibition Party was formed in 1869, and the Anti-Saloon League was founded in 1893. In 1880, Neal S. Dow was the National Prohibition Party candidate for president. He came in fourth.

In the later1800s, the temperance movement was largely driven by the Women's Christian Temperance Union as well as by self-serving ministers who preached against alcohol. As with many preachers, they were also likely dealing with their own learned guilt and shame.

The Women's Christian Temperance Movement was founded in 1880. It was said to have been organized to protect women from abusive husbands, to improve the state of the poor, and to eliminate public drunkenness and alcohol-fueled violence. But it became much more than that. Many religious fanatics became members, and used their association to preach their moral concepts to anyone who would listen, and to many of those who didn't want to. The organization went on to form the Department of Scientific Temperance Instruction, with the goal of getting schools to teach against alcohol consumption, which they did by lobbying for legislation in every state of the union.

Industrialist John D. Rockefeller took such an interest in the temperance movement to outlaw alcohol that he donated an estimated $25 million to the cause. But, it wasn't so much that Rockefeller wanted to stop people from getting drunk. Even though he liked people to think otherwise, it was known that Rockefeller was a drinker. Instead, he wanted to eliminate alcohol from the market for other reasons.

In 1870, Rockefeller had founded Standard Oil Company, which was a petroleum fuel producer based in Cleveland, Ohio. Much of what they produced in those early years of the company was kerosene, which was used in lamps. The product line of Standard Oil quickly expanded. In 1872 the combustion engine was invented, and it ran on ethanol (plant alcohol). It could also be run on petroleum gasoline.

In 1880 it was Rockefeller's money that got Kansas to add a Prohibition Amendment to its constitution.

In 1892 the diesel engine was invented by Rudolph Diesel, and it ran on plant oils. It could also be run on petroleum oil. While kerosene lamps became less popular with the invention and use of the electric light bulb, Standard Oil saw the demand for engine fuel increase as the use of motorized vehicles became popular.

Using his political connections, Rockefeller manipulated the markets to create a monopoly in oil refineries. This was another reason why Rockefeller wanted alcohol out of the picture. His interest in getting alcohol off the market was about eliminating the ethanol as a competition as an engine fuel. Through his Standard Oil Company, and then through investments in other industries, Rockefeller became the richest person in the world. Sometime between 1910 and 1920, it is estimated that he became the world's first billionaire.

Rockefeller was a supporter of the legendary temperance advocate named Carrie A. Nation, a large woman who was known to carry a hatchet into saloons and destroy the bar and the alcohol stock.

Born Carry Moore, Nation was a product of a troubled family with a history of mental illness ruled over by a mother who is said to have experienced phases where she thought she was Queen Victoria. Because of her mother's mental issues, Carry was often tended to by the family slaves and lacked a formal education. On November 21, 1867 she married Dr. Charles Gloyd, but separated even before their daughter, Charlein, was born. Gloyd, who was an alcoholic, died in 1869.

In 1877, Carry married a lawyer and minister named David A. Nation who was 19 years her senior. After her marriage, Carry began using the name Carrie A. Nation. After a cotton farm they had purchased in Texas failed, the Nation's moved to Medicine Lodge, Kansas. In their new town, her husband became a preacher as Carrie ran a hotel. It was also where Carrie founded a branch of the Women's Christian Temperance Union.

After organizing her branch of the Women's Christian Temperance Union, the group began holding protests outside of local saloons. As the group got more creative with their protests, they learned that they got more attention from newspapers. Eventually Nation began bringing an organ with her to serenade saloon patrons with leering gospel lyrics meant to shame drinkers into sobriety and the doorway of her husband's church.

On June 5, 1990, Nation had what she considered to be a message from God to, "Take something in your hands, and throw at these places in Kiowa and smash them." She interpreted this as meaning that she needed to damage the saloons in the town of Kiowa. At first she and her followers brought rocks with them to shatter the bottles of booze in the saloons they raided. Being arrested for her protests didn't stop her. At a half-joking suggestion of her minister husband, Nation began carrying a hatchet and used it to shatter the bottles in the saloons while her followers stood by singing church hymns.

To raise funds, Nation went on speaking tours, sold souvenir hatchets and publicity photos, and published a pamphlet called *The Smasher's Mail*, and a newspaper named *The Hatchet*.

73

After raiding saloons in downtown Kansas City, in April 1901 Nation was fined $500 and banned from entering the city. Her husband also divorced her.

After collapsing while giving a speech in Eureka Springs, Arkansas, Nation died on June 9, 1911 and was buried in Belton, Missouri. The Women's Christian Temperance Union paid for her headstone, which reads, "Faithful to the cause of Prohibition, she hath done what she could."

Those behind the temperance movement pressured school systems and textbook publishers to include anti-alcohol messages in their lessons. By the late 1800s anti-alcohol lessons were required in schools around the country using text approved by the Scientific Temperance Instruction movement. In the early 1900s they stepped up their efforts to outlaw alcohol throughout the country. While some of the claims they made about what alcohol could do to a person's health were based on truth, the temperance activists greatly distorted the facts.

> "The liquor traffic is the most fiendish, corrupt and hell-soaked institution that ever crawled out of the slime of the eternal pit. It is the open sore of this land."
> – Reverend Mark A. Matthews, Seattle, 1909

Michigan passed a law on May 1, 1918, that outlawed alcohol. They later changed their state law to make the fourth liquor offense punishable with a life sentence. In 1929 the dangerous person they slammed with this charge was 48-year-old, whiskey-drinking, moonshine-selling mother of ten, Etta May Miller. This put both parents of those ten children in prison because Etta's husband Alvin was also in prison for violating the Prohibition laws. On Etta's appeal the arresting officer confessed that the police planted the liquor found in the Miller home.

> "Our only regret is that the woman was not sentenced to life imprisonment before her ten children were born. When one has violated the Constitution four times, he or she should be segregated from society to prevent the production of subnormal offspring."
> – The General Secretary of the Board of Temperance, Prohibition and Public Morals, on the conviction of Etta May Miller

The temperance leaders were known to be anti-immigration, anti-European, anti-Black, anti-Mexican, anti-Catholic, and anti-Semitic. And they were influential in getting laws passed that agreed with their so-called high morals. They did this by pressuring voters and candidates, sending massive letters and telegraphs to Congress with falsified signatures, and publishing and handing out literature. They dressed children in white and used them to help hold public protests against alcohol at the places where it was sold. They testified at Congressional subcommittee hearings, which entered their words into the Congressional Record. They took copies of this and distributed it as factual information when they knew they were not truthful in their testimony. Their actions were key in passage of the Eighteenth Amendment.

Benefiting most from Prohibition was the petroleum industry, because if alcohol became illegal, so too would ethanol. The Mafia, "organized crime" organizations, and those who otherwise worked against the laws, also benefited as they took control of the underground market to supply alcohol to anyone who wanted it.

While the U.S. Pharmacopoeia omitted alcohol as a medicine in 1916, alcohol was still a part of many prescription drugs, and this too provided reason to manufacture alcohol, which then ended up in the underground market.

Companies permitted to create alcohol for industrial purposes, such as for use in paints and cosmetics, also got in on the game by making alcohol for the underground market. The Prohibition Bureau required industrial alcohol to be uningestable, thus much of the industrial alcohol had been mixed with poisons or made to taste horrible so that people wouldn't drink it. Some people did drink the poisoned alcohol and suffered the consequences, including some who died.

Many people learned to make alcohol after it became unavailable for sale, and this caused the deaths of some who created and/or drank lethal concoctions. Some companies sold personal distilleries, which weren't illegal.

> "The prestige of government has undoubtedly been lowered considerably by the Prohibition law. For nothing is more destructive of respect for the government and the law of the land than passing laws which cannot be enforced. It is an open secret that the dangerous increase of crime in this country is closely connected with this."
> – Albert Einstein, 1921

Private but illegal clubs called speakeasies opened where visitors could get drunk, and perhaps gamble as well as get laid. Boats took people out to ships anchored off the coasts, including in the Great Lakes, where the people could gamble, dance, and drink. The ships also functioned as safe havens for those smuggling alcohol in from Europe and Canada. Other smugglers used "fast crab" boats to bring the smuggled goods to shore, or left them just off shore marked by buoys for the onshore contact to gather later. In other words, people continued to drink alcohol.

75

Al Capone was on the rise in Chicago, and alcohol Prohibition got him there. His clubs served alcohol, provided jazz entertainment, and became havens for gambling and prostitution. As his wealth grew, so did the government's focus on him. But he knew he had them under his control. After the famous 1929 St. Valentine's Day Massacre, which resulted in the death of six men, Capone's empire spread throughout the Midwest. This is because the target of the attack, George "Bug" Moran, left the region. During the depression, Capone's organization ran soup kitchens that did more for Chicago's poor than the government. The back rooms of these soup kitchens also functioned as parlors for Capone's various business interests. He knew that thousands of hungry poor people would not put up with police raiding kitchens giving out free food. He also had his hands in the pockets of various city officials.

Hoover directed Andrew Mellon to get Capone. As U.S. Treasury Secretary, Mellon was over both the Prohibition Unit and the Internal Revenue Service. Using the now legendary Prohibition Agent, Eliot Ness, and his mythically flawless (but realistically corrupt) team of "Untouchables," the Prohibition Unit worked to close down Capone's alcohol stills and breweries. Using U.S. Attorney E.Q. Johnson, the IRS got a warrant to seize Capone's financial records.

The government was finally able to arrest Capone after finding his records to be both incomplete and inconsistent. He was charged with 22 counts of tax evasion, and thousands of violations of the Volstead Act. In 1931, Capone was convicted of tax evasion. He was fined $500,000 and given a severe sentence of 11 years. After his appeals failed, his sentence began in 1932.

While the very public conviction of Capone brought people to fear the IRS, the public also viewed the government's frame-up job of Capone to be somewhat ludicrous. The Hoover administration was not well liked. His handling of a protest held by tens of thousands of World War I veterans in Washington, D.C. during the summer of 1932 further damaged his reputation. A U.S. military Calvary, led by Gen. Douglas MacArthur, was ordered to shoot at the protestors. Several protestors were killed.

The Capone trial also further damaged the reputation of Andrew Mellon. Already unpopular because of his handling of events (including Prohibition) that led to the Stock Market Crash, Mellon left is position as Secretary of the Treasury on February 12, 1932. As I detail in other parts of this book, Mellon was a key figure in the destruction of the hemp industry. During the Roosevelt administration, Mellon was investigated for tax fraud.

After Eliot Ness moved to Cleveland, Ohio, he became the Director of Public Safety in 1935, which put him in charge of both the police and fire departments. Ness worked to modernize the departments while cleaning up the city's corruption and crime. He also kept busy working to break down

Cleveland's established mob network. From 1935 to 1938 the police department was working to figure out who was leaving dismembered torsos in various parts of the city. The serial murders remain unsolved and are the topic of the 2001 book, "Torso." During this period, Ness, the former and legendary Prohibition Agent, was known for his public displays of drunken behavior. The Great Lakes Brewing Company named a beer after him. The Brewpub bar has never repaired the bullet holes Ness shot into the bar. His personal life was unraveling and he divorced his wife in 1938. After leaving his job in 1941, in 1942 he moved to Washington, D.C., where he worked to break up prostitution rings largely supported by military and government personnel. Moving back to Cleveland to work for a safe company, Ness failed in a run for mayor in 1947. At age 54, Ness died in 1957 of a heart attack.

While suffering from syphilis, Capone was released early from prison and was treated in a Baltimore hospital. He spent his last years in Palm Island, Florida, where he died of a heart attack on January 25, 1947.

On the East coast, the prohibition laws helped the Kennedy family to become richer. Joe Kennedy, who was already rich from banking, various business investments, and stock and commodity trading, apparently sold bootlegged and smuggled imported liquor during Prohibition. Some say he didn't. But, he sure had accumulated a large stash of liquor during Prohibition, which he sold after Prohibition ended. In addition to his dabbling in the stock market, during which he practiced what we is now illegal and what we now call "insider trading," he invested money in Chicago real estate, including in the country's largest office building, the Merchandise Mart; in a Florida racetrack; in Hollywood studios; and the Pantages Theatre chain. His involvement with actress Gloria Swanson is legendary. He also helped Franklin Roosevelt win the election. When Roosevelt was asked why he appointed a crook like Joe Kennedy to head and straighten out the U.S. Securities and Exchange Commission, Roosevelt is said to have replied, "Takes one to catch one." When Prohibition ended, Kennedy's company, Sumerset Importers, had signed deals to become the exclusive American importers of Gordon's Gin and Dewar's Scotch. Kennedy was known for saying outlandish things about Jews. Those comments and his lack of support for Britain during WWII dashed his hopes of becoming the U.S. President. He was an early supporter of Joe McCarthy, who once dated Joe's daughter, Patricia. Robert Kennedy once served as a senior staff member on McCarthy's investigations subcommittee. In 1957, *Fortune* magazine estimated Kennedy's wealth to be in the range of $200 to $400 million, which meant he was among the richest people in the world. His fortune, and his political, business, and underworld contacts helped get his son, John, elected to the White House. Joe wanted his first son, Joe Jr., to become president, and he was grooming him for the position. But Joe Jr. was killed carrying out a bombing mission in 1944.

From its beginning to its end, Prohibition was a national disaster. Like many laws, it made the poor people poorer, and rich people richer. While the people were suffering from the nation's ailing economy, the government was spending hundreds of millions on enforcing the Prohibition laws. The costs included building jails. They also included hiring, and training officers, who often became corrupt by the easy money to be made in making and selling liquor, or protecting those who did. Many police officers, politicians, and government workers got involved in smuggling and bootlegging ventures. Unfortunately, people, including many police officers, died as a result of the laws against alcohol. Local governments lost out on tax revenue that would otherwise have been flowing in if alcohol had remained legal. Prohibition was an enormous waste of money and lives.

"People of wealth, business men, and professional men and their families, and, perhaps, the higher paid working men and their families, are drinking in large numbers in quite frank disregard of the declared policy of the National Prohibition Act."
– Commission of Enquiry in their report, 1931. The eleven-member Commission included the president of Radcliff, Ada Comstock, and had been appointed by the Hoover administration to study the Prohibition laws. Hoover worked to hold this information until after his election so that it would not interfere with his support from the "dry voters."

Shades of the end of Prohibition came early. On May 4, 1923, the governor of New York, Al Smith, repealed the New York Enforcement Act. If the federal government wanted the bootleggers busted in New York, they would have to do it themselves, but that task was also considered to be too expensive for the feds. Having the state of New York fail to enforce the Prohibition law was seen as a major step toward failure of Prohibition.

"Prohibition only drives drunkenness behind doors and into dark places, and does not cure it, or even diminish it."
– Mark Twain, in a letter to the *Alta Californian* newspaper, May 28, 1867

"There is as much chance of repealing the Eighteenth Amendment as there is for a hummingbird to fly to the planet Mars with the

Washington Monument tied to its tail."
– Texas Senator Marris Shepard, who co-authored the Prohibition Amendment

By the time alcohol Prohibition was repealed by the Twenty-First Amendment on December 5, 1933, the petroleum industry had gained a stronghold on supplying fuel for planes, trains, trucks, tractors, ships, motorcycles, and automobiles. Ethanol and plant-based fuels were not being invested in. Fossil fuels and the billionaires who ran the companies that supplied them ruled the market. This set the stage for the massive fossil fuel pollution and subsequent problems the world is experiencing today.

The dependence on petroleum turned the U.S. away from being an agrarian (largely a farming and rural) country and into being an industrial country.

Plant fuels remain easy to produce. But the government keeps its laws preventing the best fuel plant, hemp, from being farmed on U.S. soil.

Those who would be able to grow hemp would be able to experience the great benefit from it – if industrial hemp farming were legal.

It should be clear to anyone knowing the facts about hemp that it must be included in any serious discussion about getting society off fossil fuels.

# Hemp Benefits Small Farms

"My friend across the border in Manitoba, Canada, is making money raising industrial hemp. I am losing money by raising wheat."
– Farmer and North Dakota State Representative David Monson

Hemp plants are good for the soil. The roots of the plant mine nutrients from below the soil, bringing them up to the top of the plant, where the nutrients end up in the leaves. The leaves are naturally high in nitrogen, a soil nutrient. As the plant grows, it continually sheds its leaves, providing for a buildup of the soil base. When hemp is harvested it is often cut and left in the fields for a number of days. During this time more leaves fall off, giving the topsoil a nutritive boost. Even when the plant is not left in the field, the leaves that are removed in the processing can be composted and returned to the soil as a nutrient. Because hemp improves soil and needs no harsh chemicals to grow, it is an excellent crop to grow in seasonal rotation with other crops.

"A limiting factor in sustainable agriculture is the lack of profitable rotation crops. Hemp could be quite profitable as it fits well into the corn-soybean rotation. The University of Minnesota has suggested that the corn-soybean rotation is unsustainable. Farmers are losing money and equity on the corn-soybean rotation. In North Dakota, farmers have been making more money by selling wheat straw to particleboard [manufacturing] plants than from the wheat itself. Due to the bulkiness of hemp fiber, processing facilities will have to be built near the production areas. This will provide new jobs and investment in rural America."
– North American Industrial Hemp Council, NAIHC.org; 2006

"The nation that destroys its soil destroys itself."
– Franklin D. Roosevelt

Another way hemp plants are beneficial to farms is that hemp "chokes out" weeds. For fiber, the plant is typically grown in rows that are only four inches apart. Because it creates a lot of shade and grows so densely, it prevents weeds from growing to adulthood, thus sprouting the weed seeds, but preventing more seeds from forming because many of the weeds die before they are able to produce seed. The result is that after the hemp is harvested, the soil is ideal for planting with another crop but without the problem of weeds. This reduces the use of toxic herbicides (weed killers) that are carcinogenic and a major source of land, aquifer, and water pollution.

More than half of the hemp farms in Canada do use herbicides and other farming chemicals, but the demand for organic hemp is a driving force for farmers to use organic farming methods. Hemp grown using chemical fertilizers yields more seeds, which bring in more money per acre. This means that organic hemp seed products cost more for consumers. As the demand for organic hemp increases, the farmers are developing ways to successfully grow and harvest hemp with greater yields using organic methods that will satisfy the organic market. As more farmers grow organic hemp, the prices improve for consumers.

Hemp can also be used to provide fast-growing ground cover in areas where fire and floods have left land barren and susceptible to erosion. The deep root system of the hemp plant helps prevent erosion of the soil. After the hemp is harvested it leaves behind loose soil that is perfect for growing other plants.

Now that the tobacco industry is finally losing some of its undeserved appeal for investors, it would be a good thing if the tobacco farmers could start growing hemp instead of tobacco on part or all of their land. Whereas growing tobacco is labor-intensive and requires massive amounts of fertilizer, often in the form of manure, hemp is a relatively easy crop to grow, and leaves the soil in better shape than before the hemp crop was planted. Turning a tobacco farm into a hemp farm would be an easy transition and the crop would have an instant market as it can be sold to the numerous companies that already import raw hemp materials from other countries. The farmland already exists, and hemp flourishes in the same climate as tobacco, corn, oats, wheat, flax, cotton, and soybeans – which make up a large chunk of the world's farmlands. Hemp would make an excellent rotation crop with these other crops.

"Seeding should not begin until soil temperatures have reached a minimum of 42-46°F (6-8°C). Hemp seed germinates within 24 to 48 hours, and emerges in five to seven days with good moisture and warm temperature. Hemp grown for fiber should be seeded as early as possible while hemp for grain should be seeded later to minimize the height of the stalk.

… Fiber hemp is normally ready to harvest in 70 to 90 days after seeding.

… Retting is carried out in the field and depending on the weather it takes 14 to 21 days to be completed. During retting, the stems need to be turned one or two times in order to allow for even retting, since the stems close to the ground will remain green while the top ones are

retted and turn brown. Retting is complete when the fibres turn golden
or grayish colour and separate easily from wood in finer fibers."
— *A Cropping Guide for Farmers: Industrial Hemp Production*, by Peter
Dragla M. Sc., Redgetown College, University of Guelph, Kenex
Research Associate; Kenex.com/FarmersGuide.html; quoted in *A
Practical Guide to Hemp*, HempLobby.org

"[Hemp] could make the very difference between the survival of
the family farm and its extinction. It is much more valuable than corn
or other grains and has many markets."
— Willie Nelson

Farmers may be interested in growing hemp as a rotation crop to help
build the soil base, rest the land, prevent flooding, kill off noxious and
invasive weeds, work as wind blocks, and provide a bonus crop between
crop seasons. Hemp grows in all 50 states and this can help local economies
flourish, become less dependent on outside sources, and create their own
fuel. Family farmers and small companies can benefit financially by creating
markets for their hemp products.

Hemp yields approximately three to four tons of dry stalks per acre,
and up to more than four times more fiber than some types of trees
commonly used for paper. This is similar to the kenaf plant, but hemp has a
much greater range of uses. The kenaf plant is also not frost resistant, and
has a longer growing season than hemp. Thus, hemp can be established as a
superior crop.

Commercial, genetically engineered trees can produce more biomass
and pulp per acre than hemp. Genetically engineered forest can also
produce as much as six or more tons of biomass per acre annually. But the
environmental problems caused by genetically engineered trees greatly
surpass the benefits. (To learn more about the dangers of genetic
engineering of plants, access: SeedsOfDeception.com.)

"Cotton uses half of all the chemicals that are used in American
agriculture every year! That's around 30 million pounds annually. That's
not good for the soil, air, water, or you. Hemp, on the other hand, is
largely critter resistant, chokes out weeds effectively, and can grow in
conditions that would make a cottonseed yell 'uncle!' Hemp fiber is at
least three times as strong [as cotton] and it's nice and soft when spun
into fabric."
— Rob Moseley, Kentucky Hemp Outfitters, KentuckyHemp.com

Hemp is easier to grow than cotton. Hemp has few natural predators,
but cotton fields are typically sprayed with large quantities of pesticides,

herbicides, and defoliants. Cotton farms also use chemical growth regulators that trigger even growth of the crop. Switching to hemp from cotton farming would eliminate the thousands of tons of pesticides, herbicides, and defoliants used on non-organic cotton fields every year – the very same chemicals that poison groundwater, rivers, lakes, and oceans.

"Industrial hemp processing produces different materials depending on which element of the plant is the major goal of the production. In most hemp growing areas of Europe the crop is being grown densely to produce long strong fibers for the specialty papers sector, and reinforcement fibers for the automotive trade. In China it is grown in the same way to produce fiber for the textile industry. In other regions such as Poland, and in Canada, the production of hemp seed is more developed. This means that the volume of stems produced is much less than it would be when the plant is grown for multiple uses to provide fibers, wood, and seed as it is in France."
 – Steve Allin, in the article Building with Cannabis: The Hemp House I Built and the Book That Came from It, *Cannabis Culture* magazine, November/December 2006; CannabusCulture.com. Allin is the author of *Building with Hemp*; HempBuilding.com

Hemp farming needs to be decriminalized. Farmers should be able to grow it without threat of prosecution, and to sell it freely to manufacturers of the thousands of products that can be made with hemp fiber, pulp, cellulose, oil, protein, and resin.

In February 1938, *Popular Mechanics* magazine recognized the absurdity of importing fabrics that could be made domestically. In its Billion Dollar Crop article, *Popular Mechanics* reported that "Our imports of foreign fabrics and fibers average about $200,000,000 per year; in raw fibers alone we imported over $50,000,000 in the first six months of 1937. All this income can be made available for Americans." (The article largely was based on information written in an October 12, 1937 letter from H.W. Bellrose, president of the World Fibre Corporation, to Elizabeth Bass, district supervisor of the Federal Bureau of Narcotics.)

Today as the worldwide hemp industry is expanding, it would benefit the U.S. to stop importing hemp, and to start growing it and processing it domestically. Hemp industries in other countries won't suffer if they stop exporting their hemp to the U.S. This is because the hemp market is expanding so quickly that domestic markets will eventually require all of that hemp, and more.

# Hemp for Paper Saves Forests and Protects Wildlife, Water, Land, and Air

"You can make every grade of paper from toilet paper to newspaper at one-fourth the cost."
– Jack Herer, author of *The Emperor Wears No Clothes;* JackHerer.com

"Hemp paper is stronger and has greater folding endurance than wood pulp paper."
– Lyster H. Dewey and Jason L. Merrill. *Bulletin #404,* U.S. Department of Agriculture, 1916

"Hemp makes terrific paper and cutting it down is what it's planted for in the first place. Hemp paper is stronger and more recyclable than tree-based paper. Wood pulp has a high concentration of lignin, a bonding agent that makes wood pulp hard to work with when making paper. Never fear! Dioxin is here! (Dioxin is) one of the most toxic substances known to man, but it sure does break down lignin and, unfortunately, everything else. Hemp doesn't need dioxin (to be used during the paper-making process) because (hemp) doesn't have as much lignin (as wood does) in its hurd (i.e., its woody core)."
– Rob Moseley, Kentucky Hemp Outfitters, KentuckyHemp.com

"The paper industry is seeking new sources of pulp with depleting timber resources. 'Forest Product Extenders' is the term given by the industry, for agricultural fibers used in manufacture of products, continuing the life of the forests. The combination of long and short fibers of hemp allows it to be a prime raw material for paper-making. Fine Bible paper, cigarette papers, and bank notes have for centuries been made from hemp."
– Practical Guide to Hemp, HempLobby.org

"Because of both its chemical and physical composition, hemp can produce high pulp yields and can be pulped without use of the Kraft process (used for chemical pulping of wood and long-fiber specialty papers) which uses sulfur compounds that are environmentally toxic. Also, as with other non-wood pulp, hemp can be bleached with peroxide and through other processes that do not involve chlorine. The environmentally preferable pulping processes are those, such as the Organosolv process, where processing chemicals and waste products

84

can be recovered and reused either within the pulping mill or as marketable byproducts like fuel or fertilizer."
 – March 2008 Reason Foundation Study on Hemp, Illegally Green: Environmental Costs of Hemp Prohibition. Policy Study 367, by Skaidra Smith-Heisters

Since hemp has become illegal, and trees have been used as the main source of materials to make paper, the forests of the world and wildlife dependent on those forests have been devastated. Cutting down millions of trees for paper year after year has resulted in the extinction of plants and animals, and the polluting of streams, rivers, ponds, lakes, and oceans from land stripped of trees. Additionally, wood pulp paper manufacturing plants use toxic chemicals that also contribute to pollution of land and water. Many paper manufacturing mills still dump their untreated pollution directly into streams, rivers, lakes, and the ocean.

Because of its low lignin content, hemp takes fewer chemicals than wood pulp does to convert into paper and cardboard. Hemp is naturally whiter than tree fiber, which means that it can be bleached using environmentally benign hydrogen peroxide. Wood pulp is bleached with chlorine bleach, which generates toxic dioxin. With fewer chemicals used to make hemp from paper the result is a cleaner and safer environment.

Additional benefits of hemp paper is that the fibers in hemp are much longer, making a stronger paper than what is made using the short fibers in wood. Hemp paper is acid-free, which means it lasts longer than paper that has been bleached.

A growing threat to the environment is the cultivation of genetically engineered trees, as well as the increased use of pesticides on many tree farms and on tree plantations. A majority of these trees are being grown to make products that could be made with hemp.

International Paper is one company that uses pesticides on their farmed trees that are cut down for paper pulp and fiberboard. This has caused great harm to bee populations. A reduction in bee populations sounds like a very soft threat, but it is quite serious. All populations of the estimated 4,500 species of bees in North America have been on steep decline, and much of this can be blamed on chemicals used on tree and food farms. Bee pollination results in many of the foods that humans survive on as well as a large amount of the food that wildlife consume. The wild bee populations need to be protected. Chemical pesticides that kill bees should be outlawed. (To learn more about the dangers of genetic engineering of plants, access: DeedsOfDeception.com. To learn more about the collapse of bee populations, access: VanishingBees.com.)

"75 to 90 percent of all paper used from at least A.D. 100 to 1883 was made of cannabis/hemp. Books (including Bibles), money, and newspapers all over the world have been mainly printed on cannabis/hemp for as long as these things have existed in human history."
– Jack Herer, author of *The Emperor Wears No Clothes*; JackHerer.com

"Industrial hemp production has recently been the subject of increasing study around the world. In the Pacific Northwest, regional paper and wood products companies are becoming more interested in agricultural fiber sources to meet their raw material needs. Hemp is one among many possible agricultural products that could supplement or replace fiber currently supplied by foreign and domestic wood species. … There is little doubt that industrial hemp can be successfully cultivated in some areas of the Pacific Northwest.
… Until legislative restrictions are removed from hemp, it is unlikely that investments in improved production technology will be made or that the required industrial infrastructure will be developed."
– Feasibility of Industrial Hemp Production in the United States Pacific Northwest; Oregon State University, Department of Crop and Soil Science; May 1998, by Daryl T. Ehrensing

"Tough and durable, hemp content paper can be finished to a smooth-surfaced sheet with as good as or better print qualities than virgin wood-based paper. The markets for hemp content paper are growing, including not only high-quality post-consumer waste printer paper, but also ecological product packaging, brochures, and promotional materials for progressive businesses."
– Hemp Industries Association, TheHIA.org

"Farming 10,000 acres of hemp will provide as much paper, building materials and pulp as 41,000 acres of forest."
– *USDA Bulletin 404* issued in **1916 [!]**, the result of a study seeking solutions to the problem that America was using up its forests. The study concluded that hemp was the solution to saving our trees and wildlife. More modern figures using today's technological breakthroughs in farming, and in hemp and tree production, while still impressive, and favoring hemp, are not as dramatic as those stated in 1916. However, when the environmental benefits of growing, processing, and using hemp for paper are compared to growing, processing, and using trees for paper are taken into consideration, hemp wins by a landslide. Deforesting land leads to

landslides, the extinction of species, poisoned rivers and lakes, and global warming.

"Using hemp can eliminate our dependence on trees. One acre of hemp produces the same amount of paper as four acres of trees, four times a year, at 1/4th the cost of wood pulp paper and with 1/5th the pollution. Hemp only takes 90-100 days to mature for harvest, while most trees take 50 to 500 years. Hemp paper can be recycled ten times, as opposed to three times for most tree-based paper. Hemp paper production can reduce wastewater contamination normally associated in paper production. Hemp production reduces the need for acids, and lends itself to environmentally friendly bleaching instead of harsh chlorine compounds. Hemp paper does not yellow with age and is acid free. 1,500-year-old hemp paper has been found."
– *Hemp: A True Gift from God(ess)*, by Dr. Heather Anne Harder, SeattleHempFest.com/Facts. For the record, certain trees, especially those in genetically engineered tree forests managed by lumber and paper companies can produce more pulp for paper than hemp. The claim that one acre of hemp can produce the same amount of four acres of trees holds true under certain conditions, and only within certain temperate regions. Many regions of the U.S. could produce two crops of hemp per year, and certain limited regions can produce four crops per year – depending on for what the hemp is being grown. Hemp grown for seed requires a longer growing period, and it also needs to be planted wider apart than hemp that is being grown for fiber or pulp. The abundance of hemp is relative to temperate zone, season, and water and soil conditions.

A Hungarian named Dr. Ivan Bocsa began studying hemp in 1949 when he was hired as an assistant to Dr. Rudolf Fleischmann, founder of the GATE Agricultural Research Institute in Kompolt, Hungary. Fleischman had been studying hemp since 1920. Along with a German hemp consultant named Michael Karus, Bocsa is the co-author of the technical book, *The Cultivation of Hemp: Botany, Varieties, Cultivation, and Harvesting*. Using a variety of hemp that Fleischmann had developed, Bocsa bred a variety of hemp named Kompolti, which is ideal for use in paper manufacturing.

"I think we'll see hemp paper as the biggest area of growth, followed by textiles, and then followed by insulation. But we need to have a lot of factories upgraded before this can really happen. Still, this

is a very exciting time, and there are great things happening right now. We can be very hopeful."
– Dr. Ivan Bocsa, From Hungary with Love, by Deborah Kirk, *Hemp Times* magazine, 1999

Hemp and other plants like kenaf, switchgrass, jute, and bamboo should be the main sources of pulp for paper and cardboard.

Other paper fiber plants include everything from banana leaf, flax, rice straw, bluegrass stubble, wheat, and typical lawn cuttings. Hemp, bamboo, and even coconut husks and palm fiber are excellent raw materials for manufacturing fiberboard, plywood, and flooring that is stronger and environmentally safer than wood. Hemp is the most environmentally safe of all plant fibers that can be used for paper, construction board, paneling board, and base flooring. Bamboo is another environmentally sustainable source for paper. Any of these would be better to use for paper rather than having to cut down a forest every time J. K. Rowling finishes another book, and every time Oprah gives her stamp of approval on a new book.

"Wood-based paper manufacturing, which has replaced the use of agricultural fibers like hemp for papermaking, is the fourth most energy-intensive industry in the United States today, accounting for 5.6 percent of industrial carbon dioxide emissions in 2005. Paper manufacturing from wood pulp also typically requires the use of sulphur and chlorine, chemicals known to cause environmental harm. The high chemical and energy requirements of wood pulping result from the need to remove the lignin content (a type of plant glue) and isolate the useful cellulose present in the raw material. The balance of cellulose to lignin is more favorable in fiber crops, and hemp is a prime example."
– March 2008 Reason Foundation Study on Hemp, Illegally Green: Environmental Costs of Hemp Prohibition. Policy Study 367, by Skaidra Smith-Heisters

We should stop cutting down the forests of the world to manufacture wood and paper products. Most of the oldest trees on the planet, from Australia to Asia, Africa, the Americas, and Europe, have been cut down in the last 150 years, and relatively few remain.

Please access VoteHemp.com to learn how you can support the movement to legalize industrial hemp farming in the U.S.

# Hemp Seeds for Nutrition

In addition to all of the benefits hemp provides in the areas of fuel, construction materials, cleaning the air, producing oxygen, improving soil quality, reducing the use of toxic farm chemicals, protecting forests, providing material for clothing, and localizing economies, hemp is an excellent source of nutrition.

Hemp seeds do not contain tetrahydrocannabinol (THC), the psychoactive drug properties of the adult marijuana plant. There is often some very trace amount of THC residue on the seed hulls from the flowers. But this is a minimal amount that would not contribute to a person getting high from consuming hemp seeds or hemp oil. It is also not enough to cause a person to fail a drug test, even if they were to consume hemp foods every day.

Raw hemp seeds contain enzymes and biophotons, which are essential to life. They also contain amino acids and essential fatty acids in the ratios humans need to maintain optimal health.

The amino acids in raw hemp seeds are of the highest quality. Amino acids are the building blocks of protein. The human body needs a constant supply of amino acids. Raw hemp seeds, raw hemp seed powder, and the cold-pressed oil extracted from the seeds provide amino acids.

The body cannot maintain vibrant health without a continual supply of quality dietary amino acids.

Raw hemp seeds are especially rich in omega 3 fatty acids, which are lacking in the diets of people who largely consume fast food, processed food, cooked food, and animal protein-rich diets. A person doesn't need to consume the clarified oil of the hemp seeds to obtain the essential fatty acids of the seeds. The oil is in the seeds, and consuming the seeds, such as by tossing some fractured raw hemp seeds onto a salad, provides the full spectrum of nutrients contained in the seeds, including the beneficial oils.

People who follow a diet that is lacking in amino acids and essential fatty acids experience a less vibrant total physical appearance, which would include the skin, hair, nails, and eyes. Collagen protein is the most abundant protein in the body and is largely dependent on a constant supply of amino acids. Collagen is often cited as the protein that provides for skin health, strength, elasticity, and beauty. Collagen plays a part in the health of all body tissues, from the bones and teeth to the hair and nails. It also is present in the corneas and lenses of the eyes.

Raw hemp seeds provide the essential fatty acid and amino acid nutrients in excellent form and ratio for the body to maintain vibrant, strong, elastic, and healthy tissues.

89

Raw hemp oil also provides nutrients that maintain the collagen protein in the blood vessels, and that help to maintain a healthy cholesterol level. The essential fatty acids in raw hemp seed oil assists in the transference and metabolism of fat-soluble nutrients throughout the body. The globule edestins protein found in hemp is similar to the globulin of blood plasma that is essential to the formation of antibodies that fight off disease. Hemp seeds contain a ration of immune-boosting globulins higher than any other food plant. These are utilized as a nutrient when hemp is consumed and work in the formation of antibodies.

"Hemp seed oil appears to be one of nature's most perfectly balanced EFA [essential fatty acids] oils. It contains both EFAs in the right proportion for long-term use, and also contains gamma-linolenic acid (GLA). It is the only vegetable oil with this combination."
– Udo Erasmus, *Fats That Heal, Fats That Kill;* UdoErasmus.com

The gamma-linoleic acid (GLA) nutrient in raw hemp seeds is also found in mother's milk. GLA is also present in black currant oil, borage oil, and primrose oil. GLA is good for the skin, hair, nails, and tissue growth, and it reduces inflammation. Along with all the other stellar quality nutrients in raw hemp seeds, the GLA content means milk produced from raw hemp seeds is an excellent food for babies (unlike soy milk, which is not so good for babies).

"Hemp seeds contain up to 24 percent protein. A handful of seed provides the minimum daily requirement of protein for adults."
– Ed Rosenthal, *Hemp Today*, page 101

Raw hemp seeds are also a quality source of calcium, phosphorus, potassium, vitamin A, vitamin E, thiamin (B1), niacin, and trace nutrients including iron, manganese, magnesium, and zinc.

Heating hemp seeds degrades and/or destroys some of the nutrients in the seeds.

"You can basically divide (hemp seed nutrition) roughly into three components. There are essential fatty acids in the oil – omega-6, omega-3, omega-9 – and also minor fatty acids like gamma linolenic acid and stearidonic acid. So that's one-third of its composition. Another one-third consists mostly of fiber, both soluble and insoluble. And it's also one-third protein.
… There are some oils on the market – hemp oil, crushed from the hemp seed. Again, that has the same ratio of omega-6 to omega-3 – which it's most known for – as well as the other omegas that I

described, and we can talk more about that. So there are oils. People also take the entire seed and shell it – that is, take the shell off the inside and you then just have the soft interior. So you're removing a lot of the carbs and leaving primarily protein and oil. Then you can make protein powders from them by removing the oil and milling the rest into something like flour, then sifting it to remove more of the carbs so that you're left with a higher protein fraction. I make all of those products and I make them certified-organic. In addition to that, I incorporate hemp seeds into more commonly used foods, like energy bars and salad dressings."

– Ruth Shamai, RuthsHempFoods.com; in interview with Mike Adams, Health Benefits of Hemp Foods, NewsTarget.com; August 23, 2005

Hemp oil contains more of the essential fatty acids than any food oil. In addition, no food oil provides the ideal balance of EFAs that hemp seeds provide. With a minimal 35 percent oil content, hemp seed oil is only 8 percent saturated fatty acid while also being 55 percent linoleic acid (omega-6), 25 percent of the greatly beneficial alphalinolenic acid (omega-3), and 1.7 percent gamma linoleic acid (GLA: Super omega-6). Hemp also contains the important stearidonic acid (an omega-3). These constituents are essential to the human body in building a strong immune system. The linoleic acids found in hemp seeds are vital to the transfer of nutrients and oxygen throughout the body, to the health of cell membranes, and to the removal of toxins. The EFAs in raw hemp seeds also lower cholesterol, improve brain function, keep the joints healthy, and maintain nerve health.

Victoria Boutenko points out in her book, *Green for Life*, that people that follow a diet rich in omega 3 fatty acids are more likely to maintain a healthful weight. Omega 3 fatty acids are in fresh foods such as fresh leafy green vegetables, germinated buckwheat, germinated chia, raw walnuts, and raw hemp seeds. Victoria is a big advocate of green smoothies, which consist of fruit, green leafy vegetables, and water blended at high speed. Victoria also wrote a book titled *Green Smoothie Revolution*. Drinking a green smoothie every day is one way to assure an adequate dose of omega 3s. Omega 3s are susceptible to spoilage, so companies producing manufactured or processed foods like foods that contain fewer omega 3s. It has also been found that farm animals consuming their natural diet, such as cows that are let to graze on grass and wildflowers in meadows have a higher amount of omega 3s in their body tissues than farmed animals that are kept in cages in factory farms and that are fed an unnatural diet of grains and high-protein processed feed. To maintain vibrant health, be sure to include raw green leafy vegetables as part of your daily intake. (See my book, *Sunfood Diet Infusion*, for more information on this topic.)

"The omega-3 molecule is unique in its ability to rapidly change its shape. This exceptional flexibility of omega-3s is passed to organs that absorb it. Omega-3s thin the blood of humans and animals as well as the sap of plants. As a result of these qualities, omega-3s are utilized by the fastest functioning organs in the body. For example, omega-3s enable our hearts to beat properly, our blood to flow freely, our eyes to see, and our brains to make decisions faster and more clearly."
– Victoria Boutenko, author of Green for Life. RawFamily.com

You may have heard that the heart-healthy oils in fish are superior nutritional oils because they contain eicosapentaenoic acid (EPA) and docosahexaenoic acid (DHA) (omega-3 fatty acids). But fish are often contaminated with heavy metals from polluted waters. Most fish on the planet are also over-fished. Many of the fish sold in markets come from fish farms, which are not sustainable, damage local environments, risk contaminating wild stocks, and are often fed unhealthful diets that include dye to make their flesh appear healthy. Farmed fish are also treated with antibiotics, which can play with your own immune system when you consume the farmed fish. Some of the ALA in hemp converts into EPA or DHA inside the human body, thus providing nutrients that can be obtained from eating fish. People don't need to be killing and consuming fish to get those nutrients; raw hemp oil, green leafy vegetables, sea vegetables, and certain other plant substances provide the nutrients in a way that is more healthful and sustainable.

According to research detailed in the book *Fats That Heal, Fats That Kill* by Udo Erasmus, deficiencies in essential fatty acids play a role in a variety of health problems, including allergies, arthritis, bone depletion, cancer, cardiovascular disease, depression, diabetes, glandular atrophy, hair and nail problems, liver disease, multiple sclerosis, poor wound healing, pre-menstrual syndrome, skin issues, sleep disorders, slowed brain function, sterility, stress, weakened immune system, and weight problems.

Because of its high unsaturated fat content, hemp seed oil should be refrigerated. It is not good for frying or sautéing (fried and sautéed foods are not healthful anyway – especially when compared to raw, fresh fruits and vegetables). But, hemp seed oil is good for many other food uses, including as an ingredient in salad dressings, hummus, dips, spreads, and sauces. A growing number of baked foods found in natural foods stores contain hemp seed oil as well as hemp seed flour.

I don't typically use much refined oil of any sort. I believe a lower fat diet is best. We naturally obtain oils from the fruits and vegetables we eat. Even lettuce and lemons contain quality oils, as do all edible plants, including raw seeds, and raw nuts. If you do choose to use oil in your food, raw hemp seed oil is a very good choice. Raw flax seed oils is also a good choice, but hemp oil contains a better balance of omega 3s.

Hemp seeds can be used to make non-dairy milk, which is of a better quality than soymilk. The high levels of plant estrogens in soymilk are not ideal for daily consumption by men. Hemp milk can be made by high-speed blending hulled raw hemp seeds combined with vanilla, water, dates or honey, and, if desired, a pinch of sea or pink salt. For added minerals, I add a pinch of powdered dulse or kelp. Some people also blend in one or two raw Brazil nuts because the selenium in Brazil nuts is good for male fertility (but eating more than several Brazil nuts in a week can provide too much selenium, which can cause brittle nails, skin rashes, upset stomach, and other issues). The essential fatty acids in the raw hemp seeds as well as in the raw Brazil nuts help to increase testosterone. The amino acid profile combination of the hemp seeds and Brazil nuts are an excellent source of protein. The minerals in the kelp and dulse, as well as those in the Brazil nuts combined with the globule edestins and raw enzymes of the hemp seeds provide other high quality nutrition. This hemp milk can also be blended with berries, peaches, or other natural ingredients, such as powdered raw carob, which provide antioxidants. This milk is nutritionally far superior to cow milk, and much safer for the environment.

Currently it is illegal to possess raw, live (viable) hemp seeds in the U.S. All whole hemp seeds that are brought into the U.S. must be fractured, or heated, or fumigated to kill them so that they can't sprout. The heat and fumigation damages the nutrients of the seed, greatly lowering the quality of some of the nutrients while killing others.

Vacuum-packed, raw, dehulled, and fractured hemp seeds are available in many natural foods markets. These hemp kernels are of a color similar to sesame seeds, have a nutty flavor, and must be refrigerated to preserve the oils and nutrients that become less stable once the seed's hull (outer layer) has been removed.

When a person purchases hemp seed oil at a natural foods store or other venue in the U.S., that oil has either been brought into the U.S. in oil form after the raw seeds have been pressed, or the oil is from seeds that were killed before they were brought into the country and then crushed for their oil once the seeds were imported. Many companies that make hemp oil then sell the leftover, fiber- and nutrient-rich crushed hemp seed "meal" to companies that make food products, including dog food.

It is better to consume raw hemp seed oil that was pressed from living seeds than it is to consume oil that has been heated, or that is from seeds that had been fumigated. The fresher the oil, the more healthful it is. The oil is fragile and breaks down easily when exposed to heat or light. Keeping it refrigerated in a dark glass bottle will help to preserve it.

If hemp were legal to grow in the U.S., the nutritional value of the oil would be of a higher quality and the price of the seeds would be lower. Farmers, the environment, wildlife, and people would all benefit from this on many levels.

"Hemp seeds contain 25 percent high quality protein and 40 percent fat in the form of an excellent quality oil.

… [Hemp seed oil] has a remarkable fatty acid profile, being high in the desirable omega-3s and also delivering some GLA (gamma-linolenic acid) that is absent from the fats we normally eat. Nutritionally oriented doctors believe all of these compounds to be beneficial to health.

Hemp oil contains 57 percent linoleic (LA) and 19 percent linolenic (LNA) acids, in the three-to-one ratio that matches our nutritional needs. These are the essential fatty acids (EFAs) – so-called because the body cannot make them and must get them from external sources."

– *Therapeutic Hemp Oil*, by Andrew Weil, M.D., Ratical.com/Renewables/TheraphHOil.html

"Of all the 300,000 species of plants on Earth, no other plant source can compare with the nutritional value of cannabis/hemp/marijuana seeds. It is the only plant on Earth that provides us with the number one source, and the perfect balance of essential amino acids, essential fatty acids, globulin edestin protein, and essential oils all combined in one plant, and in a form which is most naturally digestible to our bodies."

– Jack Herer, author of *The Emperor Wears No Clothes*; JackHerer.com

"Studies by Dr. Joanna Budwig, M.D. (nominated for the Nobel Peace Prize every year since 1979) have shown unparalleled results in the use of essential fatty acids in the treatment of terminal cancer patients. What are essential fatty acids? The term 'essential' is the tip-off. Truly, there can be no life anywhere without the essential oils, linoleic and linoleic acids. These essential oils support the immune system and guard against viral and other insults to the immune system. Studies are in progress using the essential oils to support the immune systems with victims of HIV. So far they have been extremely promising.

What is the richest source of the essential oil? Yes, you guessed it, the seeds of the cannabis hemp plant. The seeds contain 25 percent

94

LNA acid and 51 percent LA acid. What better proof of the life-giving values of the now illegal seed?

Fortunately, when the Creator made the hemp plant there were no politicians and lobbies for multinational corporations around to advise, and no ignorant congressional committees sitting in executive session to declare it illegal.

What the world needs now is intelligent legalization of cannabis hemp, especially for medical intervention."

– William Eidelman, M.D., UCLA and R. Lee Hamilton, Ed.D, Ph.D. Medical Researchers-Biochemists, UCLA Emeritus, March 20, 1992


But why is hemp illegal, and how and when did that happen? I'll get to that. First, lets talk about...

# Banning Hemp Foods in America

"The industry should have been focused on marketplace promotion and consumer education rather than flushing over $200,000 down the drain battling pointless Drug Enforcement Administration hysteria."
– Eric Steenstra, Executive Director of Vote Hemp;
VoteHemp.com; February 2004

With all the evidence that hemp is a highly nutritious food substance with no other plant providing such balanced levels of healthful substances, what did the George W. Bush administration and the Drug Enforcement Administration try to do about foods and other products containing hemp? They aggressively worked to ban hemp foods from being imported into or manufactured or sold in the U.S.

If the DEA had succeeded, anyone importing hemp or hemp products, or possessing hemp or products containing hemp would face the risk of criminal prosecution – even though hemp is not a drug, and it can't get you high.

The DEA later made revisions to limit the products they sought to ban to those of food products and not industrial products or other items not intended for human consumption that contained derivatives of the hemp plant. This meant, for instance, that you could not import, sell, purchase, or consume hemp protein bars, but you could import, sell, purchase, and use shampoo and conditioner containing hemp oil.

"On October 9, 2001, without public notice or opportunity for comment, the Drug Enforcement Administration issued an interpretive rule purporting to make hemp foods containing any trace of naturally occurring tetrahydrocannabinol (THC), the active ingredient found in marijuana, immediately illegal under the Controlled Substances Act (CSA) of 1971. Because trace THC does not pose any potential for abuse as a drug, the U.S. Congress had exempted non-viable hemp seed and oil from control under the CSA. Similarly, Congress exempted poppy seeds from the CSA, although they contain trace opiates otherwise subject to control.

Sterilized hemp seeds have been available in the U.S. for decades and are recognized as an exceptional source of protein, omega-3 and omega-6 essential fatty acids (EFAs) and Vitamin E. Independent studies and reviews conducted by foreign governments have confirmed that trace THC found in the increasingly popular hemp foods cannot cause psychoactivity or other health effects, or result in a confirmed positive urine test for marijuana, even when unrealistically high amounts of hemp seed and oil are consumed daily. Hemp seeds and oil are as likely to be abused as poppy seed bagels for their trace opiate content, or fruit juices because of their trace alcohol content. Yet, the DEA has not tried to ban poppy seed bagels despite their trace opiates that have interfered with workplace drug testing, which hemp foods do not. The hemp industry is reassuring retailers and consumers that hemp food products should remain on the shelves, as victory in court is virtually certain. David Bronner, chairman of the Hemp Industries Association's Food and Oil Committee, says, 'Based on the law and common sense, we expect that the Court will find that DEA's rules are obviously unfounded and arbitrary.'

… Keep in mind that eating hemp foods in the hope of achieving a 'high' is as likely to succeed as eating corn to get drunk. The notion that eating hemp foods in anything short of super-human amounts will cause false positives in drug screening is farcical as well."

– *Hemp Industry vs. DEA in U.S. Court*, a press release by Kentucky Hemp Outfitters, KentuckyHemp.com; January 7, 2002

The George W. Bush administration along with the Drug Enforcement Administration and the conservative right-wing Family Research Council (FRC) worked together on this goal to ban all food and other products containing hemp.

The FRC is aligned with hyper conservative viewpoints limiting free speech and a free society. The actions of the FRC are devised with the intention of creating what they envision as a more moral society. They claim to support Christian values. By researching the activities of the FRC a person may easily conclude that the FRC is working to create a society that isn't based on values they claim Jesus would advocate.

It is frightening that a group that is as misinformed and closed-minded as the FRC could have so much influence on national policy.

With reasoning based on nonsense, the FRC considered that allowing hemp foods to be sold in America was a gateway to legalizing marijuana. They promoted the theory that hemp products are a looming threat to a drug-free society.

"Despite Bush administration propaganda, hemp foods contain insignificant levels of THC (tetrahyrdocannabinol), the chemical in marijuana that results in psychotropic effects. In that sense, eating hemp foods does not interfere with workplace drug tests, and, in fact, the THC levels in hemp foods are below that of opiates found in poppy seeds in muffins and breads."

– Organic Consumers Association, Organic Bytes #40; September 29, 2004; OrganicConsumers.org

If the FRC had done some simple research they could easily have concluded that one can't get high from foods containing hemp. Nor could one get stoned from burning or ingesting hemp products.

In response to the ban, the Hemp Industries Association (HIA) filed a petition challenging the Drug Enforcement Administration. The HIA had good reason to do so. The association is made up of hemp growers and companies that import, manufacture, and sell hemp products. At that time the association included Dr. Bronner's Magic Soaps, Nature's Path Foods, Hempzels, and Ruth Hemp Foods, as well as Hemp Oil Canada, Kenex, the Organic Consumers Association, and some other businesses.

If the DEA had been successful in banning hemp foods, thousands of people would have lost their jobs and Americans would have been unable to enjoy the nutritional and health benefits of hemp foods and supplements. The Canadian hemp industry would also have suffered – because the U.S. has been the chief importer of Canadian-grown hemp and its extracts, pulp, and fibers.

During the lawsuit the U.S. government spent millions of dollars to make hemp food products illegal. Manufacturers, importers, bakeries, distributors, and stores lost millions of dollars because hundreds of products containing hemp were pulled from store shelves. Some stores, including my local natural foods market, removed all hemp products for fear that they too would become targets of the DEA and would be brought into expensive legal situations.

"On March 21, while most Americans were captivated by the U.S.-led invasion of Iraq, the Drug Enforcement Administration (DEA) published their final rules on hemp foods. The new 'Final Rule' essentially bans the sale of all hemp food products by April 21, 2003, and is virtually identical to an 'Interpretive Rule' issued on October 9, 2001 that never went into effect because of a U.S. Court of Appeals for the Ninth Circuit Stay issued on March 7, 2002. Today, the Hemp Industries Association (HIA) and several hemp food and cosmetic manufacturers will petition the Ninth Circuit to once again prevent the DEA from ending the legal sale of hemp seed and oil in the U.S."

– From *Organic Consumers Association and Natural Foods Industry Slam Drug Enforcement Administration on Ban on Hemp Foods: Stay on DEA Rule Continues; Hemp Industry Confident DEA Harassment to End Soon,* Mary 23, 2003; HempInidustries.org; OrganicConsumers.org

Luckily the courts saw through the DEA lies and then ruled in favor of hemp.

On February 6, 2004, the Ninth Circuit Court of Appeals made its ruling on the case of Hemp Industries Association v. Drug Enforcement Administration, number 01-71662. The ruling was that the Drug Enforcement Administration couldn't ban hemp products. While recognizing that the DEA has regulatory authority over marijuana and synthetically derived THC, the court ruled that the agency did not follow the law in asserting authority over all hemp food products. The court recognized that hemp has no potential for drug use and it ruled that the DEA couldn't regulate naturally occurring THC not contained within or derived from marijuana. Noting that it is not possible to get high from products containing trace amounts of THC, the court recognized that hemp is an industrial plant related to marijuana and that the fiber of the plant has been used to make many products that are useful to society.

"A poppy seed has trace amounts of opiates, but they don't hassle [the bakers] of poppy seed bagels. No one is smoking industrial hemp."
– David Bronner of Dr. Bronner's Magic Soaps, Escondido, California; 2005; DrBronner.com

"A good analogy would be industrial hemp has about as much THC content as the poppy seeds that your bagel has opium.
… What wisdom is there in a public policy that forces manufacturers in the U.S. to send their dollars abroad?"
– California State Assemblyman Mark Leno, appearing in KGO-TV/DT San Francisco news report about his co-sponsoring of the 2007 California Industrial Hemp Farming Act; February 19, 2007

"It doesn't matter. It could be half of a half of a half percent. If it's THC, it's illegal under federal statutes."
– Javier Pena, Drug Enforcement Administration special agent, expressing his absurd viewpoints while appearing on a KGO-TV/DT San Francisco news report on the reintroduction of the California Industrial Hemp Farming. He was responding to a comment that industrial hemp has about as much THC as poppy seeds have opium; February 19, 2007. Opium is also illegal, but we allow poppy seeds to be sold in grocery stores, at bakeries, and even poppy seed muffins to be served in schools.

Imagine the preposterous scenarios that could have taken place if the DEA had succeeded in banning all hemp foods. They could have broken down your door and burst in to arrest you for eating a salad containing dressing made of hemp oil. You could have been arrested while you rested after a jog or a bike ride because you were consuming a nutritional drink or food bar containing hemp seed protein powder. If you were stopped while driving and found to be carrying a sandwich made with bread containing hemp seeds your car could have been impounded. If you were sitting in a park having a family picnic and you had hemp chips with that salsa, you would be breaking the narcotics laws. Churches raising money by having community breakfasts that happened to be serving pancakes containing hemp seed flour would have been in big trouble.

"It's high in fiber, high in protein, vitamin E, essential fatty acids. It's high in everything, but you don't get high from it."
– Lynn Gordon of French Meadow Bakery & Café, Minneapolis, Minnesota. They have been making hemp bread since 2000. FrenchMeadow.com

"This is a huge victory for the hemp industry. The Bush administration decision not to appeal the Ninth Circuit's decision from earlier this year means the three-year-old legal battle over hemp seed products is finally over. The three-judge panel in the Ninth Circuit unanimously ruled that the DEA ignored the specific Congressional exemption in the Controlled Substances Act (CSA) that excludes hemp fiber, seed, and oil from control along with poppy seeds. The Court viewed as insignificant and irrelevant harmless trace amounts of THC in hemp seed, just like harmless trace amounts of opiates in poppy seeds."
– David Bronner, Chair of the Hemp Industries Association's Food and Oil Committee and President of Alpsnack/Dr. Bronner's Magic Soaps; February 2004; DrBronner.com

"More and more health foods containing omega-3 rich hemp nut and oil will be appearing on store shelves since the legal status is no longer an issue.
Americans are looking for healthy alternative sources of omega-3 to supplement their diets due to concerns regarding trace mercury in fish and fish oil supplements.
Right now the U.S. marketplace is supplied by hemp seed grown and processed in Canada and Europe.
We will now work to convince Congress it is time for the U.S. to

again allow American farmers to grow industrial hemp and participate in this lucrative growth market."

– Alexis Baden-Mayer, Director of Government Affairs for Vote Hemp; February 2004; VoteHemp.com

"Now that the DEA cloud over the (hemp) market has lifted, sales are really exploding."

– David Bronner of Dr. Bronner's Magic Soaps, Escondido, California; 2005; DrBronner.com

# States Working to Change Hemp Farming Laws

The misunderstanding of what hemp is and what it can be used for is perhaps the biggest hurdle in the issue of getting the public behind the push to legalize industrial hemp farming.

If people understood the potential of hemp in what it can do for the economy and environment they would very likely support changing the laws banning its cultivation.

Legalization of hemp farming in the U.S. would improve the situation for family farmers, likely result in more family farms independent of corporate infusion, make the country more independent, and keep money in the U.S. that is currently going to hemp industries in other countries. It would also help the environment, protect forests and wildlife, result in a reduction in the use of farming chemicals, build healthier soil, and protect streams, rivers, lakes, aquifers, and oceans.

There are over 30 industrialized countries that allow farmers to grow hemp. Even though Canada had as much as 25,000 acres of industrial hemp growing during 2010, the U.S. continues to outlaw the growing of hemp within its borders, even though the U.S. is the world's number one importer of hemp products to the tune of over $300,000,000 in 2006.

"Industrial hemp is being grown in Canada, just a few miles from the United States border. Raw hemp is being imported into the U.S. for the manufacture of products. A growing market exists for Omega-3 rich hemp seed and oil products including snack foods, body care, and supplements. Several thousand businesses, including Fortune 1000 firms, are participating in this market. With raw materials for these products being imported, U.S. farmers are deprived of the economic benefits stemming from these new markets."
– North American Industrial Hemp Council, NAIHC.org

In February of 2006, North Dakota Agricultural Commissioner Roger Johnson and three agricultural commissioners from three other states flew to Washington, D.C. to meet with Drug Enforcement Administration officials to explore rules for allowing farmers to grow industrial hemp.

On March 9, 2006, North Dakota Governor John Hoeven signed House Bill 1492, directing North Dakota State University to begin collecting and storing hemp seed for the day when hemp farming will be legal in that state.

As of summer 2006, seven states had passed pro-hemp farming laws, including Hawaii, Kentucky, Maine, Maryland, Montana, North Dakota, and West Virginia. Other states that were working to pass bills permitting hemp farming included California, New Hampshire, and Oregon.

On September 30, 2006, California Governor Arnold Schwarzenegger vetoed a bill to legalize hemp farming in that state. While some loathed Schwarzenegger's decision, others agreed with it because of the genetic engineering issues. Hemp bills should specify that the crop should be protected from genetic engineering, and that genetically engineered hemp should not be permitted. (See Appendix 3 to read a letter from Jack Herer to Schwarzenegger, and the press release from Vote Hemp.)

> "Over-regulation of industrial hemp cultivation—for example, laws requiring that hemp seed be purchased from a certified monopoly, that legal hemp varieties contain 'terminator genes,' or that buyers must be identified before farm licenses are issued—should be avoided. The potential for illicit marijuana cultivation is not considered a significant obstacle to industrial hemp farming in any other developed democracy in the world."
> – March 2008 Reason Foundation Study on Hemp, Illegally Green: Environmental Costs of Hemp Prohibition. Policy Study 367, by Skaidra Smith-Heisters

I am against the genetic engineering of plants. I would be in favor of a bill that clearly states that genetically engineered hemp could never be planted. For more on genetic engineering, see the book *The Food Revolution* by John Robbins (FoodRevolution.com), see the documentary *The Future of Food* (TheFutureOfFood.com), contact the Organic Consumers Association (OrganicConsumers.org), access MonsantoWatch.org, and join the group Millions Against Monsanto.

Arnold Schwarzenegger, who has years of pot smoking experience, made a stupid comment about hemp that may either display his ignorance about hemp, a sad attempt at humor, or his goal to spread misinformation about hemp. He made the ridiculous comment when he appeared on the ecology-themed episode of the MTV show *Pimp My Ride*, which takes cars, trucks, and vans and transforms them into hot rods. Upon finding the 1965 Chevy Impala he submitted to be transformed into a biofuel hot rod contained hemp fabric seats, Schwarzenegger made the comment that he made hemp illegal in California. He made a "joke" that someone could end up smoking the seats. An unfortunate choice of words from someone who has the power to approve or veto a bill that could allow hemp farming in one of the largest and most populated states in the country and that ranks in the top ten world economies. To his benefit, he did appear on the show to promote biofuel vehicles, which the Impala was made into with the installation of a diesel engine capable of running on plant oils.

The California Industrial Hemp Farming Act was reintroduced in February 2007. Its sponsors were conservative Republican Assemblyman Chuck Devore and liberal Democrat Assemblyman Mark Leno.

In response to the reintroduction of the California bill, John Lovell of the California Narcotic Law Officers Association stated: "The problem becomes those people who are illicitly growing marijuana and who will use hemp as a blind, if you will, to conceal their marijuana activities." It should be quite clear to someone such as Lovell that marijuana growers wouldn't want their plants anywhere near hemp plants because the pollen from the hemp would pollinate the marijuana and make the marijuana drug content weaker. Maybe Lovell is being evasive in expressing his viewpoints in order to continue the big lie for career sake. Or, maybe he is ignorant about the hemp issue, which would be surprising. Or, perhaps, all of the above.

The bill didn't make it into law.

> "It's absolutely criminal that American farmers, the most productive and efficient farmers on the planet, cannot be allowed to grow a naturally occurring plant that grows wild in America."
> – California's conservative Republican Assemblyman Chuck Devore, appearing on ABC KGO-TV/DT San Francisco the day before reintroducing the California Industrial Farming Act of 2007, which he co-authored with liberal Democrat Assemblyman Mark Leno; February 19, 2007

On January 4, 2007, an industrial hemp farming bill was introduced in New Hampshire. The bill, HB 424, was the seventh hemp farming bill to be introduced in that state in the past nine years. It was referred to the House Environment and Agriculture Committee with the note that "the development and use of industrial hemp can serve to improve the state's economy and agricultural viability, and the production of industrial hemp can be regulated so as not to interfere with the strict regulation of controlled substances in the state."

For each person who is educated about hemp there seems to be a room filled with those who don't understand the issue. Unfortunately the rooms are often the meeting and hearing rooms of lawmakers whose words usually expose their ignorance on the topic of hemp.

When Idaho Agricultural Committee Chairman Representative Tom Trail (R-Moscow, ID) introduced a resolution to urge the U.S. Congress to eliminate federal barriers to industrial hemp farming, the resolution was killed. Lawmakers expressed their ignorant concern that legalizing hemp farming would make it easy for farmers to grow marijuana with the hemp. As Vote Hemp explained it, "Apparently, they weren't aware that marijuana growers don't want to have their specially selected female plants anywhere near industrial hemp, whose male plants would ruin the illicit crop with hemp pollen. The threat industrial hemp poses to marijuana is so serious that last year [2006] in California, legal medical marijuana growers vocally opposed an industrial hemp bill because it didn't contain a clause they desired that would have limited commercial industrial hemp production to agricultural areas of the state where marijuana isn't widely cultivated."

As mentioned earlier, in January 2007, North Dakota began issuing permits to allow hemp farming, but hemp farming remains illegal under federal law. On February 13, 2007 North Dakota's Agricultural Commissioner Roger Johnson delivered two industrial hemp farming applications to the Drug Enforcement Administration. The applications were filled out by two farmers, Wayne Hauge, and more interestingly North Dakota State Representative and Assistant Majority Leader David Monson, a Republican. Johnson said that the DEA officials were "reluctant to accept the applications."

"I felt that we've got a long way to go with the DEA. They made it quite clear that they still do not understand or believe the distinction between industrial hemp and marijuana. That's a pretty fundamental issue."
– Roger Johnson, North Dakota Agricultural Commissioner, after submitting industrial hemp farming applications to the Drug Enforcement Administration; February 2007

On February 13, 2007, a Republican Representative, Dr. Ron Paul from Texas, introduced the Industrial Hemp Farming Act of 2007 (H.R. 1009) into Congress. Written with the help of Vote Hemp, if it had been voted into law, it would have removed restrictions on the cultivation of hemp. In addition to Paul, the sponsors of the bill included nine representatives from seven states, including Congressman Dennis Kucinich, chair of the Domestic Policy subcommittee. As chair of that committee Kucinich could hold hearings on federal barriers to the farming of industrial hemp.

Paul had introduced the Federal Industrial Hemp Farming Act in 2005, but that was defeated. When that bill had been introduced, a luncheon was held that served hemp foods. Speaking at the luncheon were supporters of the bill, including North Dakota Agriculture Commissioner Roger Johnson and North Dakota State Representative David Monson.

When I spoke with Monson in November 2006 he said that he would file a lawsuit against the federal government if they deny his permit to grow hemp in North Dakota. And he did.

"The DEA has the power to waive federal registration for state-licensed industrial hemp farmers, but if they won't, it's up to Congress

to keep the promise our government made to industrial hemp farmers in 1937 when they passed the first federal law regulating marijuana – that they [the farmers] could go ahead raising hemp just as they always had."
– VoteHemp.com, February 2007. Comment refers to the farmers being told in 1937 that they could keep growing hemp. But after the Marijuana Tax Act of 1937 was passed, the Federal Bureau of Narcotics required that all hemp grown be stripped of its leaves, and only the stalks could be sold. When the stalks were sold a heavy tax had to be paid. This greatly increased the cost of producing hemp. This damaged the emerging hemp industry of the 1930s. Investors were lost and the hemp industry folded under pressure and harassment by the Federal Bureau of Narcotics, which was working to protect the interests of the paper, fossil fuel, pharmaceutical, petrochemical, and other industries.

"Let's not be naïve, the pro-dope people have been pushing hemp for 20 years because they know that if they can have hemp fields, they can have marijuana fields. It's stoner logic."
– Tom Riley, White House Office on National Drug Control Policy, responding to the introduction of the 2005 Federal Industrial Hemp Farming Act; November 2005

"It's a silly argument. Does (Representative Dave Monson) sound like a druggie?
… It's legal for us to import hemp stalks and the seed and turn them into clothes and food, but it's not legal for us to grow it. What's the sense in that?"
– Roger Johnson, North Dakota Agricultural Commissioner; November 2005

"It is indefensible that the United States government prevents American farmers from growing this crop. The prohibition subsidizes farmers in countries from Canada to Romania by eliminating American competition and encourages jobs in industries such as food, auto parts, and clothing that utilize industrial hemp to be located overseas instead of in the United States.
By passing the Industrial Hemp Farming Act the House of Representatives can help American farmers and reduce the trade deficit – all without spending a single taxpayer dollar."
– Republican Representative Dr. Ron Paul of Texas, introducing the Industrial Hemp Farming Act of 2007 to Congress, February 13, 2007

"The DEA has taken the Controlled Substances Act's antiquated definition of marijuana out of context and used it as an excuse to ban industrial hemp farming. The Industrial Hemp Farming Act of 2007 will bring us back to more rational times when the government regulated marijuana, but told farmers they could go ahead and continue raising hemp just as they always had,"

– Eric Steenstra, President of Vote Hemp, February 14, 2007; VoteHemp.com

**Tuesday, October 13, 2009; VoteHemp.com**
**Farmers, Hemp Industry Leaders Arrested for Planting Industrial Hemp at DEA Headquarters in Act of Civil Disobedience to Protest 'Reefer Madness'**

Fed Up Captains of Hemp Industry Plant Hemp Seed on DEA's Lawn with Ceremonial Shovels

DEA's Continued Blockade of State Industrial Hemp Programs Violates Common Sense as well as Obama's Presidential Directive to Federal Agencies to Respect States' Rights

WASHINGTON, DC — At approximately 10:00 AM this morning, North Dakota farmer Wayne Hauge, Vermont farmer Will Allen, and fed up American entrepreneurs, who have dedicated their livelihoods to developing and marketing healthy, environmentally-friendly hemp products, for the first time turned to public civil disobedience with the planting of industrial hemp seed at DEA headquarters to protest the ban on hemp farming in the United States. Even though the U.S. is the largest market for hemp products in the world, and industrial hemp is farmed throughout Europe, Asia and Canada, not a single American farmer has the right to grow the versatile crop which is used for food, clothing, body care, paper, building materials, auto paneling and more.

Hoping to focus the attention of the Obama Administration on halting DEA interference, North Dakota Farmer Wayne Hauge; Founder of Cedar Circle Organic Farm in Vermont Will Allen; Hemp Industries Association (HIA) President Steve Levine; Dr. Bronner's Magic Soaps President David Bronner; Vote Hemp Communications Director Adam Eidinger and Founder of Livity Outernational Hemp Clothing, Issac Nichelson were arrested while digging up the DEA's lawn to plant industrial hemp seed imported from Canada. At this time, they are currently being held in Arlington County jail and are awaiting charges. They are expected to be released later this afternoon and will be available for interviews upon release. The six protesters planted hemp seeds with ceremonial chrome shovels engraved with: Hemp

Planting Oct. 2009 ~ DEA Headquarters ~ American Farmers Shall Grow Hemp Again Reefer Madness Will Be Buried

Mr. Hauge is licensed by North Dakota to cultivate and process non-drug industrial hemp, just as Canadian farmers across the border have done profitably for over ten years supplying the booming U.S. market. However, the DEA refuses to distinguish non-drug industrial hemp cultivars grown for millennia for seed and fiber and has unconstitutionally blocked all state hemp programs such as North Dakota's. Mr. Hauge, along with North Dakota State Rep. David Monson, sued the DEA in the U.S. District Court of North Dakota in 2007, and the case is currently before the Eighth Circuit Court of Appeals. "In recent years there has been strong growth in demand for hemp in the U.S., but the American farmer is being left out while Canadian, European and Chinese farmers fill the void created by outdated federal policy," said fourth-generation farmer Hauge. "When hemp is legalized, land grant universities across the nation will develop cultivars suitable to different growing regions to enhance yield and explore innovative uses such as cellulosic ethanol."

Pictures and video of the action for free and unrestricted use, along with hemp farming footage and background information are available upon request in hardcopy and online. An HIA produced video of the action will also be posted, after 6:00 PM on 10/13 at: www.votehemp.com/DEAhempplanting.html

In the back drop of the spectacle at DEA headquarters, dozens of hemp business owners in town attending the HIA convention over the weekend fanned out across Capitol Hill to lobby lawmakers in support of hemp legislation introduced by Representatives Ron Paul (R-TX) and Barney Frank (D-MA) that would permit states to cultivate non-drug industrial hemp under state industrial hemp programs. Nine states have such programs, but their implementation has been blocked by DEA bureaucratic intransigence. This spring, however, President Obama instructed federal agencies to respect state laws in a presidential directive on federal pre-emption:

"Executive departments and agencies should be mindful that in our federal system, the citizens of the several States have distinctive circumstances and values, and that in many instances it is appropriate for them to apply to themselves rules and principles that reflect these circumstances and values. As Justice Brandeis explained more than 70 years ago, 'it is one of the happy incidents of the federal system that a single courageous state may, if its citizens choose, serve as a

laboratory and try novel social and economic experiments without risk to the rest of the country.'"
– Source:
www.whitehouse.gov/the_press_office/Presidential-Memorandum-Regarding-Preemption/

Vote Hemp and the HIA are dedicated to a free market for low-THC industrial hemp and to changes in current policy to allow U.S. farmers to once again grow this agricultural crop. Dr. Bronner's Magic Soaps President and Vote Hemp Director David Bronner stated: "Dr. Bronner's has grown into the leading natural soap brand in the U.S. since incorporating hemp oil in 1999, due in significant part to the unsurpassed smoothness it gives our soaps. As an American business, we want to give our money to American farmers and save on import and freight costs. In this difficult economy, we can no longer indulge the DEA's self-serving hemp hysteria."

On Tuesday, May 18, 2010 North Dakota Speaker of the House, David Monson, and North Dakota farmer Wayne Hauge filed a legal action against the Drug Enforcement Administration in the U.S. Court of Appeals for the District of Columbia Circuit. In announcing the filing by Monson and Hague, Vote Hemp explained, "The DEA has delayed the approval of the farmers' application for federal licenses to grow industrial hemp for more than 3 years. Both farmers have received state licenses to grow hemp for the past four growing seasons under North Dakota's industrial hemp program. Monson and Hague are seeking federal registration that would enable them to cultivate oilseed and fiber varieties as farmers in Canada and Europe already do." Vote Hemp when on to explain that, "For over a decade, North Dakotans have tried to implement non-drug industrial hemp farming under a state licensing program. Even though the state does not require farmers to obtain permission from the Drug Enforcement Administration to grow hemp, Monson and Hauge have done so to ensure that their farms will not be raided by federal drug control agents. Eric Steenstra, president of Vote Hemp, explained that, "If the lawsuit is successful, Monson and Hauge will force the DEA to implement reasonable and timely procedures for granting licenses for the cultivation of industrial hemp."

"In this time of economic hardship, American farmers should not be hamstrung by an irrational and counterproductive federal policy that preempts legitimate and rational state prerogatives to grow nondrug industrial hemp."
David Monson, North Dakota Speaker of the House, May 2010

As of this writing, in late 2010, the federal laws outlawing hemp farming in America still stand. Even if states allow hemp farming, the federal government could put an end to it by tilling it under and taking legal action against those involved with cultivating it.

The Drug Enforcement Administration restrictions on the possible farming of industrial hemp in North Dakota include the following outlandish measures to "alleviate law enforcement concerns":

- Farmers must consent to a criminal background check, including fingerprints
- Who the farmer sells to and how much is sold must be documented within 30 days of sale
- The location of the hemp field must be provided using geopositioning (GPS) coordinates
- Planted hemp must contain less than three-tenths of one percent tetrahydrocannabinol (THC)

"While North Dakota's progress could get hung up by DEA disapproval, lawyers with the hemp industry are preparing a court challenge if the DEA fails to cooperate with North Dakota or California when hemp legislation becomes law. The legal theory supporting the right of these states to regulate hemp farming stems from language in the Controlled Substances Act, which exempts hemp from federal control. Using this legal theory the Hemp Industries Association created a legal precedent when the group [which represents 300 hemp businesses] won their lawsuit in 2004 against [the] DEA, protecting sales of hemp foods and body care the agency tried to ban."
– Adam Eldinger, May 12, 2006; OrganicConsumer.org

"Although the United States permits trade in nonviable hemp seed, oil, and fiber, it is the only major industrialized nation that prohibits the growing and processing of hemp."
– Hemp Industries Association, TheHIA.org

"We currently import hemp products from China, Thailand, England, France, Spain, Holland, Germany, Hungary, Poland, Ukraine, Canada, and Australia. Hemp is grown legally in most industrialized countries of the world. What do these countries know that we don't?"
– *Hemp: A True Gift from God(ess)*, by Dr. Heather Anne Harder; SeattleHempFest.com/Facts

"Used to make rope, build and insulate houses, form the interior panels of cars and even provide the fuel to power them, industrial hemp is also a popular ingredient in organic foods. Sales of industrial hemp foods in natural products supermarkets are growing by 50 percent each year. Seventy-seven percent of all sales of hemp food and body care products are earned by California companies, but California farmers are still out of the loop."

– Organic Consumers Association, OrganicConsumers.org; 2006

# Hemp's History in America

"This may be hard to believe in the middle of the War on Drugs, but the first law concerning marijuana [hemp] in the colonies at Jamestown in 1619 ordered farmers to grow Indian hemp. Massachusetts passed a compulsory 'grow' law in 1631. Connecticut followed in 1632. The Chesapeake Colonies ordered their farmers, by law, to grow marijuana [hemp] in the mid-eighteenth-century. [Town] names like Hempstead or Hemp Hill dot the American landscape, and reflect areas of intense marijuana cultivation."
– Hugh Downs, ABC News, 1991

"Make the most you can of the Indian hempseed. Sow it everywhere."
– George Washington, in a letter to his farm manager, 1794

"What was done with the seed saved from the India hemp last summer? It ought, all of it, to have been sown again; that not only a stock of seed sufficient for my own purposes might have been raised, but to have disseminated the seed to others; as it is more valuable than the common hemp."
– George Washington, in a letter to his farm manager William Pearce, May 29, 1796

"Let particular care be taken of the India Hemp seed, and as much good ground, allotted for its reception next year as is competent to sow."
– George Washington, in letter to his farm manager William Pearce, November 5, 1796

[hemp is] "an article of importance enough to warrant the employment of extraordinary means in its favor."
– Alexander Hamilton, 1791, first secretary of the U.S. Treasury

"The fact well established in the system of agriculture is that the best hemp and the best tobacco grow on the same kind of soil. The former article is of the first necessity to the commerce and marine, in other words, to the wealth and protection of the country. The latter, never useful and sometimes pernicious, derives its estimation from caprice, and its best value from the taxes to which it was formerly exposed. The preference to be given will result from a comparison of

them: Hemp employs in its rudest form more labor than tobacco, but being a material for manufactures of various sorts, becomes afterwards the means of support to numbers of people, hence it is to be preferred in a populous country."
– Thomas Jefferson, March 16, 1791

"Flax is so injurious to our lands and of so scanty produce that I have never attempted it. Hemp, on the other hand, is abundantly productive and will grow forever on the same spot."
– Thomas Jefferson, December 1815

Throughout history the use of hemp has been closely associated with human societies. From China to Africa to Europe, hemp has been known as a versatile plant. Hemp has also been found in mounds built by ancient people in what is now the state of Ohio.

The relationship between hemp and what would become the United States of America is an interesting one.

Nobody seems to know exactly how hemp came to the Americas. Some think it may have been by way of birds or other wildlife. Others think it was brought by the Chinese, the Vikings, or other travelers.

What is known is that hemp is what brought Europe to America.

The sails of clipper ships were made of hemp fabric, and the maps and logbooks on board were made of hemp paper. By 1545 hemp was being cultivated in Chile, and varieties containing psychoactive substances were being grown in Central America where it became known as a spiritually enlightening substance.

Hemp was planted at Jamestown in 1607. Because hemp was such an important crop it is not unlikely that the Spanish planted hemp seed in Santa Fe, New Mexico, in 1610.

By 1611 by order of King James I, hemp farming was required of the colonists in northeastern America. While many colonists turned to growing tobacco because that crop commanded higher prices, it is known that hemp was one of the first crops to be cultivated in the New World, and continued to be an important crop for hundreds of years. In 1619 the Virginia Company ordered the colonists to grow hemp. In addition to Pilgrims, the *Mayflower* carried bundles of hemp seed to America in 1620. The Puritans grew hemp and found that it grew better in the soil and climate of their new land than it did in Europe. The Virginia General Assembly of 1619 required colonists to grow hemp. Other specific laws requiring hemp farming were passed in the colonies. In 1637 the General Assembly Court of Hartford ruled "every family within this plantation shall procure and plant this present year one spoonful of English hemp seed in some soyle." By 1635, Colonists in Salem, Massachusetts had built a "rope walk" (rope factory),

113

and by 1639 they were required to grow hemp for their own use as well as for trade. Other rope factories were being built in settlements along the Atlantic coast (in 1854 Henry Wadsworth Longfellow wrote his poem *The Ropewalk* about a hemp factory). In the late 1600s William Rittenhouse and William Bradford built the Rittenhouse mill alongside Wissahickon Creek near Philadelphia, Pennsylvania. They began making paper out of hemp rags. England was pleased that hemp grew so well in America, and it was imported back to England in exchange for other goods. By the late 1600s hemp was being used as a form of payment for goods and debts.

> "Industrial hemp was a cornerstone crop in early America. In fact, due to its versatility, Americans were legally bound to grow it during the Colonial Era and Early Republic."
> – Organic Consumers Association, *Organic Bytes #55*; April 12, 2005; OrganicConsumers.org

Farmers learned early that hemp could improve soil quality while choking weeds. This is one of the many reasons why hemp became so popular in the early years of what was to become the U.S. Hemp was used by farmers as a rotation crop and helped farmers manage their land.

France required the early Quebecois to grow hemp that was to be sent back to France. While the Europeans had been cultivating hemp in Canada since 1606, it apparently was not enough. The story goes that in 1666 King Louis XIV's representative in Quebec encouraged the growing of hemp by seizing all the thread from the colonists. In a letter, the king's representative, Jean Talon, wrote, "I will only distribute it [the thread] to those who agree to return a stated quantity of hemp."

England would soon find out how well hemp grew in the rich soil across the Atlantic.

Britain's reliance on hemp grown in the colonies helped turn the tides of politics. The colonists were growing hemp, sending the raw materials to England, then having to import the products made from the hemp back to America. This was because England had banned weaving and spinning in the colonies. The colonists were also required to purchase wool products imported from England. The colonists reasoned that they shouldn't have to buy materials made from what they were growing.

By the 1600s the colonists had been making their own fabric, rope, sails, and other materials from hemp. When the British Parliament passed the Wool Act of 1699 forbidding the colonists to import wool for spinning, the colonists simply began to rely more on making their fabrics from flax and hemp.

The American textile industry began to flourish as Irish textile workers began immigrating to America. Ireland had both hemp and wool industries,

114

and these workers were a benefit to the American businesses that hired them. With their own textile industry, the colonists were becoming more independent.

By the 1760s Britain tried to enforce heavier tariffs on goods being imported into the colonies.

In 1765 the Massachusetts House of Representatives paid Edmund Quincy to write "A Treatise of Hemp-Husbandry." It stated that the most important materials were hemp and flax.

In Thomas Paine's *Common Sense* he wrote that hemp was important in gaining America's independence.

The colonists had been making their own paper from flax and cotton, and mostly from the most abundant crop, which was hemp.

George Washington grew hemp at Mt. Vernon and was an outspoken advocate for its use in textiles, paper, oils, and other uses to help America gain its independence.

By 1760 the British had essentially taken control of India, and by 1763 they had defeated France. With those tasks accomplished, the British government turned their attention to gaining more control over America. Having established their presence in India and Ireland, where hemp grew in abundance, Britain no longer was dependant on American hemp. But it knew that America held other resources, and a growing number of colonies, each of which could be taxed to raise revenue.

While increasing its military foothold in America, Britain took measures to regulate the resources, finances, and import/export businesses in America. It did so by creating a number of laws, including those that taxed the colonists to help finance British rule over America. As it was worded in Parliament, these revenue-raising regulations were "for defraying the expenses of defending, protecting, and securing" both the colonies and the Kingdom. In other words, the colonists were being taxed not only to finance Britain's rule in America, but also to fund Britain's rule in other lands. Revenue was also needed because, since the end of the French and Indian War in 1763 (also known as the Seven Years War), Britain sought to maintain an army of 10,000 troops in the colonies, and more in Canada and the British West Indies.

To avoid conflict with the Indigenous societies, the colonists were supposed to stop migrating west of the Appalachian Ridge. To maintain the agreement, thousands of British troops were stationed in the west to both regulate commerce with the Native peoples and keep Whites from settling in "Indian territory." Some Whites, and also those Blacks who had been slaves did move into the territory of the Indigenous societies, not to live separately, but to become part of the communities. In the 1700s, what was then the "Western frontier," and what are now the Midwest and mountain states of America were becoming more of a mix than many people today

115

seem to understand. There were immigrants from Spain, France, Germany, and other European countries living with and adopting the lifestyles of the Indigenous peoples. Many of the immigrants found the Indigenous cultures to be more agreeable, tolerant, fair, and peaceful than what they left behind in European societies, including in the so-called "civilized" colonies. Also, some Chinese immigrants had been adopted into Indigenous groups, especially in the 1800s after having left the brutal conditions of the labor forces undertaking the construction of the railroads. When the Whites were slaughtering the Native Americans, they were also slaughtering some of the European and Asian immigrants who had become part of the Indigenous communities, some were thought of as tainted blood because they had mingled and had children with the Native Americans.

Many of those living in the colonies viewed the Parliamentary Acts dictatorial. Colonists felt they were being ruled over with no say in how their government was to be run. And they were being taxed without having a say in how the tax laws were to be formed. They felt that, and I'll say this in my best American English, nobody from the colonies was speaking for them in Parliament. In other words, it was taxation without representation and without consenting colonial legislatures.

On April 5, 1764 the Parliament of Great Britain passed the Sugar Act. Also known as the American Revenue Act, the Sugar Act placed a three-cent tax on foreign-refined sugar, increased taxes on coffee, indigo, and certain types of wine while banning the importation of rum from non-British islands, and of wine from France. This was an attempt to overhaul an earlier Act, the Sugar and Molasses Act of 1733, which was ineffective and a great failure, and had expired in 1763. The Sugar Act reduced the tax on molasses by half, with the reasoning that the tax would be easier to pay. But, the colonists, who were experiencing economic hardships, were not happy with the Sugar Act. But, their loss was the gain of the British West Indies. This Act was a failure for Britain because increased American domestic manufacturing, and decreased America's reliance on imported goods. In August of 1764, a group of Boston merchants agreed to stop purchasing certain imported British goods.

Also in 1764, Parliament passed the Currency Act. This Act was meant to protect British creditors from being paid with inflated colonial currency. The Act required colonial currency to be based on gold and silver with a one-to-one ratio value equal to British currency.

The Sugar Act was repealed in 1766. In its place, Parliament enacted the Revenue Act of 1766, which reduced the tax on molasses to one pence per gallon, including from British or foreign sources.

On March 22, 1765, Parliament passed the Stamp Act, and it became law on November 1st of that year. The Act required all contracts, court and legal document, permits, newspapers, and playing cards produced or sold in the colonies to carry a tax stamp. Legal documents lacking a legal stamp were to be considered null and void. Countries, particularly in Europe and within Great Britain, had long since enacted Stamp Acts to raise government revenue, so it was no surprise that Britain enacted a Stamp Act for the American colonies. Stamp Acts had already been considered for the colonies, but this was the first time Britain had passed and sought to enforce such an Act in the colonies. The Stamp Act was another way that Britain sought to both gain control over America while also maintaining the colonial military presence.

In the March 1765 Parliamentary debates to negotiate the formation of the Stamp Act, Charles Townshend posed, "Will these Americans, children planted by our care, nourished of strength and opulence, and protected by our arms, will they grudge to contribute their mite to relieve us from heavy weight of the burden which we lie under?"

The actions of the colonists after the Stamp Act became law pretty much answered Townshend's assumptive question.

Tonwshend's view that Britain nourished the colonists with such delicate care was hardly how the colonists viewed Britain. Many of the colonists had never set food in England or on any other foreign soil. An increasing number of colonists had been born in America, and it was all they knew. Having some country across an ocean trying to rule over them was not something they viewed lightly.

Many of the colonists viewed Britain's growing interests in ruling over them, including the British military forces, as a warning. They also did not like the wording of the Stamp Act in that it mentioned "ecclesiastical jurisdiction." Many of the colonists, or their ancestors, came to America to escape the presence of the Anglican Church. Although the colonies did not have Anglican bishops presiding in the courts, some American Anglican Church members in the north were promoting the prospects of a greater church presence. The colonists largely did not care for the idea of Anglican bishops presiding in court. And they did not want the British admiralty courts to take over the colonial courts.

The Stamp Act impacted everyone in all of the colonies, and it became a common concern that all could relate to. Merchant and landowner groups in the colonies began to correspond and become more organized. In June 1764, a five-member Committee of Correspondence was formed in Massachusetts. The Committee was to coordinate information and activities in response to the Stamp Act. In October 1764, a similar committee was also formed in Rhode Island. Hundreds of merchants in New York City organized and agreed to stop importing British goods. Demonstrations and violent protests arose against the Stamp Act and these caused the Stamp Distributors to resign. In response to the Stamp Act, the colonists organized and sent protest petitions to Parliament and the King.

"If taxes are laid upon us in any shape without our having a legal representation where they are laid, are we not reduced from the character of free subjects to the miserable state of tributary slaves?"
– Samuel Adams, Boston, May 1964

If any of the leaders in Parliament lacked an understanding of how the colonists were becoming organized and rallying behind a growing number of their own domestic concerns, the response to the Stamp Act brought them to understand.

Because they were losing money caused by the refusal of Americans to import British goods, manufacturers and merchants in Brittan also spoke out against the Stamp Act. This helped to bring Parliament to repeal the Act on March 17, 1766, and the King agreed to it.

The protests and concerns of colonists that resulted in response to the Stamp Act directly influenced the organization of the Sons of Liberty. Within months there were branches with delegates in colonies from New Hampshire to Georgia. This was another step toward American independence. Four of the delegates were signers of the Declaration of Independence.

In persisting to carry on its rule over the colonies, and affirming its right to tax and to create laws governing the residents of the colonies, on March 18, 1766 Parliament passed the Declatory Act. To put it simply, this Act was also not welcomed by the colonists and helped them to become even more organized and independent.

The colonists also did not care for the Townshend Acts. These were a group of Acts passed in 1767 and 1768. They were far-reaching in that they covered taxes, trade regulations, and legal issues, including judges and governors who were to be independent of colonial control.

In response to the Townshend Acts, John Dickinson wrote a series of twelve essays titled, "Letters from a Farmer in Pennsylvania." The first essay appeared in December 1767. They advised people to avoid paying the taxes imposed by the Townshend Acts as paying the taxes would lead to other taxes, which would all impose hardships on the colonists. Dickenson sent copies of his essays to James Otis of the Massachusetts Bay Colony. Eventually the Massachusetts House of Representatives petitioned King George to repeal the Revenue Act. The Massachusetts House of Representatives also sent out the Massachusetts Circular Letter to other colonial assemblies, which then also petitioned the King.

Dickenson's essays were printed on hemp paper, and it is likely that the paper was produced at the paper mill owned by Benjamin Franklin, who flew his kite using hemp string. The colonists were supposed to be purchasing their paper from Britain. Franklin was the leading producer of paper, and his hemp paper helped reduce Britain's rule over the colonies. As Britain's aggression toward the colonists increased, so did the amount of goods that America was producing for its own use, including hemp for fabric, oil, fuel, paper, paint, varnish, food, bedding, insulation, and animal bedding.

The various Acts passed by Parliament to establish their domain over the American colonists backfired. How the colonists reacted, including the Boston Massacre, the Boston Tea Party, the colonial boycott of British goods, and various other agreements, resolutions, meetings, protests, and events, brought about the American Revolutionary War.

Since it took control of Ireland and India, England had access to all the hemp it needed. But the growing number of military and trade ships among European countries needed hemp sails, hemp rope, hemp caulking, and hemp oil. By the 1770s America was exporting hemp to Europe and using this to purchase weaponry for the War of Independence. America had also formed an alliance with France, which was importing hemp from America.

The first American flags were made out of hemp fabric. The Declaration of Independence was written on Dutch hemp paper, as was the Bill of Rights. The first two drafts of the U.S. Constitution were on hemp paper, with the final draft being on animal skin.

As the U.S. established its own military, more hemp was grown for paper, clothing, uniforms, tents, bedding, blankets, lamp oil, sails, rigging, and caulking.

In 1781, Benedict Arnold, who originally fought for the American Continental Army, but switched sides, led British troops to destroy a hemp rope manufacturing facility in Warwick, Virginia. This was done because the rope being produced was used for America's military forces.

In 1777 Edward Antil wrote *Observations on the Raising and Dressing of Hemp*. In this he wrote that hemp is worthy of the attention "of every trading man who truly loves his country."

"Flax and hemp: Manufacturers of these articles have so much affinity to each other, and they are so often blended, that they may with advantage be considered in conjunction."
– Alexander Hamilton

American money was once printed on hemp paper. President John Quincy Adams wrote a report in 1810 titled *On the Culture and Preparing of Hemp in Russia*.

While some say that hemp was second to cotton as the most important agricultural crop in the U.S., they aren't taking into consideration that hemp provided more than just fabric. Unlike cotton, hemp also provided oil that is better than cotton oil because hemp oil has more uses, and hemp also provides food and paper. To its benefit, hemp fabric takes longer to degrade under the sun than cotton fabric, and its fibers are longer and stronger than cotton fibers. Because of this, hemp makes better and stronger fabrics for outside use, including sails, nets, tents, and rope. With that, hemp could easily be considered as the most important crop in the early days of the U.S. Interestingly, cotton bales were often wrapped in hemp fabric because hemp fabric is sturdier than cotton fabric. Hemp twine was also used to tie the cotton bales. Only after slavery ended, which greatly reduced hemp farming, did cotton bales begin commonly to be tied with wire.

While hemp was important in the U.S., it also remained an important article of trade in Europe. By the late 1700s Russia, on the back of serf labor, had developed a hemp industry that became their number one export, supplying many countries with hemp products. As both military and merchant shipping fleets grew, the demand for hemp sails and rigging continued to grow, and this greatly benefited Russia's hemp industry.

After the French monarchy was overthrown in the French Revolution of the late 1700s, the British navy blockaded the French in the early 1800s in fear that the working class would also oust the British monarchy.

Napoleon partially financed his military by selling the Louisiana Territory to the U.S. This greatly increased the landmass of the U.S. and gave Napoleon leverage. He formed an alliance with the Russian czar Alexander. The signing of the Treaty of Tilset in 1807 was a great strategy. It cut off Russia's trade with England. The British navy fleet as well as the merchant ships needed a constant supply of hemp sails and rope and had long built a reliance on Russia's quality hemp. England then considered any ship that traded with Napoleon's Continental System to be an enemy, which meant that American ships were subjected to blockade and seizure.

While some American sailors from seized ships were sent back to the U.S., others, in one way or another, became part of the British navy. The British used American ships to purchase the hemp products from Russia that the Brits needed for their navy fleet. Napoleon became aware of these dealings that provided England's navy with hemp sails and rigging. In 1810 Napoleon insisted that it be stopped, but the czar refused as his country was greatly benefiting from the trade. Then Napoleon invaded Russia to destroy the hemp crops and to work to stop the supplies of hemp fabric and rigging going to British navy ships.

Meanwhile, England continued to stop American ships from trading with the European continent, continued its blockade, and forced ships to purchase supplies from Mediterranean ports, including from Napoleon and his allies, who needed the trade.

As America suffered from these blockades and seizures, Congress debated going to war, which included plans to permanently or temporarily take part or all of Canada. By this time the U.S. had been planting many acres of hemp to supply both its domestic needs and those of its growing navy.

On June 18, 1812, the U.S. Congress voted to go to war with Britain.

In Europe, Napoleon's armies suffered great losses, mostly due to exposure and inadequate supplies.

In the U.S. Britain burned Washington, D.C. But Britain faltered as its military was stretched too thin with war against a well-fortified U.S. navy while also fighting against France.

On December 24, 1814, Britain and the U.S. signed the Ghent treaty in Belgium. Britain agreed never to interfere with American merchant ships. The U.S. agreed to give up on its idea of taking Canada.

Unfortunately, the news that the war was over hadn't reached New Orleans, where the Americans defeated British armies in January 1815; two weeks after the treaty had been signed. But the treaty wasn't finalized until February 18.

The U.S. was finally at peace with England. It also demilitarized the border with Canada.

As the United States settled in to being its own country, the population of the country expanded westward. As it did, hemp was being utilized in many different ways.

The covered wagons used to cross the Great Plains were covered with hemp fabric, and hempseed oil was used to lubricate the axles, to treat the wood, and to fuel the lamps. The clothing of the pioneers was made of hemp, flax, and cotton.

"In the 1800s, Kentucky regularly accounted for one-half of the industrial hemp production in the United States."
–A History of the Hemp Industry in Kentucky, by James F. Hopkins; University of Kentucky Press, 1951

Americans were literally wrapped in hemp. Millions of American soldiers have worn hemp fabric clothing and shoes. Although early work jeans were originally made from thick cotton, some of the first denim jeans made by the German-born dry goods merchant Levi Strauss were made of discarded hemp-sail fabric from clipper ships in San Francisco. He also made cotton jeans at the same time. He fastened them with copper pocket rivets to improve their durability for California gold rush miners.

By mid-1800s there were hemp farms from Massachusetts to California. In addition to "amber waves of grain," America the Beautiful should have mentioned the significant brilliant fields of green hemp.

It was during the middle 1800s that the industrialists began emerging as major financial and political players. With massive numbers of people

121

migrating west, the railroads became a major business. Tracks were laid across the continent using cheap labor, including horribly abused Chinese immigrants. Those who owned the railroad companies became wealthy. The owner of the New York Central Railroad, Cornelius Vanderbilt, became the richest person in America. Other players, including those who made their fortunes in the petroleum industries, which, as I explain elsewhere, played a major role in creating laws that obliterated the hemp industry while making them even wealthier.

Hemp farming and the production of hemp products peaked in the middle of the nineteenth-century. At that time it was being made into everything from clothing, food, animal feed, paper, rope, and wood preservative, to lantern fuel and lubricant oil.

The hemp industry was flourishing. In 1852 money allocated by Congress was used to build a hemp rope factory in Memphis. Some people in the southern states saw this as a slight because the South had more cotton farms, while the northern states had hemp farms.

Abraham Lincoln's wife, Mary Todd, was from a hemp farming family.

And that was the era when the North fought with the South.

Some people held the opinion that the north wanted to abolish slavery because it would make cotton more expensive to produce, and would level out the competition between the southern cotton industry and northern hemp industry. To validate their point, they mention that the economic competition between hemp and cotton was obviously an issue in the Civil War based on the fact that invading Confederate armies targeted and destroyed hemp processing facilities. But, when taking many other factors into consideration, it is unlikely that hemp was a major factor. Hemp had many more uses than cotton as it was used to create a stronger and more versatile fabric while also providing seed oil for fuel, paint, varnish, wood preservative, and food. Hemp grew easily in all states, while cotton grew only in the warmer climates. What really increased the production of cotton was the invention and use of the machines used to process it. Until the 1900s, there was no machine that could process large quantities of hemp. Also of note is that there were some slaves used in the north, including in the hemp industry. Slavery wasn't only a southern thing.

The southern states were at a disadvantage as they had a lack of skilled workers in a competitive workforce. It was mostly slaves that were used for the labor in the south, while the north had fewer slaves and more workers who were paid to do their jobs and did so at more competitive wages that may have been considered low, but they weren't as low as slavery. The lack of a skilled workforce, and of diverse industries, and the development of the railroads to the west all played a part in the fall of the south and of a united country.

However, hemp did have a role in the war as it supplied fabric and other materials for both sides. But hemp also played another role in this war, which included the 1861 *Battle of the Hemp Bales.*

Lexington, Missouri was home to hemp farms and factories that processed hemp. Northern troops had set up fort at a Masonic college on a hill near the town of Lexington. The rebel soldiers took shelter behind rolled bales of hemp taken from storage barns and wet down to absorb gunfire. Winning the Battle of the Hemp Bales on September 26, the Confederates had temporarily gained control of the state. Seventy-three soldiers were killed in the battle. To this day, the Lafayette County courthouse still features a cannonball imbedded in a column of its face.

"Kentuckians sometimes referred to hemp as a 'Nigger crop,' owing to the belief that no one understood its eccentricities as well or was as expert in handling it as the Negro. A Kentuckian stated in 1836 that it was almost impossible to hire workmen to break a crop of hemp because the work was 'very dirty, and so laborious that scarcely any White man will work at it,' and he continued by saying that the task was done entirely by slave labor."

– James F. Hopkins, *A History of the Hemp Industry in Kentucky,* Lexington: University of Kentucky Press, 1951

Farms in the South used slave labor to plant, grow, harvest, and process hemp. They often grew it next to fields of other crops including corn, wheat, and tobacco. This was particularly true in Kentucky and Missouri, which were the leaders in American hemp production of the 1800s. Female slaves were often used in manufacturing products from hemp, including fabric and rope. Many slaves who earned their freedom did so while working on hemp plantations. As the Civil War ended and slavery was abolished, the hemp industry shrank as the cost of farming and processing hemp increased. There was no machine that had been invented to speed up the processing of hemp as had been done with cotton and wool. The invention of the steam engine and its increasingly common use in ships in the late 1800s reduced the demand for hemp fabric sails and rigging. Many farms that had grown hemp went on to grow other crops, including tobacco, while others took on cattle and dairy farming, or sold their farms, or turned them into industrial sites.

Unfortunately, in collusion with the government, the paper industry turned to using trees for paper. The destruction of the forests sped up in sync with the advances in paper technology.

According to the American Forest and Paper Association, in the early 1800s a Frenchman by the name of Nicholas-Louis Robert invented the

123

Fourdrinier machine that sped up the paper manufacturing process by using pulverized hemp and plant matter spread across a continuous wire screen.

By the mid-1800s a German chemist by the name of D.F. Dahl invented a way of creating paper from tree pulp. His process worked in combination with a sulfite process developed in 1866 by an American named Benjamin Tilghman. In 1874 a paper mill in Sweden began using this process. Named the *kraft* process, it used sulfites to dissolve the lignans in wood. The process spread to America with the 1911 construction of the first *kraft* process paper mill in Pensacola, Florida. The process was especially successful with the wood of the southern pine. The spread of this paper-making process using wood further impacted the future of hemp, leading to the destruction of millions of acres of ancient forests throughout North America – a practice that continues today.

Although hemp farming continued after slavery ended, it had become a trickle compared to the hemp industry of the mid-1800s.

"Several [varieties of hemp] are grown in this country, that cultivated in Kentucky and having a hollow stem, being the most common. China hemp, with slender stems, growing very erect, has a wide range of culture. Smyrna hemp is adapted to cultivation over a still wider range and Japanese hemp is beginning to be cultivated, particularly in California, where it reaches a height of 15 feet. Russian and Italian seed have been experimented with, but the former produces a short stalk, while the latter only grows to a medium height. A small quantity of Piedmontese hemp seed from Italy was distributed by the Department in 1893, having been received through the Chicago Exposition."
– U.S. Department of Agriculture, Office of Fiber Investigations. *Report No. 8*, Page 7; 1896

# The Revival of the Hemp Industry in Early 1900s U.S.

"In Nebraska, where the [hemp] industry is being established, a new and important step has been taken in cutting the crop with an ordinary mowing machine. A simple attachment which bends the stalks over in the direction in which the machine is going facilitates the cutting... The cost of cutting hemp in this manner is 50 cents per acre, as compared with $3 to $4 per acre, the rates paid for cutting by hand in Kentucky."
    – U.S. Department of Agriculture: *Yearbook of Agriculture*, page 23; 1902

"The most important fact to be recorded in connection with the hemp industry during the past year is the successful operation of a machine brake in the fields of Kentucky. This machine breaks the retted stalks and cleans the fiber, producing clean, straight fiber equal to the best grades prepared on hand brakes, and it has a capacity of 1,000 pounds or more of clean fiber per hour. So far as we have any record, this is the first machine having sufficient capacity to be commercially practical that has cleaned bast fiber in an entirely satisfactory manner."
    – U.S. Department of Agriculture: *Report of Office of Fiber Investigations; Bureau of Plant Industry*, page 145; 1905

In October 1904, some hope for a renewed hemp paper industry came by way of a Canadian publication, *Pulp Paper Magazine*. An article titled Paper from Refuse Hemp Stalks suggested that hemp was an excellent papermaking material. This was different from the hemp paper of the past, which had been made from discarded hemp fabric. This time it was the raw hemp material that would be used directly as a substance for making paper. Another article, Hemp Waste for Paper, appeared in the March 1906 edition. Then another article was published mentioning hemp for paper. This one, written by W.B. Snow, was titled *Quality of Paper for Permanent Use*. It appeared in the March 1908 edition of *Paper Trade Journal*.

The U.S. Department of Agriculture published a pamphlet in 1908 titled *Papermaking Materials and Their Conservation*. This and an article appearing in the 1910 yearbook of the Department of Agriculture, Utilization of Crop Plants in Paper Making, mentioned hemp as a future source of paper material. The Department of Agriculture also published information suggesting hemp for paper in a 1911 pamphlet by C.J. Brand titled *Crop Plants for Papermaking*. The 1910 yearbook article, also by C.J.

125

Brand, stated that, "In addition to the waste materials that are available, evidence has been gathered that certain crops can probably be grown at a profit to both the grower and manufacturer, solely for paper making purposes. One of the most promising is hemp."

In 1916 the Department of Agriculture published *Bulletin No. 404: Hemp Hurds As a Paper-Making Material*. This included a number of studies by different authors advocating the use of hemp for paper. Hemp hurds are the inner pulp of the hemp stalk. They had previously been considered a useless waste product of hemp fiber processing. Two authors of articles appearing in Bulletin No. 404 were Dr. Lyster H. Dewey and Jason L. Merrill. While acknowledging a problem with the number of trees needed to support the paper industry, the bulletin concluded that the hemp industry had dwindled to the point that it was not large enough to supply the needs of the country's growing paper industry.

"Every tract of 10,000 acres which is devoted to hemp raising year by year is equivalent to a sustained pulp-producing capacity of 40,500 acres of average pulp-wood lands. In other words, in order to secure additional raw materials for the production of 25 tons of fiber per day there exists the possibility of utilizing the agricultural waste already produced on 10,000 acres of hemp lands instead of securing, holding, reforesting, and protecting 40,500 acres of pulp-wood lands."
– Jason L. Merrill, *Bulletin No. 404: Hemp Hurds As a Paper-Making Material;* Department of Agriculture, 1916. As noted earlier, these facts have changed, but still play in favor of hemp, when various facts and figures are taken into consideration.

Merrill's research into hemp paper production concluded that, "After several trials, under conditions of treatment and manufacture which are regarded as favorable in comparison with those used with pulpwood, paper was produced which received very favorable comment both from investigators and from the trade, and which, according to official tests, would be classified a No. 1 machine-finishing paper."

"The crop of hempseed last fall, estimated at about 45,000 bushels, is the largest produced in the United States since 1859. A very large proportion of it was from improved strains developed by this bureau in the hempseed selection plants at Arlington and Yarrow Farms."
– U.S. Department of Agriculture, Bureau of Plant Industry; *Report of the Chief,* page 12; 1917

Further studies were conducted on alternatives to wood pulp for paper. Notably were those of Ernest Becker and C.G. Schwalbe. These German scientists published a study in 1919 titled *The Chemical Composition of Flax and Hemp Chaff*. They concluded that hemp hurds, which they called *chaff*, was a superior material for paper. Other German scientists by the names of A. Zschenderlein and B. Rassow published a study titled *Nature of Hemp Wood*, an extract of which appeared in the October 1921 issue of *Paper Trade Journal*. The study also reported on the excellent qualities of hemp for paper production.

"When the work with hemp was begun in Wisconsin, there were no satisfactory machines for harvesting, spreading, binding, or breaking. All of these processes were performed by hand. Due to such methods, the hemp industry in the United States had all but disappeared. As it was realized from the very beginning of the work in Wisconsin that no permanent progress could be made so long as it was necessary to depend upon hand labor, immediate attention was given to solving the problem of power machinery. Nearly every kind of hemp machine was studied and tested. The obstacles were great, but through the cooperation of experienced hemp men and one large harvesting machinery company, this problem has been nearly solved. The hemp crop can now be handled entirely by machinery."
– By Andrew Wright, Wisconsin's Hemp Industry's field agent of fiber investigations, *Wisconsin Agricultural Experiment Station Bulletin # 293*, Page 5; 1918

"The work of breeding improved strains of hemp is being continued at Arlington Farm, Va., and all previous records were broken in the selection plats of 1919. The three best strains, Kymington, Chington and Tochimington, averaged, respectively, 14 feet 11 inches, 15 feet 5 inches, and 15 feet 9 inches, while the tallest individual plant was 19 feet. The improvement by selection is shown not alone in increased height but also in longer internodes, yielding fiber of better quality and increased quantity."
– U.S. Department of Agriculture, Bureau of Plant Industry; *Report of the Chief*, page 26; 1920

By the 1920s the U.S. hemp industry dwindled to a few farms in the Midwest that chiefly survived by supplying hemp fiber for the U.S. Navy. At the same time, the military was increasing its reliance on imported Manila hemp.

By the 1920s the farm industry was also suffering. In exploring potential ways of increasing revenue the possibilities of making paper from farm waste were considered. The farm waste included discarded corn stalks, flax, and, in the Midwest, hemp hurds discarded by companies producing hemp fiber for rope and twine. In the late 1920s the topic had been brought up in the halls of Congress as a way of reducing the import of paper materials from Canada, and to develop an alternative source of material for paper production. More studies also appeared about the promising qualities of hemp hurds as a replacement for tree pulp in paper production. One study, Physical and Chemical Characteristics of Hemp Stalks and Seed Flax Straw, was authored by E.R. Schafer and F.A. Simmonds and presented at the American Chemical Society meeting held in Minneapolis in September 1929. The study encouraged further study into the use of hemp for paper.

With the goal of advancing the hemp farming industry in his state, on January 25, 1927, Iowa Representative Cyrenus Cole went before the House and introduced a $50,000 appropriations bill for the Bureau of Standards to research potential industrial uses of farm waste as an alternative to wood pulp for paper. By that time the U.S. had been importing the majority of its paper from Canada, and the U.S. farm industry was suffering from overproduction after Europe had restored its farm production after WWI. In presenting the bill, Cole reasoned, "Can these vast [farm] wastes be utilized? Is there anything that we can make out of them?" And he added, "We must find more uses for our so-called raw products."

Cole was aware of research being conducted at Iowa College where compressed wood as well as paper and chemicals were being created out of farm waste products, including wheat straw and corn husks. Cole held a meeting with Iowa College President Herman Knapp, chemist Dr. O.R. Sweeney, Dr. George K. Burgess, director of the Bureau of Standards, and future U.S. President Herbert Hoover, who was then Secretary of Commerce. Developing paper products from farm waste and hemp pulp would have reduced the importation of paper from Canada while improving conditions for American farmers.

"Our farm problems arise from what I may call an unbalance. For two generations, or ever since the enactment of the homestead laws and the land grant college laws, we have been stressing production. Under these enactments we have thrown open vast new areas of fertile lands and we have applied every effort to the increase of production. We now find that we can have overproduction, and overproduction creates the surplus that we are now trying to deal with.

We must now put the stress on the other end. I mean on marketing and consumption. We paid all too little attention to these essential things in the equation of prosperity. We must find new markets, and new markets may not mean going across the seas with shiploads of our products, but in finding new uses for the abundant crops."

– Cyrenus Cole, Iowa State Representative, appearing before 2nd session of the 69th Congress to argue for his appropriations bill to fund the research and development of products from farm waste and crops; 1927

Although Cole's appropriations bill to fund research and development of products, including paper, from farm waste and crops was approved by Congress, the U.S. Department of Agriculture successfully worked to strike the $50,000 appropriation from the bill on the basis that it would be funding research into sources of alternative paper and construction materials already conducted by the Department of Agriculture's Bureau of Forestry and Forestry Products. In reality, the Bureau of Forestry had only conducted studies using tree pulp, and not crops. Secretary of Commerce Hoover successfully convinced President Calvin Coolidge to use executive order to reinstate the $50,000 in funding.

Within a year the Bureau of Standards was investigating the potential of farm waste products for paper and wood alternatives.

In 1928 Bill S. 4834 was introduced to Congress by Senator Thomas Schall of Minnesota. This bill was aimed at funding the construction of factories that would produce paper and building materials out of farm waste, including corn stalk and straw. Schall knew about the possibilities of using hemp for producing paper, and he mentioned so in his printed statements in the *Congressional Record* debating the bill he introduced. The bill was defeated in committee. In 1929 Schall introduced Bill S. 561, which was similar to Bill S. 4834, but that bill also died in committee.

"In 1929 three selected varieties of hemp (Michigan Early, Chinamington and Simple Leaf) were grown in comparison with unselected common Kentucky seed near Juneau, Wisconsin Each of the varieties had been developed by 10 years or more of selection from the progeny of individual plants. The yields of fiber per acre were as follows: Simple Leaf, 360 pounds; Michigan Early, 694 pounds; Chinamington, 1,054 pounds; common Kentucky, 680 pounds."
– U.S. Department of Agriculture, Bureau of Plant Industry; *Annual Report*, page 27; 1929

By 1930 the very small hemp industry was still skipping along by supplying hemp mostly for rope and twine. That year the May issue of *Paper Trade Journal* published an article by R. Schafer and F.A. Simmonds titled "Physical and Chemical Characteristics of Hemp Stalks and Seed Flax Straw."

The promise of hemp's use and the possibility of a future market kept some people interested enough in the industry to work on developing hemp harvesting and processing machinery. The president of the World Fibre Corporation, a businessman named Harry W. Bellrose, owned a patent to a hemp processing machine known as the Selvig decorticator. It was invented by an engineer named John N. Selvig. In 1933 Bellrose sold the rights to use the Selvig decorticator within Minnesota to a businessman, Frank E. Holton. As a former employee of National Citizens Bank of Mankato, Minnesota, Holton received help from the bank and members of its board in funding his hemp farming business.

"A survey commissioned by the Federal Bureau of Narcotics reported that 'from 1880 to 1933 the hemp grown in the United States had declined from 15,000 to 1,200 acres, and that the price of line hemp had dropped.' But the Bureau's surveys at the time also showed that the trend in hemp acreage was suddenly reversing, with just a few companies contracting for the 6,400 acres of hemp planted in 1934, increasing to 10,900 acres in 1937. The markedly increased interest in hemp was a result of speculation that technological breakthroughs in the processing of hemp for fiber and the growing market for cellulose for use in paper, explosives, rayon, cellophane, and plastic products would open new markets for hemp."

– March 2008 Reason Foundation Study on Hemp, Illegally Green: Environmental Costs of Hemp Prohibition. Policy Study 367, by Skaidra Smith-Heisters

The Northwest Hemp Corporation was incorporated in Minnesota in October 1933. Farmers were contracted and began planting over 6,000 acres of hemp the following spring. The new farming venture was a learning experience for those unfamiliar with harvesting and processing hemp. In 1935 the cultivation expanded to other farms. Holton proved to be a problematic businessperson. National Citizen's Bank unsuccessfully tried to force him out of the business.

Another businessman interested in the hemp industry was M.J. Connolly. Along with Holton and Citizens National Bank, the Blue Earth State Bank of Minnesota backed a new hemp business named National Cellulose Corporation, which took over Northwest Hemp Corporation in October 1935. Under Connolly's management, the company began processing the hemp the farmers had already grown and that had been held in storage and in the fields.

This startup hemp company experienced more problems because no one would purchase the processed hemp hurds. Papermaking companies were set up for wood pulp, which used a different process than that needed to manufacture paper from hemp. The company was also forced to change its name when it was found that another company was already using the name National Cellulose Corporation. The new name was Hemp Chemical Corporation.

130

Other hemp companies were starting in the Midwest, including in the Nebraska Fiber Corporation, which quickly folded, and another by the name of Amhempco Corporation, which was incorporated in New Jersey. The investors in Amhempco were the Mason jar manufacturers, the Ball Brothers. Their partners were the Sloan Brothers, who owned a carpet company in New York and whose aim was to use the hemp fiber in their products.

The Amhempco Corporation set up on land in Danville, Illinois. This was once used by the Cornstalks Products Company, which was in business to create paper products from farm waste. Amhempco planted hemp in 1935 and worked to create products from it. Without the capital needed to invest in machinery, the company stalled. Part of the reason for this was due to the activities of the Federal Bureau of Narcotics.

As I will explain, at this time the campaign to rid the country of marijuana was under full swing by the Federal Bureau of Narcotics. This interfered with those planning to invest in and produce hemp products.

Also impacting investor interest in the development of alternative sources of paper and building products were the activities of the Bureau of Forestry.

Both the campaign by the Federal Bureau of Narcotics and the Bureau of Forestry were directly related to the renewed interest in hemp farming and the potential for hemp products.

There were reasons why the FBN and the Bureau of Forestry worked against the hemp industry. Keep reading, and you will understand why this was so.

# A Little About Marijuana

Before I go on about the topic of hemp and how it became illegal, I'd like to provide a some information about the issue of marijuana.

You don't have to be for the legalization of marijuana if you are for the legalization of industrial hemp farming. The two issues can remain under law as separate issues, and not one and the same. In other words, you can be a hemp legalization advocate without advocating for a change in the marijuana laws.

One of the reasons that this book is not endorsed by Vote Hemp, a lobbying group in Washington, D.C., is that Vote Hemp chooses to remain centered on the issue of the legalization of industrial hemp farming, and does not endorse books or organizations that may express a viewpoint advocating a change in the law as it applies to marijuana.

I don't see how I could write hemp without also covering some aspects of the marijuana issue. As I mention elsewhere, anyone who would like to know more about marijuana should read the book *Cannabis: A History,* by Martin Booth.

Those considering smoking marijuana should make themselves aware of the laws relating to the substance. They would also likely do themselves a favor by studying up on both the possible pros and cons of marijuana, including in issues relating to health and marijuana law.

There are so many rumors about marijuana that the number of mistruths surrounding its use and effects are legendary. One that I heard growing up was that marijuana causes chromosomal damage, which can turn you into an imbecile as well as cause horrible birth defects in your children. Out of all of the information I have studied, I could find no evidence to back these claims. However, I found ample amounts of information that petroleum and its byproducts, as well as farming and industrial and household chemicals made from petroleum, do cause brain damage and birth deformities.

No matter what your age, if you live in the U.S., you can lose some of your rights if you have a felony drug conviction on your record. Under a law that took effect in 2000, this includes being banned from receiving federal financial aid for college for up to a year after a student has been convicted. Some of those with lesser drug offenses become eligible for the funds only after they have completed a drug treatment program. Those with three drug-use convictions or two drug-sale convictions are permanently banned from receiving federal college aid.

It seems to me that denying financial aid for education to someone who is trying to advance his or her life by going to college would not be constructive for the person or society. Those who want to go to school should be able to get all the help they can find, and not be denied financial aid based on a drug conviction. It is also odd that convicted murderers and rapists who have served their time in prison are not denied financial aid for college, nor should they be denied it.

"It's a very poor way for the government to fight the War on Drugs. I don't think that the government should find more and more ways to deprive students of a means to an education."
– David Israel Wasserman, Associated Students of Berkeley. In protest to the federal government's denial of financial aid to those with drug convictions, the ASB opened up a $400-per-year scholarship program of the student government to include those with drug convictions on their records. Students must maintain a 2.5 grade-point average, perform 20 hours of community service, and then contribute to the program after becoming financially stable after graduation. Berkeley Students Counter Federal Drug Rule, by Seema Mehta, *Los Angeles Times*, January 26, 2007

"If you are enabling self-destructive behavior by supporting it, condoning it, or even paying for it, you're probably not helping the person get the help they need to deal with their disease."
– David Murray, chief scientist with the George W. Bush White House Office on national Drug Control Policy. In response to the news that the Associated Students of Berkeley will allow financial aid to those with drug convictions. Berkeley Students Counter Federal Drug Rule, by Seema Mehta, *Los Angeles Times*, January, 26, 2007

**Those considering the use of marijuana should consider the negative aspects of its use, including potential legal and social issues.**

1. You can lose school grants and scholarships.

2. You can be denied acceptance to certain internship programs.

3. In certain circumstances, you can lose your job.

4. In certain circumstances, you can lose your professional license.

5. In certain circumstances, you can lose your health insurance.

6. You can be denied welfare as well as inclusion in other government programs.

7. If you live in government-subsidized housing and are caught with marijuana, you can lose your home.

8. In 1996, Congress passed a law allowing the Temporary Aid for Needy Families program to permanently deny food stamps or cash assistance to people convicted of possessing or selling drugs. However, most states opted out of the ban.

9. A conviction of one person may cause a member of their family to lose their job if they are employed in certain professions.

10. Some say that marijuana induces insomnia, and others say it helps them to sleep.

11. Some who have used marijuana say they have experienced paranoia or "mental discomfort," as if the people they are with dislike them and are mildly conspiring against them.

   Some say marijuana gives them the uncomfortable feeling of being a self-parody. Other say that it makes them feel the opposite, inverse-paranoia, where they think everyone likes them and is out to do them good.

   Some people say that getting high makes them enjoy being around people and animals.

12. Smoking or ingesting cannabis often causes reddening of the eyes (conjunctival vascular congestion), which can allow others to know or suspect that you are high, including employers or law enforcement officers. (Marijuana does not cause pupil dilation.)

13. It is illegal to drive while under the influence of marijuana.

14. Some say that marijuana debilitates them because it seems to reduce their motivation, fogs their memory, causes them to procrastinate on important issues, and otherwise makes them lazy. Others say that it stimulates them and they use it before they go bike riding, snowboarding, swimming, hiking, or working out. Others do it prior to engaging in a creative endeavor, or enjoying what others have created, such as art, music, literature, theatre, film, or dance.

15. Getting high on marijuana can give a person "the munchies," which amounts to the desire to eat more calories than they need. People who get the munchies often choose low-quality foods that degrade their health, such as those high in fat and sugar. Some people attribute their weight issues to their use of smoking marijuana.

    On the other hand, this is also why marijuana can be used medicinally by people who suffer from anorexia or AIDS wasting syndrome, or who experience loss of appetite while undergoing cancer treatment.

    Some people say that they don't get hungry when they smoke marijuana, and that they only want to drink water.

16. While marijuana is not physically addictive and does not cause the type of withdrawal symptoms experienced by hard or "addictive" drugs (cocaine, heroin, morphine, meth, alcohol, nicotine, etc.), some people say that a person who uses marijuana may form a psychological dependence.

17. Because marijuana can increase heart rate, it may cause uncomfortable sensations in those sensitive to changes in blood pressure.

18. Marijuana smoke contains carbon monoxide, cyanide, and tar, which can play a role in respiratory disorders.

19. People on waiting lists for organ transplants have been denied a transplant partially based on their use of marijuana. This includes patients who have held a medical prescription for marijuana.

    The United Network for Organ Sharing oversees the transplant system in the U.S. They do not make the rules of which patient gets a transplant. Instead, they leave it up to the medical staff at each hospital where transplants are performed.

    Health insurance companies may require potential organ transplant patients to undergo drug tests. A positive result for any sort of illegal substance can result in the cancellation of the insurance, or refusal to pay for the transplant.

Some hospital organ transplant boards consider the use of marijuana to be a sign that the patient is likely to become addicted to other drugs. Some cite that the introduction of smoke into the lungs can impact the immune system, which is already challenged in someone who has undergone an organ transplant and is on anti-rejection drugs. Others believe that molds found on tobacco and marijuana may lead to an aspergillosis infection in a patient who has undergone a transplant.

Some hospital transplant boards will allow a patient with a history of marijuana use to undergo an organ transplant if the patient stays clean for a number of months and/or enters a drug rehab program.

20. Using marijuana can interfere with relationships.

21. Some people have stated that marijuana was a factor in alienating them from friends and family, and in deepening troubled relationships. It is likely that they already had issues that they weren't managing, and perhaps marijuana use added another layer to their life problems.

22. Marijuana use can be used against you in a divorce or child custody case.

23. Some speak about the money they have spent on marijuana, and say they would have been much better off if they had invested the money, saved it, or spent it in other ways.

24. Some say that the professional and legal problems marijuana caused them ruined their life.

25. In the U.S. you can be sentenced to as much as life in prison for breaking certain marijuana laws.

26. You can drink any variety of alcohol till you puke and pass out and remain sick for several days, but if you are caught smoking one puff of a marijuana joint you are sharing with friends in the privacy of your own home, you may get as much as 20 years in prison.

27. If you have enough weed that it appears you may be selling it, you can be sentenced to several years in prison.

28. If you were caught exchanging weed within 1,000 feet of a school or public housing facility, or within 100 feet of a youth center, your sentence can be doubled. You would also not be eligible for probation or early parole. Rules may be more strict in the area where you are busted.

29. If you are caught growing marijuana you can lose the property you own where the weed was found growing. The government can also take away other personal property, including cars, boats, jewelry, furniture, and electronics.

30. Any marijuana seeds you have may be counted as a plant, which can increase your prison term.

31. Some countries, such as Malaysia, Singapore, and China, have been known to execute those who break certain marijuana laws.

*Take note:*
*I, the author of this book, am not an attorney, a doctor, or a person who works in law enforcement.*
*Marijuana laws are complicated and they vary from state-to-state, and from country-to-country. Getting caught breaking marijuana laws may greatly complicate your life.*
*Those who think they may be in a situation that could appear to be in violation of marijuana laws should educate themselves about the laws. I have listed organizations that deal with various aspects of the marijuana issue in the resources section at the back of this book.*

Those who are using weed to escape life's problems may be compounding their difficulties and possibly making them worse. Some would counter this with the view that marijuana could allow people to view their problems from a different angle, and perhaps this perception will help them come to an understanding on how to handle the issues with which they are concerned.

Some may say that they spend less time and energy under the influence of marijuana doing things that are active, interesting, stimulating, and satisfying than many people who are sober all of the time, but who choose to spend their free time watching television and accomplishing nothing but weight gain and slothfulness.

If the use of weed stifles a person's talents or intellect, that also is a detriment. As mentioned later in the book, there are many great works of art that have been created while the artist was under the influence of something, but that does not mean that a person couldn't succeed in creating something amazing without being under the influence.

People who believe marijuana puts them in a state of consciousness during which they can function better with life should consider that the drug might only bring out what is already within a person. Perhaps their life would work better if they would learn how to release this desirable aspect of their being without the use of drugs.

Spending money on weed while neglecting basic needs is another drawback. If people claim they are smoking weed because they can't cope with their financial situation, perhaps they should consider the amount of money and time they are spending on the marijuana.

It should be easy to understand why nobody should be operating an automobile or other heavy equipment, or making serious life decisions while under the influence of marijuana, or any mind-altering substance.

Some marijuana decriminalization/legalization advocates seem to give the message that everyone should smoke pot every day. There are certainly people who should not be smoking pot, such as doctors performing surgery. Children shouldn't have access to it for nonmedical reasons, and the choice to smoke or consume it for recreational, artistic, and/or spiritual reasons should be an adult decision.

Plenty of information can be had about the benefits and risks of smoking marijuana. Just the act of breathing smoke into the lungs should be an indication that it might not be the best thing to do. Chronic users of marijuana may increase their likelihood of experiencing various ailments, including bronchitis, emphysema, and collapsed lung.

A 2007 study of 339 test subjects by the New Zealand Medical Research Institute and that was published in the journal Thorax concluded that a subject group with a long-term history of pot smoking had a 1.3 percent rate of emphysema. A subject group who smoked both marijuana and cigarettes had a 16.3 rate, and a subject group with a history of smoking only cigarettes had an 18.9 rate of emphysema. The study included four groups, nonsmokers, cigarette smokers who didn't smoke weed, cigarette smokers who also smoked weed, and weed smokers who didn't smoke weed. The study found that those who smoked pot on a regular basis had above average rates of coughing, wheezing, chest tightness, and phlegm. They also showed signs of damage to the finer airways within the lungs.

"Marijuana smoke contains some of the same, and sometimes eve more, of the cancer-causing chemicals found in tobacco smoke. Studies show that someone who smoked five joints per day may be taking in as many cancer-causing chemicals as someone who smokes a full pack of cigarettes every day."
– National Institutes of Health.

Maybe I'm not as knowledgeable about the typical habits of marijuana smokers as I think I am. But, it seems to me that smoking 5 joints a day every day would be more than extreme. I'm guessing that the average person who smokes marijuana likely smokes a small fraction of what the above studies are suggesting. That isn't to say that people who smoke weed shouldn't consider possible physical health issues associated with the practice.

Some say that they avoid any potential respiratory matters in relation to weed by choosing instead to put the marijuana in food rather than smoke it, or to use a vaporizer rather than a pipe or joint. But they still should consider other issues that may result from being high.

When marijuana is grown using synthetic fertilizers, pesticides, fungicides, and other fossil-based chemicals there is no doubt that the smoke from that pot is more toxic than weed that was grown using nothing but organic soil, water, and Sun.

Using a lighter to light pot can cause inhalation of burning butane, which is harmful. Those who choose to smoke weed should consider lighting it with a match, or using a vaporizer.

However, I do think it is criminal that people are in jail for the possession of cannabis, and that the government spends billions of dollars on trying to control a substance that anyone can get if he or she wants it. The U.S. spends more money per marijuana prisoner than it does per schoolchild. There are many important things we can be doing with the billions we spend on trying to stop people from smoking pot.

The majority of people busted under pot laws are under the age of 25, and the U.S. spends more money on each of them than we do on individual college students. It would be less expensive and more beneficial to society to put these so-called marijuana criminals through college than it would be to send them to prison.

"Education is the most powerful weapon which you can use to change the world."
– Nelson Mandela

It should be very obvious that the U.S. has a problem with priorities in relation to what it spends on the war on drugs, and what it spends on schools and the environment. What do you say about a country that spends more on prisons than on schools?

According to a report by the Pew Center's Public Safety Performance Project of the Pew Center on the States, at the beginning of 2008, there were 2,319,258 Americans were in prison or jail. That means that the U.S. incarcerates more people in both population and per capita than any other country. The number of prisoners keeps going up, and so do the costs. In the two decades ending in 2007, the U.S. went from spending $11 billion per year to spending $49 billion per year on the jail and prison industries. According to the Pew report, the inmate population in the state of Kentucky increased 600 percent in 30 years. California, which is in an enormous budgetary crisis, spent $8.8 billion on prisons in 2007. In the same year, Oregon spent 10.9 percent of its general fund on prisons.

Perhaps what are considered to be crimes should be thought of as something else, and handled in a different way that doesn't include locking people in prisons – where they learn to do real crime.

"Let us reform our schools, and we shall find little need of reform in our prisons."
– John Ruskin

Consider the possibility that many of the young people who are busted for selling marijuana are involved in "sales" because they are trying to make money they could make if they had skills to be learned in a trade school, tech school, or other school. If it were easier for them to go to college they may not be involved in selling cannabis. On the other hand, there are likely a number of students who pay their tuition by selling weed on the side.

Here are some facts provided by Common Sense for Drug Policy (CSDP.org):

"From 1984 to 1996, California built 21 new prisons, and only one new university."
– Ambrosio, T. & Schiraldi, V., Trends in State Spending, 1987-1995, Executive Summary-February 1997; Washington, D.C.: The Justice Policy Institute, 1997

"California state government expenditures on prisons increased 30 percent from 1987 to 1995, while spending on higher education decreased by 18 percent."
– National Association of State Budget Officers, 1995 State Expenditures Report; Washington, D.C.: National Association of State Budget Officers, 1996

"The total number of State and Federal inmates grew from 400,000 in 1982 to nearly 1,300,000 in 1999. This was accompanied by the opening of over 600 state and at least 51 federal correctional facilities. The number of local jail inmates also tripled, from approximately 200,000 in 1982 to 600,000 in 1999. Adults on probation increased

140

from over 1.3 to nearly 3.8 million persons. Overall corrections employment more than doubled from nearly 300,000 to over 716,000 during this period."
– Gifford, Sidra Lea, US Department of Justice, Bureau of Justice Statistics, Justice Expenditure and Employment in the United States, 1999; Washington, DC: US Department of Justice, February 2002; Page 7

"Department of corrections data show that about a fourth of those initially imprisoned for nonviolent crimes are sentenced for a second time for committing a violent offense. Whatever else it reflects, this pattern highlights the possibility that prison serves to transmit violent habits and values rather than to reduce them."
– Craig Haney, Ph.D., and Philip Zimbardo, Ph.D., The Past and Future of U.S. Prison Policy: Twenty-five Years After the Stanford Prison Experiment; American Psychologist, Vol. 53, No. 7; July 1998; page 720

The marijuana sales industry is always going to be here because the plant can be grown in hidden gardens or "grow rooms."

Nobody really knows how big the marijuana market is because it is mostly done subversively. According to Ed Rosenthal, co-author of the 2003 book *Why Marijuana Should Be Legal*, the marijuana sales industry was doing about $25 billion in business per year at the time he was writing his book. Marijuana laws have helped increase the price of it and it has long been considered to be the biggest cash crop in the states of California, Hawaii, and Kentucky. A study conducted by the former head of the National Organization for the Reform of Marijuana Laws that was released on December 18, 2006 concluded that the U.S. marijuana business exceeds $35 billion. This figure would mean that marijuana is America's biggest cash crop above corn ($23 billion), soybeans ($17.6 billion), hay ($12.2 billion), vegetables ($11.1 billion), and wheat ($7.4 billion).

"Despite years of effort by law enforcement, they're not getting rid of it. Not only is the problem worse in terms of magnitude of cultivation, but also production has spread all around the country. To say the genie is out of the bottle is a profound understatement.
… Marijuana has become a pervasive and ineradicable part of the economy of the United States.
… The contribution of this market to the nation's gross domestic product is overlooked in the debate over effective control.
… Like all profitable agricultural crops marijuana adds resources and value to the economy.

... The focus of public policy should be how to effectively control this market through regulation and taxation in order to achieve immediate and realistic goals, such as reducing teenage access."
– Jon Gettman, public policy analyst and former head of the National Organization for the Reform of Marijuana Laws (NORML); author of report concluding that America's top moneymaking crop is marijuana; December 18, 2006. The study based its figures on government reports and purposefully worked to give a low estimate of the possible cash value of marijuana being produced in America.

As expected, Tom Riley, the spokesman for the U.S. Office of National Drug Control Policy, rejected Gettman's suggestion that marijuana should become legal and taxed. He stated that more teenagers are in treatment centers for marijuana issues than for all other drugs. He failed to mention that courts are ordering teenagers into treatment, which is the reason for the increase.

Some may ask why there are more people going into treatment centers for marijuana use.

"Although admissions to drug rehabilitation clinics among marijuana users have increased dramatically since the mid-1990s, 'this rise in marijuana admissions is due to a proportional increase in the number of people arrested by law enforcement for marijuana violations and subsequently referred to drug treatment by the criminal justice system.' Primarily, these are young people arrested for minor possession offenses, brought before a criminal judge (or drug court), and ordered to rehabilitation in lieu of jail or juvenile detention. As such, this data is in no way indicative of whether the person referred to treatment is suffering from any symptoms of dependence associated with marijuana use; most individuals are ordered to attend supervised drug treatment simply to avoid jail time."
– Marijuana: Myth vs. Fact, National Organization for the Reform of Marijuana Laws, NORML.org, quoting from the Drug and Alcohol Services Information System report, March 29, 2005, Treatment Referral Sources for Adolescent Marijuana Users. U.S. Office of Applied Studies, Substance Abuse and Mental Health Services Administration; Washington, DC

Some studies conclude that not only is marijuana smoke far less likely than tobacco to cause health problems, it may even prevent some.

142

"We hypothesized that there would be a positive association between marijuana use and lung cancer, and that the association would be more positive with heavier use. What we found instead was no association at all, and even a suggestion of some protective effect."
– Dr. Donald Tashkin, Study Finds No Cancer-Marijuana Connection, by Marc Kaufman, *Washington Post*, May 26, 2006.
    Tashkin, et al. presented the study *Marijuana Use and Lung Cancer: Results of a Case-Control Study*, the American Thoracic Society International Conference, May 24, 2006. The study was funded by the National Institute on Drug Abuse (NIDA). It involved 1,200 people in Los Angeles who had lung, neck or head cancer, and an additional 1,040 people without cancer matched by age, sex, and neighborhood. "Conclusion: We did not observe a positive association of marijuana use – even heavy long-term use – with lung cancer."

Meanwhile, tobacco cigarettes are sold throughout the country to any adult who wants them, are more addictive than cocaine and heroin, result in billions of dollars in health costs, and every year tobacco use leads to more than 400,000 miserable deaths. The U.S. tobacco industry collected $88 billion in 2006.

As I was writing this book, my neighbor, the granddaughter of Al Capone, was diagnosed with lung cancer. Over the next several months the cancer ravaged her body as it spread throughout her tissues. The last several weeks of her life were agonizing as she became extremely thin and had to be cared for around the clock. In the last days, her suffering intensified and she spent her last few days moaning in misery. Then, she died. This was a woman who started smoking cigarettes when she was a teenager, but quit ten years before her death. As an indication of the addictive qualities of cigarettes, as her daughter was taking care of her during the last weeks, the daughter took breaks several times a day to sit outside and smoke cigarettes.

Alcohol, which is similarly available to adults, also causes massive health problems, is an issue in the majority of domestic abuse cases, is often part of child abuse and neglect, plays a central role in tens of thousands of fatal car accidents, results in billions of dollars in health costs, and kills well over 100,000 Americans every year. (I am one who thinks drunk driving laws should be stricter, and should allow no one with over a .04 level of alcohol concentration to get behind the wheel of a car. Currently, the state of California's legal driving limit is .08. Studies have shown that some driving skills become impaired at .05 or less.) Alcohol pollution, in the form of broken bottles, bottle caps, beer cans, packaging, and advertising litters the American landscape.

Many studies have concluded that alcohol is more dangerous than other drugs. Clearly, alcohol causes more problems then other drugs, not only because it is the most common drug. Alcohol is often cited in the breakup of families, to job loss, to homelessness, to crimes that result in jail and imprisonment, and to the need for social services. When drunk in excess, alcohol causes a variety of health problems, and can damage all of the organs of the body, especially the brain. A study published in the November 1, 2010 edition of the medical journal, Lancet, and that was conducted by Britain's Centre for Crime and Justice Studies ranked alcohol at the top of the list of the most problematic drugs. Substances taken into consideration included alcohol, cocaine, heroin, ecstasy, LSD, and marijuana. The drugs that were lowest on the list were marijuana and LSD, which are both not physically addictive.

"I just can't stop smoking cigarettes for the life of me. I'm as addicted to that as the biggest junkie is addicted to heroin. But then, millions of us are.

… I consider booze to be far more harmful than any other available drug, far more damaging to the body, to the mind, to the person's attitude."

– Keith Richards, interviewed by Victor Bockris, Heroin, Old Age, Rhythm and Blues, *High Times* magazine, January 1978

"We could sit here with any number of policemen and doctors and they would all tell you if everybody who had a dependence on alcohol changed their mind and had a dependence on weed, the world would be a much easier place to live in."

– Singer George Michael to ITV talk show host Michael Parkinson, May 2007

Over-the-counter drugs, such as aspirin, kill tens of thousands of Americans, and prescription drugs play a part in even more deaths. According to a study published in the September 18, 2006 issue of the *Journal of the American Medical Association*, every year at least 700,000 Americans enter emergency rooms while experiencing adverse reactions to prescription drugs. The researchers agreed that 700,000 is a very conservative figure. Bad reactions to prescription drugs are often not recognized.

"To draw a real world comparison, millions of Americans safely use ibuprofen as an effective pain reliever. However, among a minority of the population who suffer from liver and kidney problems,

ibuprofen presents a legitimate and substantial health risk. However, this fact does not call for the criminalization of ibuprofen."
– Cannabis, Mental Health and Context: The Case for Regulation, by Paul Armentano, Senior Policy Analyst, National Organization for the Reform of Marijuana Laws/NORML Foundation; January 27, 2006; NORML.org

There is no record of anyone dying from an overdose of marijuana.

"Nearly all medications have toxic, potentially lethal effects. But marijuana is not such a substance. There is no record in the extensive medical literature describing a proven, documented cannabis-induced fatality.
Marijuana, in its natural form, is one of the safest therapeutically active substances known to man.
... Marijuana has been accepted as capable of relieving distress of great numbers of very ill people, and doing so with safety under medical supervision. It would be unreasonable, arbitrary and capricious for [the] DEA to continue to stand between those sufferers and the benefits of this substance in light of the evidence in this record."
– DEA Administrative Law Judge Francis L. Young, September 8, 1988

"There is no conclusive evidence that marijuana causes cancer in humans, including cancers usually related to tobacco use."
– *Marijuana and Medicine: Assessing the Science Base*, National Academy of Sciences, Institute of Medicine, 1999; page 5

Interestingly, as mentioned earlier, some studies have concluded that smoking weed doesn't appear to lead to lung cancer. One theory speculating why this may be so is that there could be something in the marijuana smoke that protects the lungs, and perhaps helps the lungs to slough off old cells. Other studies have concluded that there may be anticancer substances in weed. However, I am not suggesting that people should use this as an excuse to smoke weed.

Some of the health problems caused by tobacco were recognized early on when tobacco was first brought to Europe from America. In 1604 King James worked to prohibit tobacco by placing a high tax on the stuff. The result of this was an underground market served by tobacco smugglers. In 1608 James changed the taxation on tobacco to allow it, giving the Earl of Montgomery, Phillip Herbert, the right to collect the tax. That lasted until James canceled that arrangement in 1615 and worked a taxation that favored keeping tobacco at a price that prevented smuggling. By this time the American colonists were increasing their tobacco acreage to satisfy the British and the European markets. But it was not welcome in all parts. Some countries treated it with disdain and punished those found in possession of it. In 1634 Moscow created a law under which some who used tobacco could be hanged. India and Iran punished tobacco smokers with physical torture and/or disfigurement. Even so, the tobacco trade continued to grow to feed those who became addicted to it. By 1700 there were hundreds of ships being used to carry tobacco to European ports while in America the African slaves were being used to farm it on plantations that spread across the south. In the 1700s there were also some Americans who were outspoken against the use of tobacco, considering it a filthy habit that led to the consumption of hard liquor. In 1798, one of the signers of the Declaration of Independence, Dr. Benjamin Rush, spoke against tobacco in a document titled "Observations upon the influence of the habitual use of tobacco upon health, morals, and property." Nothing much came of these antitobacco opinions because America was making too much money from tobacco to stop it, including many politicians who owned tobacco farms where slaves labored.

Today of course the laws governing tobacco have been changed. It is now a multibillion-dollar industry that is beneficial to governments because tobacco sales bring in large tax revenues. However, when used as advertised, tobacco leads to serious health problems that burden society with huge medical costs.

Marijuana has taken a different path.

As mentioned elsewhere in the book, cannabis has been used as medicine for thousands of years. Even in the U.S. cannabis was a common medicine until after World War I. During that war the U.S. government guaranteed its own supply of medicinal cannabis by contracting with farmers in Pennsylvania, South Carolina, and Virginia. The U.S. did this to maintain its supply of medicinal cannabis because it was aware that the war could cut off supplies of cannabis from other countries.

In modern times, medicinal uses of marijuana have been established for the relief of migraine headache, ocular migraine, cancer pain and nausea, anxiety, AIDS wasting syndrome, arthritis, asthma, anorexia, chronic pain, epilepsy, fibromyalgia, hepatitis C, insomnia, lupus, menstrual cramps, multiple sclerosis, paralysis, paraplegia, quadriplegia, and Tourette's syndrome.

It is proven that marijuana reduces the intraocular (eye) pressure associated with glaucoma and that it can save the vision of those suffering from that condition.

"Our results indicate that cannabinoid receptors are important in the pathology of AD [Alzheimer's disease] and that cannabinoids

146

[substance in marijuana] succeed in preventing the neurodegenerative
process occurring in the disease."
– Prevention of Alzheimer's Disease Pathology by Cannabinoids:
Neuroprotection Mediated by Blockage of Microglial Activation,
Maria L. de Ceballos, Ph.D., et al., the *Journal of Neuroscience*, Vol. 25
No. 8; February 23, 2005

Studies have concluded that marijuana shows qualities that appear to be
beneficial for those suffering from Alzheimer's disease. Researchers at the
Scripps Research Institute in California concluded that marijuana could
prevent the progression of Alzheimer's disease. Marijuana's active
ingredient, delta-9-tetrahydrocannabinol (THC) was first identified by two
Israeli chemists, Raphael Mechoulam and Yehiel Gaoni, in 1964. THC is
effective at blocking clumps of protein that can inhibit cognition and
memory, which is more effective than commercial prescription drugs in
preventing the breaking down of the neurotransmitter acetylcholine.
(*Molecular Pharmaceutics* journal; A Molecular Link Between the Active
Component of Marijuana and Alzheimer's Disease Pathology; Aug. 9, 2006)

"After reviewing the recommendations of an expert panel, we have
decided to add Agitation of Alzheimer's Disease to the list of medical
conditions for which a doctor may write a statement of support for the
medical use of marijuana."
– The Oregon Department of Health Services; June 14, 2000 press
release

Many of the studies that have identified the medicinal benefits of
marijuana were initially meant to find harm potentially caused by marijuana.
This has caused conflict with those conducting the studies and institutions
or agencies funding the studies.

"I was hired by the government to provide scientific evidence that
marijuana was harmful. As I studied the subject, I began to realize that
marijuana was once widely used as a safe and effective medicine. But
the government had a different agenda, and I had to resign."
– Dr. Tod Mikuriya, former director of marijuana research for the
U.S. government quoted in *Why Marijuana Should Be Legal*, by Ed
Rosenthal & Steve Kuby with S. Newhart; Green-
Aid.com/EdRosenthal.htm

While it is often cited that marijuana has some effect on memory,
short- and/or or long-term, it is known that many of the most common
prescription drugs do have a negative impact on memory. These drugs

include those given for depression, heart disease, cancer, anxiety, breathing difficulties, spasms, sleep, ulcers, and pain. Perhaps if people are looking to block medicinal substances based on information that they interfere with memory, they should consider a long list of medications that are more commonly used than marijuana, and which are prescribed by doctors as "legitimate" drugs. Many of these drugs also interact with each other, increasing the likelihood of adverse effects.

Studies on the health effects of marijuana use will continue. Anyone who chooses to partake of the substance would be wise to consider the findings.

There is more on marijuana, medical marijuana, and the massively expensive and corrupt War on Drugs later in the book.

Those interested in the legalities of marijuana should read the book *Why Marijuana Should Be Legal*, by Ed Rosenthal, Steve Kubby, and S. Newhart.

Those interested in more background about marijuana should read the book *Cannabis: A History*, by Martin Booth.

The book that many people consider to be the one that ignited the drive to change the laws covering marijuana and hemp is Jack Herer's *The Emperor Wears No Clothes*. Before he died, Jack read the manuscript of this book, and approved of what it said.

## Lies and Corporate Ties:
## The Politicians and Businessmen
## Who Worked Together to Outlaw Hemp

The Pure Food and Drug Act of 1906 had been passed to require the listing of certain substances, including cocaine, morphine, opium, and cannabis on patent medicines sold over state borders.

By way of the Smoking Opium Exclusion Act, which was passed by the U.S. Congress in 1909, opium had been limited to import by pharmaceutical companies. The law was used as an argument at the Shanghai Opium Conference of 1909 to urge other countries to place similar limits on the opium market. It was also the first law in the U.S. to make a certain drug substance illegal to import, possess, or sell outside of a licensed pharmaceutical business.

The first laws in the U.S. against opium had to do with the Chinese opium dens in San Francisco and other parts of California in the 1880s. Those laws had more to do with the anti-Chinese sentiment in California because the Caucasians were mad at the railroad companies for using Chinese immigrant laborers, and angry that Chinese were "taking jobs" away from White gold miners and other labor forces. Taxes were placed on Chinese who worked in the fishing and mining industries. The prejudice was also fueled by intolerance of a people who were of a different culture and religion.

In People vs. George Hall, the California Supreme Court ruled in 1854 that Chinese could not testify against Whites. In 1860, Chinese children were segregated from the White students. When the Burlingame Treaty was signed in 1868, which increased trade between the U.S. and China, and allowed the Chinese to legally immigrate, more hostilities arose. The Chinese labor force was also blamed for the 1868 recession because many believed the Chinese were flooding the labor force and lowering the pay rates for everyone by working for low wages.

The depression of the 1870s resulted in more friction between the Whites and the Chinese laborers, with the Whites blaming the Chinese for the ailing economy. Flare-ups against the Chinese living in California resulted in public hangings of Chinese laborers. Boycotts were called for against Chinese-made products, Chinese-owned businesses, and Chinese laborers.

Not all Whites were against Chinese, but those who were began to get organized. While some churches defended the Chinese, others, including many in the Catholic Church, spoke out against Chinese immigration and labor. A California Irish man named Dennis Kearney used the slogan of

149

"The Chinese Must Go!" to organize the Workingman's Party. The group held that the Chinese must be excluded from society and sent back to China. In 1871, a mob of Caucasians killed a group of Chinese by hanging them in the Chinatown section of Los Angeles. Others were stabbed and burned in their homes. As anti-Chinese groups formed around the West, violent anti-Chinese protests also occurred in other states, including in Oregon, Washington, and Colorado.

In the 1870s, California passed laws determining how many Chinese could live in a house or apartment, how long Chinese prisoners could keep their pony tails, and laws against Chinese prostitution (which was largely supported by Caucasians). And of course, laws against Chinese opium dens.

California had no laws against Caucasians going to saloons and getting as drunk as they wanted to get and fight with each other. But there were laws made against Chinese opium dens, which allowed authorities to arrest Chinese, confiscate their property, and ruin their lives.

History is filled with examples of a certain type people who think they are better than others denying the basic rights of and doing horrible things to those they view as beneath them. The squalor the poor live in often is related to the wealth hoarding of the mansion-dwellers and the laws they create – while the rich get wealthy on the backs of the poor.

Hamilton Wright, the person credited with getting the U.S. Congress to pass the 1909 law restricting opium went on to lobby for the passage of other laws to control cocaine. Wright spread rumors to get people to back him. One of his most notable claims was that cocaine use drove Black men to seek out sex with White women. Wright was partly successful in getting laws enacted that put some control on certain substances. His interaction with Congressman Francis Burton Harrison helped lead the way to the Harrison Narcotic Act of 1914, which required that records be kept of medicinal drug dispensing and the transactions of those dealing with them, and that such transactions be taxed. The department of the government in charge of collecting the tax was the U.S. Treasury, which set up a narcotics division. Under the advice of the American Medical Association and the National Association of Retail Druggists, cannabis, which was a common over-the-counter medication for headaches and glaucoma, was not included as a controlled substance. At that time cannabis was a medication that was known for its safety and no addictive qualities.

The limits of the Harrison Act increased the price of cocaine, opium, and morphine while turning more people onto the less expensive, safer, and more available cannabis as a recreational substance.

As the demand for cannabis increased, so did the importation of it from lands where it easily grew, such as the fertile and warm soils of Cuba, the islands in the Caribbean, and in Central America. Sailors involved in transporting other goods had the option of making extra income from importing cannabis.

The first law in the U.S. placing limits on cannabis was not a federal law, but one enacted in the state of Louisiana in 1911. That law prevented pharmacists from refilling prescriptions for medications containing cannabis, cocaine, or opium.

In an act against Mexican immigrants who were often seen as users of marijuana and falsely accused of violence, in 1914 the border town of El Paso, Texas, banned the sale and possession of marijuana within its borders. Many believe this was driven by racism against the Mexicans who were the underclass living in the poverty-stricken areas where they carried on the culture of their homeland. There was hatred against the Mexicans who were viewed as problematic and they were accused of flooding the job market and causing unemployment to surge. In reality their poverty drove them to take low wage jobs that nobody else wanted, especially in factories and on corporate farms that were not a part of labor unions. The law against marijuana was passed using lies that marijuana drove the Mexicans as well as the Blacks to become violent and to cause problems for White women.

Other cities learned that this was one way they could work against immigrants, creating a crime where one had not existed, and making a potential problem for immigrants wanting to locate within a city.

As a result of complaints from the El Paso city authorities to their federal government representatives, on September 25, 1915, the U.S. Treasury Department Decision 35719 instituted a ban on the nonmedicinal importation of cannabis. No scientific evidence was used in this decision and it was based on xenophobic misinformation. However, the borders of the country were hardly secured against the importation of much of anything. Because cannabis is so easy to grow, its cultivation was not stopped, and it was commonly sold in stores throughout Texas and the Southwest for both medicinal and recreational use.

New York City took its own steps to control drugs, and in the 1930s added cannabis to a list of drugs that could be obtained only through prescription. But, being a port city, cannabis wasn't the easiest substance to control. Whoever wanted it could get it, especially since it grows very easily in the New York countryside.

States took it upon themselves to pass their own laws against cannabis, often with lobbyists and legislatures using racist and alarmist wording to plead their case to outlaw the substance. Anyone who wasn't Caucasian was suspect, especially if they followed the culture of their homelands.

Some of those who wanted laws passed against cannabis were those who wanted to put restrictions on immigrants, such as Asians, Mexicans, and those not looked at as true Americans, including African Americans.

151

Others had their own agenda.

The pharmaceutical companies knew that if they could influence the creation of laws limiting cannabis to the pharmaceutical market they could then make more money by controlling the substance. Additionally, law enforcement departments realized they could have their budgets increased to help control cannabis, if cannabis were made illegal.

"Within the last year we in California have been getting a large influx of Hindoos and they have in turn started quite a demand for Cannabis indica; they are a very undesirable lot and the habit is growing in California very fast."
– Henry J. Finger, California Board of Pharmacy, in a letter to Hamilton Wright, July 2, 1911

The first state to pass an antimarijuana law was Utah in 1915. Mormons had been introduced to the plant in Mormon settlements in Mexico, where church members had been sent to spread their gospel.

Wyoming and California also passed antimarijuana laws in 1915, followed by Texas in 1919.

Those presenting their case to legislatures often used blatantly racist wording to state their viewpoints, associating the use of marijuana with those they considered to be lowlifes, including musicians, artists, laborers, and specifically Native Americans, Mexicans, and African Americans. When the law was being considered in Texas, a senator arguing for passage stated, "All Mexicans are crazy, and this stuff is what makes them crazy."

Prohibition on alcohol in the 1920s increased the demand for marijuana.

In 1921 U.S. military personnel serving in San Antonio were forbidden to use or possess marijuana. There was no way to drug test the personnel, because the tests had not yet been developed, and there was no way to really stop them from partaking of marijuana, because it was so easy to obtain.

"1925: Concerned by the high number of 'goof butts' being smoked by off-duty servicemen in Panama, the U.S. government sponsors the 'Panama Canal Zone Report.' The report concludes that marijuana does not pose a problem, and recommends that no criminal penalties be applied to its use or sale."
– *Greenkind Magazine*, July 2006; GreenKind.net

After a number of military personnel in the Panama Canal Zone were found to be smoking marijuana, in 1925 the U.S. Army Medical Corps undertook a study. Military personnel including two military police officers, four military doctors, and some soldiers were involved in the trials. The study concluded that, "There is no evidence that marihuana as grown and used here is a 'habit-forming' drug in the sense in which the term is applied to alcohol, opium, cocaine, etc., or that it has any appreciably deleterious influence on the individual using it." The study advised that the substance not be banned. After further study, which came to the same conclusion, the military still took action to ban marijuana possession on its bases in 1930.

In the 1920s there were several more states considering laws to ban marijuana. In 1923, laws banning marijuana were passed in Arkansas, Iowa, Nevada, Oregon, and Washington. Montana and Nebraska made marijuana illegal in 1927. Of course, these laws couldn't stop people from using it.

In Montana a legislator was quoted in the *Butte Montana Standard* as saying, "When some beet field peon takes a few traces of this stuff he thinks he has just been elected president of Mexico, so he starts out to execute all his political enemies."

One doctor who versed opposition to the laws being made against marijuana was a Dr. W.W. Stockberger of the Bureau of Plant Industry. In a 1926 edition of *Literary Digest* Dr. Stockberger is quoted as saying, "The reported effects of the drug on Mexicans, making them want to 'clean up the town,' do not jibe very well with the effects of cannabis, which so far as we have reports, simply causes temporary elation, followed by depression and heavy sleep."

Alabama also passed antimarijuana legislation in 1927, placing a fine of $500 and a maximum penalty of six months in prison on those who violated the law. Of course, this also did not stop people from growing or smoking marijuana, but only got people to conceal it.

Adhering to the voluntary guidelines of the Geneva International Convention on Narcotic Control set up at the International Opium Conference held in Geneva in November 1924, the Mexican government also passed restrictions on cannabis in 1925, but the laws had little effect.

Other countries were also coming on board the anticannabis crusade. England outlawed cannabis for nonmedical use on September 28, 1928. It did this by adding it to the list of substances in the Dangerous Drug Act.

Canada had outlawed opium in 1908 and cocaine in 1911, but placed no limits on cannabis until passage of the Opium and Narcotics Drug Act of 1923.

Canada was one of the last frontiers for the spread of cannabis culture. What Canadians knew about it wasn't limited to the outlandish news stories first printed in U.S. media.

"Persons using marijuana smoke the dried leaves of the plant, which has the effect of driving them completely insane. The addict loses all sense of moral responsibility. Addicts to this drug, while under

153

its influence, are immune to pain, become raving maniacs, and are liable to kill or indulge in any form of violence to other persons."
– Emily F. Murphy

Canada had its own little propaganda darling in the form of a priest's wife named Emily F. Murphy. From a well-to-do family, Murphy had family connections to those who formed the laws, including her politician grandfather, an uncle who was a Supreme Court judge, and another a senator.

Murphy helped spread racist and distorted viewpoints about those who used cannabis and about what it did to those who smoked it.

To her credit, Murphy fought for the property rights of married women. Additionally, in 1929 she was a member of The Valiant Five, a group of women who successfully fought for the specification that women were "persons" under the law, and therefore eligible to be appointed to the Senate. Under the British North American Act of 1867 women were not considered to be persons. Murphy had been rejected as a Senatorial candidate by a number of prime ministers. Another woman, Cairine Wilson, who wasn't a member of The Valiant Five, became the first female senator in Canada. There is a monument of statues of each of the five women on Ottawa's Parliament Hill. They have also been featured on the back of Canada's $50 bill.

In 1916 Murphy became the first female police magistrate. Although Murphy was involved in the women's rights movement to do away with ridiculous laws and standards, she also held some preposterous views. She expressed them in writing for *Maclean's Magazine* under the pseudonym of Janey Canuck. Her articles were popular and, according to Murphy, triggered a number of letters to the magazine. Among her claims was that the Assyrians, Chinese, Greeks, and Negroes who were selling "dope" were going to weaken the White race through addiction and then take over the world. She had toured Vancouver's opium dens and compared opium smoking "Chinamen" to cellar rats, referred to them as "black-haired beasts," and encouraged people to insist that the Chinese be excluded from the continent. She was against immigration, and thought "lesser humans" should be sterilized so that the population of the world could be controlled, which she reasoned would stop war.

Murphy claimed that there were two million drug addicts on the North American continent. This claim was surely a wild guess at best since even today there is still no way of knowing how many drug addicts there are on any continent. She also warned against the "Negroes coming into Canada" who were working to control the "White men." The Canadian government largely considered the rumors Murphy spread, treating them as factual, and using them to pass their law against cannabis. Her racist words helped to establish laws against marijuana.

"All honest men and orderly persons should rightly know that there are men and women who batten and fatten on the agony of the unfortunate drug-addict-palmerworms and human caterpillars who should be trodden underfoot like the despicable grubs that they are."
– Emily F. Murphy, from her book *The Black Candle*, May 1922

As drug laws were created on the North American continent to control cocaine and opium, recreational use of marijuana increased.

Just as in any of the major port towns, marijuana was easy to get in The Big Easy – New Orleans. Sailors made extra money bringing in stocks of marijuana grown in the West Indies and the Caribbean. Immigrants from these regions also brought their culture and customs with them, including the use of marijuana. Reefer was commonly used among the blues and jazz community. As the musicians began to travel to other cities, they brought their music and marijuana with them.

The great Louis Armstrong was born in 1900 in an area called Storeyville. It was a section of town with a number of jazz and blues clubs accompanied by gambling, prostitution and alcohol.

Using the prevalence of cannabis as one of the reasons for their actions, in 1917 the New Orleans authorities raided Storeyville, effectively closing down the so-called dens of iniquity. One has to wonder if the point of the action was more driven by racism. It certainly worked against the disenfranchised that already had been denied so much, and were just starting to develop their culture. That act helped spread the music and culture of New Orleans into St. Louis, Kansas City, Memphis, Chicago, Detroit, Cincinnati, Cleveland, and other cities.

In the 1920s New Orleans authorities acted to place limits on cannabis. Even though Caucasians were not unfamiliar with the recreational use of cannabis, the immigrant communities as well as other non-Whites were often targets of the cannabis laws. In 1927 the Louisiana state legislature outlawed the sale and possession of cannabis and placed a steep fine of $5,000 or a six-month prison sentence on those caught breaking the law.

The racist comments in relation to cannabis were not limited to the backwoods and southern states of the U.S. Other publications ran stories that today look like some sort of comical form of journalism more likely to appear in today's mockunewspaper *The Onion*.

"A widow and her four children have been driven insane by eating the marijuana plant, according to doctors, who say that there is no hope of saving the children's lives and that the mother will be insane for the

rest of her life. The tragedy occurred while the body of the father, who had been killed, was still in a hospital. The mother was without money to buy other food for the children, whose ages range from three to 15, so they gathered some herbs and vegetables growing in the yard for their dinner. Two hours after the mother and children had eaten the plants, they were stricken. Neighbors, hearing outbursts of crazed laughter, rushed to the house to find the entire family insane. Examination revealed that the narcotic marihuana was growing among the garden vegetables."
  – Mexican Family Go Insane, a news story about a Mexico City family, The *New York Times;* July 6, 1927

"The debasing and baneful influence of hashish and opium is not restricted to individuals but has manifested itself in nations and races as well. The dominant race and most enlightened countries are alcoholic, whilst the races and nations addicted to hemp and opium, some of which once attained to heights of culture and civilizations have deteriorated both mentally and physically."
  – Dr. A. E. Fossier, The Marihuana Menace, *New Orleans Medical and Surgical Journal*, 1931

By 1934 there were antimarijuana laws in 33 states. Even so, cannabis continued to be used as a medication, and as an ingredient in patent medicines.

The first antimarijuana legislation to be introduced on a federal level was S. 2075 sponsored by Senator Morris Sheppard of Texas in 1929. The bill would have altered the Narcotic Drugs Export and Import Act of 1922 to include marijuana. Colorado Senator Lawrence Phipps requested that a study be done to determine the consequence of these changes. The Surgeon General undertook a study and issued a report titled *Preliminary Report on Indian Hemp and Peyote.*

"In the year 1090, there was founded in Persia the religious and military order of the Assassins, whose history is one of cruelty, barbarity, and murder, and for good reason: the members were confirmed users of hashish, or marijuana, and it is from the Arabs' 'hashish' that we have the English word 'assassin.'"
  – Harry Anslinger using more outlandish claims to argue for creating laws against marijuana. He carried on the lies of the Roman Pope Innocent VIII, who in 1484 issued a precedent declaring marijuana to be an "unholy sacrament," and a substance used by heretics and Satanic worshippers. He claimed that Arabic culture and Arabs who smoked hashish were ruining society.

Interestingly, the report dug up old rumors about marijuana, including the myth of the Assassins (explained later), and relied on alarmist newspaper stories of the day that claimed marijuana instigated violence in the underclass. Marijuana had not yet been subjected to the propaganda of the soon-to-form Federal Bureau of Narcotics. People were relatively uninformed about marijuana, which was still used only by a small segment of society. S. 2075 failed in attracting enough sponsors and didn't make it past committee hearings.

But things were about to change.

# William Randolph Hearst

The laws prohibiting U.S. farmers from growing industrial hemp were designed to appear as if they were banning the use of marijuana. The laws were made following a huge public campaign by William Randolph Hearst in cooperation with other businessmen, politicians, and government employees working under them who both promoted the misconceptions of hemp and greatly distorted the so-called dangers of marijuana to the point of cynical absurdity.

In the 1920s most folks didn't know what exactly got people stoned, but many did know there was a difference between the tall hemp plant that was grown for industrial uses and the much shorter, bushier, and stickier plant grown for the purpose of getting stoned. As mentioned elsewhere, marijuana's active ingredient, delta-9-tetrahydrocannabinol (THC) was not identified until 1964 when two Israeli chemists, Raphael Mechoulam and Yehiel Gaoni, conducted studies on the plant.

A newspaper mogul and land baron, Hearst owned a government permit to "harvest" hundreds of thousand of acres of trees in America's northwest – trees on U.S. public land that he got permission to cut down by manipulating lawmakers. Because Hearst owned so many newspapers, politicians knew that it was in the best interest of their careers to stay on his good side.

Hearst was known as a businessman who would go after anything he wanted. In 1915, shortly after his wife gave birth to twins, Hearst met a chorus girl in New York City. With his wife, Millicent, refusing to divorce him, Hearst continued his affair with the showgirl, Marion Davies.

Hearst had been building his empire for decades. By the 1920s he had owned 22 daily newspapers, 15 weekly papers, and several magazines. He learned that printing stories about crime sold newspapers and magazines, even if the crimes weren't based on truth or were great distortions of reality. The more salacious the stories, the better they were for sales.

To sell newspapers, all that was needed were stories that people wanted to read, even if those stories were made up. People pay more attention to stories revolving around the topics of corruption, crime, punishment, prostitution, sex, drugs, and lewd or immoral behavior. Even better if the stories contained more than one of those topics.

Hearst wasn't the first to publish exaggerated articles about cannabis, but he is often cited as the most successful at it.

*The Illustrated Police News* published articles that often distorted facts to captivate readers' imaginations. The December 1876 issue contained a story about a "hasheesh house" in Manhattan where upper-class women spent

158

their days secretly indulging in degenerate behavior (hashish is made from cannabis resin, and is stronger than regular cannabis). In those days there were some of these hash dens in major cities, often frequented by a variety of people, including the upper-class and business people. Some of the hash used in these smoking dens was mixed with opiates, and stupidly with alkaloids derived from datura (jimsonweed), a mild hallucinogen that can also be fatal. Stories of people becoming ill or dying in these hash dens had nothing to do with the hashish, but instead had to do with the substances that had been mixed into it.

The Victorian era was hardly as solidly composed of the closed-minded and self-righteous as people may believe. Starting in the 1860s candy made of crystallized maple syrup and hashish was produced by the Ganjah Wallah Hasheesh Candy Company in New York, and it was sold by the great American retail institution, Sears Roebuck and Company. A tent at the America's Centennial Exposition in Philadelphia was made up as a Turkish Hashish Exposition where visitors could sample hashish.

Another often-cited article about hashish houses appeared in the November 1883 issue of *Harpers Monthly* magazine. The article was titled "A Hashish-House in New York: The Curious Adventures of an Individual Who Indulged in a Few Pipefulls of the Narcotic Hemp." It was anonymously written by a Doctor Kane who, in a likely attempt to deal with his own issues, took up a mission to warn society of cannabis. The article described his visit to a somewhat exotically furnished den of a hasheesh house that supposedly existed in Hell's Kitchen. There, upper-class visitors dressed in smoking robes and lazed on mattress-covered floors. He wrote, "Upon them were carelessly strewn rugs and mats of Persian and Turkish handicraft, and soft pillows in heaps. Above the level of these vans there ran, all about the room, a series of huge mirrors framed with gilded serpents intercoiled, effectually shutting off the windows."

In his publications, Hearst brought these exaggerated stories to a new level, and with a self-serving purpose. Some of the first drug-related stories he published were tinged by racism and focused on the Chinese immigrants who worked on the railroads in and around San Francisco. The ridiculous stories sold newspapers, but weren't based on fact. They made the claim that the Chinese were creating opium addicts out of White women and enslaving them in prostitution rings. Drugs, sex, and illicit behavior made for interesting newspaper stories, which were the entertainment of the day for those seeking an escape from mundanity.

A writer who often wrote some of the Hearst news stories was a woman named Annie Laurie. This was a pseudonym for a Hearst journalist by the name of Winifred Black. It is unclear if Black wrote all of the stories attributed to "Laurie," or if other writers, including Hearst, wrote part or all of them.

Laurie's sensationalistic stories often focused on drugs as well as crimes related to drugs – because that was what sold newspapers. In October 1921 Laurie wrote a series of articles about drug crimes, drug rings, the menace that drugs were becoming to society, and people involved in deviant behavior while under the influence of morphine, cocaine, and heroin.

One Laurie story published on January 20, 1923, was headlined, "Path to Penitentiary Paved by Lives of Men Debauched at Early Age by Narcotics: Prison Physicians Warn That Importation and Sale of Deviating Drugs Must Stop or America's Youth Will Wallow in Vice." The story went on to describe a drug ring sending dealers to farming communities. It labeled the dealers as a "Creeping Johnny," which is a name used for the tropical disease malaria. The story proposed, "Would you like to see him face-to-face, this Creeping Johnny that is menacing us and our children with his slow, silent, smiling, cruel, secret advance?" The article goes on, "That you can never do, for it is part of the secret of his power that he himself is always invisible. But come with me, into the Street of the Living Dead, and I will show you some of his victims."

Such stories in a present day newspaper would be laughed at, but in the era when newspapers were the mass media, the stories were taken seriously. People were more innocent then. They were easily influenced to believe in the unknown dangers lurking in society, and especially the dangers of the big bad city spreading into distant communities.

Hearst publications printed so many of these stories that they played a part in establishing Narcotic Education Week, with the first taking place in February 1927.

In cooperation with this new annual event, Hearst published another series telling how drug addicts will become "wild beasts of savage cruelty, absolutely impervious to any human pity or sympathy of any kind" if their drugs were taken away. This article went on to claim that, "Many of the most brutal murders in America have been committed under the urge for morphine." It told of how, "A harmless, good-natured boy of 17 will take two or three sniffs of snow [drugs] and turn into a cold-blooded, cruel, bloodthirsty bandit ready to hold up his own father and kill his own mother to get money enough to go out and buy some more snow."

Because of the way people bought up newspapers to follow the real or fictionalized scandals, business was good for the Hearst Empire.

While spending money to produce movies in which his lover, Davies, was the star, Hearst also built an extravagant beach mansion for her in Santa Monica, California. The mansion was finished in 1928. The compound of several structures, including the main mansion and its guest homes, contained 110 bedroom, 55 baths, and 37 fireplaces. Thirty full-time servants worked at the monstrosity that featured a 110-foot saltwater pool spanned by a bridge made of Venetian marble. Hearst had imported entire rooms from European locations, including a ballroom from Venice and a tavern from Surrey, England, and had them installed into the mansion. It is estimated that the same mansion built today would cost over $100 million. Extravagant movie star parties were held there with circus performers and as many as 2,000 costumed guests. When Davies wanted to have a merry-go-round installed for a party but found there was no room for it, Hearst simply had a wall torn down for the occasion, then had the wall rebuilt when the merry-go-round was taken away. Davies liked to have fun, even when she wasn't surrounded by rich friends. She was known to invite the local surfers to her pool, assuring them that it was okay to swim naked if they felt like it.

Hearst also built an enormous mansion on a mountain overlooking the central California coast. That mansion, which Hearst named San Simeon, is now a museum and one of the most popular tourist attractions in the state.

The Santa Monica beach mansion was sold off and eventually demolished in the late 1950s. Parts of the compound still remain, including the pool, which the city of Santa Monica has turned into a public swimming pool.

In the late 1930s, after years of extravagant spending, Hearst's assets were mortgaged and he was at the brink of financial insolvency. He needed something that would change his financial situation, and fast. After she sold jewelry, stocks, and real estate, it is estimated that Davies, who became one of the richest women in Hollywood, helped Hearst with a gift of $1 million.

The money wasn't enough to quell Hearst's white-knuckled desperation. He needed something really big to happen to solidify his future.

The plan was in the works.

Hearst had lost some 800,000 acres of Mexican timberland because of the rebel Mexican general, Doroteo Arango Arambula, who is now known as General Pancho Villa.

Born under the Mexican caste system, Doroteo was denied the right to own land and he worked as a *campesino* (sharecropper). As a teenager it is said that he killed a landowner who was involved in some way with Doroteo's sister. Some say the sister was raped. Afterwards, Doroteo took to running from the law and joined with others doing the same. He changed his name to Francisco Villa. This name is said to be that of a man who was known to steal from the rich and give to the poor. With his rebel army, Villa became sort of a folk hero for the poor. He and his army took control of land owned by the rich, including foreigners, during the Mexican Revolution and gave it to the poor as well as to soldiers in his army. Villa rose to become governor of Chihuahua and presided over the bloodiest battle in the revolution. The folksong, *La Cucaracha*, or one of the many versions of it, is about a footsoldier serving under Villa not having any "marijuana to smoke." It is said that the slang term for a marijuana cigarette, a "roach," is derived from that song.

Losing that Mexican timberland in 1914 didn't stop Hearst from building his empire, and may have given him a stronger drive to do so. To increase the value of his lumber and the paper companies he partnered with, Hearst and others manipulated lawmakers to pass laws prohibiting hemp. As mentioned, at the time the hemp industry was undergoing a revival as a crop that could be used to make paper. To do this, he used his newspapers to spread sensationalistic "yellow journalism" stories about the dangers of marijuana, a relative to the hemp plant, and helped to standardize the use of the Mexican slang word "marijuana" to describe the psychoactive variety of the cannabis plant. In his newspapers the word was spelled "marihuana." (It is not the Spanish word for cannabis.) (Yellow journalism had to do with the way the paper stock used for Hearst newspapers turned yellow as it aged.)

People speculate about where the word *marijuana* or *marihuana* originated. It may have been some mixture of the Aztec word *mallihuan* with a Spanish inflection. Or the Tepehaun Indian name for the plant, *Santa Rosa* or *Santa Maria*, and/or some reference to the Mexican army slang term for prostitutes, *Maria y Juana* (Mary and Jane). Or, depending on what you believe, named after a female soldier in Pancho Villa's army named Mary.

South and Central Americans may have been introduced to cannabis and/or hemp by early Portuguese, Spanish, or African travelers or slaves, or others, or by way of plants growing from seeds dropped by birds. It grows well in the warm, wet climates, and especially at higher elevations, which Central America has in abundance. By the middle of the nineteenth-century cannabis had spread throughout much of South and Central America. By the early 1900s many had realized a market for exporting it into the U.S.

It was helpful to Hearst's cause to use the Mexican terminology. Mexican workers, especially in the southern states, were considered to be invaders who were stealing jobs from Caucasian Americans during the Depression. Many Mexicans, as well as some other Central Americans, had been immigrating into U.S. cities and towns where they worked on farms, ranches, and places that paid low wages, including nonunion employers – which also created strife. Corporate farms, a threat to family farms, often hired low-wage workers, including those in destitute financial straits, or who were otherwise disenfranchised. The immigrants, although hardworking, were often subjected to racist comments and hate-driven violence. Hearst, who hated Mexicans, helped spread this belief that Mexicans were at fault for taking jobs from Caucasians. As mentioned earlier, his use of the term "the devil marijuana weed" along with false claims about the plant and about the dangers of Mexicans, helped to sell newspapers and make Hearst wealthy.

162

"Marihuana is a short cut to the insane asylum. Smoke marihuana cigarettes for a month and what was once your brain will be nothing but a storehouse of horrid specters. Hasheesh makes a murderer who kills for the love of killing out of the mildest mannered man who ever laughed at the idea that any habit could ever get him."
– From an article appearing in Hearst newspapers

Perhaps too often, people do not question and often believe things they read in the newspaper. This is also true with people in authority, who may then act on the information they read, then create laws based on misinformation or blatant lies.

Hearst owned many newspapers and had a tendency to publish biased articles to sway public opinion on a variety of issues, and especially in ways that benefited Hearst.

# Harry Anslinger

An important person in the story of how hemp and cannabis became illegal is the ambitious government employee and dutiful corporate puppet named Harry Jacob Anslinger. Born to a Swiss immigrant family in Altoona, Pennsylvania, on May 20, 1892, this power-hungry man was the assistant Prohibition Commissioner in the Bureau of Prohibition. Blinded in one eye since childhood, it appears that he subscribed to the theory that if one tells a lie enough times it will become truth to those who hear it. It also appears that the lie could become believable to the person telling it.

Anslinger's father, Robert, was a railroad security guard who helped his son get a job, also as a railroad security guard. After Harry Anslinger graduated from college he was hired by the railroad as an arson investigator and statistician.

During World War I Anslinger worked in the War Department headquarters in Washington where his job involved government contracts with weapons manufacturers. Later, while working for the State Department, he was sent to the American embassy in the Netherlands where his fluency in the German language was utilized in intelligence work.

As the vice-consul in the German town of Hamburg, Anslinger was involved in busting a group of workers on oceangoing merchant ships who were smuggling drugs into the U.S. He also worked in Venezuela and the Bahamas, where he was involved in busting European-based merchant ships smuggling alcohol into the U.S. during Prohibition.

By 1929 Anslinger had been promoted as the assistant commissioner in the narcotics task force of the U.S. Treasury Department's Prohibition Bureau. This was a department of the Treasury set up as the Inland Revenue Bureau in 1914 to enforce tax laws established by the Harrison Act, which taxed and required registration of the sale of coca, opium, and related derivatives by those who imported, produced, or sold them as pharmaceuticals.

On August 12, 1930, Anslinger was appointed to be the first commissioner of the Treasury Department's new Federal Bureau of Narcotics. That department was created from an office already established under the Prohibition Unit, but had to be reestablished after the former head, Colonel Levi G. Nutt, and officers in the department had been removed when they were found to have been involved in mishandling crime records and were associating with a New York mobster named Arnold Rothstein.

Anslinger's Federal Bureau of Narcotics enforced laws governing both legal (prescription) and illegal drugs (cocaine, heroin, opium, morphine). As the bureau set about strengthening the enforcement of drug laws, cannabis

164

was eyed as a substance that should also be controlled. As I will explain, the reasoning for focusing on placing laws on cannabis was not based on a drug problem. Even the U.S. Treasury's own annual report for 1931 expressed the opinion that, "A great deal of public interest has been aroused by newspaper articles appearing from time to time on the evils of the abuse of marihuana, or Indian hemp. This publicity tends to magnify the extent of the evil and lends color to the inference that there is an alarming spread of the improper use of the drug, whereas the actual increase in such use may not have been inordinately large."

Why and how did the treasury change its stance?

Anslinger was the person often credited with being chiefly responsible for demonizing marijuana and hemp. He remained in his job for 32 years, retiring when he turned 70. Some say President John F. Kennedy fired Anslinger. For two years after leaving the Federal Bureau of Narcotics, Anslinger was the U.S. Representative to the United Nations Narcotics Commission.

Some say that Anslinger was only doing his job, and that he was bound by strict standards set to avoid any conflict of interest under rules established in response to the former mess created under Colonel Levi G. Nutt. But if you consider what Anslinger did, and to whom he was related, it is quite easy to see that there were clear conflicts of interest. Take a look at what he did, and who benefited from his actions:

One way to increase the budget of your department when you are head of a branch of the U.S. government is to make certain that your job looks really important. To ensure that your job is secure, you also connect with those who will help it remain that way. When you see other departments of the government as your competitors, you make sure that your department does not get stuck in the shadow.

Another department of the government that was involved in law enforcement was the Federal Bureau of Investigation (FBI). The legendary J. Edgar Hoover was the head of that department and he was quite aggressive in his role. He cooperated with the media of the day to get press coverage whenever he busted a mobster. Romanticizing cops and robbers made for interesting reading, sold newspapers, and helped establish the department as an important branch of the government that was actively working to protect citizens from evil, dangerous, bad people. Hoover was king of perpetuating the hero syndrome, successfully placing himself on the throne of adulation as the conqueror of bad people.

While Hoover was a master of manipulating government and public opinion to bolster and romanticize his position, Anslinger, while far from masterful, wasn't far behind on his impact in the formation of laws and the creation of governmental standards.

165

After a problematic period of underfunding as a result of the Great Depression, Anslinger learned ways of manipulating government to increase the budget of the Federal Bureau of Narcotics. Under Anslinger the Federal Bureau of Narcotics eventually built a national and international network of officers and undercover agents working to enforce drug laws. These were the very same laws he helped to strengthen or create by using hype and lies as well as his connections to and work with corrupt politicians, government employees, and wealthy business people.

It can be said that Hoover and his FBI stood as Anslinger's best prototype of how to run a government crime department. The agenda seemed to be to do whatever it takes to secure the position. Postulating as an important figure at every opportunity was the standard practice, even if you had to lie, cheat, and steal to do so. Anslinger even appeared as himself as the important Federal Bureau of Narcotics head in a 1948 Hollywood movie titled *To the End of the Earth*, which used Federal Bureau of Narcotics files to build the story line.

This was the era of the promotion of the virtues of work. The country had been through President Herbert Hoover, an orphan who became the first student at Stanford University, went on to become a worldwide mining expert; headed European relief efforts after WWI; became the Secretary of Commerce; headed relief efforts of the Great Mississippi Flood, and served in the White House from 1929-33. He was also a relative of future War on Drugs President Richard M. Nixon, and he worked to organize the Federal Bureau of Prisons. During his time as Secretary of Commerce, Hoover voiced support for Prohibition as a "noble experiment," and as president he worked to prosecute Mafia heads that broke the Prohibition laws. Secretly, Hoover paid visit to the Belgian Embassy to converse and enjoy drinking wine on what was legally foreign soil.

Hoover believed that there were technical solutions to economic and social problems. One thing Hoover did was use the Commerce Department to establish a cooperative partnership between government and business, including the banking, utilities, navigation, corporate farming, and petroleum industries. He wanted efficiency and product and design standards, as well as to increase international trade by opening government offices in other countries to assist American companies in conducting business (cheap labor, and access to resources in foreign land = corporate meddling). Corporate welfare was coming into play, providing financial aid to large businesses and benefiting the wealthy. But he also increased taxes on the wealthy and on corporations, and doubled the estate tax. After Hoover had been put out of office, many of his theories stuck, and others were still being promoted, forging a strong bond between government and corporate interests.

The industrialization of the country was idealized and mass consumerism was on its way in. Factories were kicking into gear manufacturing mass-marketed products. Trains, planes, trucks, automobiles, and engine-driven ships sped up transportation and communication. It was Hoover's 1928 campaign slogan that there would be, "A chicken in every pot and a car in every garage." An industrious country with a strong workforce, a vibrant economy, and a well-organized military was a strong and righteous country. Those who worked hard were good citizens. Any display of what could be interpreted as laziness was unpatriotic. A person's value was based on the wealth they generated. Family values were based around contribution to the workforce. Upstanding businessmen were to be idolized. The rule of money took hold of politics. Anything that could possibly take people away from hard work and industriousness was bad. Vices were to be looked down on, and to be punished. All of this helped to make those who promoted this work ethic, the White male billionaire businessmen and their White male politician friends, to become richer on the backs of those who worked in the factories and on increasing numbers of corporate-owned farms, many of which were worked by minorities living on the fringes of the uppity, xenophobic, and WASP society that controlled the money, the laws, and the access to good schools, job promotions, and privilege. Those who were rich were consolidating businesses to become wealthy. It was the era that the Mafia also gained strength working behind the scenes to supply alcohol while establishing its own form of underground government. And the workforce kept expanding with increasingly large numbers of people working for the companies that were being financially linked to the wealthy, such as the war profiteer Jack Pierpont "J.P." Morgan, as well as Henry Ford, Andrew Mellon, William Randolph Hearst, and major petroleum, coal, steel, railroad, banking, tobacco, and farming interests. Monetary gain for the wealthy took precedence over the safety and health interests of the general populace, as well as the environment.

Entwined in the mix of government leaders and the wealthy were those who knew how to exploit these social conditions to their own advantage.

It was in 1934 that Anslinger began to aggressively campaign to strengthen and broaden laws to ban marijuana. This also worked to increase the stature of the Federal Bureau of Narcotics to be perceived as an important government department, and subsequently worked to increase government funding for the Federal Bureau of Narcotics. Not only that, but Anslinger's campaign helped increase the awareness of drug laws in state, county, and city law departments. This meant that local police departments took up the cause of busting those who broke marijuana laws. With local law enforcement busting drug offenders, the Federal Bureau of Narcotics could spend less on maintaining, equipping, and paying staff.

When Prohibition ended on December 5, 1933 this freed up money spent on enforcing laws against alcohol, and brought more money into enforcing drug laws.

The busting of drug criminals also worked in the interests of the newly thriving alcohol industry, which helped to finance antimarijuana propaganda, including the 1936 film *Reefer Madness*, which used exaggerated high drama and distortions to warn young people against the so-called evils of smoking weed. The film centers on marijuana-smoking young adults corrupting others by throwing marijuana parties. One livid character in the film ends up in an insane asylum with a mind supposedly ruined by marijuana. The film fails at its goal of warning against substance abuse, but succeeds at being oddly entertaining.

Demonizing marijuana worked in the favor of the alcohol industry. If people didn't, or couldn't, spend money on drugs, they could spend more on alcohol.

"The hemp breeding work, carried on by the Bureau for more than 20 years, was discontinued in 1933, but practical results are still evident in commercial fields. A hemp grower in Kentucky reported a yield of 1,750 pounds per acre of clean, dew-retted fiber from 100 acres of the pedigreed variety Chinamington grown in 1934. This is more than twice the average yield obtained from ordinary unselected hemp seed."
– Annual Reports of the Department of Agriculture, page 6; U.S. Department of Agriculture, 1935

With a clear view of from where the money flowed into his department, and realizing how he could increase the funding, by 1935 Anslinger was coming down hard on marijuana.

What is interesting is that Anslinger worked against companies that wanted to create different uses for the marijuana and hemp plant, and refused to allow scientific institutions from having access to the plant for scientific studies. He was behind the discontinuation of government funding for hemp breeding work. Why did he do this? Let's explore the possibilities.

# 1937 Perjury Before Congress

By January 1937 Anslinger's campaign against marijuana, which was really about industrial hemp, had reached its high point. That was when the U.S. Treasury Department held meetings on the issue of marijuana. There, Anslinger boasted of its evils. He did so using false information about crimes, and used no scientific evidence, but did use falsified medical terminology about the dangers of marijuana. In other words, he committed perjury.

There were reasons Anslinger didn't make clear why he was focusing on marijuana. He had more than just the alcohol industry on his side.

"If the hideous monster Frankenstein came face to face with the monster marihuana he would drop dead of fright."
– Harry Anslinger, speaking to the Women's National Exposition of Arts and Industries in New York City

The Hearst "yellow journalism" newspaper report of this went on to say:

"This is not an overstatement.
Users of the marihuana weed are committing a large percentage of the atrocious crimes blotting the daily picture of American life.
It is reducing thousands of boys to criminal insanity."

Anslinger exposed his prejudices through the ridiculous comments, distortions, and lies he used to argue for making marijuana illegal. The criminal perpetrators he wrote about were often African, Mexican, or immigrants who weren't homogenized Caucasians. When Caucasians were mentioned they tended to be the innocent ones who were susceptible to corruption, or those who had been corrupted and went on to a life of bad judgment and/or criminal behavior. Anslinger's words sketched darker-skinned people as inherently bad. He was known to refer to Blacks as *ginger-colored niggers*, even going so far as to use the term in a government-issued pamphlet, which created an uproar that threatened his career. That experience apparently got him to use slightly more acceptable wording, but with the same outrageous reasoning.

"There are 100,000 total marijuana smokers in the U.S., and most are Negroes, Hispanics, Filipinos, and entertainers. Their Satanic music, jazz, and swing, result from marijuana use. This marijuana causes White women to seek sexual relations with Negroes, entertainers, and many

others… The primary reason to outlaw marijuana is its effect on the degenerate races."
– Harry Anslinger, testifying before U.S. Senate, 1937

Anslinger had no idea how many people used cannabis. There was, and there still is, no way of knowing. At best, the figure he states was based on a combination of guesses, and certainly was not based on reality. His claim that "most" smokers of cannabis were of darker skin and/or entertainers was total nonsense. His wording displayed his prejudice. It also shows the spin he was trying to put on the issue, to freak out the homogenized Caucasian populace in a way that would get them to act accordingly.

"Girls began to pull off their clothes. Men weaved naked over them; soon the entire room was one of the wildest sexuality. Ordinary intercourse and several forms of perversion were going on at once, girl to girl, man to man, woman to woman."
– Anonymous 1937 news article about marijuana users, which is attributed to Harry Anslinger and his campaign to vilify marijuana at any cost

"When officers arrived, at the home they found the youth staggering about in a human slaughterhouse. With an axe he had killed his father, mother, two brothers, and a sister. He seemed to be in a daze. He had no recollection of having committed the multiple crimes. The officers knew him ordinarily as a sane, rather quiet young man; now he was pitifully crazed. They sought the reason. The boy said he had been in the habit of smoking something which youthful friends called 'muggle' a childish name for marihuana."
– Harry Anslinger article in American Magazine, July 1937

A person's own psychological profile can often be displayed when he or she makes degrading comments about people based on assumed sexual relations. Perhaps Anslinger's constant focus on sexual acts revealed more of what was going on in his thought patterns. Maybe he had some interesting experiences in his life that made him write the sorts of things that he wrote. Or maybe it was only taken from his imagination and desires. Oh, but why? Self-hate? Guilt? Shame?

Hearst's phony and freakishly weird news stories were used by Anslinger to get Congress to criminalize marijuana and the hemp industry. There was no scientific evidence presented. The law was created based on outlandish lies. President Franklin D. Roosevelt signed it into law on August 2, 1937. It placed an extraordinary tax on industrial hemp as well as medicinal cannabis, and classified cannabis as a narcotic.

170

That is the short story. But let's explore how it happened.
Keep reading.

# The Tangled Web of Corruption and Lies

Why outlaw the most useful crop in the world, hemp, while outlawing marijuana? The so-called evils of marijuana were used to outlaw them both. Why?

In the 1930s the E.I. Du Pont De Nemours & Company developed an improved process for making paper from trees using sulfuric acid with the chemicals produced by Du Pont. This quickly became a huge financial windfall for the company as all of the tree pulp companies used these chemicals, including the International Paper and Power Company, which was tied to one of the world's richest men, J.P. Morgan, Jr.

With Du Pont's invention, pulp from trees greatly increased in value as did the value of the Du Pont Company and its associates, and these would increase even more if hemp were to become illegal.

It is important to remember here that Hearst owned the government permit to "harvest" trees from millions of acres of U.S. forests.

Du Pont also developed a product made from petroleum. It's called plastic, which can also be made from hemp derivatives (and from corn and soy, and other plants).

Further tying Du Pont profits to the success of the petroleum industry was their patent on tetraethyl lead for use as a petrofuel additive. As mentioned earlier in the book, hemp cellulose can be used to make ethanol for gas engines, and hemp seed oil can be used to fuel diesel engines.

In 1935, Du Pont scientists discovered a way of making nylon from coal. Nylon can also be made from hemp.

Du Pont had lobbyists working to get the Treasury Department to place a prohibition on hemp. Lammont Du Pont also had a very good friend who had been head of the Treasury Department, which oversaw the Federal Bureau of Narcotics, which worked to ruin the hemp farming industry by using lies and propaganda to force passage of the Marijuana Tax Act of 1937, covered in the following chapters.

Among the differences between nylon and plastic made from petroleum and the same products made from hemp is that hemp does not require the drilling or mining, processing, and environmental damage caused by the petroleum and coal industries.

Petroleum was the type of fuel used with Du Pont's petrofuel additive. The potential of hemp in that it could be used to make ethanol and hemp diesel fuel also posed a threat to the profits of the gasoline and diesel fuel industry, which was where many of the wealthy (read: friends of the politically connected) had their money invested. Many politicians owned land where oil wells were drilled, and they stood to make a lot of money if petroleum remained as the number one fuel for cars, trucks, motorcycles, planes, ships, and other vehicles.

Lammont Du Pont and his company knew the company inventions would be more valuable if competing materials could be eliminated from the marketplace. With hemp being a plant that could be used to make plastics, nylon, rope, fabric, military supplies, fuel, and paper, it is not hard to see why Du Pont, J.P. Morgan, Hearst, large paper companies, as well as certain other key business people, politicians, and government employees wanted hemp out of the picture as soon as possible. They lobbied Herman Oliphant, chief counsel of the U.S. Treasury Department, to devise a way to eliminate hemp from the marketplace, which would secure their financial interests.

Before we explain the twist, let's talk about a machine.

# The Machine They Didn't Want to Be Invented

"The Federal Government in 1841 authorized a bounty, which allowed for the payment of not more than $280 per ton for American water-retted hemp, provided it was suitable for naval cordage. Many of the planters prepared large pools and water-retted the hemp they produced. But the work was so hard on Negroes that the practice was abandoned. Many Negroes died of pneumonia contracted from working in the hemp-pools in the winter, and the mortality became so great among hemp hands that the increase in value of the hemp did not equal the loss in Negroes."

– From HempFood.com, *American Hemp Culture Verbatim*; quoting from *History of Agriculture in the Northern United States: 1620-1860*, by P.W. Bidwell and J. I. Falconer, 1941; Page 365

For centuries the processing of the raw hemp plant was labor intensive. In various parts of the world the hemp crop is left in the field to partially rot and/or is put into a water pit to make it easier to separate the pulp from the fiber.

Thomas Jefferson, the chief author of the Declaration of Independence, had been growing hemp on his plantation, which was worked by slaves. Jefferson knew how important hemp was as a crop used to make so many items of use to the new country, and that it helped the country become more independent. He was troubled that the processing of the hemp stalks was, as he wrote in his journal, "so laborious, and so much complained of by our laborers, that I have given it up."

Jefferson began to tinker with ideas of how hemp could be less "laborious." In December of 1815 he wrote in a letter that a, "method of removing the difficulty of preparing hemp occurred to me, so simple and so cheap. I modified a threshing machine to turn a very strong hemp-break, much stronger and heavier than those for the hand."

Jefferson's hemp-break machine was granted the first U.S. patent.

Jefferson's invention didn't amount to much. Over the years other hemp processing machines were invented. A Philadelphia man named David Myerle purchased the patent for a machine developed by a Boston man named Robert Graves, and in 1838 Myerle opened a hemp processing plant in Louisville, Kentucky, which was the center of America's hemp farming industry. Graves' company sold hemp rope to the U.S. military, which helped satisfy the 1842 Congressional mandate to use as much domestically produced materials as possible. In 1841 a Virginia man named Andrew Caldwell made a machine that separated hemp fiber and made yarn. A New Yorker named G.F. Schaffer took out a patent in 1861 that was used on both hemp and flax. Unfortunately, none of these machines was very successful, and hemp was still being imported from Russia. One reason for this continued reliance on Russian hemp was that the foreign hemp was water-retted, which created stronger fiber, while U.S. hemp was more often retted by leaving it in the field to partially rot by way of the elements.

For a number of reasons it was important to develop a machine that sped up the processing of hemp. As mentioned, hemp that was left in the field to partially rot before it could be separated into pulp and fiber created weaker fabric than hemp that was produced by the drying and water pit retting method, which purposefully partially rotted the stalk to separate the hurd from the fiber. Processing hemp from freshly harvested hemp into useable material could take from months to more than a year. Creating a machine to improve the process would ideally speed up production and lower the cost.

American slaves were used to perform the labor-intensive farming required to grow, harvest, and process hemp. This was especially true with the hemp farms in Kentucky.

After the slaves were freed, the cost of hemp farming and processing greatly increased. There were regional hemp farming industries that started up after the release of the slaves, including in California and the Midwest, but these quickly died off as cotton, petroleum, and trees became more popular for materials formerly derived from hemp: fabric, oil, fuel, and paper. Unfortunately for the forests of the planet it was in the 1800s that tree pulp became the most popular ingredient in the manufacture of paper. The newer western states being added to the Union were sources of petroleum, forestry, and minerals, and also provided land for growing cotton.

Another reason hemp lost favor was that, since the late 1800s, the military forces of various countries were replacing their sailing ships with engine-powered ships made of steel. In the U.S., it was the "Iron Clad" steam-ships the Monitor and the Merrimac. Those ships were the dawn of a whole different shipbuilding industry, one that relied on mass quantities of iron ore and coal mined from deep in the ground, and not from hemp grown from the soil. This also meant replacing hemp rope with metal chains and cable. Although the military use of hemp for clothing, parachutes, cordage, and rope continued, much of the hemp began to be imported from the Philippines.

As mentioned, the cost of harvesting and processing hemp rose dramatically after the end of slavery. This greatly impacted the hemp farming industry. Fewer acres of hemp were being grown, and the cotton industry became industrialized with machinery that did much of the hard

175

work formerly done by slaves. Because Britain was importing cotton grown on American plantations worked by slaves, Britain had an economic interest in the Civil War. This is one reason why the British were supplying weaponry to the Confederate army.

Before the 1800s, cotton fabric made up less than ten percent of fabric produced in America. Cotton became more common as a fabric after the invention of the 1793 cotton gin styled on the Eli Whitney design (as opposed to earlier cotton processing machines). Over the next several decades, America's yearly production of cotton went from thousands of tons to hundreds of thousands of tons. The number of slaves being used on the plantations also dramatically increased from hundreds of thousands to millions.

Because of the dramatic increase in petroleum drilling 1860s, combined with a huge downturn in the hemp farming industry as cotton took over, by the late 1800s, petroleum kerosene became a popular lamp fuel, and then petroleum gasoline became the most popular fuel for the new invention called the "combustible engine" (even though the engines were designed to run on ethanol made from plants). With less hemp being grown, tree pulp became the number one material for paper (and America's forests have suffered ever since, with over 95% of the old growth forests being clearcut). The emerging railroad system also greatly reduced the use of hemp fabric-covered wagons, which also used hemp seed oil for axle lubricant, lamp fuel, and wood sealant. The growing use of electric light bulbs reduced the use of lamp oil (and whale fat as a fuel).

In 1882 some manufacturers and merchants tried to revive the hemp industry by forming the American Flax and Hemp Spinners and Growers Association. This New York group lobbied the U.S. government to help fund the revival.

It wasn't until 1915 that an efficient hemp-processing machine was invented.

"The time will come when wood cannot be used for paper any more. It will be too expensive or forbidden. We have got to look for something that can be produced annually."
– George W. Schlichten

A German immigrant named George W. Schlichten was repulsed by the cutting down of America's pristine forests for the creation of paper. After years of toiling he succeeded in doing what many people before him had tried to do. He designed and created a machine that sped up the processing of the hemp plant.

The "decorticator" was patented on July 1, 1915. The machine made it easy to process large amounts of hemp, separating the fiber, pulp, and seeds, and eliminated the labor-intensive retting stage. It had the potential of making hemp the number one agricultural product in the country for paper, fabric, and seed oil. It would once again make it easy to grow hemp for paper, and prevent the loss of forests while protecting the water systems and wildlife that depend on healthy forests.

As his machine was put to use in a mill owned by John D. Rockefeller, Schlichten apparently realized the value of his machine. When Rockefeller offered to purchase exclusive rights to Schlichten's invention, Schlichten turned him down. Maybe that was a big mistake, not only for Schlichten, but also for the hemp industry and the environment. It was difficult to find investors during the financially stressful times the country was experiencing.

When Henry Timken, a wealthy businessman and owner of the Timken Roller Bearing Company, found out about Schlichten's invention, he invited Schlichten to plant 100 acres of hemp on the Timken ranch in Imperial Valley, California. The crop became a news item and was filmed by Hearst's media group that produced weekly newsreels for theatres.

E.W. Scripps, an owner of the Scripps-Howard newspaper chain, The United Press Syndicate, and a large newsprint company, caught news of this invention and invited Schlichten to his headquarters in San Diego. There, Schlichten met with Scripps' assistants on August 3, 1917. In the meeting Schlichten spoke of how much damage was being done to the environment by cutting down trees for paper, and he spoke of how using hemp for paper would save the forests.

Unlike Hearst, Scripps was very interested in the decorticator as it could lower the cost of producing his newspapers since hemp pulp paper would be about 50 percent less expensive than paper made from tree pulp. As the owner of a bunch of newspapers, Scripps needed a whole lot of paper on a regular basis. Even though he had huge timber companies operating in the Northwest, Scripps saw that hemp could potentially greatly improve his company profits.

"I have spent many hours with G.W. Schlichten, the inventor of the decorticating machine. Friday and Saturday last I spent with him at the Timken Ranch in Imperial Valley, while a portion of his first crop of hemp was being run through his machine. I have seen a wonderful, yet simple, invention. I believe it will revolutionize many of the processes of feeding, clothing, and supplying other wants of mankind."
– Henry Timken, in a letter to E.W. Scripps and his associate, Milton McRae; San Diego, CA, August 28, 1917

"The hemp hurd is a practical success and will make paper of a higher grade than ordinary news stock."
– George W. Schlichten

177

But the decorticator and the ensuing problems with taxation and business in a financially difficult time, combined with bad advice, caused Scripps to lose money and interest in the possibility of developing tons of newsprint from hemp processed with the decorticator.

Without a financial backer, Schlichten's interest in his own invention faded, and on February 3, 1923, he died a financially destitute man in California. In the late 1930s Schlichten's patent on his invention had expired.

Other inventors had patented decorticator machines that were used in the government hemp farming programs of the 1940s, which I cover later in the book.

This scenario of the potential for the decorticator machines also became a possible threat to companies that would have lost money if hemp once again became a popular crop to grow for fuel, paper, chemicals, plastic, paint, oil, fiber, and fabric.

In 1938 the decorticator was written about in both *Popular Mechanics* and *Mechanical Engineering*. These articles built great interest in the decorticator and what it could do to supply the needs of industry. How this article appeared and the source of information in the article is also another part of the twisted puzzle of the hemp industry and how it became criminalized.

"A machine has been invented which solves a problem more than 6,000 years old. The machine is designed to remove the fiber-bearing cortex from the rest of the stalk, making hemp fiber available for use without a prohibitive amount of human labor. Hemp is the standard fiber of the world. It has great tensile strength and durability. It is used to produce more than 5,000 textile products... ranging from rope to fine laces. And the woody material remaining after the fiber has been removed contains more than 77 percent cellulose, and can be used to produce more than 25,000 products ranging from dynamite to cellophane."
– From the article New Billion Dollar Crop, *Popular Mechanics*, 1938. The article largely was based on information written in an October 12, 1937 letter from H.W. Bellrose, president of the World Fibre Corporation to Elizabeth Bass, district supervisor of the Federal Bureau of Narcotics

# The Twist

Here is a major part of the twist that destroyed the emerging U.S. hemp industry of the 1930s, placing such a burdensome tax on hemp that investors and farmers lost interest in hemp, and farmers lost the opportunity to grow an incredible crop.

Who was the banker for the Du Pont Chemical Company? Andrew Mellon. He was also head of Mellon Financial Corporation, a major shareholder in the Gulf Oil (petroleum) company, a major shareholder in a Pennsylvania coal mining company, and a shareholder in utility companies that used coal to create electricity. Along with John D. Rockefeller, J.P. Morgan, Jr., and Henry Ford, Mellon was considered to be among the richest people in the U.S. He helped Du Pont purchase General Motors (their competitor, Ford Motor Company, was working to develop fuels and synthetic materials from hemp and other crops).

What position did Andrew Mellon hold in the U.S. Government? He was the Secretary of the U.S. Treasury.

What did Mellon do to help the oil industry? He worked to create laws giving tax breaks to the petroleum industry. He also put events into play that set the petroleum industry in a position to become the number one source of fuel used in the world.

Who was the boss of Harry J. Anslinger, America's first unofficial drug czar when Anslinger was appointed to Commissioner of the Federal Bureau of Narcotics? Andrew Mellon. (The term "Drug Czar" was first used for William Bennett, director of the White House Office of National Drug Policy decades later. Some say it was used earlier under Carter's administration when Peter Bourne was placed in the newly created position of Director of the National Drug Control Policy.)

What was Anslinger's familial relationship to his boss, Andrew Mellon, who appointed Anslinger to what turned into a 32-year job? Mellon was the uncle of Anslinger's fiancée and future wife, Martha Denniston, whose family gained wealth through the steel industry. The steel industry was also set to make enormous profits from the automobile industry (Henry Ford wanted to make the body panels, fabrics, and plastics in automobiles out of hemp resin, hemp fabric, and hemp fiberglass, while only making the chassis' and engines out of steel, which would not have been good for the steel industry).

Who went before Congress using fake news articles published in Hearst-owned newspapers to get Congress to outlaw hemp? Harry J. Anslinger.

Who wrote some of the sensationalistic news articles that appeared in the Hearst papers? Anslinger and Hearst.

What did Anslinger do to make sure members of Congress read the Hearst news articles about marijuana? Anslinger and his assistants handed out free copies of Hearst newspapers in the halls of Congress.

Who had major investments in the tree pulp paper industry? Hearst and J.P. Morgan. What company developed chemicals for both tree pulp paper and manufacturing and the petroleum industry? Du Pont. Who would make more money if Du Pont made more money? Mellon.

# How They Did It

On October 30, 1929, a bill sponsored by a senator from Texas was introduced to amend the Narcotics Drugs Import and Export Act of 1922 so that it would include cannabis. The Bureau of Prohibition rejected the bill on the basis that cannabis was grown domestically. Similar action to add cannabis to America's first federal drug law, the 1914 Harrison Narcotic Act, which controlled opium, coca and their derivatives, was also rejected.

Cannabis had obviously not been a perceived problem when the Harrison Act was drawn up. But at that time Hearst didn't need it to be, nor did Mellon, or Du Pont.

By the late 1920s, the potential for hemp in making fuel for gas and diesel engines had become a threat to the profits of the petroleum industry. The potential of a revitalized hemp industry was also a looming threat to those making money in the tree pulp paper industry.

The International Paper Company also had a large stake in getting rid of hemp. One of the richest men in America, J.P. Morgan and the bank J.P. Morgan & Company held interest in this company. Mellon Bank had financial ties to J.P. Morgan.

From 1927 to 1935 the International Paper Company was called the International Paper and Power Company, doubling the reasoning behind its support to ban hemp farming. The company produced the pulp that was made into much of the nation's newsprint. This gave it a tie-in with the dominant media of the day, the newspaper industry. Not only was the International Paper Company opposed to the development of hemp for paper, it was also opposed to and worked against the development of making paper out of farm waste, such as corn stalks.

The U.S. government's Bureau of Forestry and Forest Products also had a huge interest in making sure trees remained the most popular material for paper and building products, both of which could be made from hemp (plywood made from hemp fiber and resin is four times stronger than plywood made from tree wood, and is less susceptible to rot and infestation). The U.S. government owned millions of acres of forestland and had conducted its own research into which trees would be best for the production of paper. Those working in the government departments controlling the U.S. forests held interest in keeping wood pulp as the chief source for material for paper. Their department budgets would increase as the demand for both tree pulp and building materials increased.

For years the Bureau of Forestry dismissed studies concluding that hemp and farm waste were perfect materials for making paper. Information was available at least as early as 1910 indicating that hemp was an ideal material for paper. The 1910 *Yearbook of the United States Department of*

181

*Agriculture* included the C.J. Brand study, Utilization of Crop Plants in Paper Making, which stated, "In addition to the waste materials that are available, evidence has been gathered that certain crops can probably be grown at a profit to both the grower and manufacturer, solely for paper-making purposes. One of the most promising of these is hemp."

Furthering its actions discouraging investment in the hemp industry, in April 1931 the U.S. government's Bureau of Plant Industry of the Department of Agriculture issued a statement discouraging farmers from cultivating hemp. The Bureau of Plant Industry withdrew its support from its research into industrial hemp in 1933. The research studies were being conducted by Dr. Andrew H. Wright and Dr. Lyster H. Dewey.

Under the Roosevelt administration, starting in 1935 the Civilian Conservation Corps was used to plant hundreds of thousands of acres of Southern Pine trees on government forestland in southern states. The trees were planted specifically for the benefit of the paper pulp and lumber industries and to make the U.S. less dependant on Canadian tree products. It was the specific type of tree the government's researchers found to be excellent for paper pulp and building material. News of this was published in the June 7, 1934, edition of the *New York Times* in an article titled Roosevelt Approves Development of New Southern Industry. Investors quickly followed, including the St. Regis Paper Company, J.P. Morgan, Du Pont, Great Northern Paper Company, and the International Paper Company. This stands as another example of how large corporations and the wealthy men who were affiliated with them manipulated government to spend millions of U.S. dollars to their benefit. It also shows why the same men and companies wanted to do away with the emerging hemp industry.

At one point the International Paper Company was involved in a stock deal with Hearst. But, because of a 1929 Federal Trade Commission investigation authorized by Senate Resolution 292, which was introduced by Senator Thomas Schall of Minnesota, the two companies liquidated their stock deal. But in 1930, Hearst and other newspaper publishers invested in the newsprint companies. This was reported in the September 19, 1930, issue of the *New York Times* in an article titled Hearst Interests Acquire Canada Stock: Relinquishing Shares in Their Own Subsidiary. By the mid-30s the tangled web of newspaper companies investing in newsprint companies that made their paper from wood pulp increased the reasoning to get rid of an alternative raw material source of paper. Perhaps this is why the March 10, 1929, edition of the *New York Times* printed the article titled Cornstalk Paper Not Satisfactory. As if they had to convince investors that putting their money into companies developing non-tree paper was a bad idea, which it wasn't. In an article published on March 24, 1929, the *New York Times* published an article quoting R.S. Kellog of the Newsprint Institute, who was critical of the development of paper from farm crops.

To say the least, The Newsprint Institute was not the most reliable source for unbiased information on the best raw material for paper.

The plan to get rid of the competition, hemp, was in the works.

A way had to be created to make hemp into such a problem that it needed to be outlawed. What better way than to give its close relative plant an image overhaul, with a new slang name, and to label it as a destroyer of sanity and society?

As mentioned earlier, August 12, 1930, was the day the Federal Bureau of Narcotics was established under the Treasury Department. Harry J. Anslinger was appointed as its commissioner. Anslinger had contacted the American Drug Manufacturers Association and the American Medical Association, proposing strict limits on cannabis. Both associations were against the limits, and both wanted cannabis to remain available as a medicine.

As a way to establish uniformity in record keeping as it applied to medications, in 1922 the American Medical Association drafted the early stages of guidelines to standardize the way prescription drugs were prescribed and controlled. The medical community was aware that some of the very same substances they prescribed as medicine were also being misused and sometimes played a part in crime. Newspapers dramatizing front-page stories about crime to increase circulation often presented the image of drug-crazed addicts committing various crimes.

In 1923 representatives from the American Medical Association as well as pharmaceutical companies gathered and approved a draft of the proposed guidelines.

In 1925 the National Conference of Commissioners for Uniform State Laws gathered. Composed of governor appointees from each state, the commission also drafted a measure that would place controls on medications. Known as the Uniform State Narcotic Act of 1925, this document included cannabis as one of the substances to be controlled. But the act did not become law. Instead, another draft of the act was composed in 1928, which did not apply the same strict rules to cannabis as it did to other controlled substances. Other drafts were composed in 1929 and 1930.

The September 12, 1932, conference held to recompose the Uniform Narcotic Drug Act included representatives of the AMA, Department of State, the Public Health Service, the Federal Bureau of Narcotics, and the National Association of Retail Druggists. The AMA Bill was drafted and was prepared for presentation to the National Conference of State Commissioners in October. The National Association of Retail Druggists (NARD) attorney, E. Brookmeyer, opposed Section 12 of the measure to include the control of cannabis in the AMA Bill. Because of the NARD opposition to Section 12, it was deleted from the act.

On October 8, 1932, a meeting was held called The National Conference on Commissions on the Uniform Narcotic Drug Act. They accepted a revised draft of the bill, which classified cannabis as a narcotic with a similar status as opium. With the goal of getting state legislatures to adopt the proposed law, Anslinger directed the agents of the Federal Bureau of Narcotics to work with the sponsors of the Uniform Act to lobby the legislatures and conduct a campaign to tilt public opinion in favor of the act.

One of Anslinger's sources to compose his propaganda demonizing marijuana was the 1929 Wickersham Commission Report on Crime and the Foreign Born. Within the report was the Warnhuis Study which associated marijuana with crime and Mexicans. Anslinger also relied on sensationalistic Hearst news stories as if the stories were fact, when he clearly knew they were not. He also used police reports that related to crimes allegedly committed by minorities.

"Those who are accustomed to habitual use of the drug [marijuana] are said eventually to develop a delirious rage after its administration during which they are temporarily, at least, irresponsible, and prone to commit violent crimes."
– Anslinger's Bureau of Narcotics brochure, 1932

Finding a newspaper industry eager for sensationalistic stories, Anslinger's Federal Bureau of Narcotics used this to their advantage. If they could stir the public into a frenzy about so-called drug-crazed criminals, then the lawmakers would be pressured to act, including by approving legislation criminalizing the use of cannabis. In September and October 1931 *The Christian Science Monitor* published articles using information provided by the Federal Bureau of Narcotics.

But the country as a whole had more important issues to deal with than the random violence that might be caused by mythical drug-addicted criminals. These were not the best of financial times for the country. To adopt and enforce such a law as the Uniform Act would have been quite expensive. What all of this proposed legislation did was increase the public awareness and curiosity about this substance that was now being called *marihuana*. When the Uniform Narcotic Drug Act was passed in 1932 it applied weak regulations to cannabis, leaving individual states to decide how to control the substance within their borders.

As all of this was taking place, it remained in the interests of certain American businessmen, politicians, and government workers to kill hemp farming, hemp research, the inventions and redesign of machinery that greatly improved hemp farming and processing; and the development of hemp products and extracts that could interfere with the profits of the wood pulp industry, the petroleum industry, the coal industry, and the emerging plastics industry.

In his quest to spread mistruths about hemp and cannabis, Anslinger found a friend in William Randolph Hearst. Hearst had the need to increase the financial worth of the millions of acres of trees he had a permit to harvest from federal land, and to increase the worth of the paper companies he had interest in. Anslinger had the need to make hemp illegal, because his family and their business and political associates needed hemp out of the picture. Hearst already had a history of printing outrageous stories that would sell newspapers. But then he had an even better, and more self-serving reason to print salacious stories that would increase circulation. He had financial problems, and he needed to save his empire. It was a perfect match. Anslinger needed to get the public and those in authority to view marijuana as a huge and growing problem. There is no better way to do this than through the mass media. Hearst's publishing empire provided the perfect avenue because, in that time before radio and TV, Hearst newspapers and magazines were the mass media.

While in the past the Hearst papers printed stories about all the other drugs, such as heroin and cocaine, the new focus was on cannabis, which they called marihuana, and hashish, which is made from cannabis resin.

Hearst already had some experience in publishing bizarre stories about marihuana. One story appearing in Hearst publications on February 25, 1928, was headlined, "Marihuana Causes New Peril: Weed Drives Friends to Murder." In the same month another story told of how a person on marihuana would grab a knife and "run through the streets, hacking and killing everyone." It went on to say that a person could "grow enough marihuana in a window box to drive the whole population of the United States stark, staring, raving mad."

With Anslinger, Hearst took his marihuana stories a bit further.

Crazy stories were drawn up to spread the news that marijuana turned boys into ax murderers, and made people kill random strangers and fight with police. Hearst's yellow journalism described horror stories to create public fear of the horrible monster drug, marihuana.

"Marihuana influences Negroes to look at White people in the eye, step on White men's shadows, and look at a White woman twice."
– Hearst newspaper story on marihuana printed nationwide, 1934

Much to Anslinger's chagrin, few states did much to enforce the Uniform Narcotic Drug Act. The states were to vote on the optional marijuana clause and by April 1934 only Florida, Nevada, New York, and New Jersey had voted for the clause. The Act also denied Anslinger's Federal Bureau of Narcotics jurisdiction over cannabis.

In July 1933 Anslinger sent all federal legislatures a Federal Bureau of Narcotics White Paper titled *Official Statement on the Need for Uniform Drug Act*. In it he expressed his views that marijuana needed to be added to the act.

Anslinger's interest in hemp was apparent in that he sourced the Department of Agriculture for information on the hemp industry. In December 1933 Anslinger received a report written by Dr. Andrew H. Wright and Dr. Lyster H. Dewey. It was titled *Hemp Fiber Production*. It gave a bleak picture of the hemp industry, mostly because the industry had not received the interest of investors or financial backing of research and development, and it had trickled to a small number of farms, and mostly in Wisconsin.

When news of potential legislation placing limits on cannabis reached Dr. Wright and Dr. Dewey, in the spring of 1934 they contacted the Federal Bureau of Narcotics seeking information on how the legislation might affect industrial hemp. Wright and Dewey knew that hemp showed economic potential as an alternative source for paper, building materials, and other products (fabric, fuel, animal feed, etc.).

Wright and Dewey received a response from Anslinger on April 7, 1934. Anslinger mentioned the 1927 Nebraska law that outlawed the cultivation of marijuana, and he explained that the Federal Bureau of Narcotics did not have jurisdiction over cannabis, but that it was working to add a clause to the Uniform Narcotic Drug Act that would require the growers and producers of cannabis to be licensed. Anslinger advised that the Wisconsin State Legislature enact a "regulatory measure to ensure that the flowering tops of the plant" were not used for "improper or nonmedical use." Anslinger was purposely confusing the difference between industrial hemp and marijuana.

One way Anslinger learned about the renewed interest in industrial hemp was through correspondence with Wright and Dewey. As researchers working on developing hemp strains, these two were at the center of the interest among investors as a potentially huge new source for cellulose, fiber, and oil products that would compete with certain industries, including lumber, paper, fabric, plastics, and petroleum.

Anslinger also learned of the growing hemp industry through Helen Howell Moorehead. She was a member of the Foreign Policy Association and secretary of the League of Nations Opium and Dangerous Drug Advisory Committee. After learning through the Department of Agriculture that there were hemp farms being set up in Illinois, Iowa, Minnesota, and Wisconsin that were using the improved hemp-processing machinery to produce saleable hemp materials, Moorehead shared the information with Anslinger.

Apparently people in certain industries weren't happy with the fact that there were suddenly thousands of acres of hemp being planted in the Midwest. Under Anslinger's direction, the Federal Bureau of Narcotics began requesting and receiving reports from the Bureau of Plant Industry, which was tracking the progress of the new hemp industry.

Literature in trade publications as well as in commercial magazines was helping to fuel interest in "alternative" crops and farm waste that could be used to create various industrial materials. *Popular Mechanics* magazine featured at least two articles covering this topic. The May 1930 issue featured an article titled Money from Farm Waste. The September 1934 issue included an article titled New Uses for Old Crops. Throughout the 1930s the *Paper Trade Journal* regularly featured articles and studies mentioning hemp as an ideal material for paper.

In 1935 Anslinger began a new plan to tilt public opinion in favor of outlawing the use of marijuana. The propaganda mill to make the public fear marijuana went into overdrive. Information was spread in the press that marijuana was destroying youth, a threat to good people everywhere, and triggered crime, caused insanity, and was used by the underclass. He provided misleading information to a variety of groups that he knew would also cooperate if they were led to believe that this marijuana substance was a menace to society. Among the groups he worked with were the National Councils of Catholic Men and Women, The Women's Christian Temperance Union (which had a history of being funded by the petroleum industry to help outlaw alcohol – because alcohol could be used in engines), the National Parent Teacher Association, and the General Federation of Women's Clubs. At this point marijuana was not well known, and relatively few Americans knew about its use. But what they were learning about it was information based on lies being spread by the Federal Bureau of Narcotics and others interested in destroying the hemp industry.

These actions to build public awareness of this so-called threat just so happened to coincide with renewed interest in hemp farming in the Midwest. It also was in sync with the emerging wood pulp industry and those investing in it, including the International Paper Company, the Du Pont Company, and Hearst. These actions stand as a perfect example of how industry pressures government to form public policy using exaggeration and lies to benefit corporate interests. It is government for the few at a cost to many. In this case: the entire planet, which soon would bathe in greenhouse gasses spewed by millions of engines burning petroleum.

In June 1936 the Conference for the Suppression of Illicit Traffic in Dangerous Drugs was held in Geneva. Stuart Fuller of the State Department accompanied Anslinger to the Conference where they

187

proposed to add a ban on cannabis to the international treaty. All of the other nations rejected the proposal.

Other plans were in the works.

Back home, Anslinger had known about a pamphlet produced by the U.S. Department of Agriculture.

*Farmer's Bulletin No. 663* provided farmers with information about how to cultivate both hemp and poppies for the pharmaceutical industry. Under Anslinger's direction, the pamphlet was removed from circulation.

"Police officials in cities of those states where it is most widely used estimate that fifty percent of the violent crimes committed in districts occupied by Mexicans, Spaniards, Latin-Americans, Greeks, and Negroes may be traced to this evil."
– Federal Bureau of Narcotics propaganda, 1935

In September 1936 the *Chicago Tribune* published an article by Frank Ridgway about its own hemp farming titled, Day by Day Story of the Experimental Farms. On September 28, 1936, Anslinger sent a letter of concern about this article to Elizabeth Bass, the district supervisor of the Federal Bureau of Narcotics office in Chicago. She then met with a worker on the *Chicago Tribune*'s experimental farm and questioned him about the planed uses of the hemp crop.

Reporting back to Anslinger, Bass was then instructed to visit the farmers who were growing hemp. He also asked her to "Ascertain the demand for the machine that was used to harvest marijuana. Find out the places in the U.S. where there is such a demand. Find just what the hemp is used for in those sections."

In her November 3, 1936 letter that is now in the Marijuana Tax Act of 1937 files of the National Archives, Bass shared her view with Anslinger that, "Objections raised by the manufacturing druggists who have slight need of the extracts of the cannabis in medicinal compounds will be trifling when compared with the country-wide protests that will be raised as with one voice by the experimental stations everywhere developing the use of the fibers of the cannabis plant stems for every variety of textile." In other words, Bass was telling Anslinger that a ban on growing hemp would be a major problem for a lot of farmers, investors, and other businesspeople.

On November 4, 1936, the *Chicago Tribune* printed another article by Frank Ridgway about the newspaper's experimental hemp farm. The Marijuana Tax Act of 1937 files of the National Archives show that Bass sent Anslinger a copy of this article on November 6, 1936.

In 1937 three new hemp companies formed in Minnesota. These included the Central Fibre Corporation, the Champagne Paper Company, and Chempco, Inc. Additionally, the Amhempco Corp. of Danville, Illinois,

188

which began hemp farming in 1935, became the largest of all the new hemp companies as it had planted over 7,000 acres of hemp in 1937. More bankers, farmers, and investors became interested in this growing industry. Some of the farms were using hemp harvesting machines made by the John W. Deere Co. of Moline, Illinois.

The April 12, 1937 edition of the *Washington Herald* published an article in which Anslinger again compared marihuana to "the hideous monster Frankenstein." The Hearst newspapers and magazines often shared stories, so one story, or a slightly different version of it, might be printed in other Hearst publications in cities across the U.S.

Furthering his propaganda machine, Anslinger used a study conducted by a French pharmacist named Dr. Jules Bouquet. The study was conducted in the North African province of Tunisia. The study was titled the *SubCommittee on Cannabis of the League of Nations Advisory Committee on Traffic in Opium and Other Dangerous Drugs.* Anyone reading Bouquet's words today should be able to detect more than a hair of racism, yet Anslinger relied on these same words as if they were scientific conclusions that would support the proposed legislation against marijuana.

"The basis of the Moslem character is indolence. These people love idleness and day-dreaming, and to the majority of them work is the most unpleasant of all necessities. Inordinately vain-glorious, thirsting for every pleasure, they are manifestly unable to realize more than a small fraction of their desires. Their unrestrained imagination supplies the rest. Hemp, which enhances the imagination, is the narcotic best adapted to their mentality. The hashish addict can dream of the life he longs for. Under the influence of the drug he becomes wealthy, the owner of a well-filled harem, the delightful cool gardens, of a board richly supplied with exquisite and copious viands. His every longing is satisfied, happiness is his. When the period of intoxication is over and he is again faced with the drab realities of his normal shabby life, his one desire is to find a corner where he may sleep until a new orgy of hemp brings him back to the realm of illusions."
– Dr. Jules Bouguet, a French hospital pharmacist, author of study on cannabis use in Tunisia for the Sub-Committee on Cannabis of the League of Nations Advisory Committee on Traffic in Opium and Other Dangerous Drugs

Anslinger revived and exploited the questionable story of the "assassins." This story evolved over the years and had something to do with Marco Polo's travels in Persia. Polo's *Il Milione (The Travels of Marco Polo)* recounts how he heard about a brutal group of people living in mountains of northern Persia under the rule of an Islamic dissident master, Hasan bin-

Sabah, who required his followers to kill anyone at his command. The followers are said to have been users of hashish and were called the *hashshishin*, which became the word *assassin*, and the followers as *The Order of Assassins*. But Anslinger's use of the myth of the Old Man of the Mountain and the assassin terminology had more to do with distorting this myth into getting people to believe that marijuana makes people want to kill, or that the substance is an "assassin of youth." On the contrary, marijuana and hashish are more likely to induce a placid state.

It is clear that Anslinger was using falsehoods and boldface lies to destroy the hemp industry.

A Mankato, Minnesota, attorney named G.P. Smith was interested in investing in the growing hemp industry of the Midwest. Hearing about the proposed new law that would restrict hemp farming, he wrote a letter to Minnesota Congressman Elmer J. Ryan.

In the June 12, 1937 letter Smith stated, "We are unable to understand why such a bill should be proposed because, according to our information, it could serve no good purpose and would embarrass, if not kill, an important agricultural development."

Ryan passed the letter along to Anslinger's Federal Bureau of Narcotics.

Anslinger packed a letter with lies and distortions and sent it to Congressman Ryan reassuring him that the proposed bill would allow for the hemp industry to continue while bringing "out into the open all production and sale of the tops, leaves, and seeds of the hemp plant which contain the dangerous drug marijuana and to prevent, if possible, the illicit production and sale of these tops, leaves, and seeds."

Anslinger knew he was not telling the truth. He was aware of the studies about hemp, and that it held promise of becoming a huge industry. He also had a clear understanding of the difference between industrial hemp and marijuana. And he continued on with his campaign to end the cultivation of hemp by passage of the Marijuana Tax Act so that the financial interests of certain industries would be protected. By April the Marijuana Tax Act had already been drafted.

"The sprawling body of a young girl lay crushed on the sidewalk the other day after a plunge from the fifth story of a Chicago apartment house. Everyone called it suicide but actually it was murder. The killer was a narcotic known to America as marihuana, and history as hashish. It is a narcotic used in the form of cigarettes, comparatively new to the United States and as dangerous as a coiled rattlesnake."
– Marijuana Assassin of Youth, *American Magazine*, July 1937; credited to Harry Anslinger

"In Los Angeles, a youth was walking along a downtown street after inhaling a marihuana cigarette. For many addicts, merely a portion of 'reefer' is enough to induce intoxication. Suddenly, for no reason, he decided that someone had threatened to kill him and that his life at that very moment was in danger. Wildly he looked about him. The only person in sight was an aged bootblack. Drug-crazed nerve centers conjured the innocent old shoe-shiner into a destroying monster. Mad with fright, the addict hurried to his room and got a gun. He killed the old man, and then, later babbled his grief over what had been wanton, uncontrolled murder. 'I thought someone was after me, he said. 'That's the only reason I did it. I had never seen the old fellow before. Something just told me to kill him!' That's marijuana."

– Harry Anslinger antimarijuana propaganda published by Hearst, 1937

The propaganda worked. The public fear brought the states and law enforcement to encourage the Secretary of the Treasury, Henry Morgenthau, Jr., to come up with a solution for this greatly exaggerated concern that marijuana was going to destroy the youth of America and cause incurable insanity in those who dared partake of the drug. (Morgenthau took over as Secretary of the Treasury from Andrew Mellon in 1932.)

Herman Oliphant was the general counsel of the treasury. He was assigned the task of drafting a law that would rid society of marijuana. Failing to create legislation that was unlikely to be judged in conformity with constitutional standards, Oliphant had already been considering the National Firearms Act as well as the Harrison Narcotics Act. Finding that the National Firearms Act effectively imposed a large tax on machine guns, and that Congress upheld it on March 29, 1937, Oliphant found what he thought could be a constitutionally acceptable way to put an end to hemp farming and the marijuana market. Seeing that a large tax on machine guns was ruled constitutional in the case of the National Fire Arms Act, Oliphant believed that the same could be done for hemp and marijuana.

Secretly, Anslinger and Oliphant drafted the Marijuana Tax Act. Dismissing any advice they received from the medical and scientific community, Anslinger and Oliphant continued to work on their plan to present the Marijuana Tax Act to Congress.

In April 1937, using fake news stories and doctored information that was truly a pack of lies, treasury attorney S.G. Tipton provided the case in support of the Marijuana Tax Act. It was presented to a six-member House Ways and Means Committee on April 14. The committee was selected because it presented bills to the House of Representatives free of consideration or debate from other congressional committees. This way

191

representatives from districts where hemp was grown would not be able to oppose the legislation.

Robert L. Doughton of North Carolina chaired the House committee presented with HR 6385. He was a friend of the Du Pont family. When Doughton called the Ways and Means Committee hearing into order on May 11, 1937, he described HR 6385 as a "bill to impose an occupational excise tax upon certain dealers in marihuana, to impose a transfer tax upon certain dealings in marihuana, and to safeguard the [tax] revenue therefrom by registry and recording." He used the terminology that they wanted him to use, referring to cannabis as marihuana, thus sticking to the agenda to outlaw the cannabis plant, and its relation, hemp.

The Treasury Department's own assistant counsel, Clinton Hester, presented more lies to the committee by stating, "The purpose of HR 6385 is to employ the federal taxing power not only to raise revenue from the marihuana traffic, but also to discourage the current and widespread undesirable use of marihuana by smokers and drug addicts, and thus drive the traffic into channels where the plant will be put to valuable industrial, medical, and scientific uses." Of course that made no sense because the bill would effectively apply prohibitive taxes on the plant in such a way that it wouldn't be traded, and there would be no revenue raised. Hester wasn't stupid. He was simply saying the words that he was told to say because there was huge money to be made by his associates if the bill became law.

Anslinger testified at the Ways and Means Committee hearing with some more lies and outlandish reasoning when he said, "This traffic in marijuana is increasing to such an extent that it has become the cause for the greatest national concern. In medical schools the physician-to-be is taught that without opium, medicine would be like a one-armed man. That is true, because you cannot get along without opium. But here is a drug that is not like opium. Opium has all the good of Dr. Jekyll and all the evil of Mr. Hyde. This drug (marijuana) is entirely the monster Hyde, the harmful effect of which cannot be measured."

"I think it is an established fact that prolonged use leads to insanity in certain cases."
– Dr. Carl Voegtlin, chief of the Division of Pharmacology of the National Institutes of Health, lying as he testified at the Ways and Means Committee hearing on marijuana, April 1937. Voegtlin used no scientific evidence because studies had been blocked under Anslinger's reign as head of the Federal Bureau of Narcotics, which denied scientific institutions the use of marijuana in scientific studies.

Dr. William C. Woodward, an attorney and director of the American Medical Association's Bureau of Legal Medicine spoke against the bill, and attacked it as based on unsound research. He clearly was of the opinion that cannabis should be kept on the market as a medicine, and even spoke against the "marihuana" terminology being used at the meeting. Woodward smartly questioned the claims made by, the prefabricated testimony of, and the unfactual newspaper articles presented by Anslinger. Woodward expressed his concern with the way the proposed law had been created without the use of scientific evidence, and with no input from various agencies and departments that could present statistics supporting or dismissing Anslinger's claims. Unfortunately, Woodward also displayed some measure of belief in the newspaper articles, a sign of the trust people had in journalism at that time.

"That there is a certain amount of narcotic addiction of an objectionable character no one will deny. The newspapers have called attention to it so prominently that there must be some grounds for statements. It has surprised me, however, that the facts on which these statements have been based have not been brought before this committee by competent primary evidence. We are referred to newspaper publications concerning the prevalence of marihuana addiction. We are told that the use of marihuana causes crime.

But yet no one has been produced from the Bureau of Prisons to show the number of prisoners who have been found addicted to the marihuana habit. An informed inquiry shows that the Bureau of Prisons has no evidence on that point.

You have been told that schoolchildren are great users of marihuana cigarettes. No one has been summoned from the Children's Bureau to show the nature and extent of the habit, among children.

Inquiry of the Children's Bureau shows that they have had no occasion to investigate it and know nothing particularly of it.

Inquiry of the Office of Education – and they certainly should know something of the prevalence of the habit among the schoolchildren of the country, if there is a prevalent habit – indicates that they have had no occasion to investigate and know nothing of it.

Moreover, there is in the Treasury Department itself, the Public Health Service, with its Division of Mental Hygiene. The Division of Mental Hygiene was, in the first place, the Division of Narcotics. It was converted into the Division of Mental Hygiene, I think, about 1930. That particular bureau has control at the present time of the narcotics farms that were created about 1929 or 1930 and came into operation a few years later. No one has been summoned from that bureau to give evidence on that point.

Informal inquiry by me indicates that they have had no record of any marihuana or cannabis addicts who have ever been committed to those farms.

The bureau of Public Health Service has also a division of pharmacology. If you desire evidence as to the pharmacology of cannabis, that obviously is the place where you can get direct and primary evidence, rather than the indirect hearsay evidence.

...There is nothing in the medical use of cannabis that has any relation to cannabis addiction. I use the word 'cannabis' in preference to 'marihuana,' because cannabis is the correct term for describing the plant and its products. The term 'marihuana' is a mongrel word that has crept into this country over the Mexican border and has no general meaning, except as it relates to the use of cannabis preparations in smoking.

... We cannot understand yet, Mr. Chairman, why this bill should have been prepared in secret for two years without any intimation, even, to the profession, that it was being prepared."
– Dr. William C. Woodward, arguing against passage of the Marijuana Tax Act of 1937

Woodward's corrective words and displeasure with the proposed law were not welcome. The Chairman, Doughton, reproached Dr. Woodward by reading newspaper articles as if the articles were fact. But the articles contained lies about marijuana and fabricated stories about crimes committed by people who supposedly smoked marijuana. The chairman (friend of Du Pont) essentially dismissed Dr. Woodward's argument and said that without the proposed law "we would have no civilization whatever."

The general counsel for the National Oil Seed Institute, Ralph Loziers, argued against the law at the House hearing. He reasoned that hemp seed "is used in all the Oriental nations and also in a part of Russia as food. It is grown in their fields and used as oatmeal. Millions of people every day are using hemp seed in the Orient as food. They have been doing that for many generations, especially in periods of famine."

A representative of the Sherwin Williams Paint Co. testified that by 1935 his company was using 58,000 tons of hemp seed to press for the oils used in paints.

Because of the testimony of a representative from a birdseed company, who said that hemp seed was a main component of his product and beneficial to the plumage, hemp seed was excluded from the bill, and remained legal to sell for bird and animal feed.

On June 14, 1937 HR 6385 was presented to the full House. The representatives were presented with some of the fabricated information about how marijuana was ruining society, destroying the minds of the country's youth, and increasing crime.

The act was passed by the House and went to the Senate Committee on Finance, which conducted their hearing on July 12, 1937.

Who chaired the Senate Committee on Finance that was presented with HR 6385? Prentice Brown of Michigan. Who were Brown's friends? The Du Pont family.

Anslinger spoke as a witness and again used his fabricated news stories to argue for the bill. He also dismissed concerns that the bill would negatively affect the industrial hemp industry.

Several hemp industry leaders were there to present their case. Wisconsin's Rens Hemp Company founder, Matt Rens, argued for a reduction in the proposed tax. He was supported in his argument by the superintendent of the Danville, Illinois, AmHempCo Corporation.

The Hemp Chemical Corporation was also represented by a spokesman at the hearing. His words give an idea of how new was this whole concept of a relationship between hemp and a so-called dangerous drug that was going to ruin society. He said that people "did not know until two months ago that the hemp which they grew there contained marihuana. Until this agitation came up they did not dream of it." His words indicate how Anslinger's campaign had successfully confused and misinformed even the most involved industry leaders.

"We have to contract our seed from growers [with] acreage [that] runs anywhere from a quarter of an acre up, and we have no objection to the bill. In fact, any attempt to prevent the passage of a bill to protect the narcotic traffic would be unethical and un-American. That is not the point, but we do believe that a tax of $5 is going to be prohibitive for the small [raw hemp materials] dealer as well as the man that grows the crop, because he will average, I do not know what the acreage will be, but they raise as little as two acres."
– Superintendent of AmHempCo Corporation of Illinois

Anslinger's side came to a compromise to appease the hemp industry. This was that the hemp industry could still sell its hemp stalks, *if* the stalks were free of foliage, including the leaves and budding tops before the stalks could be transferred to the processor or other company purchasing the hemp stalks. But he knew that removing the foliage from each hemp stalk would be labor intensive and cost prohibitive, further impacting the farmers and making it unlikely that their businesses could survive the extra labor cost. He also knew that industrial hemp would not get a person high.

The House ignored the information presented by Dr. William C. Woodward of the AMA who clearly argued against every aspect of the proposed law. It also ignored the arguments by hemp industry leaders to lower the proposed tax. When a New York member of the house asked the Speaker what the bill was about. Speaker Sam Rayburn answered, "I don't know. It has something to do with a thing called marijuana. I believe it's a narcotic of some kind." The House member asked, "Mr. Speaker, does the American Medical Association support this bill?" A member on the committee rose and answered with a lie, and got Doctor Woodward's name wrong. "Their Doctor Wentworth came down here. They support this bill 100 percent." Interestingly, after little debate and apparently believing in or supporting the lies, the purchased and manipulated members of Congress unanimously passed the bill. They did so at the end of a Friday afternoon session when some of those who would have been at the meeting had left for the summer weekend.

The propaganda used to make people believe in the horrible demon monster, marijuana, worked. Section 14 of the Tax Act granted the Federal Bureau of Narcotics the jurisdiction over marijuana.

In the self-righteous halls of the politicos one needs to present what political society views as exemplary characteristics, and vote in a way that will be good for the political career. One's social standing and financial connections are more important than whether or not the vote is based on factual evidence. The bills being considered in those early days building up to marijuana prohibition were not based on scientific evidence or matters of health. They were based on prejudices and crooked politics, and they were especially rooted in corporate greed.

President Franklin Roosevelt signed The Marihuana Tax Act of 1937 into law on August 2, 1937. It took effect October 1.

Andrew Mellon, perhaps the chief conspirator of this scenario, did not live to see this law enacted because he died on August 27.

The act placed extraordinarily high taxes on hemp and medicinal marijuana. It required that anyone who grew, transported, sold, or prescribed marijuana pay a tax of one hundred dollars per ounce on any exchange. Hemp was taxed at one dollar per ounce. Hemp farmers were also required to remove the foliage of the hemp stalks before transferring ownership of the hemp. As a tax law, not a narcotics law, it effectively made hemp too costly to farm, process, or sell.

"President Roosevelt signed today a bill to curb traffic in the narcotic, marihuana, through heavy taxes on transactions."
– *The New York Times*

So you see, the U.S. government hemp and marijuana laws were formed using lies.

196

# The Aftermath

The hemp industry in the U.S. was demolished. Farmers who had already suffered through the Great Depression then lost the potential of making money from hemp, which is a perfect rotation crop that easily grows in every state in the U.S.

Over the following months farmers and hemp companies in the Midwest were soon found by the Federal Bureau of Narcotics to be in violation of the Marijuana Tax Act. The tax burden worked. Investors in hemp farming and processing were discouraged and most dropped out. Banks failed to back the companies. Most farmers stopped planting hemp. The Federal Bureau of Narcotics made it difficult for farmers and hemp companies to transfer ownership of the hemp they had already grown.

The hemp farmers and business people who still worked to continue the hemp industry under the new laws were in a constant battle with the Federal Bureau of Narcotics to comply with the new standards and taxes. Federal Bureau of Narcotics officers often made trips to farms to investigate the farming practices. This could be described as harassment. Interestingly, hemp farms and hemp businesses in Wisconsin that had contracts to supply hemp products to the U.S. government for military uses, especially for the Navy, were not kept under the watchful eyes of field supervisors of the Federal Bureau of Narcotics.

Some hemp companies in Minnesota threatened to sue the government to compensate the companies for their business losses. In Anslinger's flippant response to this situation during the summer of 1938 he wrote, "This hemp may be sold under the provisions of the Marijuana Tax Act provided that it is substantially free of flowering tops and leaves without respect to the transfer of the act. Accordingly, the passage of the Marihuana Tax Act of 1937 did not destroy the market for hemp."

> "Tell Mr. Anslinger that he can go to the region below and let him present the country with a spectacle of arresting half a thousand farmers in Minnesota for selling an agricultural crop grown off from their farms which were grown long before Congress ever thought of the Marihuana Act."
> – Ojai A. Lende, in a letter to Minnesota Senator Henrik Shipstead, March 31, 1939. Lende was an attorney representing farmers that were trying to deal with this new law that was destroying their businesses.

The year after the U.S. passed the Marihuana Tax Act, Canada also outlawed hemp farming and did so using lies about marijuana. Canadians also lost their source for medicinal cannabis because they relied on cannabis farms located in South Carolina to supply them with the medical grade product.

In the early 1940s, apparently under the pressure of Anslinger, cannabis was taken out of the U.S. pharmacopoeia. Most doctors had already stopped prescribing it because the Tax Act had made it too expensive and problematic. Pharmaceutical companies could then sell more medicine because a most common medicine, marijuana, was essentially taken off the market.

Which companies suddenly became a lot more valuable when hemp became too costly to grow? The International Paper Company; the St. Regis Paper Company; the Du Pont Chemical Company that produced the chemicals used by the tree paper companies; the oil companies; and the one owned by William Randolph Hearst. Although he died on August 27, 1937, Andrew Mellon's companies, and his heirs and business associates, didn't make out so badly in the deal, either.

Some members of Congress also just so happened to benefit financially by voting the way Hearst, Du Pont, Mellon, and Anslinger wanted them to vote. Many members of Congress put their fortunes in cotton, petroleum, lumber, paper, and other ventures that benefited from the elimination of hemp farming.

With unfounded claims such as, "Marihuana is an addictive drug which produces in its users insanity, criminality, and death," and "Marihuana leads to pacifism and community brainwashing," Anslinger used outrageous lies to advocate and strengthen the laws, and distorted any reasoning in his favor to get funding for his department. His decades-long career was set, but he could always be aided by keeping his so-called important job in the news. One was to go after the high-profile people.

Anslinger's Federal Bureau of Narcotics received more funding to deal with the control of marijuana, but placed more pressure on states and local governments to enforce the marijuana laws while the Federal Bureau of Narcotics focused on other drug crimes.

When 58-year-old Samuel Caldwell of Denver was the first to be arrested for breaking the Marijuana Tax Act law, Anslinger traveled to be present at the court hearing on October 8, 1937. Caldwell was accused of selling marijuana to a 26-year-old named Moses Baca. The judge, J. Foster Symes, fined Caldwell $1,000 and sentenced him to four years labor. Baca was sentenced to 18 months. They both served their time in the U.S. penitentiary located in Leavenworth, Kansas.

"About 1935, we were stunned with the rapid wildfire spread of this drug, and by the following year it had become such a major menace as to call for the enactment of national control legislation. Nearly every state had suffered from the insidious invasion of this drug. It spread to new circles not previously contaminated by drug addiction – to young, impressionable people."

– Harry Anslinger, speaking before a meeting with the *New York Herald Tribune*, 1938

# The U.S. Used Hemp to Fight WWII

"Last week the War Production Board approved plans for planting in the United States 300,000 acres of hemp (the only one of the fibers which will grow in this climate) and for building 71 processing mills. Plantings will be concentrated in Kentucky, Indiana, Illinois, Wisconsin, Minnesota, and Iowa, with the processing plants in approximately the same areas.

This program should assure an adequate supply by the time stocks run out, for hemp is normally only a four-month crop. Farmers like it, too, because it helps control weeds, needs no tending until harvest, and leaves the soil in good condition."
– Hemp, *Newsweek* magazine, October 16, 1942

"In 1942, 14,000 acres of fiber hemp were harvested in the U.S. The goal for 1943 is 300,000 acres."
– *Hemp for Victory*, an industrial film that had nearly been erased from the government's records until hemp activist Jack Herer found it listed in the records of the Library of Congress. The film was produced by the U.S. Department of Agriculture to teach farmers how to grow and process hemp to help with the war effort, providing American troops with hemp clothing, tents, and parachutes, and military ships with rope. So patriotic was the growing of hemp that farmers and their sons who grew hemp under government contract were exempt from having to serve in the war. Access: JackHerrer.com.

"We will not allow American farmers to grow hemp."
– General Barry McCaffrey, U.S. drug czar, 1999

Why did the U.S. Department of Agriculture make a film titled *Hemp for Victory* that taught U.S. farmers how to grow and process hemp in the early 1940s? Why did the government issue federal registration contract documents with a tax stamp for about 20,000 U.S. farmers to be able to grow hemp at that time? Why did the government hand out a pamphlet to farmers titled *Hemp: A War Crop*? Why did the U.S. government send bundles of hemp seeds to farmers who contracted to grow hemp? Why did the War Hemp Industries Corporation build forty-two mills for processing hemp in the Midwest between 1942 and 1945? At the same time, why was the U.S. government distributing *Farmer's Bulletin No. 1935*, which encouraged farmers to grow hemp? Why did the U.S. government print thousands of posters featuring an image of an idealistic military man

200

standing on a naval ship and the words "Grow Hemp for the War"? Why did the U.S. government exempt farmers and their sons who grew hemp from military service?

Why? The Japanese had cut off America's supply of Asian hemp. Hemp farming was then being advocated as a way to keep America independent and provide a product that could be used for rope, fabric, parachute cordage, shoelaces, and other military uses, including mops to clean the decks. At that time members of 4H clubs were encouraged to grow hemp to supply seeds for the government to distribute to farmers. The University of Kentucky's agricultural department published a pamphlet titled *The Hemp Seed Project for 4-H Clubs*. With it, children were given seed packets to grow hemp. This helped to supply enough seed for U.S. farmers to grow over 30,000 acres of hemp.

"When a farmer signs a contract to grow hemp in the government program of 1943, he also signs an application for a registration, and no further application is necessary. The registration must be renewed each year beginning July 1. This so-called 'license' permits a farmer to obtain viable hemp seed from a registered firm dealing in hemp, to plant and grow the crop, and to deliver mature, retted hemp stalks to a hemp mill.

Hemp is now a strategic war crop. It is needed for making strong, durable twines and ropes, formerly made of fibers imported from the Philippines and the Netherlands East Indies.

Your government is sponsoring the expansion of the hemp industry, and farmers will be assisted in the production, handling, and marketing of this crop.

By growing hemp in 1943, farmers in Minnesota, Iowa, Wisconsin, Illinois, Indiana, and Kentucky can serve their country and also have good prospects of profit for themselves.

Hemp should be planted on the most productive land on the farm – land that would make 50 to 70 bushels of corn per acre.

It is not a hard crop to grow. It is planted with a grain drill and harvested with special machinery rented from the hemp mills.

It is allowed to lie on the ground until the outer part of the stalks has rotted, freeing the fibers. This process is called dew retting.

The most important step in hemp farming is to stop the retting process at the proper time.

This bulletin tells how to grow and harvest hemp. For more information write the Bureau of Plant Industry, United States Department of Agriculture, or to your state experiment station, or consult your county agent or county Agricultural War Board.

Hemp is an annual plant that grows from seed each year, and therefore it can be brought readily into production. It produces twice as much fiber per acre as flax, the only other fiber that is its equal in strength and durability and that is known to be suitable for culture and preparation on machinery in this country."
– From the opening of *Hemp: Farmers' Bulletin No. 1935*, distributed to farmers by the U.S. Department of Agriculture in the 1940s

"The plant itself is large and powerful, and its output is multifaceted. It grows higher than man, very quickly. All parts of its body can be utilized: the fiber strand, the smooth seed, the woody part and the narrow leaf. Every part is dedicated to serve the four-year plan...
The woody part of this large plant is not to be thrown out, since it can easily be used for surface coatings for the finest floors. It also provides paper and cardboard, building materials and wall paneling. Further processing will even produce wood sugar and wood gas...
Anyone who grows hemp today need not fear a lack of a market. Because hemp, as useful as it is, will be purchased in unlimited amounts...
He who grows hemp with industrious hands helps himself and the fatherland."
– From the German government's World War II *Humorous Hemp Primer*, published by the Reich's Nutritional Institute, Berlin, 1943. The comical but sincere booklet encouraged farmers to grow hemp, and companies to manufacture products from hemp, such as hammocks to romance their lovers. The full text of it is included in Jack Herer's 1985 book *The Emperor Wears No Clothes*. Access: JackHerer.com.

Under pressure from the petroleum industry, the flax industry, the cotton industry, the paper industry, and others with a financial interest in killing the American hemp industry of the 1940s, the U.S. government ended the hemp farming program when WWII ended.
What happened when World War II ended? America went back to its hemp restrictions that started in 1937. The farmers who were growing hemp were told to stop, their government contracts were canceled, government hemp processing plants were closed, and America again started importing hemp products from other countries.

"Many commodities which came to replace traditional uses of industrial hemp in the United States in the last century and a half also carried considerable environmental baggage.

Cotton and polyester production are two good examples of industries that replaced industrial hemp. Both are high-performance materials with unique qualities. Polyester fiber manufacturing requires six times the average energy required to produce either cotton or industrial hemp fiber, generating particulate pollution, as well as carbon dioxide, nitrogen oxides, sulphur oxides, and carbon monoxide. Cotton is one of the most water- and pesticide-intensive crops in the world. The United States is the second largest producer of cotton, accounting for roughly a fifth of world production. Health effects due to pesticide use are a concern for both humans and wildlife, particularly bird and amphibian species. One researcher has estimated environmental and societal damages as a result of pesticide use in the United States at a value of $9.6 billion annually.

Because industrial hemp has far greater natural pest and weed resistance than cotton does, fewer inputs (farming chemicals: fertilizers, pesticides, herbicides) are needed for economic cultivation of this crop. Even new technologies that allow for more precise application of pesticides and genetic engineering for herbicide-tolerant and insect-protected cotton still leave cotton well outside the environmental performance range of hemp."

– March 2008 Reason Foundation Study on Hemp, Illegally Green: Environmental Costs of Hemp Prohibition. Policy Study 367, by Skaidra Smith-Heisters

One organization that worked to help spread rumors claiming hemp was a drug and ruinous to society was the Flax and Fibre Institute of America. On March 30, 1943, the managing director of the institute, Howard D. Salins, wrote a widely distributed letter consisting of a desperate rant filled with ridiculous lies. He claimed hemp was a dangerous narcotic, and the increased acreage being used to grow hemp during the war was robbing the nation of land where food should be grown to the point that it was going to result in a food shortage. He had been lobbying various members of Congress and members of government agricultural offices to put an end to hemp farming. His interests were financial. Hemp oil and fiber could be used in place of flax.

"In one of the most dastardly propositions ever 'cooked' up, the U.S. Department of Agriculture and the War Production Board are manipulating the proposition of a promotion and scheme to grow and produce hemp from a plant, outlawed by law, that is the fount of the insiduous [sic] drug known as Marijuana, the worst and most serious source of all (dope) narcotic evils afflicting children, in the schools and outside, and grown-ups alike in all walks of life. The fiber itself from

203

this plant is worthless. The seeds from this plant fly far and wide. The resultant wild growth becomes dangerously uncontrollable. In the face of shortage and scarcity of labor, foodstuffs, linseed oil, fibers and other critical materials which are peculiarly being denied us, these corruptors [*sic*] of American life are now engaged in the promoting of 350,000 acres, erecting 100 buildings and building a large volume of equipment and machinery in a number of Mid-Western States for the production of this narcotic (dope) plant product, all of which must reach the staggering cost of $500,000,000 and end in catastrophic failure. A number of land-grant educational institutions are in on this racket. The Commodity Credit Corporation and the War Production Board and the Defense Plant Corporation, through their own created socalled [*sic*] 'War Hemp Industries, Inc., Agency,' something new in the New Deal bureaucratic set-up, are running this (dope) narcotic show with private racketeers as undercover men. Large profits have been made already by them on the seeds by cheating and gipping [*sic*] the government. The financial 'kill' is figured to be colossal for all the participants. The kill to agriculture, industry, (the choicest and most fertile land or soils are being demanded) and health and welfare of the American people is going to reach disastrous proportions from which recovery may never be found possible.

... This whole hemp marijuana racket will be dumped out of existence right after the war is over in accordance to with [*sic*] a statement from Washington, D.C., but obviously not before the 'kill' in taxpayers' money has been made and the narcotic has been spread to dope them."

– Excerpted from letter by Howard D. Salins, Managing Director, Flax and Fibre Institute of America, March 30, 1943

Anslinger's idea for using cannabis to fight the war was a bit different from the Hemp for Victory campaign. In 1942, with Anslinger's cooperation, the U.S. investigated the possibility that marijuana could be used to help fight the war. In cooperation with the Federal Bureau of Narcotics, the U.S. Office of Strategic Services tested marijuana as a truth serum for interrogating possible spies, traitors, and captives. The test subjects displayed behavior that wasn't what the OSS had planned. The subjects displayed a variety of behaviors associated with being stoned, including laughter, non-stop talking, hunger, paranoia, contemplative silence, and sleepiness. Apparently curious about the behavior of the test subjects, some of the agents apparently also partook of the serum. (The Office of Strategic Services eventually morphed into the Central Intelligence Agency.)

When the war was over, the government began sending out work crews and hiring destitute day laborers to rid the countryside of wild "ditch weed" hemp plants. This was a task that was ongoing because birds, streams, and rivers were so good at spreading the seeds. It is a process that continues today. Even the National Guard is used to cut down and destroy clusters of feral hemp.

In 2005 the DEA claimed to have killed 223,000,000 cannabis plants in the U.S., the majority being wild strains (called *ruderalis,* which is a Russian word applied to hemp that has acclimated to its environment), and the rest through "drug busts" of people growing cannabis. This killing of wild and benign cannabis plants is another example of how the government wastes money on trying to control marijuana. These wild strains of hemp can't get you high, are spread through wind, water, and wildlife, and are abundant in many areas. Funding for this eradication program should be canceled. The money can be spent on something that would benefit society, such as in protecting the environment and wildlife rather than destroying part of it.

What did a lot of the southern farmers start to grow after they stopped growing hemp? The labor-intensive and soil-nutrient-robbing crop called tobacco. The use of tobacco leads to millions of miserable cancer deaths around the world, and more deaths in the U.S. every year than all deaths from illegal drugs in the past century. Not only does the U.S. government allow farmers to grow tobacco, the government gives corporate welfare to tobacco farmers in the form of subsidies, thus tax dollars are supporting the tobacco industry – which fuels the cancer industry, etc.

People argue that we can't stop subsidizing the tobacco industry because it employs so many people. But we most certainly can. Everywhere tobacco is grown is excellent land for hemp farming, which would create many thousands of jobs and stop money from flowing out of the country to import hemp. And it would help localize economies as they can use locally-grown hemp to produce fuel, food, fabric, insulation, plywood, and paints and finishes. Cutting tobacco subsidies would also save the government huge amounts of money.

"Recipients of Tobacco Subsidies from farms in United States totaled $528,207,000 from 1995-2004."
– Environmental Working Group's Farm Subsidy Database, EWG.org

In 1952, during the Korean War, the U.S. government reissued the hemp farming manual. They were prepared to have it ready for mass publication to distribute to farmers. It was to be accompanied by massive amounts of hemp seeds that had been kept in dry storage. The U.S. government was once again ready to encourage farmers to grow hemp in case Communist China cut off a large portion of America's access to foreign hemp fiber. This time the government was also going to allow for the production of hemp fuel for diesel engines. The hemp fuel scenario was considered as a way to make the U.S. independent from offshore petroleum sources.

But the hemp program was never revived. Unfortunately, to this day the U.S. continues to rely on poisonous petroleum for diesel fuel, and most of it is imported from other nations. Petroleum-based diesel fuel causes great harm to the environment and lungs. Additionally, a large chunk of the government money being spent to subsidize corn for ethanol should be spent on building a hemp and cellulosic fuel industry, which would also be safer than corn for the environment.

The last legal hemp crops in America were grown in central Wisconsin in 1957. The crops were purchased by Matt Rens Hemp Company in Brandon, Wisconsin. The farms were shut down in 1958.

# Anslinger, La Guardia, and Lindesmith

From the beginning not everyone was in agreement about what the federal government was doing to control marijuana, its Federal Bureau of Narcotics propaganda, nor the reasoning behind treating cannabis smokers as criminals.

In 1938, New York City's mayor, Fiorello "Frank" La Guardia, cooperated with the New York City Police Department and the New York Academy of Medicine to conduct a study on marijuana. The mayor's committee was chaired by Dr. George B. Wallace and included dozens of professionals in the fields of pharmacology, psychiatry, and sociology. Study headquarters were set up at Goldwater Memorial Hospital.

It wasn't so much that marijuana was very prevalent in New York City; it wasn't. But La Guardia felt that the government hadn't told the truth about the substance. He was correct, they hadn't. So the city government undertook this study to pursue the truth of the matter.

The immigrant community Anslinger's propaganda often targeted in his vilification of marijuana use was relatively small in New York City. While growing, the city didn't have quite the mix of people that it has today. Although there was a marijuana presence, it was commonly used in "tea houses" or "tea pads," which were often the residence of someone who sold the stuff. Sometimes there was an admission fee to get into the casual party.

Marijuana was also used in some of the New York City nightclubs, including those in the growing jazz and blues communities in Harlem.

One young man who sold weed in Harlem was named Malcolm Little. In 1946 Little was arrested in Boston on charges of armed burglary. In prison he studied the teachings of Elijah Muhammad. He became Malcolm X, with the X standing for his lost African name.

Some of the people used for the La Guardia study were prisoners serving time at Riker's Island. Some had even been convicted on marijuana charges. Taken to Goldwater Memorial Hospital, the prisoners got to smoke weed, eat, and listen to music, and were subjected to tests conducted by the medical staff.

The La Guardia study was published in 1944 and was titled *The Marijuana Problem in the City of New York*. The September 1942 issue of the *American Journal of Psychiatry* published the first report of the study's lead physicians, Dr. Samuel Allentuck and Dr. Karl Bowman. Titled *The Psychiatric Aspects of Marihuana Intoxication*, the report concluded that the facts about marijuana causing catastrophic effects had been greatly distorted by the Federal Bureau of Narcotics. The report concluded that marijuana was

207

not addictive, did not lead to morphine, heroin, or cocaine addiction, and did not lead people to commit serious crimes. In his summary, the Committee Chairman, Dr. George B. Wallace, wrote that marijuana smokers were "of a friendly, sociable character. Aggressiveness and belligerency are not commonly seen... Marihuana does not change the basic personality structure of the individual. It lessens inhibitions and this brings out what is latent in his thoughts and emotions, but it does not evoke responses which would otherwise be totally alien to him."

"I am glad that the sociological, psychological, and medical ills commonly attributed to marihuana have been found to be exaggerated insofar as the City of New York is concerned.

... From the study as a whole, it is concluded that marihuana is not a drug of addiction, comparable to morphine, and that if tolerance is acquired, this is of a very limited degree. Furthermore, those who have been smoking marihuana for a period of years showed no mental or physical deterioration which may be attributed to the drug."
– Fiorello La Guardia, in the foreword to the study The Marihuana Problem in the City of New York, 1944

Anslinger was not happy with the report. He was also disappointed in 1946 when, after considering the La Guardia report, the Commission on Narcotic Drugs of the United Nations decided against more research into the dangers of marijuana.

Disregarding the La Guardia study, Anslinger continued on his quest to stop people from smoking marijuana. He also worked against allowing any more studies to be conducted that could be used to disprove his claims.

When sociologist Alfred Lindesmith of the University of Indiana spoke out in support of medical treatment for people with drug problems and opined that the Federal Bureau of Narcotics was spreading misinformation, Anslinger ridiculed him.

It didn't please Anslinger that Lindesmith's opinions were used in a 1948 documentary titled Drug Addict. The documentary was used to teach the Canadian police that drug addiction was a medical problem. Lindesmith's phone was tapped and Anslinger sought to connect Lindesmith to Communist organizations. This worked to quell the plans other scientists may have had to conduct research on marijuana.

While opposed to a documentary presenting an opinion different from his own, and that discredited his propaganda, Anslinger worked with Hollywood studios to approve scripts so that Hollywood movies and TV shows presented information about drugs in alignment with Anslinger's view.

Anslinger also kept working for those high-profile drug busts. He specifically wanted the publicity that would result from busting a famous musician, actor, or celebrity.

"Over 50 percent of those young addicts started on marihuana smoking. They started there and graduated to heroin; they took the needle when the thrill of marihuana was gone."
– Harry Anslinger, testifying before U.S. Congress Ways and means Committee, 1951

Under pressure from Anslinger and others, the United Nations made the absurd agreement in 1954 that marijuana was of no medical use. On March 10, 1961, the United Nations ratified its Single Convention on Narcotic Drugs and made the nonmedical use of marijuana illegal throughout the world within 25 years. However, it did not outlaw industrial hemp. The U.S. didn't sign onto the convention because it disagreed with the delayed action of the law.

Even after Anslinger left his position as head of the Federal Bureau of Narcotics in July 1962 the Bureau continued to publish outlandish nonsense about marijuana.

"It cannot be too strongly emphasized that the smoking of marijuana is a dangerous first step on the road which usually leads to enslavement by heroin."
– Federal Bureau of Narcotics antimarijuana pamphlet, 1965

# Anslinger, Musicians, Beat Writers, Kesey, Leary, and Marijuana

"The tempo of present-day music, the big apple dance and these jam sessions seem to do something to the nerves. As a result, use of marihuana is on the increase. Not only is it being used by dance band musicians, but by boys and girls who listen and dance to these bands."
– Federal Bureau of Narcotics press release published in *Minneapolis Tribune*, 1938

"I think the traffic has increased in marihuana, and unfortunately particularly among the young people. We have been running into a lot of traffic among these jazz musicians, and I am not speaking about the good musician, but the jazz type. In one place down here in North Carolina we arrested a whole orchestra, everybody in the orchestra. In Chicago we have arrested some rather prominent jazz musicians; and in New York. It is pretty widespread."
– Harry Anslinger, in a presentation to the U.S. Congress Ways and Means Appropriation Committee, 1949. He was working to get increased funding for the Federal Bureau of Narcotics. In a way it seems his words show how his fight against marijuana was a failure, and that the use of it continued despite his efforts and millions of dollars in government money used to support his Federal Bureau of Narcotics.

Anslinger, so fierce in his words pinpointing artists and musicians as marijuana smokers, had the Federal Bureau of Narcotics keep an eye on many of the top jazz musicians and entertainers of the day. While the main focus seemed to be on those who were African American, he also had some White folks under his watch, including Jackie Gleason, Kate Smith, and Milton Berle.

Anslinger kept a list of jazz bands with members who had legal problems with drugs. He also listed talent considered to have likely been users of drugs. The musicians on the list included Louis Armstrong, Count Basie, Cab Calloway, Jimmy Dorsey, Duke Ellington, Dizzy Gillespie, Lionel Hampton, Gene Krupa, and Thelonius Monk.

Armstrong had one marijuana charge on his record since being arrested along with drummer Vic Benton outside a club in California in 1931.

"It makes you feel good, man. It relaxes you, makes you forget all the bad things that happen to a Negro. It makes you feel wanted, and

210

when you're with another tea smoker it makes you feel a special sense of kinship."
– Louis "Satchmo" Armstrong

I knew Peggy Lee and she used to call me her son. She came of age in the era of Big Band, blues, and jazz music. I don't know if she ever smoked weed, but she knew about it from the time when she was starting out as a North Dakota teenager named Norma Egstrom. She told me that at one point as a teenager, because of her stepmother, Peggy didn't have a safe place to sleep. So, she slept in a bar, literally beneath the bar, where she had started to perform.

About marijuana, Peggy told me that, "You know, it wasn't called that." She had heard it called by some other names, including "muggles" and "reefer." She said, "Everyone thinks hippies discovered that stuff in the '60s, but it was all over the jazz clubs back in the 40s and 50s, and even way before that." She told me to stay away from it, and from all the other drugs, too.

Anslinger was likely interested in some of the most popular songs of the 1930s. Some of those referencing marijuana included:
- *When I Get Low I Get High*, by Chick Webb & His Orchestra
- *Gimme a Reefer*, by Bessie Smith
- *Weed Smoker's Dream*, by The Harlem Hamfats
- *Sendin' the Vipers*, by Mezz Mezzrow
- *Anybody Here Want to Buy My Cabbage?*, by Lil Johnson
- *The Stuff Is Here*, by Georgie White
- *Reefer Head Women*, by Jazz Gillum & His Jazz Boys
- *Weed*, by Bea Foote
- *Killin' Jive*, by The Cats & The Fiddle
- *Muggles*, by Louis Armstrong
- *Here Comes the Man with the Jive*, and *You'se a Viper*, by Stuff Smith & His Onyx Club Boys
- *Reefer Man*, by Baron Lee and the Blue Rhythm Band
- *That Funny Reefer Man*, and *The Man from Harlem*, by Cab Calloway
- *Mellow Stuff*, by Lil Johnson
- *That Cat Is High*, by The Ink Spots
- *Viper's Drag*, by Fats Waller
- *Wacky Dust*, by Ella Fitzgerald and the Chick Webb Orchestra
- *I'm Gonna Get High*, by Tampa Red & The Chicago Five
- *Light Up*, by Buster Bailey's Rhythm Busters
- *Reefer Hound Blues*, by Curtis Jones

- *Jack I'm Mellow*, by Trixie Smith
- *Smoking Reefers*, by Larry Adler
- *All the Jive Is Gone*, by Andy Kirk and His Twelve Clouds of Joy
- *Viper Mad*, by Sidney Bechet with the Noble Sissle's Swingers

In the 1940s there were more popular marijuana songs, including:
- *Junker's Blues*, by Champion Jack Dupree
- *Knocking Myself Out*, by Lil Green
- *Santa's Secret*, by Johnny Guarnieri & Slam Stewart
- *Texas Tea Party*, by Benny Goodman & His Orchestra
- *Sweet Marihuana Brown*, by the Barney Bigard Sextet
- *The Reefer Song*, by Fats Waller
- *Save the Roach for Me*, by Buck Washington
- *The G Man Got the T Man*, by Cee Pee Johnson

Many of these songs can be heard on a CD by The Viper Label titled *The Ultimate 30's & 40's Reefer Songs*.

While much of Anslinger's focus was on New Orleans, where many musicians either lived or spent time, and which had become a port of entry for marijuana grown on the islands and in Mexico, he also planned a nationwide roundup to arrest a number of musicians on charges of marijuana use. In addition to New Orleans, he and his Federal Bureau of Narcotics targeted jazz clubs in Chicago, Ft. Worth, St. Louis, and New York City's Harlem. Anslinger's plan was halted after his superior disapproved.

Perhaps Anslinger believed in his job too much. Perhaps he didn't understand the concept that the main reason the laws were created was to outlaw hemp so that the rich could get richer. But what he did understand was that making his office look important helped people perceive him as an important man, and his job to eradicate the devil weed from society could remain well funded by the government.

The focus on musicians and their drug use didn't end by canceling Anslinger's plan. He figured out a way to build his Federal Bureau of Narcotics. The bigger problem he made marijuana out to be, the more government money he could get allocated to run his department. Since real drugs were not enough of a "problem," there was no better way than to focus on something as prevalent as marijuana, and to work to get people to perceive it as evil.

Many musicians have served time after being busted for drugs, sometimes on false charges. In the case of Anita O'Day, it wasn't until after she served time for heroin that she actually tried heroin. She was hardly the only one who started taking hard drugs after serving time in prison.

> "The narcotics thing was just there. It was what was happening. Kept me in and out of trouble for 20 years; cost me a couple of very nice houses, the Jaguar, the self-respect, everything. I got busted the first time for marijuana and served 45 days. Next time was for pot again – I got 90 days but they gave me 45 off for good behavior. These were misdemeanors.
>
> But the third time around, I got busted for heroin. That was a bum rap – a musician set me up for it. He was able to keep out of trouble by turning someone else in every so often. They put me in jail for six months. Well, I figured I had the name, I might as well play the game. So when I got out, I decided to try it [heroin]. It's like quicksand – you never get out."
> – Anita O'Day, the "Jezebel of Jazz," in a 1973 interview with the *Los Angeles Times*

Heroin has been a major problem for the musician community. A number of musicians of all sorts have died of heroin overdoses. Marijuana has been more widely used, easier to purchase for the musicians, and easier for law enforcement to find. During Anslinger's reign the law enforcement seemed more focused on marijuana, as if busting musicians for using marijuana is going to improve society. Even so, law enforcement reaped impressive numbers of arrests – at great expense to city, county, state, and federal budgets.

In his 1946 autobiography, *Really the Blues*, musician Milton "Mezz" Mezzrow details his experiences with drugs, jazz, crime, women, and jails. He was born into a White, Jewish family in Chicago in 1899. His book tells about how he ended up in the Pontiac Reformatory after going for a ride with a friend in a stolen car. While serving his time he listened to fellow Black prisoners sing the blues in "low moanful chants morning, noon, and night."

> "I knew that I was going to spend all my time from then on sticking close to Negroes. They were my kind of people. And I was going to learn their music and play it for the rest of my days."
> – Milton "Mezz" Mezzrow, in his autobiography, *Really the Blues*

After being released from his first time in prison, Mezzrow familiarized himself with the jazz and blues community. He bought a saxophone and clarinet, learned how to play them, and performed in jazz clubs, where he became familiar with Al Capone. While not considered one of the best musicians, Mezzrow worked with what he had and made his way to jazz clubs in other cities, including New Orleans, Kansas City, Detroit, Harlem in New York City, and Paris. Along the way he proudly became known as "the first White Negro."

Mezzrow was introduced to cannabis by a friend named Patrick while staying at the Arrowhead Inn in Indiana. He preferred the weed that his friends brought up from New Orleans rather than the stuff he came across in other cities. In describing his days performing in Detroit, he wrote, "Every one of us that smoked the stuff came to the conclusion that it wasn't habit forming and couldn't be called a narcotic. We found out that at one time the government had discussed it as a drug and tried to include it in the Harrison Anti-Narcotic Act but never could dig up any scientific reason for it. There being no law against muta then, we used to roll our [marijuana] cigarettes right out in the open and light up like you would on a Camel or Chesterfield." Although he partook of them, he didn't like other drugs, such as heroin, morphine, and cocaine.

While living in New York he sold weed, became addicted to opium for four years, and was a close associate of Louis Armstrong. In his autobiography Mezzrow describes his terrifying experience detoxing from his opium addiction. After coming clean off opium, he married a Black woman, which went along with his belief that, "When you loved a girl you married her, without consulting a color chart."

Mezzrow became known as the "Muggles king," and "the Johnny Appleseed of weed." Some people of the day referred to the cannabis "reefer" joints as "mezzroles." In Stuff Smith's song, *If You're a Viper*, which was recorded by Rosetta Howard, Smith refers to a five-foot long marijuana joint as a "mighty mezz."

"I never advocated that anybody should use marihuana, and I sure don't mean to start now. Even during the years when I sold the stuff I never 'pushed' it like a salesman pushes vacuum cleaners or Fuller brushes. I had it for anybody who came asking, if he was a friend of mine. I didn't promote it anywhere, and I never gave it to kids, not even to little Frankie Walker [a young musician friend]. I sold it to grown-up friends of mine who had got to using it on their own, just like I did; it was a family affair, not any high-pressure business. Sort of everybody to their own notion, that was the whole spirit. I laid off five years ago, and if anybody asks my advice today, I tell them straight to steer clear of it because it carries a rap. That's my final word to all the cats: today I know of one very bad thing the tea can do to you – it can put you in jail. 'Nuff said."

– Milton "Mezz" Mezzrow, in his autobiography, *Really the Blues*

In 1940 Mezzrow was arrested at a jazz club at the New York World's Fair. He was charged with and convicted of possessing a stash of marijuana joints with intent to distribute. After convincing authorities that he was Black, he served time in the Black section at Riker's Island and on Hart's Island. Upon his release on September 28, 1942, he received his draft card, which listed his race as Negro, and he liked that.

Mezzrow's slang-laced book, *Really the Blues*, provides a window into the counterculture of his day. While Anslinger considered the book a "glorification of marijuana smoking," it influenced the beat generation artists, including William Burroughs, Lucien Carr, Neal Cassady, Gregory Corso, Allen Ginsberg, Dave Kammerer, Jack Kerouac, and Edie Parker, all known for living non-conformist lives.

Many of those of the Beat Generation era also became involved or experimented with other drugs.

One of the most colorful characters was Neal Cassady. Kerouac used Cassady as the basis for the character of Dean Moriarty in the novel, *On the Road*, which defined beat culture. The Grateful Dead rock group immortalized Cassady in their song "The Other One."

Cassady was the product of a troubled childhood. After his mother died when he was ten, Cassady spent his childhood in skid row hotels with his alcoholic father. At age 14 he was arrested for auto theft and was put in a reform school. More arrests, including for car theft and receiving stolen property, lead to an 11-month jail sentence. In 1945, he married and moved to New York City, where he met Jack Kerouac and Allen Ginsberg in 1947. On a return to the West coast, Cassady got married to his second wife. He was arrested at a nightclub in 1958 after offering to share some weed with an undercover agent. After his conviction, he served his sentence in San Francisco's San Quentin prison and was released in June of 1960. Rejoining his wife, they had three children and he worked for the Southern Pacific Railroad.

In the summer of 1962 Cassady met *One Flew Over The Cuckoo's Nest* author Ken Kesey and helped throw lively parties with the Hells Angels at Kesey's house in La Honda, California. In 1963 Cassady's wife divorced him, and in 1964 he drove Kesey's "magic bus" named "Further." The riders on the bus called themselves "The Merry Pranksters." Tom Wolfe turned the story about the bus trip and Kesey's adventures into a book titled *The Electric Kool-Aid Acid Test*. The main bus trip involved driving from California to New York, via Florida. In New York, Cassady introduced Kesey to Allen Ginsberg and Jack Kerouac.

Many people consider Kesey and his "Merry Pranksters" to have been about challenging the system. But others consider him to be someone who simply got caught up in the adventures of spreading LSD to the masses while leading a life of foolishness.

215

Even the most famed promoter of LSD and psilocybin mushrooms, Timothy Leary, who was no angel, was leery of Kesey's LSD parties.

In the 1950s and early 1960s Leary had been Harvard University psychology professor who, with Richard Alpert (who became known as Ram Das), became known for conducting LSD and psilocybin experiments using hundreds of Harvard students and teachers as subjects.

An associate of Leary's, Anthony Russo, told him about taking psilocybin mushrooms during a trip to Mexico. In August of 1960, Leary and Russo traveled to Cuernavaca Mexico to experience a mushroom trip under the direction of an indigenous group. Leary said that he learned more about psychology under the influence of psilocybin than he "had in the preceding fifteen years of studying doing research in psychology."

Back at Harvard, Leary and Alpert began their Harvard Psilocybin Project with the intention of understanding the effects it had on those who took the substance under the guided "trips." It was these experiments, and the positive effects they had on those that took them, that put Leary in the spotlight among the Harvard community. So many people wanted to be involved in the studies that Leary could not accompany them. Because of this, people began selling psilocybin mushrooms and LSD in and around Harvard. By 1962 Leary and Alpert had founded the International Foundation for Internal Freedom. In May 1963, Leary and Alpert were both dismissed from Harvard.

"A psychedelic experience is a journey to new realms of consciousness. The scope and content of the experience is limitless, but its characteristic features are the transcendence of verbal concepts, of space-time dimensions, and of the ego or identity. Such experiences of enlarged consciousness can occur in a variety of ways: sensory deprivation, yoga exercises, disciplined medication, religious or aesthetic ecstasies, or spontaneously. Most recently they have become available to anyone through the ingestion of psychedelic drugs such as LSD, psilocybin, mescaline, DMT, etc. Of course, the drug does not produce the transcendent experience. It merely acts as a chemical key – it opens the mind, frees the nervous system of its ordinary structures."
– Timothy Leary, Richard Alpert, and Ralph Metzner, in the book *The Psychedelic Experience*, 1964

By 1964, Leary had moved to an estate in Millbrook, a town in upstate New York, where he continued his experiments. In an interesting twist, use of the mansion had been arranged for Leary by Peggy, Billy, and Tommy Hitchcock, who were heirs to the fortune of Andrew Mellon. It was during this time that Leary and his group was having legal issues brought on by the government. The local assistant district attorney was G. Gordon Liddy, who was later in the Nixon administration, and one of the masterminds behind breaking into Democratic National Committee offices at the Watergate building in 1972, which lead to the resignation of Nixon.

When Kesey and his Merry Pranksters and their magic bus arrived at an upstate New York estate to meet with Leary, they were not welcomed. Leary didn't even come outside to meet them. In *The Electric Kool-Aid Acid Test*, Tom Wolfe wrote that Leary was in the middle of a three-day psychedelic trip, and that Leary's people would not share any acid with Kesey's people. Leary thought that LSD should be more of a spiritual experience than the sort of party drug that Kesey was treating it as. Others differ in this opinion, and claim that the Leary associates had become their own form of party animals.

In September 1966, Leary founded the League for Spiritual Discovery (LSD) and went on a tour of colleges. He saw the League as a religion and used the LSD substance as its sacrament. Another group, The Brotherhood of Eternal Love, considered Leary to be their spiritual leader.

The U.S. made LSD illegal on October 6, 1966, which has denied any research studies using the substance.

On January 14, 1967, Leary was in Kesey's turf, San Francisco, where he spoke at the "Human Be-In" gathering in Golden Gate Park. It was there that Leary spoke his legendary phrase, "Turn on, tune in, drop out." By this time Leary and Kesey had become friends, and many people started criticizing Leary for doing too much promotion, and attracting the attention of the government. Owsley Stanley, a leading supplier of LSD and the sound technician for the Grateful Dead rock group, was one who went so far as to blame Leary for the government's modern laws against drugs.

In October 1967, Leary was guest of honor at a Hollywood party where most or all of the guests were under the influence of LSD. I was at a similar party in Beverly Hills in the late 1980s during which Leary and a bunch of guests took LSD. I didn't partake, but simply observed the others and listened to their conversations. At one point Leary took a few people outside so they could stare at the stars and moon.

When Leary's daughter was arrested for marijuana possession at the U.S./Mexico border on December 20, 1965, Leary took responsibility. On March 11, 1966, he was convicted of possession under the Marijuana Tax Act, sentenced to 30 years in jail, fined $39,000, and ordered to undergo psychiatric treatment. Leary appealed the case using the argument that the Marijuana Tax Act was unconstitutional. On December 26, 1968, he was arrested in Laguna Beach, California and charged with being in possession of two marijuana cigarettes.

Leary's subsequent lawsuit against the US government resulted in the Supreme Court ruling On May 19, 1969, the Supreme Court ruled that the Marijuana Tax Act was unconstitutional.

With his conviction overturned for his 1965 border arrest, Leary declared himself a candidate for governor of California, which meant he was running against Ronald Reagan. On June 1, 1969, Leary was present when John Lennon and Yoko Ono held their "Bed-In" in Montreal. As a result, Lennon wrote Leary's campaign song, "Come Together."

Leary was still fighting his 1968 arrest, which he clamed was a set-up with the marijuana joints planted on him by the arresting officer. For that little problem, on January 21, 1970, Leary was sentenced to ten years in prison. In a truly ironic twist, when he was assigned to prison, he was given psychological tests that he himself had designed during his years as a psychologist. After being assigned as a gardener in a low-security prison, Leary escaped. Members of the Brotherhood of Eternal Love smuggled Leary and his wife to the northern African country of Algeria, where he stayed with Eldridge Cleaver of the Black Panther party.

In 1971, Leary and his wife moved to Switzerland. When Nixon found out about this, he had his attorney general, John Mitchell, convince the Swiss government to put Leary in jail. After two months in jail, and with the Swiss government refusing to extradite Leary to the U.S., Leary was allowed to live relatively freely in Switzerland.

After getting a divorce from his wife, Leary married a French socialite. In 1973, when he traveled to Kabul, Afghanistan, he was arrested on the airplane by an agent of the U.S. federal Bureau of Narcotics and Dangerous Drugs. If he had been successful in exciting the airplane, he would have been able to live freely in Afghanistan because they did not have an extradition treaty with the U.S.

When Leary was returned to the U.S., he was held on an extraordinary $5 million bail. Richard Nixon had declared Leary to be "the most dangerous man in America." (As if Nixon couldn't' be classified as such.) When Leary was in solitary confinement in California's Folsom Prison, the next prisoner over was Charles Manson. It was during this time that the FBI claimed that Leary had turned on a group of his supporters, including members of The Weather Underground, which he had not. On April 21, 1976, Governor Jerry Brown let Leary out of prison. All of this drama occurred and millions of dollars were spent because of two partially burned marijuana cigarettes.

After relocating to Los Angeles, where he moved to Laurel Canyon, in 1978, Leary married filmmaker Barbara Blum, sister of Tanya Roberts, who was a co-star on the TV series "Charlie's Angels," and later in the series "That 70s Show" (Co-starring Ashton Kutcher, who was known to have gotten stoned at a Hollywood Hills home with a certain Republican president's daughter.) In 1982, Leary and G. Gordon Liddy toured together on the lecture circuit. The tour is captured in the documentary, "Return Engagement." Over the next twenty years, Leary became known for

218

attending "rave" parties, appearing at rock festivals, and associating with the likes of Johnny Depp, who dated Leary's goddaughter, Winona Ryder. His last months were spent surrounded by a large group of friends, visitors, and followers, including some who moved into his home. Much of this was videotaped and placed on his Web site, which was continually updated. After his death, some of Leary's ashes were shot into space on the Pegasus rocket on April 21, 1997.

"We saw ourselves as anthropologists from the twenty-first century inhabiting a time module set somewhere in the dark ages of the 1960s. On this space colony we were attempting to create a new paganism and a new dedication to life as art."
– Timothy Leary

Kesey first became familiar with LSD while living at Stanford in 1959. He had learned that the Menlo Park Veterans Hospital was conducting CIA-funded lab tests on LSD, DMT, psilocybin mushrooms, mescaline, and cocaine. Kesey brought LSD back to his friends at Stanford. When Kesey's home at Stanford was sold off to become a housing tract, Kesey moved to a ranch he had purchased in the town of La Honda in the Santa Cruz Mountains. It was at La Honda that many of Kesey's wild adventures took place, including parties he hosted for the Hell's Angels. Allen Ginsberg was one of the famous people who attended some of Keseys' parties.

In 1966 Kesey was busted for possessing marijuana when he was sitting on a rooftop with Carolyn "Mountain Girl" Adams. To escape serving time, Kesey traveled to Mexico by hiding in the back of a friend's car. Many of the Pranksters followed him there. Mountain Girl avoided prison, as she was pregnant with Kesey's baby. She also traveled to Mexico to spend time with Kesey.

Eventually coming back to America and living undercover, Kesey got involved in throwing more LSD parties in the San Francisco area. After being captured by FBI agents who stopped a car he was riding in on a crowded freeway, Kesey served five months in the San Mateo County Jail. He lived the rest of his life in Oregon and made occasional appearances at events, such as at Grateful Dead and Phish rock group concerts.

Kesey's greatest contributions to the era were his books, including *Sometimes a Great Nation*, which, like *One Flew Over the Cuckoo's Nest*, was turned into a film. As far as his success at challenging the system and creating positive change, he was no Pete Seeger.

Mountain Girl went on to marry Jerry Garcia of the Grateful Dead. In 1976 she wrote a book titled *Primo Plant: Growing Sensemilla Marijuana*.

219

"The paradoxical key to this bizarre impasse of awareness is precisely that the marijuana consciousness is one that, ever so gently, shifts the center of attention from habitual shallow, purely verbal guidelines and repetitive secondhand ideological interpretations of experience to more direct, slower, absorbing, occasionally microscopically minute engagement with sensing phenomena."
– Allen Ginsberg

During Anslinger's last days as head of the Federal Bureau of Narcotics, he made Ginsberg a personal target. This was especially so after Ginsberg appeared on the John Crosby talk show on February 12, 1961. During the show Ginsberg spoke openly about his use of cannabis and how present it was in Tangier when he lived at William Burroughs' Villa Delirium in the 1950s. Crosby, anthropologist Ashley Montague, and author Norman Mailer all joined the conversation. These were well-educated White males talking on national TV about the government's harsh marijuana laws. Not something Anslinger would appreciate. The Federal Bureau of Narcotics kept a file on Ginsberg.

"From what I have read and heard it would appear that the reported increase and widespread use of marihuana by college students could be attributed in part to the influence of Allen Ginsberg and persons of his ilk. It appears that Ginsberg's writings and poetry readings on the many college campuses and avant-garde meeting places have had a strong appeal and have provided a rationale to many college students and persons in intellectual life here and abroad."
– March 1965 entry in Federal Bureau of Narcotics file on Allen Ginsberg

By 1952 Mezzrow had moved to Paris, which still carries an active jazz and blues community. He died there on August 5, 1972, and is buried in the same cemetery as Jim Morrison, *Pére LaChaise.*

"There are three groups who are bringing about the great evolution of the new age that we are going through now. They are the dope dealers, the rock musicians, and the underground artists and writers."
– Timothy Leary

Musicians busted for possession of marijuana include everyone from jazz drummer Gene Krupa, who served 84 days in San Quentin prison and paid a $500 fine in 1943 after being busted in Los Angeles, to Ray Charles, Gerry Mulligan, Paul McCartney, John Lennon, George Harrison, Yoko Ono, all of the Rolling Stones, the Grateful Dead, Neil Diamond, James

220

Brown, Bobby Brown, Gary Chapman, Art Garfunkel, Flavor Flav, David Bowie, Queen Latifa, Ray Price, David Crosby, Carlos Santana, D'Angelo, John Popper, Whitney Houston, Dionne Warwick, Faith Evans, Freddy Fender, Bo Bice, David Lee Roth, and George Michael.

"I never had that much to rebel against because my parents were always so kind of cool. I mean, what could I do? Run away and smoke a joint and go to rock concerts for the weekend? I mean, that's all they ever did."
– Actress/model Liv Tyler, daughter of Steven Tyler of Aerosmith; *Allure* magazine, June 2007

On September 18, 2006, Willie Nelson, his sister Bobbie, and his tour manager, David Anderson, were issued citations after marijuana and magic mushrooms were found on Willie's tour bus while they were traveling in Louisiana. The charges against Bobbie Nelson were dismissed. Willie and Anderson received six months probation and were fined $1,024.

"If you need some temporary help in getting through the day, cannabis is the best way."
– Willie Nelson

There is a possibility that other musicians also have used, or use marijuana. Ask Sean "Puff Daddy" Combs.

"I'd been a rather straight working-class lad, but when we started to get into pot it seemed to me quite uplifting. It didn't seem to have too many side effects like alcohol or some of the other stuff, like pills, which I pretty much kept off. I kind of liked marijuana and to me it seemed it was mind-expanding. Literally mind-expanding. So 'Got to Get You into My Life' is really a song about that. It's not about a person, it's actually about pot. It's saying, 'I'm going to do this. This is not a bad idea.' So it's actually an ode to pot, like someone else might write an ode to chocolate or a good claret."
– Paul McCartney. According to legend, the Beatles first smoked marijuana in the presence of Bob Dylan on the sixth floor of the Delmonico hotel in New York on August 28, 1964. Some people use this as some sort of international marijuana day to light up in homage to the Beatles, as if that were the day they became enlightened. In 1980 McCartney was arrested in Japan when marijuana was found in his luggage as he was touring with Wings. He spent ten days in jail before being released. He later said it was the longest time he had been separated from his beloved Linda.

"Your spirit flies when you are playing music. So, with music, you tend to look deeper and deeper inside yourself to find the music. That's why, I guess, grass was around those clubs."
– Bob Dylan, 1978. Dylan has said that he does not smoke marijuana.

"Careful attention should be given to reports that subject is heavy narcotics user and any information developed in this regard should be furnished to narcotics authorities and immediately furnished to bureau in form suitable for dissemination."
– J. Edgar Hoover, in memo given to the New York FBI office in response to President Richard Nixon's demands that John Lennon's movements and activities be closely watched by federal police organizations. Lennon was outspoken about the harsh marijuana laws and appeared with Yoko Ono at a 1969 rally protesting the ten-year sentence given to John Sinclair for possessing two marijuana cigarettes.

"I ended a few romances over the years because when I got on pot I couldn't stop talking. And finally I remember one girl who said, 'Did you come to fuck or to knit?'"
– Norman Mailer, Norman Mailer on Pot, interview by Richard Stratton, *High Times* magazine, November/December 2004

# The Spread of Cannabis and Opium

As trade was established between Europe and Asia, and points in between, so too was the knowledge of cannabis. As those from the West traveled East they learned more about the culture and the ways people of the East enjoyed themselves. Where alcohol wasn't popular, cannabis and the hashish made from its resin often was. Hashish from the Middle East and the Indian cannabis and herb drink called *bhang* were becoming popular in port towns of Europe, where the ships docked to trade goods brought back from the East. Along with the exotic imports there were rumors of where they came from and how they were grown or created. One rumor about hashish was that it was collected by sending naked plantation laborers to run through the fields, then the resin of the plant was gathered from their skin.

When Napoleon Bonaparte invaded Egypt in 1798 his soldiers were introduced to hashish. They used it as an alternative to wine, which was prohibited in the Islamic country. When authorities attempted to prevent the soldiers from using cannabis, the troops apparently continued their use, even bringing it back to France when they returned home.

The European use of cannabis increased. It was used both as a medicine that could be purchased at pharmacies and as an intoxicant that could be purchased from those who sold imported goods.

The first government action against cannabis may have been carried out in Cairo during the year 1253. That was when the local government raided and burned the cannabis gardens of the Sufis who were considered a threat to local society because of their independent culture.

It appears that the first laws aimed at controlling or outlawing cannabis were also associated with the Sufis. In 1378 the Egyptian government burned cannabis farms. Those who grew cannabis were imprisoned, and it is said that some had their teeth pulled out as punishment, and others were executed. Nearly 500 years later, in 1868 Egypt made hashish possession a capital offense, but the law wasn't effective. Some eradication efforts were made with police burning cannabis gardens, but many of the police involved in confiscating it were also reselling it. By 1884 the Cairo government allowed the local authorities to export the hash they had confiscated, but that only increased the corruption. The laws continued being ineffectual, with use and smuggling common. By the 1920s the government of Egypt was focusing on cocaine, heroin, and morphine, and placing less attention on cannabis, which was too well established in the local culture in the form of hashish, and too easy to grow, to effectively ban.

With each advance in the government's suppression of any substance came inventive ways of smuggling. By the 1930s the British head of the Egyptian Central Narcotics Intelligence Bureau, Thomas Wentworth Russell (also known as Russell Pasha), had armed the police with guns. Tragically, they took to shooting drug smugglers. As the drug trade became well organized and financed throughout Egypt, Greece, Turkey, Lebanon, Palestine, and into Europe and other countries, so too did the law enforcement working against it. It didn't suppress the demand, but did greatly increase the price while creating a drug warfare scenario.

Russell began working for the Egyptian Civil Service in 1902. He held the opinion that cannabis in the form of hashish was not a major problem, and even considered that it should be grown locally and taxed, which would stop the illegal importation of hashish, prevent money from going out of the country, and bring revenue into the local governments. He thought that hashish should not be considered in the same classification as opiates, the worst of which he considered to be heroin. However, his job was to enforce the law, including busting those who broke the Egyptian laws against hashish. A focus was placed on those who were smuggling it into the country.

Russell's success in breaking up a well-financed drug network helped him land the position of vice-president of the League of Nations Advisory Committee in 1939. That organization had spent the decade, and lots of money, working to unsuccessfully impose an international ban on the heroin trade. Ironically, this was being done by the British government which, since at least the beginning of Warren Hastings's position as governor-general of British India in 1773, had partially financed their East India Company by protecting and encouraging the production of opium so that it could make money by being sold to the East Indies and China.

In the 1830s the British House of Commons openly allowed the British East India Company to maintain their opium exporting to support the company. This was a formality. The Battle of Plassey in 1757 resulted in Britain annexing Bengal, and this solidified the British East India Company's business in India's opium exports, which had already been going on for decades. By at least 1767, it was known in the British government that the British East India Company had been exporting opium to China. British merchant and passenger ships traveling to India purchased opium there, then traveled to China to exchange the opium for other goods they could then sell in Britain, including tea, precious metals, jewels, jade, porcelain, silk, art, and other luxury and exotic items.

For more than a century, Spain had been involved in bringing opium into China with shipments of corn, tobacco, and other more useful items, including silver from South America. As the global demand for Chinese products increased, so too did the amount of opium being brought into

China from India on British ships. By the 1820s the annual importation of opium to China from British Bengal was estimated to be in the range of 900 tons. By the 1840s, businesses from several other countries were involved in the trade, including Augustine Heard & Company and Russel & Company, which were both based out of the busy docks of Boston. U.S., French, German, Dutch, and Japanese companies were in financial arrangement with the British companies, who held sway over what went in, and what went out of China's docks. The British had their own gated and guarded communities in China, especially in Canton (Guangzhou).

Eventually the Chinese farmers began to grow poppies not only to make money, but also to stop money from going to other countries, including to Britain. These situations were what caused the Opium Wars of 1839-42 and 1856-60. The British fought with the Chinese, and the Chinese government held public executions of Chinese citizens believed to have been involved in the importation, production, and sale of opium. Opium storage facilities in Canton and other areas were raided and destroyed and their contents destroyed. Britain fought the war using steam-powered ships that carried gun platforms. After taking Canton, the British vessels traveled up the Yangtze and took control of the ports. China's defeat in their fight against Britain lead to the signing of the Treaty of Nanjing, Treaty of the Bogue, and, after the second Opium War, the Treaty of Tannin. These allowed the British government to increase trade with China and forced them to cede Hong Kong to Queen Victoria for what eventually lead to a lease good for 99 years. China was also forced to repay British and other foreign merchants for their loss of opium that was destroyed by the Chinese.

Of course, none of this ended the opium trade, but increased prices, created an underground market, and helped to spread opium, and subsequently heroin, use throughout the world. Britain played a major role in this because they continued to import opium into China.

In 1840, when the House of Commons enquired about the opium production in India, they were told by banker W.B. Baring that canceling it would lead to an increase in the use of hemp (cannabis) "which was in every way more injurious than the use of the poppy." This claim was discounted by Dr. William Brooked O'Shaughnessy, professor of chemistry at the Medical College of Calcutta, India.

As he detailed in *Transactions,* the journal of the Medical and Physical Society of Calcutta, O'Shaughnessy first conducted cannabis tests on animals. After finding that the animals experienced no apparent harm, he used cannabis on people suffering from various ailments. He found that cannabis worked as "an anti-convulsive remedy of the greatest value." His work with a London pharmacist, Peter Squire, produced the medicinal extract of cannabis called Squire's Extract, which was sold as a pain reliever. A similar medicinal extract named Tilden's Extract was sold in the U.S.

By the 1880s China was growing more opium than the amount being imported. Even so, the East India Company continued to sell opium to China.

In the 1870s the British government investigated the possibility of creating laws against cannabis in India (where it was known as *ganja*). They appointed a commission to study the moral issues relating to use of the plant, to evaluate the impact it had on society, and to consider the reasoning behind placing a prohibition on the growth of the plant. A second cannabis study conducted in 1890s India involved a thousand people. The report was issued in 1894 and concluded that cannabis was relatively harmless and trying to prohibit the use of it would be unworkable. The studies found cannabis in wide use among a variety of professions in "all classes of labourers." They concluded that it was basically a nonaddictive substance that didn't contribute to crime or violence. While examining hospital records, they found that stories of patients being admitted for insanity caused by the use of cannabis were unsubstantiated. The *Report of the India Hemp Drugs Commission* concluded that banning cannabis would be unworkable, especially since the plant was wild and that it was so easy to grow that "it would be impossible to prohibit" a man "from gathering, from such a plant, the daily quota used by him and his family." The government of India grew it and licensed shops to sell it.

In 1905 the British government offered to reduce the amount of opium being brought in to China if China also agreed to reduce their production of the drug. An agreement was reached between the two governments that the opium traffic would end within ten years' time. When American authorities in the Philippines informed their superiors, the response by the State Department was to organize the Shanghai Opium Conference of 1909. Thirteen countries were represented at the conference. American representatives argued for international support of the Smoking Opium Exclusion Act, which had just been passed by the U.S. Congress to limit the import of opium to pharmaceutical companies. The American law was the country's first to make certain substances illegal to import, possess, or sell outside of a licensed pharmaceutical business. The Americans failed to get the support. The conference only resulted in an agreement between the countries to work to reduce the international production of opium and its derivatives, heroin and morphine. This did not stop the underground opium market.

At the urging of President Taft, a second international conference on opium and its derivative drugs was held. The International Opium Convention was signed at The Hauge (the third-largest city in the Netherlands) on January 23, 1912. Countries represented included China,

France, Germany, Italy, Japan, the Netherlands, Persia, Portugal, Russia, Siam, the United Kingdom, and the U.S. This resulted in another ineffectual agreement to limit the production and distribution of opium, its derivative drugs, and cocaine to authorized parties for pharmaceutical purposes. There was no supervisory board, no way to determine if member countries were taking measures to do away with the drug trade, and no definition of the amount of opium needed to maintain medical and scientific supplies. While some efforts in reducing the opium trade were temporarily successful, especially in China, this agreement did not end the underground opium market. There were too many addicts, and too many people and governments making money from the cultivation of poppies and the manufacture and distribution of the drugs. The actions of the very same governments represented at the conference show how uncommitted they were to the task of reducing the opium market, especially Britain, which continued to run the hugely profitable Indian opium trade.

In February 1909 a report was published by Britain that was the result of a study conducted to explore the possibility of ending the British-supported opium trade in India. The report (Proceedings of the Commission appointed to Enquire into Matters Relating to the Use of Opium in the Straits Settlements and the Federated Malay States. Presented to both Houses of Parliament by Command of His Majesty) concluded that ending the trade would result in a loss of half of the revenues from the Straits Settlements (territories in Southeast Asia originally included in the British East India Company beginning in 1826) and the Federated Malay States. American writer Ellen Newbold La Motte found a copy of this report in the New York Library. Her interests in the opium market were triggered by a chance meeting with a "young Hindu" on a boat as she was traveling in the Far East in 1916. This man told her how Britain was running the opium trade in Asia. Her disgust and curiosity about this led her to explore the topic as she traveled in Eastern countries. La Motte's home country, the U.S., had passed the Harrison Narcotics Act in 1914. The act, while not successful in conquering the underground drug market, was meant to restrict the use of opium drugs to medical and scientific uses within U.S. borders.

While traveling in Asia, La Motte investigated claims that the poppy production had been reduced by international trade agreements. Her conclusion was that although the opium market had been reduced in certain regions, the poppy market and the underground drug smuggling they supported were not only still present, but had also increased production after the international agreement. She also learned that what the "young Hindu" had told her about Britain running the opium market was true. She found that the British government loaned money to poppy farmers without interest, and ran opium processing plants where the poppy farmers brought their crops. The British government also ran an opium auction market in Calcutta. She wrote, "We must face the facts, and recognize clearly that the source of supply is the British government, through whose agents, official and unofficial, it is distributed."

"In British territory the cultivation of the poppy for the production of opium is mainly restricted to the United Provinces, and the manufacture of the opium from this region is a State monopoly. A limited amount is also grown in the Punjab for local consumption and to produce poppy seeds. In the monopoly districts the cultivator receives advances from Government to enable him to prepare the land for the crop, and he is bound to sell the whole of the produce at a fixed price to Government agents, by whom it is dispatched to the Government factory at Ghazipur to be prepared for the market. The chests of manufactured opium are sold by auction in Calcutta at monthly sales. A reserve is kept in hand to supply the deficiencies of bad seasons, and a considerable quantity is distributed by the Indian excise departments. Opium is also grown in many of the Native States of Rajaputana and Central India. These Native States have agreed to conform to the British system. No 6 opium may pass from them into British territory for consumption without payment of duty."
– *Statesman's Year Book* of 1916; page 140, The British Empire: India and Dependencies

In the Conclusion of her 1920 book, *The Opium Monopoly*, La Motte wrote, "We have seen that certain British colonies, Hong Kong and the Straits Settlements, for example, derive from one-third to one-half of their upkeep expenses from this (opium) traffic." She also found that France allowed and encouraged opium shops in Indo-China while refusing to allow them inside the borders of France. During World War I Britain made a loan to Persia based on opium sales.

In the closing chapter of her book La Motte wrote that the opium not sold into the Asian countries "goes out for smuggling purposes, to be distributed in devious, roundabout, underhand channels throughout the world. We [Americans] are coming in for our share in this distribution." She noted in her book that the 1907 agreement between Britain and China meant the phasing out of opium sales into China. Interestingly, she found information that more opium was then being imported into England, and it wasn't for medicine and science, but was to feed the underground market in opium, heroin, and morphine. She quotes from the *The Japan Society Bulletin* No. 60: "*The Japan Chronicle,* speaking from 'absolutely authentic information,' states that 113,000 ounces of morphia [morphine] arrived in Kobe from the United States in the first five months of 1919." It appears that the opium was brought to England. Morphine was manufactured, then it was brought into Japan on American ships. It was truly a worldwide drug market, and it was clear that Britain was working with the U.S. to evade the agreement it made with China.

By 1919, Japan was purchasing increasingly larger amounts of opium at the British-run Calcutta opium markets, then exporting opium and its derivatives into China. "In South China, morphia is sold by Chinese peddlers, each of whom carries a passport certifying that he is a native of Formosa, and therefore entitled to Japanese protection. Japanese drug stores throughout China carry large stocks of morphia. Japanese medicine vendors look to morphia for their largest profits. Wherever Japanese are predominant, there the trade flourishes." In this way, Britain was getting around its agreement to stop importing opium into China. Not just opium, but the more addictive extract, morphine, which would surely keep millions of Chinese addicted and dependant on the British opium monopoly.

"That such conditions existed were to us unheard of, and unbelievable. It seemed incredible that in this age, with the consensus of public opinion sternly opposed to the sale and distribution of habit-forming drugs, and with legislation to curb and restrict such practices incorporated in the laws of all ethical and civilized governments, that here, on the other side of the world, we should come upon opium traffic conducted as a government monopoly. Not only that, but conducted by one of the greatest and most highly civilized nations of the world, a nation which we have always looked up to as being in the very forefront of advanced, progressive and humane ideals. So shocked were we by what this young Hindu told us, that we flatly refused to believe him. We listened to what he had to say on the subject, but thinking that however earnest he might be, however sincere in his sense of outrage at such a policy, that he must of necessity be mistaken. We decided not to take his word for it, but to look into the matter for ourselves.

We did look into the matter. During a stay in the Far East of nearly a year, in which time we visited Japan, China, Hong Kong, French Indo-China, Siam and Singapore, we looked into the matter in every country we visited. Wherever possible we obtained government reports, and searched them carefully for those passages giving statistics concerning the opium trade, the amount of opium consumed, the number of shops where it was sold, and the number of divans where it was smoked. We found these shops established under government auspices, the dealers obtaining their supplies of opium from the government, and then obtaining licenses from the government to retail it. In many countries, we visited these shops and divans in person, and bought opium in them freely, just as one goes to a shop to buy cigarettes. We found a thorough and complete establishment of the opium traffic, run by the government, as a monopoly. Revenue was derived through the sale of opium, through excise taxes upon opium, and through license fees paid by the keepers of opium shops and divans. A complete, systematic arrangement, by which the foreign government profited at the expense of the subject peoples under its rule. In European countries and in America, we find the governments making every effort to repress the sale of habit-forming drugs. Here, in the Far East, a contrary attitude prevails. The government makes every effort to encourage and extend it."

– Ellen Newbold La Motte, in the introduction of her book, *The Opium Monopoly*, 1920

The same year that La Motte wrote her book, *The Opium Monopoly*, about the British government running the opium trade, Britain's Ministry of Health sent Dr. Harry Campbell to the U.S. to study the survey of the success of the Harrison Narcotics Act. Campbell concluded, "The country [U.S.] is overrun by an army of peddlers who extort exorbitant prices from the helpless victims. It appears that not only has the Harrison law failed to diminish the number of drug-takers, some contend, indeed, that it has actually worsened it; for without curtailing the supply of the drug it has sent the price up tenfold, and this has had the effect of impoverishing the poorer class of addicts and reducing them to a condition of such abject misery as to render them incapable of gaining an honest livelihood." In other words, Campbell clearly did not endorse creating a similar law in Britain. Instead, doctors in England were permitted to prescribe a "maintenance" amount of heroin to drug addicts so that the addicts would not be supporting an underground market.

Meanwhile, steps were being taken to address the worldwide underground drug trade. Some say these moves were being taken by grandstanding politicians who desired to make it appear that they were doing something while not much was actually being done. When taken into consideration who was ruling the world opium market, having politicians and their appointees oversee the enforcement of the international drug laws was about as useless as trying to cool a boiling pot with an ice cube. At least with Britain's East India Company, the government officials were largely being supported with money from drug sales.

The Paris Peace Conference resulted in the January 25, 1919, agreement to form the League of Nations with a charter, The Treaty of Versailles, being signed by 44 countries on June 28, 1919. The U.S. was not one of the original countries to join the League. The first meeting of the League was held in London on November 15, 1920.

In addition to working to prevent war and improve collective security, the League of Nations was given a supervisory role over international agreements, such as those governing drug manufacturing and importation. Within the league there was a Permanent Central Opium Board which was set up to establish a legal trade in narcotics to serve the medical and scientific communities.

When the South African government attempted to establish international cannabis laws at the 1923 gathering of the League of Nation's Advisory Committee on the Traffic in Opium and other Dangerous Drugs, the British government vetoed it because banning cannabis would result in a loss of tax revenue. Cannabis had been outlawed by the British government in southern Africa in the 1870s, but the laws were basically ignored. The owners of the diamond mines grew cannabis to provide for their workers who lived in camps. In a move to criminalize the Blacks that used cannabis, the White aristocracy of South Africa banned cannabis in 1910.

It wasn't until the International Police Commission (Interpol) was formed in Paris in 1923 that serious talk of international laws against cannabis were considered. No laws were established and the focus was on drug trafficking as part of international crime. That very same year the British still were of the opinion, expressed by Lord Inchcape in a commission report done to study the finances of the East India Company, that the amount of land under poppy cultivation should not be reduced because it is a "most important source of income" for the British government in India. The first Lord of Inchcape (James Lyle Mackay), who died in 1932, was involved in banking, shipping, export, tea, mail distribution, and jute and khaki fabric production in India. His family's business was considered to be nearly as important to the British presence in the subcontinent as the East India Company.

Under the League of Nations Advisory Committee, an International Opium Convention was signed by member states on February 19, 1925, and it went into effect on September 25, 1928. In the U.S., Congress passed a law restricting the importation of heroin. The U.S. delegates tried to persuade the league to add such measures to the convention, but were unsuccessful. Even at home the act had been criticized. The June 1926 edition of the *Illinois Medical Journal* expressed the opinion that the restriction would allow drug dealers to bring in "double the money from the poor unfortunates upon whom they prey."

Egypt tried to add a prohibition on hashish and other cannabis substances to the International Opium Convention, but delegates from India spoke against establishing limitations on cannabis because the substance was used in religious ceremonies as well as for meditation, spiritual enlightenment, or ritual. Placing a ban on cannabis was viewed as

231

unenforceable because it was a wild plant, and because so many people smoked it for both religious and social means that laws against it would be impossible to enforce. A flimsy compromise was reached that was not included in the convention. It was that member countries agreed to voluntarily ban the exportation of cannabis that they may place prohibitions on its use, and to limit shipments to what was required for "medical or scientific purposes."

Opium traffic continued. Although the International Opium Convention was to establish a Central Narcotics Board to oversee the production and sale of opium for legitimate medicinal and scientific needs, the board was never organized. Drug-producing countries had no place to report how much opium, heroin, morphine, or cocaine they produced or exported. Countries that were importing the drugs also had no place to report how much of the drugs they were importing.

In the summer of 1931 the Opium Advisory Committee agreed to limit the production of opium in drug-producing countries to a predetermined set amount based on the estimated needs of medical and scientific uses for opium, heroin, and morphine. This was known as *the Blanco formula*, named after the person who thought it up, A. E. Blanco, a British man who worked in the Chinese Customs Service office. The formula was designed to keep track of the drugs from the raw materials to the production and on to the delivery and use at medical and scientific facilities. It didn't stop the underground production or sale of the drugs.

The Conference for the Suppression of the Illicit Traffic in Dangerous Drugs was held in 1932 and worked to further encourage countries to agree to a number of restrictions on drug trafficking. Although it did not sign on to the agreement, the U.S. was the most active in working to enforce the restrictions.

By the 1939 start of World War II the international drug trade was still flourishing. The war effort also contributed to the lack of control and suppression of the drug trade as resources were focused on other matters. After the war, in 1945 the United Nations Organization replaced the League of Nations.

My point in mentioning all of this information about opium is to show that when international drug laws first began to form around the start of the twentieth century, they were concentrated on opium and its extracts, heroin and morphine, and also on cocaine, but not on cannabis. I also wanted to give some detail about how governments, including the U.S., are involved in, and profit from, the international drug trade.

Cannabis wasn't added to an international treaty to control drugs until the Single Convention on Narcotics Drugs treaty was signed in 1961. Even then the international treaty relied on member states to enforce the law. It wasn't until the reign of Nixon's administration that the U.S. implemented the treaty within its boundaries by enacting the Controlled Substances Act of 1970.

Despite the efforts to control the underground opium and cocaine markets, they continued to flourish. Growing poppies and coca to produce the drugs was simple, smuggling was relatively easy, demand for the drugs was global, and it was a billion dollar industry. Mass quantities of opium drugs and cocaine were being produced in European and American laboratories, then sold into the world drug trade. This was detailed in the 1925 book *Opium* by John Palmer Gavit, chief of the Washington Bureau of the Associated Press. In the 1934 book, *Inside Dope*, British journalist Ferdinand Tuohy further details the opium market of the day, including flaws in the Opium Advisory Committee's plans meant to control the drugs, and the story about prisoners using carrier pigeons to obtain drugs.

*The Nation* magazine was also following the international drug trade. Ellen La Motte had become a correspondent for the magazine and was writing articles about the League of Nations Opium Advisory Committee, which the press had nicknamed "The Smugglers' Reunion." The Committee's response to the exposure was to limit the access journalist correspondents had to the Commission's meetings, and to guard the printed records of the meetings.

The cannabis market had also been increasing. But because cannabis wasn't seen as an addictive drug, it was not included in the focus on either opiate drugs (opium, heroin, morphine) or cocaine. Some say that perhaps this was because cannabis could not yet make as much money for governments. This was not the case in India where the British government also encouraged the cultivation of cannabis.

In 1927 a British man named Horace Gundry Alexander, the son of the secretary of the Society for the Suppression of the Opium Traffic, traveled to the Far East to investigate the drug trade. He became an acquaintance of Gandhi, who described him as "one of the best friends India has." Alexander found that the 1926-27 report of the Excise Department of the United Provinces reported that the "downward tendency in the sales of charas [cannabis] has now been arrested." In other words, cannabis sales had increased, which improved the revenue for the British colony. Alexander commented, "Even in the limited sphere of drug and drink habits, the main guilt of the West, for which sooner or later the East will call us to account, arises from the expoert of manufactured habit-forming drugs, such as morphine and cocaine, and from the expoert of spirits. So long as we go to the East with these things in our hand, Chinese and Indians and Malays are not likely to have much use for the programme of social reform that we carry in the other."

Gandhi had a history of trying to work against the drug trade. He referred to opium as "the other oppressor," with the British government

233

being the first. When some of Gandhi's followers worked to eliminate the production of opium in their region they were arrested for "undermining the revenue" of the colony.

The Mideast-to-Europe drug trade was the topic of the book *The Hashish Crossing*. It was published in 1933 and written by a former drug smuggler named Henry de Montfreid, an Islamic convert who wrote books under the name of Abd el-Hai.

In regions outside India, Britain conveniently ignored their earlier studies on cannabis and continued to treat it as if it were a great contributor to crime, violence, and mental health issues. During World War II British forces were used to destroy many acres of cannabis in Palestine. This too did not stop the use of or demand for cannabis. But it did succeed in increasing its price while creating a crime factor in which the government tried to suppress the production and sale of cannabis. And Britain did so to protect its own interests.

Just as in modern day, the early laws against cannabis didn't stop the cultivation, distribution, or use of the plant. Ditto with poppies and the drugs created from them (opium, heroin, and morphine).

# The Boggs Act, the Narcotics Control Act, and Modern-Day Drug Laws

The Boggs Act of 1951 strengthened the domestic U.S. enforcement of the Marijuana Tax Act and the Narcotics Drug Import and Export Act. It placed harsh uniform penalties on those convicted of drug violations. Under the Boggs Act, those charged with a first offense involving cocaine, marijuana, or opiates were given two to five years in prison. Second-time offenders were given five to ten years, and third-time offenders were given ten to twenty years. Many opposed to the sentences in the act cited that the second- and third-time offenders were denied parole when even murderers and rapists could be eligible for parole. The Narcotics Control Act of 1956 also strengthened the laws against drugs.

The Boggs Act got its name from Thomas Boggs, Sr., a congressman from Louisiana who sponsored the bill because he thought the drug laws were too lenient. Drug laws were most severe in the South, where the laws were passed using arguments with racist connotation. For instance, those charged with a second marijuana offense in Georgia could receive the death penalty.

In 1956 the Narcotic Control Act was ratified and increased minimum sentences for those convicted of marijuana charges to ten years for a first offense, twenty years for a second, thirty years for a third, and forty years for a fourth. They were the same for cocaine and heroin. To help fight the crime, Federal Bureau of Narcotics agents were given guns.

During the Kennedy administration there was some talk that the personal use of marijuana would be legalized. In 1962 Kennedy's administration had organized a panel to study drug use. This resulted in the proceedings of the White House Conference on Narcotic and Drug Abuse of September 27-28, 1962. The 500-person panel published its conclusions in *The Prettyman Report*, named after chief author E. Barrett Prettyman, a judge retired from the U.S. Supreme Court of Appeals. The study said, "It is the opinion of the panel that the hazards of marijuana per se have been exaggerated and that long criminal sentences imposed on an occasional use or possession of the drug are in poor social perspective. Although marijuana has long held the reputation of inciting individuals to commit sexual offenses and other antisocial acts, the evidence is inadequate to substantiate this."

It was suggested that the U.S. laws governing marijuana should be rewritten because they were "in poor social perspective."

The Kennedy administration also advocated for repealing of mandatory penalties put into place by the Boggs Act of 1951.

235

In 1963 the Kennedy administration created a Presidential Advisory Committee on Narcotics and Drug Abuse. The committee expressed the opinion that the marijuana drug laws should be changed. The plans didn't come to fruition because Kennedy was assassinated in November.

The Lyndon B. Johnson administration was also critical of the marijuana laws. Its Commission on Law Enforcement and Administration of Justice denounced the laws that treated marijuana as harshly as the highly addictive substances cocaine and heroin.

Despite the findings and viewpoints of the White House, personal marijuana use remained illegal, and the Boggs Act remained in effect. Meanwhile, marijuana use greatly increased during the 1960s, and so did the number of people being arrested for breaking the marijuana laws.

Marijuana arrests went from 169 in 1960 to over 15,000 in 1966. More people were smoking it, more people were smuggling, growing, and selling it, and more people were getting arrested for it. It was obvious that people wanted it, liked it, and were not going to stop using it. And it was becoming more apparent than ever that the laws to control it were not working, and never could.

# 1960s, the Hippy Trail, and Nixon

During the Johnson administration the marijuana culture flourished. Thousands of military personnel serving in Southeast Asia became familiar with marijuana. Some brought packets of it home with them. Some shipped home bundles of choice cannabis in body bags. Others sent cannabis-stuffed gifts back to friends and loved ones back home. Across the U.S. and Canada there was an awakening of political activism, often with large groups of young people gathering for civil rights marches and war protests where marijuana was smoked. Others were dropping out and flocking to communes, such as in Taos, New Mexico. The communes, the rock-'n'-roll music, and the 1967 Summer of Love turned more people onto marijuana. Government actions to try to control it were a waste of money. Anyone who wanted it could get it. Yet, the arrests of those breaking the marijuana laws eclipsed those of more serious crimes. The marijuana laws were a failure from the start, and by the late 1960s it was glaringly apparent that the government was moving in the wrong direction. It should have been extremely obvious that placing pot-smoking young people in prison at the prime of their lives was not a good thing for society.

"The traffic in marijuana has increased sharply within the last three or four years. Many areas which were formerly almost free of drug abuse now report a small but persistent traffic, centering on the 'hippie elements' and college campuses. Our reports show that more than 40 percent of the new marijuana users reported to the Bureau in 1967 were under the age of 21 years."
– Henry Giordano, head of the Federal Bureau of Narcotics, testifying before Congress, 1968

In the 1960s an organization of political activists named "The Brotherhood of Eternal Love" was actively involved in smuggling cannabis into the U.S.

As the marijuana culture spread, the demand for it increased beyond what was being produced in domestic cultivation. The government was well aware that huge amounts of cannabis in various forms, including hashish and hashish oil, were being smuggled into the U.S. and Canada, including on military ships and airplanes returning from warmer climates.

In 1967, under pressure from the U.S., the United Nations ratified its Single Convention on Narcotics Drugs to outlaw marijuana throughout the world. Anslinger, although no longer in his position as the head of the Federal Bureau of Narcotics since Henry Giordano had taken his place during the Kennedy administration, attended a hearing to advise the Senate

237

to sign onto the ratification, which they did. This created the United Nations Fund for Drug Control. Known as the International Drug Control Program, it allows for worldwide policing of the drug trade. That same year the Single Convention on Narcotics Drugs was amended by the Convention on Psychotropic Substances.

With each year more people were arrested and imprisoned on marijuana charges. But one could buy cancer-inducing cigarettes and cheap alcohol at the local supermarket, liquor stores, bars, nightclubs, military bases, and even on some college campuses. By the end of the decade laws against marijuana use among college students and war protestors were being used as a tool to arrest those who spoke out against the government. Some of the young people busted on marijuana charges were given the option of jail or joining the killing machine that was the military.

> "Since the use of marijuana and other narcotics is widespread
> among members of the New Left, you should be alert to opportunities
> to have them arrested by local authorities on drug charges."
> – J. Edgar Hoover, FBI director, 1968 memo to all FBI field
> offices

The FBI and Federal Bureau of Narcotics used illegal phone taps, undercover agents, and paid informants to fight marijuana use and/or to work against those who spoke against the government. They also negotiated with those they arrested to turn in their friends and associates in exchange for shortened sentences or softer charges. Files were kept on some of the most popular musicians and celebrities of the day. Anyone speaking at a war protest or involved in the civil rights movement was suspect.

If a young person traveled to certain countries on the "Hippy Trail" where cannabis was commonly grown and used, such as Afghanistan, India, Iran, Lebanon, Morocco, Pakistan, and Turkey, they could also be subject to government attention. Airport searches were becoming increasingly common when travelers returned from those countries.

The U.S. government also attempted, but failed, to destroy the hashish market by paying millions of dollars to the Afghanistan government to eliminate cannabis farms. With countries in that region of the world increasing their reliance on income from exporting cannabis and hashish, it was virtually impossible to crush the production of cannabis. But the U.S. kept using its policing of the drug trade as rational to formulate foreign policy and relations with other countries. This was often done with the goal of gaining access to natural resources.

While the government increased its involvement in trying to eradicate cannabis cultivation in other countries, it also was spending greater resources in labor, equipment, and cash in an attempt to get rid of the domestic cultivation, sales, and use of cannabis.

All of the government's domestic and international efforts did not stop cannabis from becoming the most common illicit substance being used throughout the world.

Poet and outspoken antidrug law activist Alan Ginsberg knew what it was like to be harassed by the government. Exercising his freedom of speech through his books, and at speaking engagements on college campuses, at bookstores, and in the media brought him to the attention of the Federal Bureau of Narcotics, which kept a file on him. Once when returning to the States he was strip-searched and even the lint of his pockets was examined with a magnifying glass to see if any illegal substances could be found. People who associated with him were also subjected to the watchful eye of both the FBI and the Federal Bureau of Narcotics.

When Black Panther member Lee Otis Johnson was arrested after sharing a joint with an undercover agent in Houston in 1967, he was convicted and sentenced to thirty years in prison. A federal district appeals court dismissed the sentence after ruling that the charges were politically motivated.

"Drug use signifies the total end of the Protestant ethic: screw work, we want to know ourselves. But of course the goal is to free oneself from American society's sick notion of work, success, reward, and status and to find oneself through one's own discipline, hard work, and introspection."
– Jerry Rubin, co-founder with Abbie Hoffman of the Youth International Party (Yippies) that put a real live Landrace boar named Pig (real name: Pigasus from the Hog Farm hippie commune) on the '68 Democratic primary ballot. Hoffman once ran for mayor of Berkeley where he organized peace marches; wore an American Revolutionary War uniform when he appeared before the House Committee on Un-American Activities; led an antiwar march on the Pentagon; and, along with Hoffman and Tom Hayden, was part of the Chicago Seven who protested at the 1968 Democratic National Convention. This led to the Chicago Conspiracy Trial of 1969, which, in a government act against those who protested the administration, tried the group on trumped-up conspiracy charges. After a circus-like trial, five of them were convicted, but the ruling was eventually overturned on appeal. I was present in November 1994 when Rubin jaywalked across Wilshire Blvd. to get to his Westwood apartment building. A load of airline flight attendants were getting off a bus in front of a hotel,

239

which may have distracted some drivers. One car swerved, but
another hit Rubin. It was a terrible sound. Everyone was surprised
that he was still alive. He was rushed to UCLA Medical Center,
underwent many hours of surgery, but died two weeks later.

The youth of the country were becoming increasingly active in working
to protest the government's military actions in Southeast Asia, and the
abuse of their own rights and lives. More people became aware of
marijuana with some smoking it simply in protest of what they saw as a
corrupt government. And more people became disillusioned by the White
House administration and the war machine that was the Pentagon.

In October 1967 a group of protesters gathered outside of the
Pentagon in an attempt to focus their mind energy on eliminating the evil
from the U.S. military. And on New Years Day 1968, in the New York
apartment of *Steal This Book* author Abbie Hoffman, a group of people
gathered to smoke weed and organize the Youth International Party (YIP)
with its members becoming known as *yippies*.

Marijuana use among U.S. citizens at home was reflective of those who
were attending foreign universities, traveling in other countries, living
abroad, or fighting the war in Vietnam. The whole world was becoming
aware of marijuana. Songs, films, and other forms of art expressed this
awareness. As the popularity of cannabis spread, more people started
growing it inside the U.S. borders, often with seeds imported from other
parts of the world, including those brought home by soldiers and military
personnel returning from Vietnam and other countries.

Then there was also a young man named Thomas King Forcade
(intentionally sounds like *façade*). He was born Kenneth Gary Goodson and
served a short stint in the Air Force in 1965, but had some fake or real
incident with mental health issues and was dishonorably discharged. After
graduating with a business degree from the University of Utah, Forcade
moved to a commune in Tucson. At some point he had been involved in
smuggling marijuana from Mexico. After the law raided the commune,
Goodson changed his name to Forcade, became politically involved, and
began publishing an underground journal named *Orpheus*, which he put
together while living in a school bus. He eventually moved to New York
and helped to form the Underground Press Syndicate, an association of
alternative publications that were starting across the country to report on
issues and events not covered in the corporate press.

Then, Richard Nixon became president in 1969 and the fight for
personal freedom and the manipulation of foreign policies intensified as
Nixon declared his unobtainable goal to eliminate drug use from society.
He authorized U.S. embassies to increase their focus on the international

drug trade and allocated more money for certain countries to subsidize farmers to grow food rather than cannabis, poppies, and coca.

The Nixon administration also investigated antiestablishment organizations and publications associated with the Liberation News Service, which supplied articles to alternative publications in the Underground Press Syndicate.

During a one-month period at the end of 1969 the Nixon administration authorized Operation Intercept to intensify drug searches of vehicles entering the U.S./Mexico border gates. It was known that a large amount of Mexican-grown marijuana was entering the U.S. The well-publicized and wasteful plan was canceled after little marijuana was found and the Mexican government failed to cooperate.

What Operation Intercept did do is that it raised the price of marijuana because the growers, importers, suppliers, and others in the marijuana business saw what kind of risks they were up against. It also got young people to drink more alcohol, because it was cheaper and easier to get, and it increased the number of alcohol-related traffic deaths caused by young drivers. Statistically, people who drive under the influence of alcohol cause a great number more traffic accidents than those who are only under the influence of marijuana.

> "As you know, there is a Commission that is supposed to make recommendations to me about this subject; in this instance, however, I have such strong views that I will express them. I am against legalizing marijuana. Even if the Commission does recommend that it be legalized. I will not follow that recommendation."
> – Richard Nixon, New York Times, May 1971

As the government intensified its domestic drug enforcement it chose peculiar targets – often people and organizations that spoke out against the White House administration.

In a meeting on May 26, 1971, Nixon made these rather revealing comments to Bob Haldeman:

> "Now, this is one thing I want. I want a goddamn strong statement on marijuana. Can I get that out of this sonofabitching, uh, Domestic Council?"
> Haldeman: "Sure."
> Nixon: "I mean one on marijuana that just tears the ass out of them. I see another thing in the news summary this morning about it. You know it's a funny thing, every one of the bastards that are out for legalizing marijuana is Jewish. What the Christ is the matter with the

Jews, Bob, what is the matter with them? I suppose it's because most of them are psychiatrists, you know, there's so many, all the greatest psychiatrists are Jewish. By God we are going to hit the marijuana thing, and I want to hit it right square in the puss, I want to find a way of putting more on that."

When the feds raided the Phoenix offices of the Underground Press Syndicate they failed to find drugs, but located and took the subscription lists and other files – which some people believed was the real goal of the raid.

When the President's Commission on Obscenity and Pornography held meetings in Washington in May of 1970, Forcade made an appearance and accused the members of the commission as being "walking antiques." He presented a letter listing 45 publications that had been the focus of the administration's intimidation tactics to shut down alternative newspapers that Forcade referred to as the "new-conscious media." He told the commission, "The only obscenity is censorship." He also threw a custard pie at a congressman.

The Nixon administration kept on with its war on the underground press, on drugs, and on those associating or suspected of associating with groups or people that spoke out against the War on Drugs, the war in Vietnam, or that were working to educate the public about the inner workings of the government. Alternative presses continued to be subjected to office raids, intimidation, and having their equipment and publications destroyed. Artists and musicians continued to produce works protesting the government, advancing the antiestablishment movement. And more and more people kept being charged with breaking marijuana laws and being sentenced to prison.

To further expand its War on Drugs, the Nixon administration created the Office for Drug Abuse Law Enforcement as well as the Special Action Office for Drug Abuse Prevention. And they used the FBI's Counter Intelligence Program (COINTELPRO) to intimidate and otherwise cause problems for alternative news publications and groups, organizations, and people, such as Vietnam Veterans Against the War, that worked to educate the public about the government's tactics and that worked to encourage young people to vote.

The cultivation of hemp, which is not a drug and can't get you high, was temporarily labeled as a Schedule 1 substance under the Comprehensive Drug Abuse Prevention and Control Act that was passed by Congress in 1970. The Act classified hemp as an illegal substance with no medical value. The Act also removed mandatory sentences for marijuana possession, making it a misdemeanor. It created a five-level classification for drugs in line with a drug's perceived medical value and potential for abuse.

This ban on hemp came at a time when Richard Nixon was being advised by various scientists to legalize hemp and marijuana because the laws banning them were a tremendous waste of money and based on ludicrous claims. He obviously ignored the advice. He wanted marijuana permanently banned as a Schedule 1 substance.

On June 17, 1971 Nixon, declared his War on Drugs before Congress.

The Comprehensive Drug Abuse Prevention and Control Act established the national Commission on Marijuana and Drug Abuse. This became known as the Shafer Commission, named after its chairman, former Pennsylvania governor Raymond Shafer. Hoping to get a report that agreed with his stance on marijuana, Nixon and his advisors picked nine of the 13 commissioners.

What is interesting is that in 1971 Nixon appointed Shafer to chair the congressionally mandated National Commission on Marijuana and Drug Abuse specifically because Shafer was a conservative. To help formulate the outcome of the expected conclusions of the report, the Nixon administration also appointed a dean of a law school; a retired Chicago police captain; two senators, and two congressmen from each of the Republican and Democratic parties; and four doctors, including the head of a mental health hospital.

In Oval Office meetings, Nixon was exacting in his instruction to Shafer that the final report should be conclusively against marijuana.

What Nixon wanted wasn't always what Nixon ended up getting.

The Shafer Commission undertook a massive project that involved dozens of research projects. They considered all previous research and claims about marijuana while also conducting new research. The report was released in several stages covering various aspects of U.S. drug laws and viewpoints of many professionals. It pointed out the myths and mistruths about marijuana. Among its conclusions was that "Marihuana's relative potential for harm to the vast majority of individual users and its actual impact on society does not justify a social policy designed to seek out and firmly punish those who use it."

"… The policy-makers [who made marijuana and hemp farming illegal in 1937] knew very little about the effects or social impact of the [marijuana] drug; many of their hypotheses were speculative and, in large measure, incorrect."
    – Shafer Commission Report: Marihuana, A Signal of
    Misunderstanding: The Report of the National Commission on
    Marihuana and Drug Abuse: Chapter V: marihuana and social
    policy: A Social Control Policy for Marihuana: Discouragement or

Neutrality: 2. Continuing Scientific Uncertainty Precludes Finality;
Commissioned by President Richard M. Nixon, March 1972

Boy, was Nixon in for a surprise when the commission did just the opposite of what he wanted: Instead of sticking up for him and recommending stronger drug laws, the commission recommended decriminalizing marijuana!

Apparently dissatisfied with the conclusions of a report that his own administration commissioned, Nixon rejected the findings of the commission. He had advance word that the report was not going to back his agenda and he was prepared to work against its conclusions.

The Shafer Commission Report not only concluded that marijuana should be decriminalized for personal use, but also said that the selling or other exchange of small amounts should also be decriminalized. It concluded "marihuana use is not such a grave problem that individuals who smoke marihuana, or possess it for that purpose, should be subject to criminal procedures." The report concluded that about 40 percent of U.S. citizens aged 18 to 25 had used cannabis. It stated, "Neither the marihuana user nor the drug itself can be said to constitute a danger to public safety." Rather than blaming marijuana for dangers to health, the report stated, "a careful search of literature and testimony by health officials has not revealed a single human fatality in the U.S. proven to have resulted solely from the use of marijuana." The Commission compared the situation to alcohol Prohibition. Dr. James Carey of the University of California wrote, "There is increasing evidence that we are approaching a situation similar to that at the time when the Volstead [alcohol Prohibition] Act was repealed [on December 5, 1933]."

When Nixon was provided with the painstakingly researched report he said he tossed the study into the trash without reading it. The report was in opposition to Nixon's stance that marijuana "criminals" needed to be treated more harshly. "Enforce the law. You've got to scare them," is how Nixon put it in conversations recorded in the Oval Office.

Nixon called the commission "a bunch of do-gooders" who were "soft on marijuana." On March 21, 1972, the day before early versions of the report were released (the final report was released in 1973), Nixon made his now-famous statement: "We need, and I use the word 'all-out war,' on all fronts."

In October 1973 Arab countries became greatly displeased with how the U.S. supported Israel with weaponry during the Yom Kippur War with Egypt and Syria. The Arab countries retaliated by refusing to export their petroleum to the U.S. and its European allies. This became known as the "OPEC oil embargo," with OPEC meaning the Organization of Petroleum Exporting Countries. In the U.S., the price of a gallon of gasoline quickly rose to $1.50 per gallon. Long lines formed at gas stations. Automobiles in that era often got less than 15 miles per gallon, and most of America had become overly reliant on their automobiles.

1973 was also the year that the Nixon administration increased funding to arrest those breaking the marijuana laws. As the war abroad continued, Nixon got the government to go to war with its own citizens. In support of the Nixon administration, New York's Governor Nelson Rockefeller got the state to enact the strongest drug laws in the country. As arrests went up, so did the price of drugs. And as the price went up, so too did the number of organized crime organizations wanting to get in on the money, on protecting their territory, and on importing larger and larger quantities of drugs.

By 1974, the budget of the newly-created Drug Enforcement Agency was $719,000,000. The costs of the drug war also involved more officers, more people in court, and more people having to be sent to prisons – and this meant building more prisons.

To put it lightly, Nixon and Rockefeller, and the rest of them, were a bit disconnected from reality, and especially from the reality of what most of America was experiencing, what they considered to be important, and what they considered to be solutions to the real problems facing the nation. What the Republican leadership was doing wasn't helping the country, or the citizens, but was working against them at a time when things were already stressful.

"And let's look at the strong societies. The Russians. God damn it, they root them [homosexuals] out, they don't let them around at all. You know what I mean? I don't know what they do with them. Now, we are allowing this in this country when we show [unintelligible]. Dope? Do you think the Russians allow dope? Hell no. Not if they can allow, not if they can catch it, they send them up. You see, homosexuality, dope, immorality in general: These are the enemies of strong societies. That's why the Communists and the left-wingers are pushing the stuff, they're trying to destroy us."
– Oval Office conversation 498-5, meeting with Nixon, Haldeman, and Ehrlichman, May 13, 1971, between 10:30am and 12:30pm; transcript available at the Web site Common Sense for Drug Policy, CSDP.org/Research/NixonPot.txt. The conversation goes on with Bob Haldeman leaving the room. George Shultz enters with Chicago Mayor Richard Daley. Then Nixon goes on to express more bizarre viewpoints about marijuana.

"Now, my position is flat-out on that. I am against legalizing marijuana. Now I'm against legalizing marijuana because, I know all the

245

arguments about, well, marijuana is no worse than whiskey, or etc., etc., etc. But the point is, once you cross that line, from the straight society to the drug society – marijuana, then speed, then it's LSD, then it's heroin, etc., then you're done. But the main point is – well, well, we conduct, well, this commission will come up with a number of recommendations…"

– Nixon saying to Richard Daley that the commission will come up with a number of recommendations that back Nixon's views on marijuana.

Nixon's stance resulted in marijuana arrests increasing by more than 128,000. The year after the Shafer Commission Report was released, approximately 420,700 persons were arrested on pot charges.

As a way to formally lobby legislatures to overhaul the U.S. marijuana laws, in 1971 an attorney named Keith Stroup formed the National Organization for the Reform of Marijuana Laws. He was assisted by a donation by *Playboy* magazine founder Hugh Hefner. NORML continues to this day.

One popular marijuana case during the Nixon administration involved the arrest of music promoter, poet, and White Panther party founder John Sinclair. He was arrested in Michigan for possessing two marijuana cigarettes. In July 1969 Sinclair was sentenced to ten years in prison.

Abbie Hoffman interrupted the Who rock band during their performance at Woodstock by grabbing the microphone to speak to the crowd about Sinclair. According to various takes on the event, Pete Townsend either accidentally bumped into Hoffman, which knocked him off the stage; used his guitar to push Hoffman from the stage; or hit him on the head, which made Hoffman tumble from the stage. Townsend later apologized for whatever happened and also spoke out against the imprisonment of Sinclair.

On December 10, 1971, a benefit concert named the *Free John Now Rally* was held at the Crisler arena in Ann Arbor, Michigan. Over 15,000 people attended. Among those appearing on stage were people not so truly loved by the Nixon administration: Jerry Rubin, Allen Ginsberg, John Lennon, and Yoko Ono. The FBI and other branches of the government had been keeping files on all four of them. Together they sang a song written about and titled *John Sinclair*. Bob Seger and Stevie Wonder also performed at the rally.

The publicity worked. Three days later the Michigan Supreme Court ruled that the state's cannabis laws were unconstitutional. Sinclair was then released from prison. While in prison he wrote the books *Guitar Army* and *Music & Politics*. He went on to become the editor of the *Detroit Sun*, to record music, and to write the book of poetry *Va Tutto Bene (It's All Good)*.

The city of Ann Arbor has created some of the most lenient cannabis laws in the U.S. In 1972 the city enacted a $5 fine for possession of less than two ounces of weed. The ordinance was repealed in June 1973 as more than one hundred spectators protested by lighting joints in city council chambers and the city's mayor was smacked in the face with a pie. In April 1974 Ann Arbor voters reversed that decision and reinstated the $5 fine by amending the city charter. City police and prosecutors were restricted from referring pot charges to state or federal authorities. In 1990 the fine was increased to $25 and up to $100 or more depending on the offense.

The city of Ann Arbor hosts a "Hash Bash" on the first Saturday of April, an annual event that started in 1971 to protest Sinclair's arrest.

By the summer of 1974 the Nixon administration was unraveling. This was because of a little incident that happened on the night of June 17, 1972. It was when five men broke into the Democratic headquarters in the Watergate building. The men were working for the Committee to Re-Elect the President. This led to exposure of other illegal activities involving abuses of power, wiretapping, stealing of classified documents, plans to do other break-ins, and great efforts to cover up the mess. The ensuing investigations and hearings enlightened the masses to government corruption.

There were huge protests at the 1972 Republican National Convention held in Miami. The crowds were larger than the 1968 Democratic Convention in Chicago. The corporate news failed to report on the protests, and focused instead on the actual convention. Meanwhile, the FBI's Counter-intelligence Program was used against those working to organize the protests. Tom Forcade was arrested on false charges of planning to bomb the Miami convention center. He was later cleared of the charges.

In July 1973 the Nixon administration used Executive Order and formed the Drug Enforcement Administration (DEA) by combining the Bureau of Narcotics and Dangerous Drugs, the Office for Drug Abuse Law Enforcement, the Special Action Office for Drug Abuse Prevention, and the Office of National Narcotics Intelligence.

While most of the DEA's focus is on a domestic War on Drugs, its influence and activities are global. In 2007 the DEA had over 250 field offices in the U.S. and over 70 foreign offices in over 55 countries. It hasn't stopped drug use, but has increased the price of drugs while also increasing prison populations throughout the world and fueling the organized crime elements of the drug trade.

In well-deserved international disgrace, Nixon left office on August 9, 1974.

Shafer remained in the opinion that marijuana should be decriminalized, including during his time serving as special counsel on the

247

staff of Vice-President Nelson Rockefeller from August 1974 to January 1977.

# Cannabis in Canada and England

Because marijuana was increasingly being used north of the border the Canadians initiated their own studies on marijuana by forming the Commission of Inquiry into NonMedical Use of Drugs. That commission became known as the Le Dain Commission, after its chairman Gerald Le Dain, dean of York University's Osgoode Hall Law School in Toronto.

In 1972 the Le Dain Commission published a report titled *Cannabis*. The report largely agreed with the findings of the Shafer Commission report, but it advised keeping the sale of cannabis illegal as a way of discouraging its use. The Canadian laws against cannabis were much softer than those of the U.S., allowing judges to dismiss some cases and charge a fine or assign probation to lesser marijuana charges. Canadian police placed more focus on hard drugs.

There was also cannabis drama happening on the other side of the Atlantic.

On April 7, 1967, England appointed a committee led by Lady Barbara Wootton (also known as Baroness Wootton) to study the marijuana issues in that country. They were also assigned to report on LSD, which was growing in popularity since it had been accidentally discovered in 1943 by chemist Albert Hofmann when he was studying the medicinal uses of a fungus commonly found on grains (This is written about in Hoffman's 1979 book, *LSD: my problem child*, and in the popular 1954 Aldous Huxley book of essays, *The Doors of Perception,* which was read by Jim Morrison. While riding in a Volkswagen and smoking a joint with his band mates, Morrison told them he thought the name of their band should be The Doors). The official title of Wootton's committee was the Sub-Committee on Hallucinogens of the Home Office Advisory Committee on Drug Dependence. A social scientist, Wootton had been a court magistrate, the head of a university department in social work, and governor of the BBC.

As in other countries, marijuana was becoming increasingly popular in England, and so were the number of people being arrested for it. It was no longer viewed as an issue of the lower class. The upper class was becoming well aware that their children were smoking marijuana. It was no secret that cannabis was being smoked by students at Oxford, by members of the ruling class, and that it was being smuggled into the country in many different ways, including through British Naval ships, and by mail delivery to foreign embassies located in London.

It was also no secret that the world-famous musicians that made up The Rolling Stones and the Beatles were quite familiar with cannabis, and this was having an enormous impact on the youth culture. In 1967 there had been well-publicized drug charges brought against Keith Richards and

Mick Jagger. Richards was sentenced to a year in prison on cannabis charges and Jagger received three months for possessing some "black bomber" amphetamine pills. This resulted in large protests against the government with thousands of young people marching through London streets.

In May 1967, the Beatles released the psychedelically-charged Sergeant Pepper album and it instantly became an enormous success. Some say that it was not only inspired by LSD, but also was meant to be listened to while under the influence of LSD. Stephen Abrams of the Soma Research Association, which was involved in researching THC, has said that Paul McCartney told him to listen to the album while on LSD and wearing headphones. Two clues to the artists' connection with both LSD and marijuana is that the cover includes marijuana plants as well as an image of Aldous Huxley, the author who famously requested to be on LSD as he died in his California home on November 22, 1963.

On July 16, 1967, there was a huge "be-in" gathering in London's Hyde Park, which became known as the "Legalize Pot Rally." Poet Alan Ginsberg had attended the rally and was famously photographed giving a flower to a police officer. It was covered in the international press. Days later the Beatles were in the news again because they had paid for a July 24, 1967, ad in *The Times* advocating the reform of cannabis laws in England. The ad was sponsored by the Soma Research Association and signed by 65 people, including scientists, doctors, members of Parliament, and Francis Crick, winner of the Nobel Prize for discovering the structure of DNA. Publication of the advertisement triggered debate in the House of Commons. The advertisement gained so much attention that on Friday, July 28, 1967 the House of Commons debated the claims it made. Subsequently, on July 31, 1967, Jagger's sentence was reduced to a conditional discharge and Richards' conviction was dismissed on appeal.

Under Britain's 1964 Drugs Prevention and Misuse Act, users of cannabis could receive more severe penalties than users of highly addictive drugs like morphine and heroin. Under the National Health Service, heroin addicts can get prescriptions for the "maintenance dose" of heroin from doctors at specified clinics, which is a proven way of stifling the underground market while treating addiction as a health issue. But Britain's cannabis users could go straight to prison, and sometimes for as long as those who were convicted of murder. This was recognized as extremely unbalanced, disproportionate to the so-called crime of smoking cannabis, and did harm rather than good. Furthering concern of the upper class was that, as the Wootton Report detailed, in 1964 there were more Caucasians than Blacks arrested in England on cannabis charges.

The Wootton Sub-Committee conducted its study between April 1967 and July 1968. In October 1968, the committee submitted its report to Home Secretary James Callaghan.

In November 1967 John Lennon was tried and received a small fine for breaking the marijuana law. The publicity this received kept the marijuana debate in the news.

The "Wootton Report" was published in January 1969 and was hotly debated in Parliament on January 27. The report concluded that marijuana is "very much less dangerous than the opiates, amphetamines, and barbiturates, and also less dangerous than alcohol." It also stated, "The long asserted dangers of cannabis were exaggerated, and that the related law was socially damaging, if not unworkable." And it recommended, "Possession of a small amount should not normally be punished by imprisonment."

> "Having reviewed all the material available to us we find ourselves in agreement with the conclusions reached by the Indian Hemp Drugs Commission appointed by the Government of India (1893-1894) and the New York Mayor's Committee on Marihuana (1944) that 'the long-term consumption of cannabis in moderate doses has no harmful effects.'"
> – *The Wootton Report*, paragraph 29; January 1969

England's Home Secretary, James Callaghan, again dismissed the report as being influenced by the marijuana "lobby." In the January 27 debate in Parliament, Callaghan stated, "I think it came as a surprise, if not a shock, to most people when that notorious advertisement appeared in the Times in 1967 to find that there is a lobby for legalising cannabis. The House should recognise that this lobby exists, and my reading of the Report is that the Wootton Sub-Committee was overinfluenced by this lobby."

Callaghan's words angered members of the committee. Wootton and the chairman of the committee, Sir Edward Wayne, wrote a letter to the Times that was published on February 5, 1969. In it they defended the "distinguished colleagues" and "eminent medical men" who signed the report.

However, in 1970 Callaghan introduced legislation to adopt the recommendations of the Wootton Report. It was eventually passed as the 1971 Misuse of Drugs Act. It reduced penalties and did away with prison terms in relation to cannabis. Interestingly, it did not distinguish between suppliers and users.

> "Home Secretary James Callaghan has had a dramatic change of mind on drugs. He has decided that people who smoke 'pot' should no longer be punished as severely as those using heroin. He has gone

further by deciding that the penalties for possessing both hard and soft drugs should be cut."

– Drug Law Shock, *Sunday Mirror*, February 1, 1970

On November 19 and 26, 1972, the *Sunday Telegraph* published articles about the use of marijuana in England. Titled Cannabis on Demand: Britain's Drug Dilemma, the articles estimated that upwards of two million citizens of England were smoking pot.

In 1973 the Lord Chancellor, Lord Hailsham, told magistrates to "reserve the sentence of imprisonment for suitably flagrant cases of large scale trafficking."

The 1977 Criminal Justice Act reduced the maximum sentence on summary conviction for possession of cannabis to three months, which was one month less than the Wootton Committee advised.

# The *High Times* Era

1974 was the year Tom Forcade began publishing *High Times* magazine, which focused on the growing marijuana culture. The first issue of the magazine was published out of a basement office on West 11th Street in New York. It was created as a sort of lampoon of *Playboy* magazine. Featuring photographs of marijuana instead of naked young women, it had no paid advertisers, but quickly sold out of its first printing. Advertisers soon signed on, the offices were moved to Broadway, and the magazine grew to have a readership in the millions and distribution that spread into other countries. It was the first national magazine to provide an advertising venue for marijuana paraphernalia accompanied by some rather impressive journalism. Some thought *High Times* was corporate-backed and Wall Street's way of making money off the hippies.

The Underground Press Syndicate became the Alternative Press Syndicate and began publishing *Alternative Media* out of the offices of *High Times*. Forcade also helped to start *Punk* magazine and produced a documentary on the Sex Pistols punk rock group. Forcade continued to be involved with smuggling marijuana into the U.S. He also contributed money to the National Organization for the Reform of Marijuana Laws (NORML).

*High Times* became more and more successful as it spoke to people in ways that other publications didn't. It carried articles written by investigative reporters and covered topics not found in corporate media. It gave voice to those who believed the War on Drugs was a waste of money, an invasion of personal freedom, based on lies and political corruption, and responsible for the death of many people.

The War on Drugs was escalating while companies that made so-called legal prescription pills that also were being used recreationally were knowingly manufacturing hundreds of millions more pills than could possibly be used by the medical profession. This was great for stockholders because the pharmaceutical companies made more money with every pill they sold. These pills, including methaqualone (Quaaludes [downers]) and the diet pills (speed) known as "black beauties," were ending up on the underground market. When speed and downers are mixed together, and/or with alcohol, the result can be kidney failure, coma, or death.

While the prescription pill underground was flourishing there were those who were figuring out the difference between highly addictive street drugs, prescription pills, and the relatively tame, nonaddictive, and medicinal qualities of cannabis.

In 1975 the Supreme Court of Alaska ruled that residents of the state could possess marijuana for personal use in their own homes. In *Ravin v. Sate* the court ruled: "It appears that [the] effects of marijuana on the individual are not serious enough to justify widespread concern, at least as compared with the far more dangerous effects of alcohol, barbiturates, and amphetamines."

Meanwhile, the corporate media kept reporting on the Drug War with the cop and criminal alarmist mentality that sold newspapers.

However, news coverage of the U.S. government's activities to eradicate domestic marijuana gardens and to arrest those who broke marijuana laws worked to increase the public's awareness of marijuana. The knowledge of marijuana was saturating the culture. While the news was reporting on marijuana with restraint, other TV shows were not so frigid about the matter. With a wink, wink, marijuana was joked about on national TV, often so subtly that only those-in-the-know could understand the joke. Other times, such as on talk shows of the era, including Johnny Carson and Merv Griffin, guests, especially comedians, would show up a little too happy and the show hosts would slyly glance at the audience letting those with an understanding of what was happening know that they understood the situation.

Anyone going to a rock concert anywhere in the U.S. during the 1970s could easily understand that huge numbers of people were smoking cannabis, and enjoying it, and that tremendous amounts of marijuana were being grown, sold, and smoked within U.S. borders.

On January 1, 1976, residents of Los Angeles awoke to see the landmark mountaintop Hollywood sign transformed. Daniel Finegold, an art major at Cal State Northridge, gathered three friends and used fabric and rope to alter the sign to read "HOLLYWEED." The story was covered in the international news.

In 1976 the U.S. Food and Drug Administration started a Compassionate Investigative New Drug program that allowed for certain patients to use government-issued marijuana. Six patients were accepted to the program and were sent marijuana grown at the Marijuana Research Facility at the University of Mississippi. A man with glaucoma, Robert C. Randall, became the first legal pot smoker in the U.S. since 1937. Originally, Randall had discovered that smoking marijuana improved his vision, which he had been told he would lose because of his glaucoma. When he began growing marijuana he was arrested. Under the Compassionate Investigative New Drug program, Randall continued smoking marijuana, and was able to preserve his vision until he passed away in 2001.

Under Gerald Ford's administration the government supported operations to find and spray marijuana fields in Mexico. The toxic substance they used to do this was Paraquat (a human carcinogen that is also known as Gramaxone). The chemical wilted and killed the plants. The poison can cause a variety of adverse effects in humans, including respiratory lesions, lung scarring, convulsions, and death. In 1976 the U.S.

spent $60 million on the marijuana field spraying program. Meanwhile, Ford's kids were not un-familiar with weed, and his wife was famously addicted to prescription pills and alcohol.

The spraying of marijuana plants in Mexico spurred the growth of the "home-grown" marijuana movement. People wanted to avoid any marijuana coming in from Mexico. More and more marijuana was being grown on U.S. forestland, in backyards, and wherever else people could get away with growing the plant for three to five months.

In the late 1970s the state of New Mexico passed the first medical marijuana law in the U.S. This was after a cancer patient brought the medical marijuana issue to the attention of the state legislature. A number of cancer patients and their doctors testified in favor of the medical benefits of marijuana. In 1978 the law passed with restrictions. It allowed for chemotherapy patients to use marijuana to relieve nausea and for glaucoma patients to use it to lower the eye pressure associated with that disease which can lead to blindness. Lynn Pierson, the cancer patient who initiated the issue, died before the law took effect.

Taking the Shafer Commission Report into consideration, in 1977 President Jimmy Carter asked Congress to eliminate the criminal penalties for possession of less than one ounce of marijuana. Instead, the Carter administration proposed a $100 fine, which was backed by the American Medical Association and the American Council of Churches.

Carter's stance on drugs was damaged in 1977 when his administration's director of the National Drug Control Policy, Dr. Peter Bourne, was seen snorting cocaine with gonzo journalist Hunter S. Thompson at a Christmas party for the staff of the National Organization for the Reform of Marijuana Laws (NORML). Bourne later left his position after getting in hot water for writing a prescription for Quaaludes for a White House secretary. Some people say he meant this to happen so he would have an excuse to leave the administration after damaging Carter's drug policy plan. (Quaaludes were a very popular drug in the 1970s, and made people feel a bit drunk without the calories or alcohol. They were very easy to obtain.)

In 1979 Carter eliminated funding for the Paraquat spray program, but the Mexican government continued the practice. Carter spoke out against this because marijuana sprayed with Paraquat could cause serious health problems for those who smoked it.

"Punishment for using a drug should not be more harmful to an individual than the drug itself. Nowhere is this more clear than in the laws against the possession of marijuana in private for personal use."
– Jimmy Carter

The Carter administration was not successful in changing the law. Many attribute this to the cocaine use by Dr. Peter Bourne. After Bourne resigned, the Carter administration increased funding for drug eradication efforts in Mexico.

"In the years to come the rhetoric of the Dope War will replace rhetoric of the Cold War as the justification for foreign military intervention. Instead of sending in the marines, Washington will send in the narcs."
– Robert Singer, in his prophetic article Dope Dictators, *High Times* magazine, March 1977; HighTimes.com

Despite the laws against it, marijuana culture blossomed. The TV show *Saturday Night Live* first started airing (as *NBC's Saturday Night*) in October 1975 with humor that was often aimed directly at those who were stoned on Saturday nights. Among the performers was Bill Murray, who had been arrested on marijuana charges when he was 20.

During one 1978 episode of *Saturday Night Live* while Chevy Chase was giving the *Weekend Update* he reported the FBI had announced that a large amount of marijuana had been smuggled into New York City. Chase informed viewers that *Saturday Night Live* had decided to perform a public service by conducting analysis on the marijuana. He encouraged viewers who may have any of the marijuana to place a small amount of it in an envelope and anonymously send it to Chevy Chase, Apartment 12, 827 West 81st Street, New York, NY 10053.

Also in 1978 the Cheech and Chong movie *Up in Smoke* was released and became a huge hit. Stoner humor was in the mainstream.

A koala was sitting in a gum tree while smoking a joint when a little lizard walked past, looked up, and said, "Hey koala! What are you doing?"
The koala said, "Smoking a joint, come up and have some."
So the little lizard climbed up and sat next to the koala where they enjoyed a few joints.
After a while the little lizard said that his mouth was dry, and that he was going to get a drink from the river.
The little lizard was so stoned that he leaned too far over and fell into the river.
A crocodile saw this and swam over to the little lizard and helped him to the side. Then he asked the little lizard, "What's the matter with you?"

The little lizard explained to the crocodile that he was sitting smoking a joint with the koala in the tree, got too stoned, and then fell into the river while taking a drink.

The crocodile said that he had to check this out, then walked into the rain forest and found the tree where the koala was sitting while finishing another joint.

The crocodile looked up and said, "Hey you!"

So the koala looked down at him and said, "Shiiiiiiiiiit dude... How much water did you drink?"

The party was on. Large rock concerts held in baseball stadiums sold out largely to fans who smoked so much pot that the smoke heavy with the scent of burning cannabis wafted through and above the crowds. FM radio and stereophonic sound systems became a necessity. Just as it had been mentioned in blues and jazz songs in the 1920s-40s, marijuana was mentioned in many rock songs, and some image or reference to cannabis was often included in the art of album covers. There was no more hiding the fact that large numbers of people were smoking weed on a regular basis. It was regularly mentioned in publications including *Playboy* and *Penthouse* magazines as well as more conservative news magazines like *Time* and *Newsweek*. Marijuana influenced jewelry, clothing, and furnishings, some of it designed with a place to hide a marijuana stash. Some people spent thousands of dollars having their cars, vans, and motorcycles painted by airbrush artists in ways that suggested the coolness of marijuana culture. A bumper sticker from the era featured the phrase, "Ass, Gas, or Grass, Nobody Rides for Free." Burton Rubin was making millions from his company, E-Z Wider, which produced double-wide "cigarette" papers designed specifically for rolling marijuana cigarettes (joints).

On November 16, 1978, political activist, marijuana smuggler, and *High Times* publisher Tom Forcade's life ended with a gunshot wound to the head in his bedroom in New York. The official story is that he committed suicide. Some people believe it was homicide. He was 33. He had been troubled since the death of his friend Jack Coombs earlier that year. A plane Coombs was flying crashed or was somehow brought down into a ball of flames in Florida as Coombs was smuggling a load of Colombian marijuana into the U.S. This smuggling operation was to be part of a documentary film Forcade was making. *High Times* magazine was also in trouble because the company that had been distributing it became dysfunctional. The distribution company was owned by *Hustler* porn magazine publisher Larry Flynt. In March 1978 Flynt was shot and paralyzed outside a Georgia courthouse where he was being tried on obscenity charges. Some people believe Flynt was targeted for assassination by the government.

257

After Forcade's death, *High Times* struggled for years with its focus unfortunately drifting away from marijuana and unwisely into hard drugs. During the early Reagan years the magazine seemed to foolishly glorify cocaine, which triggered an investigation by the Justice Department to explore charges of conspiring to distribute drug paraphernalia. Under the Reagan administration, companies that sold or manufactured products that could be used in conjunction with drugs, such as marijuana pipes, bongs, rolling machines, fancy roach clips, and grow room equipment, were targeted for intimidation or closure. Many companies that had been advertising in *High Times* struggled with legal issues, or closed shop.

Eventually a new editorial staff in the late 1980s cleaned up *High Times* and brought the editorial focus back to marijuana. But many say that *High Times* had lost its editorial edge, which seemed to have moved to a rival Canadian publication, *Cannabis Culture*, which ended publication in 2009.

For over five years, the Canadian publisher of *Cannabis Culture*, Marc Emery, who was known as "the prince of pot," and was the founder of the British Columbia Marijuana Party, was targeted by the U.S. government for running a marijuana seed-selling business from a head shop in Vancouver. The U.S. authorities had listed Emery as one of the top most wanted international drug dealers. In May, 2010, 52-year-old Emery was handed over to the U.S. authorities, convicted of a single count of conspiracy to manufacture marijuana, and was sentenced to five years in prison, including four years of supervised probation.

Perhaps the main reason the DEA was after Emery was because he was helping promote the legalization of marijuana, supporting organizations doing the same, and was strongly against the corrupt laws enacted in the U.S., which trigger the creation of drug laws in other countries.

"Hundreds of thousands of dollars of Emery's illicit profits are known to have been channeled to marijuana legalization groups active in the United States and Canada. Drug legalization lobbyists have one less pot of money to rely on."
– Karen Tandy, former DEA Administrator, in July 2005 DEA press release.

The money spent on getting Emery brought to, prosecuted in, and imprisoned in the U.S. is another total waste of tax dollars, while real criminals, such as Dick Cheney, Donald Rumsfeld and associated war lord company executives, and the people who run Monsanto, are free and living the wealthy life.

Some of the more interesting articles from *High Times* can be found in a 2004 book titled *High Times Reader*.

Articles from *Cannabis Culture* magazine can be found on the Internet.

# The 80s, Reagan, and Bush

As the marijuana culture continued to flourish, so too did the government programs that tried to control it. But in the 80s it was in the hands of the militant and conservative Reagan administration.

Under its Domestic Cannabis Eradication and Suppression Program, the Reagan administration increased funding to the Paraquat spraying program in Mexico. The administration also allowed for the poison to be sprayed on marijuana fields found in U.S. national forest lands. He encouraged other countries, including Columbia, to do the same.

When the issue was raised with the Reagan administration that the poisoned marijuana still might be sold and smoked, a spokesperson said that the administration considered the poisoning by smoking Paraquat-tainted marijuana to be reasonable punishment. It is a wonder what his children thought of that opinion.

In 1982 the Reagan administration pushed for and was successful in getting an amendment made to the Posse Comitatus Act of 1878. The act placed limits on the powers of the federal government to use the military for domestic law enforcement. The Reagan administration's amendment allowed for the use of the military to enforce drug laws within U.S. borders, thus taking the country "at war with its own citizens" to a whole new and obscene level. The war included the 1982 formation of the White House Drug Abuse Policy Office and passage of the Anti-Crime Bill allowing the government to confiscate cash, cars, real estate, and other property during drug raids. The Reagan administration also created mandatory minimum sentences for those arrested on drug charges, which greatly increased prison populations – which made the prison industry happy, which got them to donate more money to the Republicans. Even persons found to possess "drug paraphernalia," such as roach clips, rolling papers, or pipes, could be charged with a drug crime.

The enforcement of the drug laws resulted in the scenario in which the government could, and did, confiscate cars, homes, boats, and other belongings from citizens who were found to have small amounts of drugs, such as a partially smoked joint. The Woods Hole Oceanographic Institution in Massachusetts had its research vessel, the R.V. *Atlantis II*, impounded for two months in San Diego when a small amount of marijuana was found in the shaving kit of a crew member. The impounding interfered with a major study.

In 1984 Columbia began poisoning marijuana fields with a toxic chemical herbicide called glyphosphate. The Reagan administration said that other countries should follow Columbia's example.

259

"Sooner or later politicians will have to stop running scared and address the evidence: cannabis per se is not a hazard to society but driving it further underground may well be."
– The Lancet (British medical journal), November 11, 1995

In 1986 the Drug Enforcement Administration began holding hearings on marijuana to consider the relevance of various claims relating to the possible medical values of it and the laws controlling it.

"I have other things to do than waste my time with stupid fears of a physician-mediated 'plague' for what should be a controlled substance of some value. Do we have major problems with physician abuse of morphine, methadone, Demerol, codeine, etc.? The problem is a psycho-social issue resembling the search for witches of an earlier era. Preventing a psychoactive drug's entry into Schedule II will not solve crime on our streets and hurts patients who can benefit from an expanded therapeutic option."
– Dr. William Regelson, testifying before Drug Enforcement Administration hearings on marijuana

By 1988 when the Convention Against Illicit Traffic in narcotic Drugs and Psychotropic Substances (the Vienna Convention) was passed, the U.S. drug war was taken internationally.

On September 6, 1988, the government's very own Chief Administrative Law Judge, Francis L. Young, issued a 69-page ruling titled *In the Matter of Marihuana Rescheduling Petition*. In it he stated, "Marijuana, in its natural form, is one of the safest therapeutically active substances known to man." He also stated that marijuana was the safest drug for many health concerns, and that it was "unreasonable, arbitrary, and capricious to keep it illegal." The National Academy of Sciences had recommended that marijuana be made legal. Judge Young asked the Drug Enforcement Administration to "reschedule" marijuana so that doctors could legally prescribe it under federal law. The DEA administrator overruled Judge Young. The Court of Appeals allowed the overruling to stand.

The DEA continues to dismiss all scientific studies concluding that marijuana has significant therapeutic uses.

"Legalizing drugs would be an unqualified national disaster. In fact, any significant relaxation of drug enforcement – for whatever reason,

however well-intentioned – would promise more use, more crime, and more trouble for desperately needed treatment and education efforts."
– White House drug czar William Bennett, in the National Drug Control Strategy, 1989

The government's drug strategies worked to manipulate public opinion in favor of more funding for the drug war much in the same way Harry Anslinger's propaganda was used to demolish the hemp industry in the 1930s. One difference in the 1980s and beyond is that the prison industry and the guard unions are making huge political donations to politicians who favor building more prisons while increasing funding for prison administrations. As the funding keeps increasing, so does the construction of jails and prisons, the manufacture of prison clothing and equipment, and uniforms. In the past 50 years, the U.S. has built more prisons than any society in the history of the world. Land of the free?

The critics of the government's actions sometimes came from people associated with conservative views. In his syndicated column, *National Review* editor William F. Buckley, Jr. challenged Bennett's concept that legalization would increase crime. Instead, Buckley argued that drug laws were more damaging than the drugs. Buckley theorized that, "If one were to remove from the price of drugs the overhead of sneaking it into the United States, killing or bribing all who stand in the way of this operation, and all who stand in the way of merchandising it in the streets, then the price of it would certainly collapse, and there would be no profit in its sale, save the modest profit of paying the licensed dispenser."

Buckley was familiar with government operations. After graduating from Yale he and his wife moved to Mexico City, where he worked as an undercover CIA agent (spy) to report on communist activities in student groups. His CIA station chief supervisor was E. Howard Hunt, who later helped fashion the Watergate break-in, which lead to the resignation of President Nixon.

Because of job offers that came in after the success of his book, *God and Man at Yale*, which criticized Yale administrators for "failing to uphold Christian ideals," Buckley left the CIA job within a year. Returning to the U.S., he became a sympathizer of Senator John McCarthy's delusional crusade to expose suspected communists in the U.S.

After the Senate discredited and censured McCarthy in 1954, Buckley got busy and started the magazine *National Review* in 1955. This is considered to be the founding of the conservative movement.

After founding his magazine, Buckley distanced himself from the right-wing John Birch Society, anti-Semites, and segregationists. This move both lost magazine subscribers and brought about a more mainstream right-wing conservative movement. Funding the magazine with his speeches and organized events, in 1966 Buckley started the political talk TV show *Firing Line*, which he hosted for 33 years.

By the early 1970s Buckley had grown his hair long and fancied riding a motorcycle around the streets of New York City. To the chagrin of the conservative movement, his magazine featured favorable comments about the Rolling Stones and the Grateful Dead rock groups. In 1972 Buckley spoke out in support of the decriminalization of marijuana and admitted to smoking it on a boat in international waters, outside of the boundaries of U.S. law enforcement. (Why, yes. Of course.)

Interestingly, Buckley was an acquaintance of Ronald Reagan, who Buckley had met in 1960. In 1966 Buckley has supported Reagan's successful campaign to become California governor. By the 1980s Buckley had become a well-known confidant of Reagan. Buckley's column in *National Review* often was specifically written to advise, support, and defend Reagan and his followers. Reagan said that he considered Buckley to be one of the most important intellectuals of his time.

Unfortunately, Reagan didn't listen to Buckley's views on the War on Drugs, and the Reagan drug policies continued to rage as a war against the U.S. citizens.

Where the Reagan administration left off, the George H.W. Bush administration took over, continuing the slide into an unwinnable, expensive, and ruinous War on Drugs.

In 1990 the Transportation Appropriations Act included the requirement that states revoke the driver's licenses for six months of anyone convicted of drug crimes. States that did not comply would risk losing federal funding for highway construction and maintenance. The George H. W. Bush administration also forced Alaska to rescind its law allowing residents of that state to possess small amounts of marijuana for personal use. The administration did this by threatening to withhold federal highway funds from the state.

On June 27, 1991 the Supreme Court ruled that states may impose a life sentence on those convicted of certain drug offenses.

In May 1991 the UN reassigned the THC substance as a Schedule II drug because it displays medical benefits. Oddly, they kept the actual plant in the Schedule I classification. THC is the main substance attributed to getting people "high," not the rest of the plant. Still, it was a small step in acknowledging that the drug had beneficial qualities. The Reagan administration didn't agree.

"Claims of marijuana's medical benefits are a cruel hoax to offer false hope to desperate people."
– Robert Bonner, Drug Enforcement Agency administrator, 1992

In the early 1992 James Mason, George H.W. Bush's chief of Public Health Service, forced the FDA's Compassionate Investigative New Drug program to stop accepting any new patients. This was at a time when many people suffering from AIDS were finding that marijuana was of great help in reducing nausea as well as increasing appetite, helping to ward off the wasting syndrome associated with AIDS.

The administration may as well have told AIDS and cancer patients to go to hell. Denying a helpful medication increased suffering and was of no benefit to society.

"If it is perceived that the Public Health Service is going around giving marijuana to folks, there would be a perception that this stuff can't be so bad."
– James Mason, chief of Public Health Service under George H. W. Bush administration, in explaining why he stopped the government's medicinal marijuana program from accepting applications from AIDS and other patients; 1992

All of these rulings and laws denied patients a valuable medicine. They also increased prison populations. Those doing time for drug "crimes" increased from 16 percent of prison populations in 1970 to 62 percent in 1994.

"The medical, scientific process is open to any drug. That includes marijuana. But you have to get through a process and demonstrate scientific validity. And in this case, to be honest, I think it's nonsense. This is mostly a Cheech and Chong show for the quasi-legalization of marijuana."
– Barry McCaffrey, misinformed and/or lying drug policy chief during the Clinton administration

"The federal antidrug effort, concentrating on police action and mandatory sentences, has in effect led to a race war, with disproportionate arrests of African Americans and Latinos. In addition, the multibillion dollar War on Drugs campaign, started under the Nixon Administration in 1972, has proved so expensive that other services suffer."
– Resolution signed by police chiefs and mayors of San Francisco and Oakland, California, May 1993

Shamefully, as I write this in late 2010, the federal laws banning medicinal marijuana as well as industrial hemp farming in America also remain in effect.

263

Why is hemp farming now illegal in the U.S.? Why is hemp stupidly classified as a drug under the Controlled Substance Act when hemp can't get a person stoned?

Keep reading.

# Strengthening and Continuing the Racist and Corrupt Laws

Outlawing hemp had nothing to do with the so-called evils of marijuana, but did effect what was financially best for some wealthy people, the companies they owned and/or worked for, and for certain politicians and government employees. It had to do with greed.

There are a few dozen varieties of the hemp plant. Only its cousin, which we call marijuana, produces leaves and flowers with high concentrations of delta-9 tetrahydrocannabinol (THC), the pleasurable psycho-active element. Other varieties of the hemp plant contain only trace amounts of THC. The hemp plant that is grown for industrial uses contains cannabidiol, which blocks the effects of THC. You can smoke as much hemp as you want, but you aren't going to get high.

So why is hemp illegal?

Meanwhile, alcohol, which is clearly addictive for many people and plays a role in most domestic violence cases, is freely served at political gatherings. Very often, the alcohol served at political functions and dinners is purchased with tax dollars.

Today the Drug Enforcement Agency (DEA) can seize the property of persons involved in so-called marijuana-related offenses. Those charged with marijuana "crimes" can also be fined, put on probation, have their children taken away, be permanently banned from receiving school funding, and sentenced to time in prison. Depending on the amount of marijuana and the circumstances involved, a person charged with breaking marijuana laws can be put in prison for life. Almost every 45 seconds a U.S. citizen is arrested on marijuana charges.

"Since its inception, the War on Drugs driven by the United States has caused misery of incalculable proportions. In the U.S., it has provoked racism, classism, and been used to incarcerate millions; destroyed both inner cities and rural regions; is responsible for thousands of deaths of both law officers and offenders; and given rise to obscene forfeiture laws intended to go after the property of drug lords but used almost exclusively on small-time and otherwise law-abiding drug users. In the name of the War on Drugs we have watched our civil rights and liberties stolen from us, including the right to be secure in our homes and our right to privacy on phones and the Internet."

– Peter Gorman in the opening paragraph of Do They Know It's Christmas: How the U.S. Drug War Prevents Peace Around the

World, *Cannabis Culture* magazine, November/December 2006; CannabisCulture.com

The result of these insane laws is that at a cost of billions of dollars, many thousands of people are sitting in prison. At times the number of marijuana convictions makes up more than 20 percent of all criminal convictions in the U.S. Many of these imprisoned people are young and in the prime of life. When they are in prison, they are unemployed, forced to cancel or delay their life progression, and are separated from their families and friends. As mentioned earlier, it costs more to keep them in prison than it would to send them to a university. Some are serving life terms simply because they broke marijuana laws that should not exist and that were formed based on lies.

"In the United States and many other nations, it is no longer possible to talk honestly and frankly about racism without talking about the War on Drugs. Few U.S. policies have had as disproportionate effect on Blacks, Latinos and other racial minorities than the War on Drugs. Every policy of the War on Drugs – from racial profiling to arrests to prosecutions to length of sentencing – is disproportionately carried out against minorities. It should come as no surprise that the United States government has used the War on Drugs to reinforce the country's historically racist attitudes towards all minorities and especially Blacks and Latinos. From its very inception the War on Drugs has been laden with racial overtones."
– The Racial History of U.S. Drug Prohibition; Drug Policy Alliance, August. 2001; DrugPolicy.org

In the U.S. the first serious laws against the use of cannabis were enforced in the cities of El Paso, Texas, and in New Orleans, Louisiana.

In 1914 El Paso banned the sale and possession of cannabis within its borders. This could be seen as a direct act against the Mexican population that composed the underclass living in poverty and that carried on the traditions and culture of their native country.

In 1927 the Louisiana legislature passed a law imposing a $500 fine or up to six months in jail for those caught with marijuana. Those arguing for creating the laws used outrageous claims, such as that using marijuana causes incurable insanity. These laws were largely enforced against the African American community, or otherwise those that are not viewed as Caucasian.

Since the passage of the first laws against marijuana the number of state and federal laws against marijuana use, possession, and/or sale have magnified, and so have the jail and prison populations of non-Whites convicted of breaking marijuana laws.

Today there remains a disproportionate number of African Americans and Latinos both charged with and convicted of drug crimes. They are in jails and prisons overcrowded with prisoners who have been arrested for minor drug charges. Very often violent criminals are released to make room for those convicted of nonviolent drug crimes. Meanwhile, the government keeps planning and building more prisons to provide room for the drug offenders.

As I was writing this, the state of California was considering an $11 billion increase in funding to expand the prison system. In 2010, California had over 167,000 prisoners and was spending $8 billion, about 11% of its budget, on the penal system, more than on higher education. Many thousands of prisoners in the system are there after having been convicted of breaking marijuana laws. This prison expansion was being planned under pressure of a governor who not only has admitted to using marijuana, but also can be seen smoking a joint on a popular video clip on the Internet site YouTube. In the clip, Arnold reclines on a sofa, takes a big drag off a joint, and slowly exhales the smoke with a most pleasurable expression on his face. The T-shirt he is wearing features the words, "Arnold is Number Uno."

While the economy is flailing, Americans are buried under debt, tens of thousands are losing their homes to foreclosure, and the auto and banking systems are a mess, billions of dollars continue to be spent on funding the domestic war on drugs. The same amount of money could otherwise improve society through protecting the environment, improving schools, building monorails in large cities to reduce petroleum use, and making the country self-sufficient.

This is done by a country with a history of helping other countries run their drug trade of heroin, opium, morphine, cocaine, and cannabis. Numerous books explore these events, including *Powderburns: Cocaine, Contras, and the Drug War*, by former DEA agent Celerino Castillo. Another is *Drugs, Oil, and War: The United States in Afghanistan, Colombia, and Indochina*, by Peter Dale Scott.

# Drugs and War

It is no secret that Air America was a CIA front that transported heroin and opium around Vietnam during the war. U.S. soldiers also used drugs to escape the tremendous horrors of that terribly wrong war, and many of them became addicted.

It is also no secret that the U.S. government protected China's opium trade in the 1960s. With the help of the CIA office in Laos, the opium from China and Southeast Asia was flown into American cities.

Similar operations have built the cocaine business out of South America, allowing funding for military operations in the Americas. Some of this has been done in cooperation with mob bosses and others living in the U.S.

The Kennedy administration and the CIA participated with the Chicago mob syndicate in planning to take Cuba by assassinating Fidel Castro. The Chicago mob made lots of money from heroin and wanted back into the Cuban casinos and night clubs that they controlled before Castro took over.

Nixon was well aware of the CIA's interaction with Turkish heroin producers to fund military operations in Turkey just as Nixon was declaring drugs as "public enemy number one."

It is no secret that the U.S. government has run a U.S. School of the Americas to provide training for those involved with political and military activities in South and Central America. The school has provided instruction in assassination, torture, corrupting vote counts, and other such activities to manipulate the government organizations of Latin America. Some who have attended the training are clearly involved in international cocaine trading to fund military and/or political activities that agree with U.S. government interests – often for the exploitation of natural resources and/or land and labor.

It is no secret that in the 1970s the Israelis were supplying guns to the Christians in exchange for hashish. And it was being done with the cooperation of other governments.

It is no secret that Bolivia's cocaine production multiplied during the 1980s with the cooperation of the CIA trainees. Peru's government is another that has been largely funded through its cocaine industry, especially during the 1990s, and in cooperation with both the CIA and DEA. The Columbian drug cartel has made money both because of and in spite of the U.S. government. Nicaragua's history is rife with U.S. intervention, drug money, and war funded with it.

Most, if not all, of the White House administrations in the last several decades have had some interaction with the international drug trade, often cooperating to get the U.S. political goals met. This may have involved simply looking the other way while the CIA played their games with politics in other countries. The games involve selling U.S. weaponry to governments that buy the equipment using drug money, and the games involve training courtesy of the CIA and U.S. military. Often these games are played at the expense of the lives of innocent people and for the benefit of multinational corporations.

President Carter stands out as an example of one who tried to stop some of the U.S. participation in worldwide drug trafficking. For instance, he cut off funding to Nicaragua's President Anastasio Somoza Garcia. Carter also wanted to do away with laws against the personal use of marijuana, which would have cut funding to prison construction because fewer people would be locked up. It would also have greatly reduced the price of marijuana, which would have made a lot of powerful people lose money. He also wanted to make the punishment for breaking drug laws no worse than any harm the drug could do to the individual.

Carter viewed the country's reliance on foreign fuel the moral equivalent of conducting warfare. He envisioned a future where people relied less on petroleum and more on plant-based fuels, solar energy, and wind turbines. His administration founded the National Renewable Energy Laboratory in Golden, Colorado. The NREL has been underfunded since the Reagan administration. In 1986 Reagan also foolishly removed the solar panels that Carter had installed on the roof of the White House (they were then moved to Unity College in Main to heat their water system). If there was ever a structure that should be held as an example of environmentally sustainable living it should be the White House. Unfortunately, this has not been the case. But, interestingly, the George W. Bush White House installed solar panels on the roof in 2002. (His "ranch" in Texas also uses a lot of green technology, including solar panels. In 2010, the Obama White House announced that more solar panels will be installed at the White house to make the place more sustainable.)

While the U.S. Bureau of Narcotics had great control on the goings-on in Afghanistan, especially during the early 1970s, it was during Carter's administration that the CIA became more involved in the Afghanistan fight against the invading Soviets.

A Texas Congressman named Charlie Wilson had a lot to do with how the U.S. funded weaponry for the Afghanistan armies throughout the 1980s to shoot down Soviet military planes and helicopters, and to blow up Soviet tanks. When this story was turned into a feature film, *Charlie Wilson's War*, starring actors Tom Hanks and Julia Roberts I was asked if I wanted to work on the movie. I am an extra in the opening scene and am briefly seen standing behind Julia Roberts as she is in an audience listing to Tom Hanks speak.

Many view the U.S. funding of the Afghanistan fighters as the U.S. working to protect its access to petroleum, and to land where petroleum pipelines could be built.

We will likely never know how involved the White House was in these decisions, or how independently the CIA was acting – such as if it were acting against the wishes of the Carter administration. To fund the Afghan fight, the CIA participated in the opium farming in Pakistan and Afghanistan. The CIA not only allowed the opium farming to expand, it also helped transport the drugs to other countries. The laws creating the drug war are what made the drug business so lucrative. The laws were in place before Carter took office. He wanted to get rid of some of them, and soften others, which, as mentioned, would have caused the drug prices to collapse.

Carter was not favored by those in power, who were more than happy to see him go. It would take volumes to describe the events that took place the day Carter left office, and how those events came to be through the people working against him behind the scenes. It wasn't a coincidence that the American hostages were released in Iran on the day Reagan took office, it was an arrangement. By whom? That's another book that someone else can write.

The Reagan administration became highly involved in the politics of Central America, specifically with activities to overthrow the Sandinistas in Nicaragua. When Congress cut off funding to the Contras, the U.S. military, CIA, DEA, U.S. Embassy in Costa Rica, and high-ranking officials in the U.S. National Security Council Staff covertly helped the Contras fund their war with cocaine through El Salvador, Costa Rica, and Panama. Large amounts of the drugs were landing in U.S. cities, with the cooperation of the U.S. government. This was all being done while Reagan was talking about fighting drugs, allowing the military and private businesses to begin urine testing to detect drug use, and his wife undertook her "Just Say No!" campaign to encourage children to stay away from drugs.

Similar to most children of modern-day presidents, at least a couple of the Reagan children weren't exactly perfect examples of drug-free citizens. Nancy took her campaign internationally, and invited First Ladies from dozens of countries to the White House for her "First Ladies Conference on Drug Abuse." Throughout the next decade it was common to see "Just Say No!" bumper stickers on police cars and school busses, and on many cars confiscated in drug busts.

In 1986, at the height of Nancy Reagan's anti-drug crusade, the Partnership for a Drug Free America (PDFA) was formed and was supported with millions in tax-deductible "charitable" donations from the petroleum, lumber, alcohol, tobacco, and pharmaceutical industries – The Petroleum, lumber, alcohol, and pharmaceutical industries had financial

270

interests in keeping industrial hemp and medicinal marijuana illegal. Saudi Arabia also donated to the "Just Say No!" campaign, after the Reagan administration agreed to sell them fighter jets. In 1997 the PDFA announced that it no longer accepted donations from the tobacco or alcoholic beverage industries. The pharmaceutical industry, which produces billions of pills that are sold on the streets, lead to addictions (even when taken as prescribed), and result in overdoses and side-effects that cause all sorts of health problems, including over one hundred thousand fatalities every year, continues to support the PDFA.

By the late 1980s, Partnership for a Drug Free America was producing a series of public service advertisement that ran in both the print and electronic media. One of the PSAs used the image of fried eggs with the slogan, "This is your brain on drugs." That particular PSA was satirized by look-alike ads featuring a pile of dog poop with the slogan, "This is your country under Reagan's leadership."

Meanwhile, the inner cities were erupting in what could be described as drug warfare between gangs, drug smugglers, and law enforcement. And prison populations were quickly increasing as more and more people were charged and convicted of drug crimes. And the endless pit of the U.S. military costs increasingly became tangled with the U.S. drug war that was spreading throughout Latin America. Reagan claimed that he didn't know about many of the activities taking place in Central America. His own daughter, actress and writer "Patti Davis" Reagan, was one of the most outspoken critics of the Administration, not only about the drug war in the U.S. and Central America, but also about U.S. policy in Columbia, and about many of Ronald and Nancy Reagan's conservative views.

A series of critical and highly criticized articles about the CIA smuggling cocaine from Central America into Los Angeles was published in the *San Jose Mercury News*. Written by the late Gary Webb, the 1996 articles, Dark Alliance, can be viewed on the Internet. Webb also came out with a book titled *Dark Alliance: The CIA, the Contras, and the Crack Cocaine Explosion*.

Another interesting book to read on this topic is *Firewall: The Iran-Contra Conspiracy and Cover-Up*, by Lawrence E. Walsh, independent counsel for the Iran-Contra investigation. Another that covers a broad range of issues relating to the drug trade and how it works is *Drug Wars and Coffeehouses: The Political Economy of the International Drug Trade*, by David R. Mares.

During Reagan's years, under CIA cooperation, Pakistan became a major supplier of heroin, with much of the heroin landing in Europe and America to fund the Northern Alliance in Afghanistan. Among the CIA allies in Afghanistan was a man named Osama bin Laden, who the CIA trained, funded, and supplied with weaponry. Bin Laden's organization

271

recruited mercenaries to fight against the Soviets. Among the substances grown to raise money for the insurgency was cannabis on slave farms in southern Sudan. Through these operations bin Laden funded his al-Qaeda. When the Soviets retreated, the aftermath left Afghanistan politically divided. These series of events are tied into U.S. political maneuverings in Iran and Iraq. This all led to the situation that exists today.

It is no secret that the U.S. government has a history of funding foreign wars, training people to fight the wars, trading weapons, and doing much of this in ways that broke all sorts of laws – and in ways that involved enormous amounts of drugs, and the deaths of many people – while other people profited from the events, including certain American companies.

Another way the U.S. has been involved in the drug trade is that the U.S. has paid subsidies to farmers (including encouraging and paying farmers to grow tobacco [an addictive health-destroying substance]) in other countries to stop them from producing heroin, cocaine, opium, and cannabis when it is politically savvy for the U.S. to do so, and eliminating the subsidies when it is in U.S. favor (or when it favors U.S. corporations and wealthy businesspeople who donate large sums to certain politicians and their parties). Of course some of these subsidies work more as political bribes because they never make it to the farmers, and instead are used as payoffs to authorities, to governments, and to military people, or to the companies owned by the same, in both the U.S. and other countries. It is no secret that the U.S. government has been involved in closing down drug farms to prevent certain groups from getting money through the international drug trade. And vice versa.

Airplanes, helicopters, guns, and other equipment provided by or through the workings of the American government to countries to control the drug trade are often used for military activities by the receiving party. Sometimes it very much appears that the supplies are given more for military activity to overthrow governments or to fight against factions the U.S. opposes.

Sometimes these activities backfire when a group that gathers funds through international drug networks with U.S. help then goes about using the money against the U.S. military or U.S. citizens traveling in foreign countries.

The drug trade involves enormous amounts of money, and where that exists, the government and corporations get involved.

All of this has been going on for decades while the administrations have presented an image to the American people that the White House is tough on drugs and is dealing rightfully.

It is a wonder what is really going on in Afghanistan. In 2007, Peter Bergen, the author of *Holy War, Inc.: Inside the Secret World of Osama bin Laden*, visited the governor's mansion in Uruzgan in Southern Afghanistan. What

272

he saw were poppy fields "stretching as far as the eyes could see." The southern parts of the country produced record amounts of opium in 2007. It is estimated that the Helmand Province has increased its opium production by nearly half. This meant that Afghanistan was supplying more than 90% of the world's opium. In the 1990s it was supplying about 70%, and less than 50% in the 1980s. This increase in Afghanistan opium is at a time when the U.S. has been keeping a huge military presence in the country, which some reasonably call an "occupation." It is also during a time that the U.S. government claims to be providing $600 million to Afghanistan to eradicate poppy farming, which creates warfare in Afghanistan with poor farmers fighting against armies and security forces funded with international money. European forces do not support the U.S. eradication policies. The U.S. stance keeps spreading the troublesome U.S. drug war standards into other countries, and into international politics. The 2007 strategy of the U.S. State Department was to spend 6% of its counter-narcotics spending in Afghanistan on funding "alternative livelihoods," such as getting farmers to grow other crops. The rest of the money was apparently meant to be spent on the intensified drug war: bullets, guns, missiles, prisons, eradication using toxic chemicals that poison the environment, etc.

In August 2007, the United Nations estimated that there were 477,000 acres of poppy fields growing in Afghanistan. It isn't like thousands of acres of poppies can't be found. But the main questions I have regarding all of this are, where has all of that money been spent, and who is benefiting by the sale of all of this opium? And also, why are they doing it, and what drove them to this point? Does it stem from oil, and a war based on such?

In October 2010, Russian antinarcotic agents joined U.S. DEA agents and some Afghanistan officials with the backing of the U.S. military to conduct a drug raid in an eastern Afghani town. They claim to have found four drug-processing labs and to have seized about $56 million worth of heroin, but how that figure was factored is likely lost in back-patting. President Hamid Karzai condemned NATO for the raid, was angry that Russians were allowed to participate in the raid within Afghanistan borders without the approval of the Islamic Republic of Afghanistan, and he demanded an investigation. While Afghanistan and Russian relations had been improving between their political leaders in Kabul and Moscow, there is still that bit of history with the 1979-80 Soviet invasion, Charlie Wilson's War, the CIA covert activities with Afghanistan-grown opium (and cannabis), and the CIA training of some group lead by some guy named Osama bin Laden, supported with drug sales, in cooperation with the CIA.

Why are the DEA and U.S. military so involved in drug raids in a distant country to the point that they are joining up with the Russians and Afghanistan officials? They may claim that the drugs go to fund so-called

273

terrorist groups, but the CIA has a history of helping to develop the Afghanistan opium fields (an cannabis fields) and trade since at least the 1980s. Oh, wait, a lot of people say that the CIA is a terrorist organization. Nevermind.

Even as I write this, Afghanistan is the world leader in both opiate drug (opium, heroin, morphine) production and hashish (from cannabis resin) production. Afghanistan presently has the largest number of U.S. soldiers within its border now than it ever has. Funny how that works.

If the purpose of the DEA and U.S. military activities is to secure the U.S. and protect its citizens, why not focus on providing security so that bombs can't by flown into U.S. cities, the way they did the very same week the Afghanistan drug raid took place during the last week of October 2010, when airplanes from Yemen landed in New York and Pennsylvania? The U.S. instantly was blaming Al Qaeda, and that was what was reported in the corporate-owned media, so that is what we are supposed to believe – because everything in the news is the truth. Right?

I'm a bit weary of the black and white definition of "Taliban" or "Al Qaeda," and "terrorists," and so forth. I also don't believe we are being told who may be supporting whatever groups are being blamed for these messy situations, what their goals are, and how they fund their activities, including how they get the materials needed to process opium into heroin – and how they go about distributing it all over the planet. I also don't advocate spraying poppy fields with chemical defoliants or herbicides, which poison the air, land, and water, damage wildlife, and raise rates of cancer and birth defects in humans.

Perhaps treating opium and other drugs the way they are treated in the Netherlands would be most beneficial, and it would make the profits of the international drug market plunge while saving many billions of dollars on the Drug War, which could then be spent on schools, healthcare, the environment, infrastructure, alternative energy technology, monorails in large cities, and other things that benefit society. A world with less reliance on foreign oil, and also on fossil fuels in general, would create a situation where other countries wouldn't have interest in raiding other countries to exploit their petroleum resources. This is another reason why industrial hemp farming should be legalized, to help create homegrown, "alternative," non-fossil fuels.

In addition to Central and South America, Vietnam, Afghanistan, and Pakistan, drugs have helped to finance political activities and so-called "crime syndicates" in Africa, Chechnya, Kosovo, Northern Ireland, Serbia, Uzbekistan, and Southeast Asia. While much of this has been financed with opium, heroin, and cocaine, huge amounts of money have been raised by supplying cannabis in its various forms to the world market.

With domestic production of cannabis in any region becoming more common with the use of interior grow rooms, cannabis has lost some of its use as a war and foreign policy fund-raiser. Prices of cannabis would dramatically decrease and billions of dollars of government money would be saved if personal use and possession of small amounts of cannabis were made legal. But maybe it serves certain people in political positions to keep up the price, similar to how the mobsters were working to control alcohol distribution and sales as well as certain politicians and corporations during the 1920s and early 1930s.

# 1990s

The War on Drugs continued into the 1990s as former CIA Director George H.W. Bush was sworn in as the 41st U.S. president in 1989. One of his more famous quotes is the one in which, like other Republican presidents, he seems to be declaring war on Americans:

"Some think there won't be enough room for them [those arrested on drug charges] in jail. We'll make room. We're almost doubling prison space. Some think there aren't enough prosecutors. We'll hire them with the largest increase in federal prosecutors in history."
– President George H.W. Bush

By the mid-90s the U.S. was spending several billion dollars per year on its failed attempts to try to control marijuana use. At that time the country was in the middle of the biggest prison-building boom the world had ever seen. In the meantime, school funding was being cut. School sports programs were being cut. School art and music programs were being cut. And the cost of going to college was going up – and still is. And more people were going to prison for marijuana charges than ever.

Some people believe that the drug war situation will change with the Obama administration, and it may. But presidents often straddle the bipartisan fence more during their first terms, and then do their most dramatic work in their second term. The changes people really want to see may not happen for a few years – if ever. However, in December 2008, President Elect Obama nominated former Iowa Governor Tom Vilsack for the position of Secretary of Agriculture. As a Senator, in 1997 Vilsack voted in committee to pass a hemp study bill. Like many politicians are now doing, Obama has admitted to smoking weed in his younger days.

"I would start with nonviolent, first-time drug offenders. The notion that we are imposing felonies on them or sending them to prison, where they are getting advanced degrees in criminality, instead of thinking about ways like drug courts that can get them back on track in their lives – it's expensive, it's counterproductive, and it doesn't make sense."
– Barack Obama, as quoted in *Rolling Stone Magazine*, July 2008

Obama's vice president, Joe Biden, has been a strong supporter of U.S. preposterous drug policy, and has served as chairman of the Senate Judiciary Committee, in which he dealt with drug policy, crime prevention, and civil liberties. U.S. drug policy has abused and neglected civil liberties

276

and Biden helped write the laws creating the Drug Czar appointee who is over national drug control policy. However, some in the hemp industry rather hopefully point out that Biden's focus was on drug rape drugs, such as Ketamine. Biden is known for being a liberal and the American Civil Liberties Union gives him a high score, including a score of 91 percent for his work in the 2008 session of Congress. It is also hopeful that Biden will wisen up and react accordingly to the great burden the War on Drugs has placed on minorities. As a teenager, Biden was involved with protesting segregation. In his first run for U.S. Senate he was positioned against a buddy of Richard Nixon, J. Caleb Boggs. Even though Biden's campaign was greatly underfunded, he won the election, which was not appreciated by the Nixon administration. An automobile accident just weeks after his election win took the life of Biden's wife and daughter, and injured his two sons. Biden was sworn into office while standing next to the hospital bed of one of his injured sons.

"Once he (Obama) is president, the (United States) will engage vigorously in theses negotiations and help to lead the world toward a new era on global cooperation on climate change."
– Al Gore speaking at the United Nations Climate Change Conference, Poznan, Poland, Friday, December 12, 2008. Days prior to this Conference, Gore had met with President-elect Obama in Chicago.

Some people are expecting Obama to form a commission to study the U.S. drug policy, and to recommend changes. If such a commission does get appointed, it is likely that it will suggest major changes in drug policy, including a wiser use of resources, changes in the justice system, and an overhaul of the laws regarding marijuana and hemp.

"Famously, Franklin Delano Roosevelt saved the United States banking system during the first seven days of his first term.
And what did he do on the eighth day? "I think this would be a good time for beer," he said.
Congress had already repealed Prohibition, pending ratification from the states. But the people needed a lift, and legalizing beer would create a million jobs. And lo, booze was back. Two days after the bill passed, Milwaukee brewers hired six hundred people and paid their first $10 million in taxes. Soon the auto industry was tooling up the first $12 million worth of delivery trucks, and brewers were pouring tens of millions into new plants."
– John H. Richardson, "Why Obama Really Might Decriminalize Marijuana," Esquire Magazine; Dec. 23, 2008

There have been subtle signs that the Obama administration is seeing through the problems of U.S. drug policy, breaking away from the same old same of the Democrat/Republican oligarchy. The administration instructed the federal government to avoid interfering with medicinal marijuana sales in states where medicinal marijuana has been approved. Maybe, if they stay in office, the Obama administration will be making wiser decisions in regards to creating a U.S. industrial hemp industry, including for food, fuel, paper, fabric, insulation, building materials, and biodegradable plastics. It can't happen soon enough.

Unfortunately, Obama has backtracked on his statements against nuclear energy that he made during his presidential campaign, and has been advocating the construction of more nuclear power plants. He should buzz off of the nuclear powerplant bandwagon and get on with getting industrial hemp approved in the U.S.

"More money has been spent trying to find something wrong with cannabis than any other vegetable material in human history."
– Terence McKenna, author of *Food of the Gods: The Search for the Original Tree of Knowledge: A Radical History of Plants, Drugs, and Human Evolution*

"When I smoked pot it was illegal, but not immoral. Now it is illegal and immoral. The law didn't change, only the morality. That's why you get to go to jail and I don't."
– Newt Gingrich, Republican Speaker of the House, 1997. This smarmy hypocrite introduced the Drug Importer Death Penalty Act that called for the life imprisonment for those importing what could be 100 doses of an illegal substance, and the death penalty for those convicted on a second offense.

The previous Democratic president, Bill Clinton, did not have a good history with how he and his administration handled the War on Drugs. It stayed strong as a war on U.S. citizens.

Marijuana arrests skyrocketed during the Clinton administration. He also initiated a $15.1 billion commitment to reduce drug use in the U.S. Both Clinton and Al Gore had admitted to smoking marijuana (Clinton famously claimed that he didn't inhale).

The Clinton/Gore drug war funding didn't do much to stop people from smoking marijuana, especially not Al Gore's son, Albert Gore III, who was busted on cannabis charges in 2003 in Bethesda, Maryland, and was busted again on July 4, 2007 in Laguna Niguel, California. Maybe the boy simply misunderstood his father's advice to "go green." Within hours of his arrest he had already spent more time in jail than Scooter Libby.

Gore is hardly the first, and not the last, politician's child to smoke weed, including the ones with the last names Kennedy, Carter, Reagan, Bush, and Bush. Movie star and husband of Demi Moore, Ashton Kutcher, told a magazine interviewer that he got stoned with Bush twins Jenna and Barbara at his Hollywood Hills home by smoking weed in a hookah pipe.

In addition to the children of presidents, the offspring of congresspersons also have a broad history of marijuana use. California Republican Congressman Duke Cunningham, who was so outspoken about strengthening the drug laws, found himself in the peculiar situation of finding that his son, Randy, was busted with 400 pounds of marijuana. Minnesota Republican Congressman Rod Grams once called the police to help find his son, Morgan. They found his son, and ten bags of marijuana in the boy's vehicle. Republican Representative Dan Burton, who backed the idea of creating laws applying the death penalty to drug dealers, asked a judge for leniency when Dan Burton II was convicted of possessing marijuana with intent to sell. There is a long list of politician's children and other family members who have been busted for breaking pot laws.

> "Politicians' children probably don't use illegal drugs more than other young people do, but they are the victims of a special irony: the laws that ensnare them are often written by their parents!"
> – Pete Brady, *Cannabis Culture* magazine, July 2004;
> CannabisCulture.com

It is likely that the great majority of politicians have either tried, or do smoke marijuana, as have and do judges who sentence people to jail for pot offenses (Chief Justice Clarence Thomas has admitted to smoking weed), and those working in law enforcement who hold jobs where they regularly arrest people on marijuana charges. During her run for government, that Tea Party charmer, Sarah Palin, admitted to having smoked weed in her younger days (Some fine varieties of marijuana are known to grow in Alaska). The drug history of George W. Bush is well known (He increased the billions of dollars being spent on the drug war). Earlier presidents who are known to have smoked cannabis include Washington, Jefferson, Madison, Monroe, Jackson, Taylor, Pierce, Lincoln, Kennedy, and probably Nixon (who had a well-known problem with alcohol, including alcohol-fueled temper tantrums and blackouts during his time in the White House). And now, Obama.

All of this drug war stuff increased the price of illegal drugs, making it enticing for those who need cash, or who at least want to make a quick ten grand. Throughout the decades there have been cases of the underground

279

drug market being helped along by those who are in professions meant to stifle the drug trade.

On January 21, 1998, federal agents charged 44 Ohio and New York police and corrections officers with helping to run the cocaine underground in northern Ohio. The arrests took place after a two-year investigation into organized crime in and around Cleveland. During the investigation the officers had escorted federal agents posing as cocaine dealers. Oops!

More common is a situation in which officers aren't involved in making money from drugs, but sometimes partake of illegal substances.

While I was writing this book I spoke with a man who worked as a police officer in the drug unit of a major American city during the 1990s. He told me that it wasn't uncommon to smoke weed with his fellow officers on the weekend after taking a little weed from batches of confiscated marijuana. He said that if it showed up in a blood test they could easily reason that he breathed it in during a drug bust or undercover investigation. But, he said, as far as he knew, the officers didn't take hard drugs like cocaine or heroin because they couldn't rationalize that. They simply liked to relax now and then with a little puff of a burning dried leaf. "No harm in that," he said. His expression was dubious when I mentioned to him that it was kind of bizarre that he was busting people for smoking marijuana when he was one who enjoyed marijuana. Or, maybe he was being elusive because he had just smoked a doobie that morning.

"If the misery of the poor be caused not by the laws of nature, but by our institutions, great is our sin."
– Charles Darwin

Those who are working to eradicate marijuana farms are faced with a new challenge. In 2004 Mexican soldiers trying to rid the Michoacan region of Mexico of pot farms discovered a genetically altered variety of marijuana. This new variety will grow back if the roots are not destroyed and it produces much more pot per acre than other varieties. It also grows year-round, which means that the authorities will no longer be able to schedule their pot farm raids for the typical harvest season. Because the plant does not die if it is sprayed with herbicides, some believe that it has been modified using the same science used to genetically modify corn, soy, and other food crops against toxic herbicides. The Mexican drug war and political corruption related to it has intensified and become increasingly violent in recent years. Over 2,000 people died in drug-related raids and drug syndicate killings in 2006. Organized drug traffickers seeking to protect their production and distribution channels are utilizing high-tech spyware. Using genetically modified plants is one of their latest uses of modern technology. Most of their equipment, including their weaponry, originates in the U.S.

"The war on drugs has been a disaster, creating failed states in the developing world even as addiction has flourished in the rich world. By any sensible measures, this 100-year struggle had been illiberal, murderous, and pointless. That is why The Economist continues to believe that the least bad policy is to legalize drugs."
– The Economist, March 7, 2009; Economist.com

# Personal Vices

> "It's estimated that the state of Oregon spends $60 million
> enforcing marijuana laws. Meanwhile the state is facing shortfalls in
> school and health care budgets. We're wasting time that should be used
> to catch real criminals and money that should be spent on our people's
> education and health care!"
> – Madeline Martinez, executive director of Oregon NORML
> (National Organization for the Reform of Marijuana Laws), 41,000
> Signatures Turned In for Lowest Priority Initiative, *Cannabis
> Community News*, Summer 2006; ORNORML.org

Some cities have voted to make personal marijuana use among its
citizens the lowest law enforcement priority. In November 2006 the city of
Santa Barbara, California, did so with apparently no incident. Voters there
overwhelmingly approved Measure P, which made smoking marijuana for
any reason the lowest priority of law enforcement.

In November 2006, when the voters in the city of Santa Monica,
California, approved a measure to make personal marijuana use the lowest
law enforcement priority, the city's new police chief, Timothy Jackman,
stated, "My officers have a lot more important things to spend their time
on, like tracking down murderers and rapists."

The day after Santa Monica voters approved the measure to place
marijuana as the lowest priority of the police department, the city erupted
into massive rioting. Teenagers who smoked weed ran through the streets
shattering store windows and overturning cars. Crazed office workers
stoned on pot threw their computers and office furniture into the streets.
Hippies under the influence of marijuana chased terrified elderly residents
through the streets. Bank workers blazing on high-grade chronic opened
the vaults, threw piles of money into the streets and lit them on fire. The
police department was overwhelmed and retreated into City Hall. Pot
smokers began smashing cars into schools and setting public buildings on
fire. Driverless trucks were rammed into gas stations, which caused the
underground storage tanks to explode. The fire department refused to enter
the riot zones. Half the city became engulfed in flames. So many people
were smoking weed that the smell of it permeated the city, and the clouds
of smoke could be seen on satellite images. Huge clouds of pot smoke were
wafting into surrounding communities, which also experienced some
rioting, looting, and instances of crazy stoned grandmothers wildly dancing
in the streets. News helicopters trying to film the uprising from the sky
were shot at by machine gun-brandishing pot-smoking hellions. Packs of
marijuana-puffing, bikini-clad surfer girls overtook, tied up, and sexually

assaulted the local lifeguards. Bong-toking retirees in high-rise condos threw bottle bombs onto passing cars. Society as the city residents had known it came to an abrupt halt.

Actually, that last paragraph may be what some people think could happen if personal marijuana use were legalized. But, the day after the law passed, nothing out of the ordinary happened in Santa Monica. Life went on as usual. The only difference was that the police department could focus on matters other than the possible crime of marijuana smoking.

When it is taken into consideration that marijuana can easily be purchased by anyone who wants it, and that it is being grown in homes, commercial buildings and secret gardens throughout North America, one would have to wonder why the government spends billions of dollars every year on trying to control the plant.

"The FBI reports that 65 to 75 percent of violent crime is alcohol related."
– Family Council on Drug Awareness, FCDA.org

"Cigarette smoking is the most important preventable cause of premature death in the United States. It accounts for nearly 440,000 of the more than 2.4 million annual deaths. Cigarette smokers have a higher risk of developing several chronic disorders. These include fatty buildups in arteries, several types of cancer and chronic obstructive pulmonary disease (lung problems). Atherosclerosis (buildup of fatty substances in the arteries) is a chief contributor to the high number of deaths from smoking. Many studies detail the evidence that cigarette smoking is a major cause of coronary heart disease, which leads to heart attack."
– American Heart Association, December 2008

"The total cost of caring for people with health problems caused by cigarette smoking – counting all sources of medical payments – is about $72.7 billion per year, according to health economists at the University of California."
– The Berkeleyan, By Patricia McBroom, Public Affairs, September 16, 1998; berkeley.edu/news/berkeleyan

"Every year, cigarette smoking causes an estimated 259,494 deaths among men and 178,408 deaths among women. The three leading causes of death attributed to cigarettes are lung-cancer, chronic obstructive pulmonary disease, and heart disease. An estimated 38,112

lung cancer and heart disease deaths annually are caused by exposure to secondhand smoke."
– Centers for Disease Control and Prevention study, 2005

Alcohol is a drug and cigarettes contain a drug called nicotine. Alcohol and cigarettes are a much greater problem than marijuana has ever been; yet alcohol and cigarettes are advertised and sold everywhere possible. Alcohol plays a part in over 60 percent of all murders, half of all driving fatalities, and the majority of domestic violence cases. Even legal drugs, which we call "prescription drugs," play a part in the deaths of more than 100,000 Americans every year. When was the last time you heard of someone dying from marijuana?

A French study that reviewed 10,748 drivers who were involved in fatal car accidents found that 28.6 percent of the accidents were attributed to alcohol and 2.5 percent were attributed to marijuana. Three percent of those in the marijuana group also had alcohol in their system.
– Cannabis intoxication and fatal road crashes in France: population-based case-control study; *British Medical Journal*, December 1, 2005 BMJ.com

Many people who drink alcohol do so because they say it "relaxes" them. That is the same reason many people smoke marijuana.
"Lushes" was a term used in the jazz and blues community of the 1920s to describe alcohol drinkers who didn't smoke reefer, but who seemed to cause a lot of problems.

"Man, they can say what they want about vipers [weed smokers], but you just dig them lushounds [alcohol drinkers] with their old antique jive, always comin' up loud and wrong, whippin' their old ladies and wastin' up all their pay, and then the next day your head feels like all the hammers in the piano is beatin' out a tune on your brain. Just look at the difference between you and them other cats, that come uptown juiced to the gills, crackin' out of line and passin' out in anybody's hallway. Don't nobody come up thataway when he picks up on some good grass."
– A friend of jazz musician Milton Mezz Mezzrow talking to Mezzrow as recalled in his 1946 autobiography, *Really the Blues*

Probably the large majority of the people involved in arresting and convicting marijuana offenders either smoke cigarettes, drink alcohol, or both. What makes the recreational activities of the enforcers of the corrupt

284

marijuana laws any better than the people they are arresting for marijuana use?

Maybe Richard Nixon explained it really well. Or maybe he didn't.

Richard Nixon: "Why in the name of God do these people take this stuff?"

John Ehrlichman: "For the same reason they drink. It's uh, they're bored, it's uh, it's a diversion."

Nixon: "Drinking is a different thing in a sense. Uh, Linkletter's point I think is well taken. He says, 'A person may drink to have a good time' "

Ehrlichman: "Mm-hmm."

Nixon: "But a person does not drink simply for the purpose of getting high. You take drugs for the purpose of getting high."

Ehrlichman: "Yep, yep."

Nixon: "There is a difference."

– Oval Office conversation 510-3 between Richard Nixon with John Ehrlichman, June 2, 1971, Time: 3:16 pm - 4:15 pm. As detailed on the Web site for Common Sense for Drug Policy, CSDP.org/News/News/Nixon.htm.

Nixon was referring to Art Linkletter, the TV personality, who became an outspoken advocate of stronger drug laws after his daughter fell to her death from a high rise building, apparently while she was under the influence of LSD. Linklater largely accused Timothy Leary of influencing his daughter to take the drug. Linkletter later changed his views on the Drug War, considering that it isn't the solution. He advised parents who found their children to be on drugs to avoid calling the police, but to stay calm, get them into a safe place, and talk them down, and try to talk some sense into them.

"Despite its lurid reputation, marijuana seems no more harmful than alcohol. Though habitual criminals often use it, psychiatrists and police narcotic experts have never been able to prove that it induces criminal tendencies in otherwise normal people. It is less habit-forming than tobacco, alcohol, or opium."

– The Weed, *Time Magazine*, July 19, 1943

"The only clinically significant medical problem that is scientifically linked to marijuana is bronchitis. Like smoking tobacco, the treatment is the same: stop smoking."

– Dr. Fred Oerther, M.D., 1991

Even the amount of jail time that a so-called marijuana offender receives is beyond unfair. A person convicted of manslaughter may spend one year in prison. A pot grower may spend five or more years in prison.

"In 1978, after 202 years of Nationhoood, there were 300,000 Americans in state and federal prisons and another 150,000 in country jails (for all crimes). There were only 45,000 prison guards nationwide. At that time, the construction of schools and universities was a thriving growth industry. At least five times more was being spent on schools than on prisons.

Suddenly, in 1978, new leadership in prison guards unions molded the previously ineffectual guards into one of the most politically powerful lobbying blocks in the country. What the guards wanted was longer and longer determinant sentences for less and less serious crimes, and with virtually no time off for good behavior to assure rapidly growing prison populations.

In the last 20 years, these powerful correctional officers unions became the largest single contributors to state legislators – and mostly to the Republican party. Now in 1998, there are more than 1,200,000 people in prison, 550,000 in jail and the penal system supports 230,000 prison guards!

Today, prison construction and prison employment are among the largest growth industries in the U.S., while federal and state spending for new schools has dwindled to less than one-fifth that of prison building expenditures.

What kind of society would rather build jails than schools?"
– Jack Herer, Los Angeles, August 6, 1998; author of *The Emperor Wears No Clothes*; JackHerer.com

The marijuana convictions do not accomplish anything other than create problems, destroy the lives of those who are convicted, and use up tax money and court time that can be used on something more useful and meaningful to society. This is done at the expense of taxpayers — not only because it costs money to convict and imprison the offenders, but also because the offenders lose their jobs and therefore cannot pay taxes while they sit in prison.

If everyone in the U.S. who has smoked pot were to be jailed, there would have to be jails built to hold tens of millions of so-called marijuana offenders.

You can be charged with any number of crimes, still hold a job, and consume lots of alcohol and be a chain smoker of cigarettes. But if you work at certain companies that do urine testing for marijuana, you can be out of a job for smoking a joint.

286

Meanwhile, schools are rightly declared to be drug-free zones, but every day American children swallow truckloads of risky prescription personality drugs known as selective serotonin reuptake inhibitors that carry the side effect of suicide. The teachers take their breaks to smoke cigarettes, which are more addictive than cocaine and heroin. In the cafeterias the children and school staff members are served junk food, fried food, candy, sodas, and foods containing saturated fat, trans fats, cholesterol, corn syrup, artificial sweeteners, and chemical food additives that destroy health, damage bone and muscles, alter brain function, compromise neural development, increase obesity, and help to cause diabetes, depression, and hormone imbalances – which results in more toxic prescription drugs being used.

"Politicians like to use the mantra of 'protecting our children' to help pass draconian drug war legislation. Most of the drug war's financial resources, however, are actually spent protecting consenting adults from themselves, while the little that is devoted to protecting young people is wasted on programs with a long history of proven failure. The drug policy reform movement should make developing effective drug education a high priority. Decades of research has consistently determined what does more harm than good: 'scare-based' prevention tactics, overuse of authority figures, talking down to people, and conveying over-the-top messages or ideas that don't conform to people's perceptions and experiences. More specifically, policymakers have hooked prevention resources to three failed programs: DARE, the National Youth AntiDrug Media Campaign, and student drug testing.

A 2003 study by the Unities States Government Accountability Office found that every evaluation of the DARE program the agency reviewed proved that 'DARE had no statistically significant long-term effect on preventing youth illicit drug use.' Numerous other studies have reached similar conclusions."
– Bill Piper, Executive Director Drug Policy Alliance, in his article Congress 2007: The Agenda Ahead, *Cannabis Culture* magazine, March/April 2007; CannabisCulture.com; DrugPolicy.org

Public schools in the U.S. seem to be doing a very good job at turning out hordes of obese children who speak one language, who have a distorted view of the world gained from taking white-washed history (blind-patriotism) classes that teach myths and lies, whose time and talents are wasted on low-quality education, and who have to sit through silly and degrading anti-drug public service announcements that only leave the schoolchildren curious to explore the drugs they are told to avoid.

"Marijuana prohibition needlessly destroys the lives and careers of literally hundreds of thousands of good, hard-working, productive citizens each year in this country. More than 700,000 Americans were arrested on marijuana charges last year, and more than five million Americans have been arrested for marijuana offenses in the past decade."
– National Organization for the Reform of Marijuana Laws, NORML.org; 2006

Over the past several decades, more and more U.S. citizens have found themselves in jail, in prison, and/or on probation for breaking drug laws. It should be obvious that the anti-drug campaigns don't work, and that the drug laws do not benefit society, but do waste billions of dollars – including on courts and on the jails and prisons needed to house all of the citizenry breaking the drug laws.

Being incarcerated in prison changes people, most often for the very worse. Hard drugs are rampant in U.S. prison systems. Many inmates who have never done hard drugs begin to do so while they are in prison. Prisons are referred to as "correctional facilities." But what they often do is harden people by exposing them to a harsh environment that damages their soul.

The laws governing the use, possession, and sale of marijuana are horrible laws. They were created using fake news stories, lies, and distorted information, and they were created using political and corporate propaganda for the benefit of the wealthy. They destroy lives. If anything can be described as evil, it is the marijuana laws that result in the arrest of hundreds of thousands of people every year, and also prevent the farming of industrial hemp that can provide the raw materials that can be used to replace products that are causing great harm to the global environment.

"This report concludes that legalization of marijuana in Massachusetts would produce an annual savings in state and local expenditure of about $120.6 million while generating tax revenue of at least $16.9 million."
– From the report: *The Budgetary Implications of Marijuana Legalization in Massachusetts*, by Jeffrey A. Miron, Professor of Economics, Boston University; August, 2003

If a relatively small state like Massachusetts can experience savings of over $135 million in state and local expenditures every year if pot were made to be a legal, taxable product, then states that are struggling with annual budgetary shortfalls, such as California, could make a big dent in their debt simply by legalizing marijuana in a way that it becomes a taxable commercial product. Industrial hemp farming could also be legalized and farmers could begin benefiting from a whole new, very needed, and environmentally sustainable crop.

But the federal government stands in the way, preventing laws from being changed, increasing the number of marijuana arrests every year, and determining that billions of dollars get spent on marijuana enforcement.

Rather than wasting billions of dollars to pay law enforcement workers to find and arrest people who possess, grow, or sell marijuana, and spending billions more to prosecute, imprison, cloth, and feed the otherwise harmless citizens, the money would be put to better use if it were spent to improve the nations' educational facilities, on giving raises to the grossly underpaid teachers who work in the American school systems, on environmental protection and preservation, on alternative fuel technology, on infrastructure improvement, and on monorail systems in the largest cities. Spending billions on those issues would improve society. Putting people in prison for marijuana charges does not.

In consideration of what could happen in a society where marijuana was legal, one has only to look at Holland where cannabis is sold in designated "coffee shops." That country has the lowest imprisonment rate in the Western world, and they are able to spend more money on social programs, healthcare, and the environment. A smaller percentage of teenagers there regularly use marijuana than do the teenagers in the U.S. The same is true for adults in Holland.

"Alcohol and tobacco cause many more deaths in users than do drugs. Decriminalization would not prevent us from treating drugs as we now treat alcohol and tobacco: prohibiting sales of drugs to minors, outlawing the advertising of drugs and similar measures. Such measures could be enforced, while outright prohibition cannot be. Moreover, if even a small fraction of the money we now spend on trying to enforce drug prohibition were devoted to treatment and rehabilitation, in an atmosphere of compassion not punishment, the reduction in drug usage and in the harm done to the users could be dramatic.

This plea comes from the bottom of my heart. Every friend of freedom, and I know you are one, must be as revolted as I am by the prospect of turning the United States into an armed camp, by the vision of jails filled with casual drug users and of an army of enforcers empowered to invade the liberty of citizens on slight evidence."

– Milton Friedman, Nobel Laureate economist in An Open Letter to [White House drug czar] Bill Bennett, *Wall Street Journal*, September 7, 1989

"I would legalize marijuana. In fact, I would change the whole drug policy. This approach of War on Drugs has not succeeded. We've spent billions of dollars on it, and we still have a problem. The problem is a public health problem. It's not a war problem. And of course our jails are overloaded with people who got picked up for a joint or what have you. That's another problem we have to deal with. As we correct that situation, these people who have been incarcerated for bad policy should be re-examined and helped to be rehabilitated. The marijuana problem is a simple one. We legalize that and you should be able to buy that at a liquor store, just like you buy alcohol. But the rest of the drug area needs attention, needs medical attention, so that when a person needs to get drugs, they can go get a prescription for a doctor. They get it, it's not a problem. Then they have to be registered and then when they are ready to be rehabilitated we have the resources to do that. Right now we don't. We catch you, throw you in jail. And that's no rehabilitation because it brings about unbelievable recidivism in the whole process."

– Democratic presidential candidate Mike Gravel, former U.S. Senate, Alaska, 1969-1981; Alaska House of Representatives, 1963-1966; On C-Span, May 3, 2007

# A Country at War With Its Own Citizens

"Potheads should be taken out and shot."
– Daryl Gates, chief, L.A. Police Department, 1988

"The government arrests more people for marijuana use each year than for all violent crimes combined."
– Marijuana Policy Project, MPP.org; 2006

"The founding fathers would be shocked at the excessive bails, fines, and punishments inflicted for violation of our drug laws. People are being jailed for twenty-five years, without the possibility of parole, for having a joint. Their homes and property are being seized because they are growing a plant. Surely this flouts the Eighth Amendment."
– *Why Marijuana Should Be Legal*, by Ed Rosenthal & Steve Kubby with S. Newhart; Green-Aid.com/EdRosenthal.htm

Since the marijuana prohibition laws went into effect in 1937, somewhere around 75,000,000 Americans have been charged with marijuana offenses. This has accomplished what? How many billions have been spent on this every year while our schools and environment are neglected?

"Prisoners sentenced for drug offenses constituted the largest group of federal inmates (55 percent) in 2001, down from 60 percent in 1995. On September 30, 2001, the date of the latest available data in the Federal Justice Statistics Program, federal prisons held 78,501 sentenced drug offenders, compared to 52,782 in 1995."
– Harrison, Paige M. & Allen J. Beck, Ph.D., U.S. Department of Justice, Bureau of Justice Statistics, Prisoners in 2002; Washington, DC: U.S. Department of Justice, July 2003; Page 11

As I write this there are around 60,000 U.S. citizens serving time in prisons because they have been convicted of breaking cannabis laws. Somewhere around three times that number are being detained as they await their case to be tried in the overcrowded courts. About 20 percent of the people in federal prisons are there on pot convictions.

The laws prohibiting marijuana are different from those that prohibited alcohol. Under alcohol Prohibition those who manufactured or sold alcohol were punished. With marijuana the users as well as the sellers and/or growers are punished. The similarity between the laws is that they create a situation where gangs and violence take place with a substance that is illegal. Mobsters gained power during alcohol Prohibition.

"I say legalization, not decriminalization… The War on Drugs is an absolute failure."
– Gary Johnson, Governor of New Mexico, speaking at The Cato Institute, October 1999

"There is no simple profile of a typical cannabis user. It's been used by millions of people from all walks of life for thousands of years for hundreds of medical, social, and religious reasons, as well as for personal relaxation. Several of our greatest [U.S.] presidents farmed hemp. About one in three American voters say they have tried it."
– Family Council on Drug Awareness, 2006; FCDA.org

Marijuana laws do not stop anyone who really wants marijuana from obtaining it. What the laws do is drive up the cost of marijuana, help to create a criminal element, and waste billions in tax dollars every year to spy on, to entrap, to carry out surveillance on, to charge, to prosecute, to imprison, and to ruin the lives of millions of U.S. citizens (including the family members of those who are sent to jail or prison).

"The War on Drugs is inarguably a complete failure, it has failed to stop or even reduce drug use, sales, or trafficking, despite decades of arrests, imprisonment, and billions of tax dollars."
– Educators for Sensible Drug Policy, EFSP.org

Some who are in favor of decriminalizing marijuana and drugs believe it would be better to put so-called drug "offenders" through drug treatment programs instead of throwing them in prisons with murderers, rapists, armed robbers, swindlers, and child molesters. It would certainly be less expensive to put people through drug treatment programs than to prosecute and jail them. It would even be much less expensive to give them college scholarships.

As long as the laws treat drug addictions as crimes, the laws will continue to fail society and waste tax dollars. And the governments will continue to be corrupted with American drug money in Columbia, Mexico, Peru, Ecuador, Panama, Burma, Nigeria, Thailand, Afghanistan, and other drug-growing regions.

Many people who do not take drugs have been and are involved in selling drugs because they know they can make money – but if they get caught they can be sent to jail for a long time.

There are also people who make money because of the U.S. drug laws. It is they who work to keep the drug war going by lobbying for passage of stricter drug laws, and opposing any sort of change that would allow for counseling, therapy, and rehabilitation instead of jail and prison. They make money from the drug laws because they make the weaponry and equipment used by the drug enforcement officers, they design and build the prisons, they make the cement and steel used to build the prisons, they represent the drug offenders in court, they are the drug-testing companies, they are the antidrug organizations that are funded by governments and private donations to fuel the War on Drugs, they are the union guards in the prisons, they are the companies supplying food and clothing for prisoners, and they are the corporations that run the prisons under government contracts.

Perhaps those who benefit the most from keeping marijuana and hemp illegal in the U.S. are the petroleum, cotton, corn, plywood, and tree pulp paper industries. They are all making money, but at what cost to society?

"Marijuana legalization would remove this behemoth financial burden from the criminal justice system, freeing up criminal justice resources to target other more serious crimes, and allowing law enforcement to focus on the highest echelons of hard-drug trafficking enterprises rather than on minor marijuana offenders who present no threat to public safety."
– Keith Stroup, Executive Director of the National Organization for the Reform of Marijuana Laws, NORML.org, 2004

As long as these laws prohibiting marijuana exist there will always be marijuana entrepreneurs in every county of the U.S., growing and selling marijuana illegally, tax free.

"The government's War on Drugs has become a wildfire that threatens to consume those fundamental rights of the individual deliberately enshrined in our Constitution."
– Chief Judge Burciaga, *U.S. v. Boyll* (1991) 774 F. Supp. 1333; quoted on JudgesAgainstTheDrugWar.org

"Governance involves choices. Every expansion of government power is a diminution of individual liberty. A balance must be struck between lawlessness and personal freedom. Some restrictions on liberty are necessary in order to have a society that is relatively free from crime and predation. The current obsession is to eliminate illicit drug use. There is no question, however, that under the so-called War on Drugs, personal freedoms and liberties are being trampled. While I may

deplore the marketing and use of illicit drugs, as well as the undesirable personal and social problems that flow therefrom, I believe that the pendulum has swung too far in the area of law enforcement and that the assault on our basic liberties and freedoms by government itself has become a far more serious and potentially destructive social problem."
– *People v. Mitchell* (1995) 650 N.E.2d 1014; Heiple, Justice, Dissenting; Supreme Court of Illinois; quoted on JudgesAgainstTheDrugWar.org

"If this nation were to win its War on Drugs at the cost of sacrificing its citizens' constitutional rights, it would be a Pyrrhic victory indeed. It ill behooves a great nation to compromise or sacrifice the freedoms of its citizens as the price of more efficient law enforcement."
– *U.S. v. Layman* (1990) 730 F. Supp, 332; Carrigan, District Judge; U.S. District Court, Dist. of Colorado; quoted on JudgesAgainstTheDrugWar.org

U.S. federal government agencies involved in trying to control marijuana:
- Air Force
- Agriculture Department
- Army
- Central Intelligence Agency
- Coast Guard
- Commerce Department
- Customs
- Department of Education
- Department of Health and Welfare
- Department of Transportation
- Drug Enforcement Administration
- Federal Bureau of Investigation
- Immigration and Naturalization
- Internal Revenue Service
- National Institute of Mental Health
- National Institute on Drug Abuse
- Navy
- Post Office
- Treasury Department
- U.S. Forestry Service

Additionally, the U.S. funds the drug war in other countries. For instance, in 2007 the U.S. gave $69 million to Mexico to help train police and prosecutors. Some members of Congress want to more than double that amount. Drug war funding from the U.S. to Columbia has been in the billions of dollars.

"Police arrested an estimated 755,187 persons for marijuana violations in 2003, according to the Federal Bureau of Investigation's annual Uniform Crime Report. The total is the highest ever recorded by the FBI, and comprised 45 percent of all drug arrests in the United States.

Marijuana arrests for 2003 increased 8 percent from the previous year, and have nearly doubled since 1993.

In the past decade, more than 6.5 million Americans have been arrested on marijuana charges, more than the entire populations of Alaska, Delaware, the District of Columbia, Montana, North Dakota, South Dakota, Vermont, and Wyoming combined."
– ChangeTheClimate.org

In 2004 there were 773,000 Americans arrested on marijuana charges. In 2009 there were 858,000 Americans arrested on marijuana charges. If the trend continues, more people will be arrested each year.

Some say that marijuana needs to be illegal because it is a dangerous drug or a gateway drug. Ask them to support their claims with fact and they will likely come up empty, or they will cite claims that are based on myths, distortions, and/or government lies.

"According to the Canadian Senate's 2002 study: 'Cannabis: Our Position for a Canadian Public Policy,' 'Cannabis itself is not a cause of other drug use.' This finding concurs with the conclusions of the U.S. National Academy of Science's Institute of Medicine 1999 study, which states that marijuana is not a 'gateway drug to the extent that it is a cause or even that it is the most significant predictor of serious drug abuse.'"
– Marijuana: Myth vs. Fact, National Organization for the Reform of Marijuana Laws, NORML.org

# Medicinal Marijuana

"Marijuana should be available to all patients who need it to help them undergo treatment for life-threatening illnesses. As long as therapy is safe and has not been proven ineffective, seriously ill patients (and their physicians) should have access to whatever they need to fight for their lives."
– *The New England Journal of Medicine*; August 7, 1997

"There is evidence to suggest that the therapeutic use of cannabis or of substances derived from it for the treatment of certain medical conditions may, after further research, prove to be helpful."
– The Report of the Expert Group on the Effects of Cannabis, British Advisory Council on the Misuse of Drugs, 1982

"*Consumer Reports* believes that, for patients with advanced AIDS and terminal cancer, the apparent benefits some derive from smoking marijuana outweigh any substantiated or even suspected risks. In the same spirit the FDA uses to hasten the approval of cancer drugs, federal laws should be relaxed in favor of states' rights to allow physicians to administer marijuana to their patients on a caring and compassionate basis."
– Consumer Reports: Marijuana as Medicine; *Consumer Reports* magazine, May 1997; ConsumerReports.org

"During his [Prince Charles'] annual visit to the Sue Ryder Home in Cheltenham, Gloucestershire, he asked Karen Drake, who has MS: 'Have you tried taking cannabis? I have heard it's the best thing for it.'"
– Prince Ponders Medicinal Value of Cannabis, *The London Times*, Dec. 1998

"When pure and administered carefully, [cannabis] is one of the of the most valuable medicines we possess."
– Sir Russell Reynolds, Queen Victoria's personal physician, writing about using cannabis to treat menstrual cramps, *The Lancet*, Britain's medical journal, 1890

"Medical marijuana? I fully support it, absolutely. Who is government to tell someone if they have AIDS or cancer, what they

should be taking?"
– James "Jesse Ventura" Janos, 38th governor of Minnesota, responding to a question asked by a University of St. Thomas political science student, 2001

"The chief opposition to the drug rests on a moral and political, and not a toxicologic, foundation."
– The *Merck Manual of Diagnosis and Therapy*, 1987

Because using marijuana too much can make some people lazy, there are those who would probably agree that regular use of marijuana is not a wise practice. However, there are many people who can benefit from marijuana.

For thousands of years marijuana has been used as a medicine throughout the world. Mention of it has been found in ancient Chinese writings.

In the 1560s a Portuguese book mentioning the medicinal uses of cannabis was published. Titled *Drugs and Medicinal Matters of India and of a Few Fruits*, the book was written by Carcia Da Orta, and was also translated into Chinese. After his death the Catholic Church in Portugal ordered the book burned because it was found that Da Orta was a Jew. In Martin Booth's excellent book, *Cannabis: A History*, he tells how Da Orta's book was saved and published in English, French, Italian, and Latin. Another Portuguese book mentioning the medical uses of cannabis followed, this one written by Cristobal Acosta and titled *A Tract about the Drugs and Medicines of the East Indies*. As Booth explains, the publication of those two books was followed by other books over the next 150 years distorting what was said in previous books. Such has been the history of cannabis, people saying one thing, and others saying the opposite, and/or taking things out of context – sometimes on purpose to serve an agenda.

By studying the writings of George Washington, it is clear that he kept a separate amount of hemp growing that produced a sticky resin, which could easily be translated to mean that he grew his own medicinal crop of hemp's sister plant. At that time, what we now call "marijuana" was used for headaches and other ailments just as we use sleeping aids, painkillers, and aspirin today.

In his journal notes from his Mount Vernon plantation, Washington wrote in May 12-13, 1765 that he had "Sowed hemp at muddy hole by swamp." On August 7, 1765, he wrote that he "Began to separate the male from the female plants." On August 29, 1766, he wrote that he was, "Pulling up the hemp. Was too late for the blossom hemp by three weeks or a month." In other words, he was trying to make sure to separate the male plants from the female plants, which would result in a stickier female plant. The reason a person would want the sticky female plant that grew away from the male plants is that the unfertilized female plant contains the substances that get you "high."

"If seed hemp and marijuana plants cross-pollinate, the resulting seed produces plants with THC levels in between the levels found in the parent plants. Growers of either plant should want to prevent this, and use a known genetic variety to grow each new crop."
– March 2008 Reason Foundation Study on Hemp, Illegally Green: Environmental Costs of Hemp Prohibition. Policy Study 367, by Skaidra Smith-Heisters

While Washington's diary entries are mentioned in many books that point out the clear evidence that Washington knew what he was doing to grow the sticky female plants, it isn't clear what he was going to do with the plants. We do know that cannabis was a common medicine. In other words, Washington got high. He may have done it for headaches, or for his aching and well-known dental situation, or for a number of reasons, including for relaxation, contemplation, and/or socialization, or to better enjoy his time with Martha.

Thomas Jefferson wrote that he smoked hemp to relieve his headaches. Anyone who knows anything about hemp knows that smoking industrial hemp doesn't relieve headaches, nor does it get you high. But, smoking a well-bred female plant that was kept away from the male plants, and that was grown to the point of having sticky resin, is what gets you high, and what relieves headaches.

As a popular medication and intoxicant during the 1830s, cannabis was taxed in Britain. As mentioned earlier, an Irish doctor named William Brooke O'Shaughnessy who worked at the Medical College of Calcutta, India, wrote and taught about the medical uses of cannabis. In the 1840s O'Shaughnessy worked with a London pharmacist named Peter Squire to create a medicinal extract of cannabis that was named Squire's Extract. It was sold in pharmacies as a pain reliever. A similar extract named Tilden's Extract was sold in the U.S. In the 1850s cannabis was added to the European pharmacopoeias. It was also added to the *United States Pharmacopoeia.*

From the middle of the nineteenth-century until the 1930s, American doctors gave cannabis to their patients who were suffering from various ailments such as headaches, nausea, and insomnia. Drug companies sold various extracts of cannabis and it became a very common medication for a variety of uses. It was during these years that cannabis was suggested as an alternative to alcohol for those who had become addicted to drinking.

One man, Frederick Hollick, claiming to be a doctor, sold cannabis extract as a secret aphrodisiac for married couples. His 1851 book, *The Marriage Guide*, contained mail-order information for those wanting to purchase his marriage aid.

Then, in 1937, the U.S. marijuana tax made cannabis much less available for doctors. In the 1940s cannabis was removed from the *United States Pharmacopoeia*. Taking its place were patented synthetic chemical drugs that could be taken in pill form, or injected into the blood stream via hypodermic needle. Highly addictive opiate drugs, which are water soluble, were used for many of the applications formerly covered by cannabis extracts. These patent drugs also made more money for the pharmaceutical companies and the doctors who prescribed and treated their patients with them.

Marijuana is currently being used illegally under federal law, but legally under state laws, as an effective therapy for helping cancer patients cope with pain and by AIDS patients suffering from AIDS-related wasting syndrome. Marijuana relieves stress; combats the muscle spasms and pain associated with multiple sclerosis; helps to relieve the pain of arthritis and fibromyalgia; and reduces the elevated eye pressure associated with glaucoma. It also reduces the nausea and vomiting experienced by patients who are undergoing chemotherapy. Marijuana stimulates the appetite, which is helpful for people who have diseases or disorders that cause them to become dangerously thin. Marijuana often quickly reduces the temporary blind spots experienced during episodes of migraine and ocular migraine. Dr. Gregory T. Carter of the University of Washington School of Medicine has found marijuana to be helpful for those with ALS (amyotrophic lateral sclerosis).

In 1992 William Devane discovered that the brain produces a cannabinoid-like neurotransmitter that has biological and behavioral effects similar to THC. This neurotransmitter also provides pleasant sensations and appears to be utilized by the body to control pain. He gave it the name anandamide. *Ananda* is a Sanskrit word that translates to the English word *bliss*. The THC in cannabis docks with the same cell receptors as anandamide.

There are more than 70 cannabinoids in the marijuana plant, and they interact with the endocannabinoid system of the human body that regulates a wide variety of processes within the human system, including those involving pain, memory, appetite, and immunity.

The receptors where both anandamide and THC dock were discovered in a 1984 study lead by Miles Herkenham at the National Institutes of Health. They found that the receptors are predominantly found on cells of the cerebral cortex and hippocampus regions of the brain, but also in the basal ganglia, in the spinal chord, and in the testes. The part of the brain where pain is modulated, the rostral ventromedial medulla, is one area that is particularly receptive to the substances in marijuana. Because there are only a certain number of receptors, this provides a situation where a person can't overdose on THC and it can't interfere with the vital life support functions (but it can increase heart rate, making it a potential problem for those with cardiovascular disease).

A 1982 study conducted by the British Advisory Council on the Misuse of Drugs published as the Expert Group on the Effects of Cannabis Use, the study said there was evidence that cannabis and substances derived from it may prove to be beneficial.

When a number of states were legalizing medical marijuana, the U.S. attorney general during the Clinton administration, Janet Reno, held a press conference announcing that the federal government would review records and revoke the registration of any physician who "recommends or prescribes schedule 1 controlled substances."

Reno was talking about rescinding the federal license to prescribe drugs from doctors who prescribe marijuana for cancer patients, AIDS patients, glaucoma patients, and others. The doctors were also warned that their practices would be excluded from the Medicare and Medicaid programs.

In October 2002 the 9th U.S. Circuit Court of Appeals unanimously ruled that the government cannot revoke a doctor's license to prescribe controlled substances when the doctor has recommended marijuana to patients. The Justice Department argued that the doctors were interfering with the War on Drugs by suggesting that their patients may find relief through marijuana. The court ruled that the policy of the Justice Department was interfering with the free-speech rights of doctors and patients. The court upheld a two-year-old court order prohibiting the government from revoking a doctor's license to dispense medicine. The ruling was hailed as a victory for free speech, for doctors, and for patients' rights.

> "An integral component of the practice of medicine is the communication between doctor and a patient. Physicians must be able to speak frankly and openly to patients."
> – Chief Circuit Judge Mary Schroeder

Doctors should not have to prescribe marijuana. What would work, and get them out of the loop of prescribing marijuana, would be to allow them to give a patient a signed document indicating the diagnosis of the patient. Any patient with certain diagnoses that fall under those health conditions known to benefit from the use of marijuana should be able to go to a compassion club or pharmacy to have a medical marijuana prescription filled. The document should also work as a legal document indicating that the person can legally obtain, possess, and grow a certain amount of marijuana for medicinal purposes.

Churches that have endorsed legalizing medical marijuana:
• Episcopal Church
• Presbyterian Church
• Progressive National Baptist Convention
• Union for Reform Judaism
• Unitarian Universalist Association
• United Church of Christ
• United Methodist Church

Ironically, while the government continues to deny marijuana to people who need it, there is a prescription pill containing a concentrated synthetic form of delta-9-THC, one of the active forms of THC in marijuana. This expensive prescription drug is called Marinol made by Solvay Pharmaceuticals of Marietta, Georgia. This synthetic chemical drug has been approved for use in the treatment of people suffering from weight loss associated with AIDS and the nausea associated with cancer chemotherapy.

Chemists had been working since at least the 1880s to create a patented cannabis extract. In 1895 a cannabis extract was made by chemists named Easterfield, Spivey, and Wood at the University of Cambridge. But their extract never caught on. With Marinol, a company finally succeeded. 2004 sales of the drug amounted to about $78 million.

> "The [pharmaceutical] drug companies want control, rather than just a ban, for they know the medicinal benefits of marijuana. They have attempted to substitute synthetic derivatives for the raw herb, because the raw herb cannot be patented, meaning they can't make money from it."
> – *Why Marijuana Should Be Legal*, by Ed Rosenthal & Steve Kubby with S. Newhart; Green-Aid.com/EdRosenthal.htm

While some patients say that Marinol is effective in doing what it is meant to do, many people who have taken Marinol say that it is too strong, takes much longer to take effect, and does not provide the same feeling as that gained from smoking or vaporizing marijuana. One reason for this is that marijuana smoke or vapor contains some other natural chemicals that don't exist in Marinol. THC is only one of more than 50 cannabinoids in the cannabis plant and any one of them may be beneficial to certain health conditions. Marijuana that is inhaled into the lungs puts THC directly into the bloodstream, while Marinol must be absorbed by the digestive system

301

before it has an effect, which may take hours. (For those who smoke marijuana, consider using a cannabis vaporizer instead of a pipe or joint.)

"The active ingredient in Marinol, delta-9-tetrahydrocannabinol, is only one of the compounds isolated in marijuana that appears to be medically beneficial to patients. Other compounds such as cannabidiol (CBD), an anticonvulsant, and cannabichromine (CBC), an anti-inflammatory, are unavailable in Marinol, and patients only have access to their therapeutic properties by using cannabis.

Patients prescribed Marinol frequently complain of its high psychoactivity. This is because patients consume the drug orally. Once swallowed, Marinol passes through the liver, where a significant proportion is converted into other chemicals. One of these, the 11-hydroxy metabolite, is four to five times more potent than THC and greatly increases the likelihood of a patient experiencing an adverse psychological reaction. In contrast, inhaled marijuana doesn't cause significant levels of the 11-hydroxy metabolite to appear in the blood."
– National Organization for the Reform of Marijuana Laws, NORML.org

There are other drugs available containing synthetic forms of substances found in marijuana, and there are more being developed. Some are pills, others are sprays and inhalants.

The International Cannabinoid Research Society is made up of over 400 researchers looking at the various substances contained in marijuana and exploring the "therapeutic opportunities" of the substances. In addition to fostering research, the ICRS works to get financial support from government and private agencies to support research and development of drugs based on the findings.

At the annual symposium of the ICRS in 1999 the British company GW Pharmaceuticals announced their research into treating multiple sclerosis with cannabis substances. Since then the company has raised hundreds of millions for funding, including from private investors, from a 2001 stock offering that brought in $48 million, and from a $65 million licensing fee with Bayer, the German pharmaceutical company.

The British government exempted GW from an international treaty forbidding the production of illegal drugs, gave GW permission to grow marijuana in greenhouses, and allowed them to test their products on human subjects. By doing all of this the company was able to develop their Sativex whole plant cannabis spray that they call "a novel prescription pharmaceutical product derived from components of the cannabis plant." GW is allowed to grow up to 30 tons of marijuana per year.

Although Sativex was developed for multiple sclerosis-related neuropathic pain, it can be prescribed "off-label" by doctors for other illnesses. The first country to approve its use was Canada in April 2005.

A medication in spray form can be better than a pill because some people have problems swallowing and keeping down pills. A cannabis spray that is absorbed by the mucous membranes of the mouth also is a good alternative for those who don't like to smoke. Another advantage to Sativex is that it contains compounds from the cannabis plant that are not included in the pills like Marinol, and some of those interacting compounds are what benefit patients. Some patients who have used it say that Sativex has a horrible taste.

A hepatitis C patient in Canada was one who was prescribed Sativex "off-label." Although his experience with the drug lasted only five days, he found that marijuana in its natural form provided him with more relief of the nausea and loss of appetite he experiences in relation to his condition.

"If I didn't have access to a safe and consistent source of whole-plant, organic cannabis, or if I found myself in a situation where smoking might be inappropriate or otherwise impossible, I would certainly consider Sativex a far superior alternative to Marinol or Cesamet [Nabilone].

Ultimately, I will continue to use cannabis in its raw form for a number of reasons, including a personal philosophy that sees me choose to eat an orange rather than taking vitamin C, and a general disinclination to using pharmaceuticals if they can be avoided. Additionally, the raw-plant, organic cannabis grown by the Vancouver Island Compassion Society appears to be more effective in controlling my nausea and increasing my appetite than Sativex; and possibly because of my ample experience with smoked-ingestion, I find it more predictable than GW's product. I consider Sativex not as a replacement for smoked-ingestion or for raw cannabis, but rather as another 'strain' and yet another viable option for medical users, many of whom might never want to smoke their medicine, or to purchase therapeutic products from anyone but a pharmacist."
– Phillipe Lucas' 5-day Sativex Trial; Daily Report and Conclusions. In his report Lucas mentions a self-made product called VICS Cannamist. For more information on this product, see the Web site of the Vancouver Island Compassion Society; TheVICS.com.

While the U.S. government funds cannabis research with the goal of finding things that are wrong with it, pharmaceutical companies and other researchers are working to develop synthetic prescription drugs that can do what marijuana does best for patients. Much of this cannabis research is done to create drugs that can bring hundreds of millions of dollars to the drug companies. In 2006 the international cannabinoid prescription drug market was estimated to be about $1 billion.

It is an odd situation where marijuana is outlawed by a government that says it is of no medical benefit, yet patients can get a prescription for a drug based on marijuana. But if marijuana remains illegal, then the pharmaceutical companies can make money from the patented drugs based on cannabis. This is one scenario that people often mention when they say that drug companies want to keep marijuana illegal so that the same drug companies can reap hundreds of millions in profits. Perhaps it is no coincidence that pharmaceutical companies donate large amounts of money to political campaigns, and spend lots more money on political lobbying.

As the benefits of medical marijuana finally become widely known and accepted, and the pharmaceuticalization of marijuana continues, law enforcement is put in the bizarre situation of supporting the biggest pot dealers of all, the pharmaceutical companies. They do this by allowing only prescription pot in pill or spray form while outlawing the use of the natural substance the drugs are based on – even when patients with the whole plant substance can very easily get a prescription for the pharmaceutical drug.

Could the drug companies be hiring people who understand America's marijuana drug laws to keep these laws in place so that the drug companies can guarantee their market share? GW has at least made some very interesting choices in whom to hire in the U.S. Look at a few facts, and judge for yourself:

It is interesting that to help win U.S. approval for Sativex, in 2005 GW hired Andrea Barthwell for an advisory board role. As a doctor, she has promoted herself as an addiction medicine specialist. She served as a U.S. deputy director in the White House Office of National Drug Control Policy. In that position, which she held from 2002 to 2004, she worked under the main drug czar, John Walters. She was against medical marijuana while she was President Bush's advisor on issues relating to medical marijuana. During that time she called medical marijuana "medical excuse marijuana." She also said, "The people who are advancing marijuana as a medicine are perpetuating a cruel hoax that exploits our compassion for the sick... They are using patients' pain and suffering in an attempt to change America's drug control policy. Marijuana is a crude plant product that most definitely is not a medicine." She also said, "Even if smoking marijuana makes people feel better, that's not enough to call it a medicine." Huh?

But then Barthwell became employed by a company producing a medicine containing the substances in marijuana. After she switched jobs she sounded as if she were defending medical marijuana – or, at least the liquefied form of it that is being sold by her employer, which will be very financially rewarding for her employer. Maybe she just likes the money they are paying her to do what they want her to do. It's a very old profession.

> "Having this product available will certainly slow down the dash to make the crude plant material available to patients across the country.
> Comparing crude marijuana to Sativex is like comparing a raging forest fire to the fire in your home's furnace. While both provide heat, one is out of control."
> – Andrea Barthwell, *Los Angeles Times*, April 20 2005

It's not like Barthwell didn't know what she said. She's a doctor. What she said when she worked for the Bush administration is on public record. She worked against medical marijuana, working to deny ailing patients from having a medicine that could relieve suffering. Then she began working for a drug company that sells what amounts to liquid marijuana that is expensive and that is likely to make many hundreds of millions of dollars for her employer. But suddenly medical marijuana is okay with her. But don't call it marijuana. It's Sativex. Maybe what matters most to her is which one puts money in her pockets.

> "Sativex is for all practical purposes liquid marijuana, so the question of whether marijuana is medicine has been settled. The only question is what form people use, and that's best left to doctors and patients.
> …In practical terms, Sativex is to marijuana as a cup of coffee is to coffee beans."
> – Bruce Mirken, Marijuana Policy Project; April 2005

GW also has hired John Pastuovic to handle U.S. public relations. In 2000 Pastuovic worked as a spokesman for the Bush-Cheney campaign in Illinois. In early 2005 he also worked to oppose passage of medical marijuana legislation in Illinois.

> "Doctors and patients should decide what medicines are best. Ten years ago, I nearly died from testicular cancer that spread into my lungs. Chemotherapy made me sick and nauseated. The standard drugs, like Marinol, didn't help.
> Marijuana blocked the nausea. As a result, I was able to continue the chemotherapy treatments. Today I've beaten the cancer, and no longer smoke marijuana. I credit marijuana as part of the treatment that saved my life."
> – James Canter, cancer survivor, Santa Rosa, California; in rebuttal to argument against proposition 215, the medical marijuana bill that

is now law in California

One of the problems with prescription drugs meant to provide the relief that natural marijuana provides is that they may not contain all of the beneficial substances that exist in whole marijuana, including substances that are not psychoactive and that may play a role in balancing and metabolizing the others. There are dozens of forms of THC and several dozen different cannabinoids contained in marijuana. Any one of these substances can be what benefits someone experiencing a certain health condition. Taking a synthetic prescription drug that is based on only one form of the substances naturally present in marijuana may not help the patient, and may lead to more problems.

"Marijuana is an effective medical treatment and is neither an addictive nor a gateway drug."
– Institute of Medicine, 1999

"For decades, politicians have said that marijuana has no proven medical value while scientists have been denied the ability to prove otherwise."
– Rick Doblin, Ph.D., president and founder of the MAPS (Multidisciplinary Association for Psychedelic Studies). Founded in 1986, the MAPS is a membership-based nonprofit research and educational organization that assists scientists to design, fund, obtain approval for and report on studies into the risks and benefits of MDMA, psychedelic drugs and marijuana. The MAPS has had two Federal Drug Administration-approved studies blocked by the National Institute of Drug Abuse; MAPS.org

The Drug Enforcement Administration continues to claim that marijuana is not a medicine while at the same time denying scientists and medical researchers access to marijuana for research purposes. As mentioned earlier, the U.S. government produces marijuana at the University of Mississippi where the plants are grown under supervision of the National Institute on Drug Abuse. It is a monopoly on the only marijuana in the country that is grown for research purposes.

On February 13, 2007, the DEA's own Administrative Law Judge Mary Ellen Bittner "recommended" that University of Massachusetts-Amherst professor Lyle Craker be allowed to grow marijuana for government-approved studies for developing prescription medicine and to evaluate marijuana in smoked or vaporized form for the purpose of establishing Federal Drug Administration guidelines. Judge Bittner, who is in a position appointed by the U.S. Department of Justice, ruled that it is in the public's interest for the DEA to grant Craker to have a Schedule 1 license with the purpose of growing marijuana for research without depending on the University of Mississippi supply. Thirty-eight Congressional representatives along with a number of medical, public policy, religious, and scientific organizations voiced support for Craker's challenge to the DEA.

"Given its narrow confines, Bittner's recommendation makes sense. It has no bearing on the DEA's licensing of researchers, which would remain in place, nor would it remove the burden of proof on scientists who want access to research-grade marijuana. It would merely prevent situations in which, the judge noted, legitimate researchers who have completed all due diligence are still refused access to research samples [of marijuana]."
– *Los Angeles Times* editorial, Not Enough Marijuana: Federal officials should allow competition in growing the drug for needed studies on its medical use, May 31, 2007

Judge Bittner's ruling was the result of a six-year fight by Craker, the MAPS (Multidisciplinary Association for Psychedelic Studies), and the ACLU (American Civil Liberties Union) to allow scientists access to research marijuana, or to allow the researchers to produce their own marijuana. In his response to the ruling, Craker said, "This ruling is a victory for science, medicine, and the public good. I hope [DEA] administrator [Karen] Tandy abides by the decision and grants me the opportunity to do my job unimpeded by drug war politics."

However, the ruling by Bittner is a recommendation, not a requirement. It is an opportunity for the DEA to stop its obstruction of scientific-based medical research on cannabis.

(For more information, access: MAPS.org/mmj/dealawsuit.html.)

"For patients who do not respond well to other medications, short-term marijuana appears to be suitable in treating conditions like chemotherapy-induced nausea and vomiting, or the wasting caused by AIDS."
– John Benson, dean of the Oregon Health Sciences University School of Medicine, co-principal investigator on Institutes of Health study on medical benefits of marijuana; quoted in Institutes of Health press release, March 1999. The report stated, "We acknowledge that there is no clear alternative for people suffering from chronic conditions that might be relieved by smoking marijuana, such as pain or AIDS wasting."

"One of marihuana's greatest advantages as a medicine is its remarkable safety. It has little effect on major physiological functions. There is no known case of a lethal overdose; marihuana is also far less addictive and far less subject to abuse than many drugs now used as muscle relaxants, hypnotics, and analgesics. The ostensible indifference of physicians should no longer be used as a justification for keeping this medicine in the shadows."
– *Journal of the American Medical Association*, June 21, 1995; Commentary; Pages 1874-1875

"Of all cancers, few are as aggressive and deadly as glioma. Glioma tumors quickly invade healthy brain tissue and are typically unresponsive to surgery and standard medical treatments. One agent they do respond to is cannabis.

Writing in the August 2005 issue of the *Journal of Neurooncology*, investigators at the California Pacific Medical Center Research Institute reported that the administration of THC on human glioblastoma multiforme cell lines decreased the proliferation of malignant cells and induced apoptosis (programmed cell death) more rapidly than did the administration of the synthetic cannabis receptor agonist, WIN-55, 212-2. Researchers also noted that THC selectively targeted malignant cells while ignoring healthy ones in a more profound manner than the synthetic alternative.

... Most recently, a scientific analysis in the October issue of the journal *Mini-Reviews in Medicinal Chemistry* noted that, in addition to THC and CBD's brain cancer-fighting ability, studies have also shown cannabinoids to halt the progression of lung carcinoma, leukemia, skin carcinoma, colorectal cancer, prostate cancer, and breast cancer.

Emerging evidence also indicates that cannabinoids may play a role in slowing the progression of certain neurodegenerative diseases, such as multiple sclerosis, Parkinson's disease, Alzheimer's, and amyotrophic lateral sclerosis (a.k.a. Lou Gehrig's Disease)."
– Cannabis and the Brain: A User's Guide, by Paul Armentano, Senior Policy Analyst, National Organization for the Reform of Marijuana Laws/NORML Foundation, February 14, 2006; NORML.org

"California NORML has recently heard increasing reports that Marinol patients are being drug tested and denied employment for use of marijuana. In particular, we have heard from legal Prop. 225 patients who were denied jobs despite presenting Marinol prescriptions after being re-tested specifically for marijuana. Until recently, Marinol and marijuana were indistinguishable on the standard drug tests, so that patients with a Marinol prescription had a valid medical excuse under federal law for testing positive for marijuana.

However, special testing techniques have been developed that make it possible to distinguish the two by testing for non-standard cannabinoids that appear in marijuana but not Marinol. Until recently, these tests were expensive and rarely used except in high-profile criminal cases. However, it appears that they are now being routinely used by certain laboratories in cases where Marinol use is claimed. In particular, we have heard reports of such testing being used to disqualify Marinol-using Prop 215 patients by the transportation industry and by Walmart.

California NORML has accordingly altered its drug testing information to warn against relying on Marinol RXs as a screen for marijuana use: canorml.org/healthfacts/testing.tips.html.

There is of course no valid scientific or health justification for allowing patients to use Marinol but not marijuana. The only purpose is to enforce compliance with the law. It is a tribute to the power and influence of the drug testing industry that they have prevailed in foisting the costs of this unnecessary and obnoxious procedure on employers."

– National Organization for the Reform of Marijuana Laws, Labs Testing for Marijuana Use by Marinol Patients, by Dale Gieringer, Ph.D., Director, California Normal; Wednesday, Dec. 24, 2008; NORML.org

If anyone is involved in growing medicinal cannabis, they should use only organic fertilizers and organic soils. Synthetic chemical fertilizers as well as soils enhanced with chemical fertilizers made from fossil fuels should not be used on a plant that is to be taken medicinally. Additionally, growers should not use pesticides, herbicides, insecticides, or fungicides. Any compost used should consist of organically grown plant substances mixed with organic soil. (See Ed Rosenthal's book *Marijuana Growing Tips*. Also, access MarijuanaGrowing.com; IslandHarvest.ca; BioBizz.NL; and the Organic Materials Review Institute at OMRI.org)

# Medical Marijuana Doctors and Pharmacies Under Attack

"If people let government decide which foods they eat and medicines they take, their bodies will soon be in as sorry a state as are the souls of those who live under tyranny."
– President Thomas Jefferson, who was a hemp farmer

Every year the Hollywood Foreign Press Association holds its Golden Globe Awards ceremony to hand out statuettes to TV and film talent. At the 64th annual ceremony that was held January 15, 2007, there was a bit of a seating problem that got taken care of before the guests were seated. Los Angeles Police Chief William J. Bratton and his wife were to be seated at the same table as the cast of the Showtime cable TV show *Weeds*, a comedy starring actress Mary-Louise Parker as a single soccer mom selling cannabis in the suburbs to make ends meet. The show organizers also made sure that the Beverly Hills Police Chief and the Los Angeles County Sheriff were seated away from the cast of *Weeds*.

In the news the same day of the ceremony was Bratton's plan to place limits on where the medical marijuana dispensaries (pharmacies) could be located in the city. At the time there were 98 of the dispensaries providing cannabis to anyone with a medical marijuana prescription as allowed by a state law passed by the 1996 Proposition 215 Compassionate Use Act and the 2004 state Senate Bill 420. Together, Prop 215 and SB 420 legalized possession and cultivation of cannabis for qualified medical patients.

In a report to the Police Commission, Bratton called for a moratorium on new facilities until rules could be established clarifying where the facilities could be located. The report included over 40 recommendations for regulating dispensaries. It called for banning dispensaries from within 1,000 feet of schools, churches, parks, and childcare facilities. It also called for the dispensary owner to keep an area of within 100 feet of the dispensary free from litter. It seems that 94 of the facilities had opened in the previous year, 2006. Bratton was concerned about some facilities that had opened near schools, and some that had been aggressively marketing their presence by placing flyers on neighborhood cars. He pledged to cooperate with the DEA in prosecuting dispensaries that break the laws.

While writing this I thought about how more than 100,000 Americans die every year from pharmaceutical prescription drugs commonly sold at drug stores that spend enormous amounts on advertising and marketing. But those are legal drugs that are often covered by private and government insurance programs, and that are feely available to anyone with a

310

prescription issued by a doctor who carries a federal drug license. Nobody dies from an overdose of marijuana. But that little fact doesn't seem to be a concern of the DEA, so having a few thousand prescription drug stores in every city and more in every suburb and town is okay with them. But a safe medication that a person can't overdose and that provides relief to ailing patients – that, the DEA doesn't like.

By some estimates, in 2009 Los Angles had one prescription drug pharmacy for every 4,000 residents. Across America there was more than one new corporate chain pharmacy opening every single day during 2006. On January 15, 2007, Los Angeles had one marijuana dispensary for every 39,200 people, but many of the people who obtain medical marijuana from dispensaries within Los Angeles travel from other counties where dispensaries are not permitted.

On January 17, 2007, Los Angeles County had 11 fewer marijuana dispensaries in operation than the day before. That is because armed DEA agents wearing bulletproof vests, gloves, sunglasses, and dust masks raided 11 of the dispensaries located in five cities. (Dust masks? Yes, dust masks.)

Included in the raids was the Farmacy in West Hollywood. That dispensary was considered to be one of the best run of all the dispensaries in L.A. It limited patients to an ounce of medical cannabis when by law patients are allowed to have up to eight ounces. It provided the medication in the form of tinctures as well as candy and baked goods so that patients could avoid smoking it, which would prevent respiratory issues. The Farmacy didn't allow patients to take their medication on the premises. It detained anyone found to be presenting a forged medical marijuana prescription or other documents. It provided medical marijuana for many AIDS, multiple sclerosis, glaucoma, and cancer patients. Some of these patients often deal with a loss of appetite, which is brought back by taking medical marijuana, preventing weight loss and helping the patients to maintain health.

"The government is just rattling their swords [by] taking down these dispensaries. Do they think they are going to stop the need for medical marijuana in California and other states? I don't think so, but by shutting down these safe access locations patients are going to have to turn to the black market."
– Attorney Bruce Margolin of Los Angeles, NORML Legal Committee member

Perhaps the DEA doesn't care about AIDS and cancer patients.

To conduct the raid, the DEA arrived with cardboard boxes printed with the words "DEA Evidence" in blue letters. They used the boxes to gather up the marijuana plants, dried marijuana, baked goods, ice cream bars, and other edible items the dispensaries sold. They also took cash and records, and detained 20 people.

Local officials in West Hollywood said they learned of the raids only as they were happening. Just the day before, the West Hollywood City Council had unanimously voted to cap the number of dispensaries in the city at four while approving an ordinance establishing permanent guidelines for the dispensaries.

The city of West Hollywood had been made well aware of the DEA tactics in dealing with marijuana dispensaries. The city had loaned more than $300,000 to the Los Angeles Cannabis Resource Center to purchase a building that was raided by the DEA in 2001. The DEA seized the building and effectively closed the dispensary that was meant to provide medicinal marijuana to people with AIDS, cancer, and other afflictions.

"We've been fighting to support the access to medicinal marijuana for many, many years and there's just a great disconnect between the federal government and communities like West Hollywood. Medicinal marijuana provides comfort and relief to people who are seriously ill and seemingly they [the DEA] view those people as drug addicts who belong in jail as opposed to people who deserve compassion and assistance."
– West Hollywood California Councilman Jeffrey Prang, in response to DEA raids on medicinal marijuana dispensaries in West Hollywood; January 17, 2007

"There are hundreds of thousands of patients in California who need safe and reliable access to a medication that their doctors recommend they use and these raids are an example of the federal government going out of its way to interfere with the lives of patients."
– Steph Sherer, founder of Americans for Safe Access; January 17, 2007

"The DEA has failed to significantly reduce marijuana consumption despite breathtaking increases in arrests and incarcerations. And its recent efforts aimed at keeping medicine from patients are shamefully transparent attempts to go after an easy target: Marijuana dispensaries operate openly, and cancer patients are limited in their ability to evade law enforcement.

The arcane classification of marijuana under the Controlled Substances Act persists despite the government's own actions and date to the contrary. In 1992, the Food and Drug Administration approved Marinol pills, which use the active ingredient in marijuana (THC) to treat nausea and vomiting. In 1999, the Institute of Medicine, part of

the National Academy of Sciences, concluded that 'the evidence is relatively strong for the [marijuana] treatment of pain and, intriguing although less well established, for movement disorders."
– Attorney Manuel S. Klausner, founder of the Reason Foundation. Sick and need pot? The Feds don't care: We need to rewrite outdated marijuana laws, not raid medical facilities, *Los Angeles Times*, January 26, 2007

It is likely a good thing to put some regulations on where a medical cannabis dispensary can locate, and on the hours that it conducts its business, but it is hardly necessary for the DEA to spend their time and resources on raiding dispensaries when the towns and cities where the dispensaries are located are quite capable of handling any problems that may occur in relation to the dispensaries. If the people have voted to allow the dispensaries, then the government should respect and represent the people. There are many other responsible ways to use tax dollars than to harass ailing people and to close down dispensaries providing a needed medicine to people who benefit from it.

During the second week of June 2007 DEA special agent Timothy J. Landrum sent a two-page letter to more than 150 Los Angeles commercial building landlords warning that they risk arrest and the loss of their properties if they continue allowing cannabis pharmacies to operate out of the buildings.

"By renting their property to individuals violating federal drug laws, they are in and of themselves violating federal law. These [letters of warning] are definitely meant to serve as a notice. What might happen as to the continuing investigations, we'll just have to see."
– Sarah Pollen, Drug Enforcement Administration spokesperson, July 2007

In July 2007 there were more than 400 cannabis pharmacies in operation inside Los Angeles city borders. Within days of the DEA warning landlords were notifying the dispensaries to close shop and move out.

On July 17, 2007 the DEA announced a set of indictments alleging that the Compassionate Caregivers chain-store dispensary operators were profiteering from illegally selling marijuana. The chain owns dispensaries in several California cities, including Bakersfield, Oakland, San Francisco, San Leanardo, Ukiah, and West Hollywood. The DEA accused the owners, James Carberry and Larry R. Kristich, of doing more than $95 million in business and purchasing expensive items including cars and Costa Rican real estate. Other dispensary owners in Corona, Morro Bay, and San Louis Obispo were also indicted.

One doctor, Armand T. Tollette Jr., was indicted and accused of writing prescriptions for minors, not conducting physical examinations, and paying finder fees for client referrals.

"These dispensary operators are no different than any other drug trafficker: They prey on people in our communities to make a profit."
– Timothy J. Landrum, DEA special agent in Los Angeles announcing the indictments against nearly a dozen California medical marijuana dispensaries, July 17, 2007.

When is the DEA going to bust regular pharmaceutical drug company owners and regular chain drug store pharmacies from profiteering on the backs of ailing people, on the backs of the elderly, and for spending money on mansions, expensive cars, vacations, vacation homes, and on country club memberships? This is not a question people may consider when they hear that the DEA is indicting chain medical marijuana pharmacy owners with profiteering. But when it is taken into consideration that the medical marijuana dispensaries are distributing a medicine that is much safer than many of the drugs sold at common chain pharmacies, it is an interesting concept to explore.

Many viewed this tactic of the DEA as a way to clamp down on the number of cannabis pharmacies that the city of Los Angeles was working to regulate. It also was viewed as a threat to safe access for those who do benefit from the medicinal use of marijuana. It would drive people back to obtaining their marijuana the old fashioned way, through street dealers and organized marijuana distributors – which puts them at risk of arrest.

On July 25, 2007 federal DEA agents again raided ten medical marijuana dispensaries in Los Angeles. This happened at the same time the City Council was holding a press conference announcing a moratorium on new medical marijuana dispensaries for at lease one year while the city worked out guidelines of where and how the dispensaries could operate within city borders.

Teams of DEA agents showed up at the dispensaries wearing M-16 rifles and some were dressed in riot gear, including bulletproof shields. Dozens of officers with the Los Angeles Police Department were used to provide "perimeter defense" at the raids. There were also undercover officers who helped stage the raids. Some of the police officers were those who were "cross-deputized" as DEA agents. During the raids agents removed marijuana in the form of the raw dried plant and pot cookies, candy and other edibles. Outside there were crowds gathering and some protesters sat in front of police cars. Some of the protesters were forcibly removed, handcuffed, carried away, body searched, and detained. The badass behavior of the DEA played out as theatre on the local nightly news.

Although DEA spokesperson Sarah Pullen said that the DEA had "been planning this for some time," the timing of the July 25 raids seemed to be less than coincidental. Los Angeles City Councilmembers were busy holding a news conference announcing that they had sent a letter to DEA administrator Karen Tandy to request that the DEA cease threatening medical marijuana dispensaries that supply medicine to the city's medical patients. Some of the people who run the medical dispensaries being raided were attending the conference at City Hall. One of the City Council-members, Dennise Zine, is a former police officer who supports patient access to medical marijuana. Dozens of people showed up to support the moratorium.

Under the atmosphere created by the raids on the medical marijuana dispensaries some patients have avoided the dispensaries and have instead turned to purchasing marijuana off the streets or through home dealers. Each choice carries its own set of risks placing ailing people in an unfair position.

Also unfair is that people who have been arrested for using marijuana for medical reasons have been denied the use of Marinol in prison. The doctors are saying the patients need the drug for a medical problem, but the government is saying the patients can't have it. Who would you rather have controlling your access to medications that may benefit your health, a doctor or someone involved with law enforcement?

"The role of physicians was not that clearly explained [in California's 1996 medical marijuana law], although it was left to physicians to be the ones, in their informed opinion, to determine whether a patient would benefit from marijuana."
– David Thornton, executive director of the California Medical Board, November 2006

Eleven states have passed laws legalizing medical marijuana. But the federal government continues to enforce the federal laws holding that marijuana is illegal and of no medicinal value. The Obama administration notified DEA and other federal offices to respect the medicinal marijuana laws in the states where they have been passed. Although there had been a decrease in the number of raids, they were still happening.

"Notwithstanding any other provision of law, no physician in this state shall be punished, or denied any right or privilege, for having recommended marijuana to a patient for medical purposes."
– Compassionate Use Act of 1996: Proposition 215: California Medical Use of Marijuana Initiative Statute

Doctors who have been prescribing marijuana to patients have found themselves hounded by legal issues. Even though the California state law states that doctors in that state should not be "punished" for recommending marijuana, the reality is that most, if not all, of them have experienced some level of being investigated by the state medical board. They have also been dealing with the federal government laws against cannabis, those who enforce those laws, and the various laws of each county and city. Even though a federal appeals court ruled that the U.S. Drug Enforcement Administration cannot target doctors on the basis of their recommending marijuana to patients, it appears that is exactly what has going on.

During the Bush administration, marijuana dispensary raids and issues relating to the doctors who recommend medicinal marijuana were much more common.

Dr. Mollie Fry is one who had her life disrupted by the federal laws. Her office and home had been raided by federal drug agents. In 2005 she was indicted by a grand jury on felony charges of conspiring to distribute marijuana.

"I assumed the fact that I had 'M.D.' at the end of my name gave me the right to make judgments about people's health.

... What did I take an oath to do? To do no harm and to alleviate pain and suffering.

... I'm going to be true to my oath, and I'm even willing to go to prison for it."
– Dr. Mollie Fry, of Cool, California; November 2006

Doctors who have been prescribing marijuana to their patients suffering from such conditions as AIDS, cancer, glaucoma, and other ailments with symptoms that clearly are relieved through marijuana, have been accused of being quacks. The doctors recommending marijuana are also accused of neglecting to prescribe synthetic chemical drugs that may relieve the same symptoms that marijuana may relieve. Having patients take synthetic chemical drugs may be good for the pharmaceutical companies, including ones that donate money to various politicians, but it doesn't mean that the chemical drugs are best for patients.

Chemical prescription drugs are often accompanied by a long list of known and risky side effects such as ulcers, stroke, heart attack, bloody stool, kidney failure, addiction, and cancers, including leukemia. Marijuana exists often as a much safer medicine. It is very common for patients to express symptom relief from marijuana not experienced from the synthetic prescription drugs. The medicine given to the patient should be a matter between the doctor and the patient, and not between pharmaceutical

316

companies, law enforcement, and politicians that benefit from donations from pharmaceutical companies.

Doctors recommending marijuana have also been accused of not conducting significantly thorough exams of patients before recommending marijuana to a patient. That may be true in many cases, but neglecting to conduct thorough exams is not something limited to doctors prescribing marijuana. How many billions of prescription pills of all varieties are being taken by patients who barely spent more than a minute or less with a doctor before that doctor prescribed a drug, and often a drug that carries serious risks?

It has been very well documented that doctors often prescribe medications of all varieties without sufficient information on patient health, and without knowing what other drugs a patient may be taking that could counteract the prescription drug, or that may interact with another drug the patient is taking, which might cause the patient to suffer grave consequences.

The doctors who recommend marijuana are often put under great scrutiny and face charges of unprofessional conduct not applicable to other doctors who neglectfully prescribe much more dangerous drugs and/or perform unnecessary and risky surgeries.

When a person goes to a pharmacy to have a prescription filled, the person they may be dealing with at many chain drug store outlets may be an employee with no formal medical training and who may be as young as 16. There have been a rash of misfiled prescriptions resulting in patient injuries, including comas, strokes, and death. Additionally, many prescription drugs carry serious risks even when taken as directed.

I know a little bit about medical malpractice. I wrote a book (*Surgery Electives*) that largely focused on the widespread medical misconduct and bad medicine that plagues America through its hospitals, insurance companies, medical training, and the marketing of surgery and drugs. Thousands of patients die or suffer horrible consequences after being misdiagnosed, or after taking harmful drugs that are often misprescribed. Many more die or are left disabled by surgeries that should never have taken place.

It is likely that there are many patients who have been recommended marijuana after a doctor did not conduct the best sort of exam. But it would be better to improve doctor education and practices rather than to prosecute doctors and deny medicine to those patients who may benefit from it.

If the so-called authorities want to improve the state of medicine, perhaps they should consider the amount of money being spent by pharmaceutical companies to romance doctors into prescribing toxic synthetic chemical drugs. They should consider the number of patients who are undergoing dangerous surgeries when the patient could have experienced better long-term health with some other form of attention and/or a dietary and/or lifestyle change. They should consider the number of patients who are taking prescribed drugs that harm health. They should consider the number of patients who have experienced the terrible consequences of taking two or more drugs that interact with each other. They should consider the billions of dollars being spent by the government to support the pharmaceutical drug industry, the hospital industry, and the insurance industry. They should consider what doctors are actually learning in school, and how allopathic medical schools often function as facilities to teach student doctors how to prescribe lucrative drugs and surgery rather than how to actually improve patient health through what causes most health problems: bad diet, lack of exercise, stress, and environmental toxins. They should improve the situation of the poor who often neglect their health because they cannot afford to see a doctor and who are one paycheck away from financial ruin if they experience illness or disability.

"As to the message we are sending to kids, NORML hopes the message we are sending is that we would not deny any effective medication to the seriously ill and dying. We routinely permit cancer patients to self-administer morphine in cancer wards all across the country; we allow physicians to prescribe amphetamines for weight loss and to use cocaine in nose and throat operations. Each of these drugs can be abused on the street, yet no one is suggesting we are sending the wrong message to kids by permitting their medical use."
– National Organization for the Reform of Marijuana Laws, NORML.org

"Marijuana is not a cure, but it can help cancer patients. Most have severe reactions to the disease and chemotherapy – commonly, severe nausea and vomiting. One in three patients discontinues treatment despite a 50 percent chance of improvement. When standard anti-nausea drugs fail, marijuana often eases patients' nausea and permits continued treatment. It can be either smoked or baked into foods.

… When one in five Americans will have cancer, and 20 million may develop glaucoma, shouldn't our government let physicians prescribe any medicine capable of relieving suffering?

… The federal government stopped supplying marijuana to patients in 1991 [actually, it stopped accepting new patients into the FDA's Compassionate Investigative New Drug Program, allowing approved patients access to government-grown marijuana from the University of Mississippi]. Now it tells patients to take Marinol, a synthetic substitute for marijuana that can cost $30,000 a year and is often less reliable and less effective.

... Marijuana is not magic. But often it is the only way to get relief. A Harvard University survey found that almost one-half of cancer doctors surveyed would prescribe marijuana to some of their patients if it were legal.

... Today, physicians are allowed to prescribe powerful drugs like morphine and codeine. It doesn't make sense that they cannot prescribe marijuana, too.

– Richard J. Cohen, M.D., Consulting Medical Oncologist, California-Pacific Medical Center, San Francisco; Ivan Silverberg, M.D., Medical Oncologist, San Francisco; Anna T. Boyce, registered nurse, Orange County; Argument in Favor of Proposition 215, the medical marijuana bill – now law in California

It is outrageous that people who are suffering from terminal health conditions cannot get access to a simple medication contained in a plant. What crime are they committing by relieving their symptoms?

Currently those patients who can benefit most from the therapeutic effects of marijuana must purchase the medication illegally. Because many of them are too ill to be mobile, they rely on friends and relatives to purchase the marijuana. This places these individuals in what might be uncomfortable and dangerous situations.

The laws that attempt to prohibit the use of marijuana were not based on any scientific studies. Instead, they were based on lies and without considering the needs of ailing or dying people. They are arcane, antiquated, and draconian laws that should never have been created.

In 1937 representatives of the American Medical Association urged Congress to keep marijuana available as a medication that doctors could prescribe. The AMA was unprepared to present their findings because they found out about the hearings to overtax marijuana just two days before the hearings occurred. The AMA was ignored by these politicians who were being manipulated by William Randolph Hearst, Du Pont, Anslinger, Andrew Mellon's interests, the paper companies, and others who benefited financially when hemp and marijuana became illegal.

"Some physicians will have the courage to challenge the continued proscription of marijuana for the sick. Eventually, their actions will force the courts to adjudicate between the rights of those at death's door and the absolute power of bureaucrats whose decisions are based more on reflexive ideology and political correctness than on compassion."

– Jerome P. Kassirer, M.D., editor, *New England Journal of Medicine*, January 30, 1997

"Cannabis should be made available even if only a few patients could get relief from it, because the risks would be so small. For example, as I mentioned, many patients with multiple sclerosis find that cannabis reduces their muscle spasms and pain. A physician may not be sure that such a patient will get more relief from marihuana than from the standard drugs baclofen, dantrolene, and diazepam – all of which are potentially dangerous or addictive – but it is almost certain that a serious toxic reaction to marihuana will not occur. Therefore the potential benefit is much greater than any potential risk."
– Dr. Lester Grinspoon, formal testimony before the Crime Subcommittee, Judiciary Committee, U.S. House of Representatives, October 1, 1997

"Marihuana worked like a charm. I disliked the 'side effect' of mental blurring (the 'main effect' for recreational users), but the sheer bliss of not experiencing nausea – and then not having to fear it for all the days intervening between treatments – was the greatest boost I received in all my year of treatment, and surely had a most important effect upon my eventual cure. It is beyond my comprehension – and I fancy I am able to comprehend a lot, including much nonsense – that any humane person would withhold such a beneficial substance from people in such great need simply because others use it for different purposes."
– from *Marihuana: The Forbidden Medicine*, by the late Stephen Jay Gould, American paleontologist. He used marijuana to prevent nausea during his treatment for abdominal mesothelioma. StephenJayGould.org

The control of a substance that provides benefits to ailing people should be in the hands of the health community, and not in the hands of the politicians and law enforcement officials. Even drugs such as cocaine and morphine, which are illegal on the streets, are often used for pain relief in medical facilities.

The U.S. government needs to reclassify cannabis from a Schedule 1 drug to a Schedule 2 drug – the same classification as morphine, cocaine, and other common medical drugs. This will allow doctors to legally prescribe cannabis to their patients that can benefit from it.

For more on marijuana, read the book *Understanding Marijuana: A New Look at the Scientific Evidence*, by Mitch Earleywine.

# The Trials of Ed Rosenthal: More Government Money Wasted

Ed Rosenthal has been a columnist for both *High Times* and *Cannabis Culture* magazines. He is the author of several books, including *Closet Cultivator: Indoor Marijuana Cultivation Made Easy*; *Marijuana Growers Handbook: The Indoor High Yield Cultivation Grow Guide*; *The Big Book of Buds: Marijuana Varieties from the World's Great Seed Breeders*; and *Ask Ed: Marijuana Law. Don't Get Busted.*

In one of its most aggressive moves to prosecute someone involved with medical marijuana, in February 2002 the U.S. Attorney charged Rosenthal with cultivation and distribution of marijuana after they had found him to be growing hundreds of plants in a warehouse.

On September 4, 1998, Rosenthal was deputized by the city of Oakland, California, as an "officer of the City of Oakland" for the purpose of cultivating marijuana for local patients, pursuant to the Oakland Municipal Code Pertaining to Medical Cannabis. Therefore, his work with the marijuana plants was in compliance with city regulations. He supplied marijuana plants to the Harm Reduction Center, a San Francisco compassion group running a dispensary providing marijuana to medical patients. In addition to the warehouse, the Harm Reduction Center and Rosenthal's residence were also raided.

What Rosenthal was doing is legal under California state law, but illegal under federal law. However, the U.S. Attorney's office found it necessary to spend a whole bunch of money to put Rosenthal through two trials.

In his first trial Rosenthal was convicted on February 1, 2003, and faced five or more years in prison and possible fines of up to 4.5 million. The prosecutors wanted him sentenced to 6 1/2 years. The judge cited unusual circumstances and Rosenthal was sentenced to the minimum time possible under the case: one day in jail. But Rosenthal was credited with time served. He was also fined $1,000.

Complicating his defense, U.S. District Court Judge Charles Breyer ruled that the evidence and witnesses Rosenthal had tried to introduce for both his first and second trial were inadmissible and irrelevant. Therefore, the jury never heard that Rosenthal had been deputized by the City of Oakland to provide medical marijuana, or that he was in compliance with city regulations. Rosenthal's defense was not permitted to present scientific testimony about the medical efficacy of marijuana, nor were they allowed to present information about state laws and local ordinances governing medical marijuana. Testimony from city council member Nate Miley was allowed in the first trial, but was not allowed in the second trial.

When the jury of the first trial learned that they were not permitted to hear the whole story, including that Rosenthal was acting on behalf of city officials, within hours of the verdict seven of the 12 jurors repudiated their verdict and criticized the court.

Upon appeal, Rosenthal's attorney, Dennis Riordan, argued in September 2005 that the trial judge's refusal to allow Rosenthal to present information regarding his work to supply cannabis to medical marijuana patients as permitted by the state and city violated Rosenthal's Sixth Amendment right to a fair trial. The three-judge panel of the Ninth Circuit Court of Appeals said, "We reject the premise that an ordinance such as the one Oakland enacted can shield a defendant from prosecution for violation of federal drug laws."

On April 26, 2006, Rosenthal's conviction was overturned on the standing that a juror engaged in misconduct by seeking outside legal advice from an attorney friend prior to the verdict. The appeals court ruled that this exchange between the juror and her attorney friend was an "improper influence."

The juror said she had called her attorney friend because she was "troubled" and "frustrated and confused" by the court presentation that was lacking information on medical marijuana and by the judge's instruction that only federal law could be considered in the case. The juror had asked her attorney friend if she could vote her conscience. Her friend told her that she should follow the instructions of the judge or she could "get into trouble." The court's opinion was that, "Jurors cannot fairly determine the outcome of a case if they believe they will face 'trouble' for a conclusion they reach as jurors." The court was of the opinion that, "A juror who genuinely fears retribution might change his or her determination of the issue for fear of being punished."

"We hold that here the communication was an improper influence upon Juror A's decision to acquit or convict."
– Ninth Circuit Court of Appeals Judge Betty Fletcher wrote for the court, joined by judges Marsha Berzon and John Gibson.

The federal prosecutors had also filed an appeal and argued that Rosenthal should have received two to five years in prison. Upon overturning Rosenthal's conviction, the Ninth Circuit said that the government's challenge to the length of Rosenthal's sentence was "moot."

On October 12, 2006, the U.S. Attorney's office in San Francisco re-indicted Rosenthal.

On May 30, 2007, the jury of the second trial split its verdict on a trial during which Rosenthal offered no defense. He was found guilty of three federal felonies, including one conspiracy count; one count of growing with intent to distribute and of distributing marijuana; and one count of using a commercial building to grow and distribute marijuana. He was found not guilty on charges relating to providing marijuana plants to the Harm Reduction Center. The jury deadlocked on a conspiracy count, which was dismissed by the U.S. Attorney's office on direction of the judge.

Nine additional money laundering and tax evasion charges that the U.S. Attorney's office brought against Rosenthal when they reindicted him in October 2006 were ruled to be vindictive prosecution and dismissed by Judge Breyer on March 14. In his ruling to dismiss, Judge Breyer said, "The government's deeds – and words – create the perception that it added the new charges to make Rosenthal look like a common criminal and thus dissipate the criticism heaped on the government after the first trial."

The U.S. Attorney's office tried to get seven medical marijuana patients to testify against Rosenthal. All seven patients rejected immunity letters from the U.S. Attorney's office, refused to answer questions, and were found in contempt of court. They were later excused by Judge Breyer after telling him that they would not testify.

"I think that this prosecution is against the will of the people, and it's actually harming the citizens of California. I believe it would be illegal and immoral for me to participate in the prosecution because of that."
– Debby Goldsberry, one of seven patients who refused to testify against Ed Rosenthal

The judge as well as the prosecutor allowed that Rosenthal would serve no jail time or have to pay a fine with the second conviction. He had already had three years of supervised release.

"The government gets medical marijuana convictions by cherry-picking juries and then preventing any meaningful defense. When it comes to medical marijuana, our federal system of justice is broken."
– Rob Amparán, attorney for Ed Rosenthal. May 30, 2007.

"If the jury had heard the whole truth, they would have acquitted me on all charges. These laws are doomed. Science and compassion will win out over politics and superstition...
Whether they know it or not, the jury voted against their own self-interest. At some point they're going to wake up and realize the enormity of what they did, and they're going to live with that for the rest of their lives the way the previous jury did..."

It's a cruel thing for the government to impose upon its citizens, the idea that they have to leave their conscience behind when they vote in the jury box. That should be part of it, and so should justice."
— Ed Rosenthal, May 30, 2007; Green-Aid.com

# Cannabis Use In Religion, Spirituality, and Artistic Expression

Throughout the history of humanity, cannabis, or some derivative of it, became popular for both entertainment and spiritual use. It has been used by everyone from the Africans to the Celts, Chinese, Egyptians, Indians, and the Romans. The Rastafarians, a religious sect with roots in Jamaica, and the Zion Coptic Church of Ethiopia, believe cannabis was grown on King Solomon's grave.

"When you smoke herb, herb reveal yourself to you. All the wickedness you do, the herb reveal it to yourself, your conscience, show up yourself clear, because herb make you meditate. Is only a natural thing and it grow like a tree."
– Bob Marley, Rastafarian and popular reggae musician

"The sacred source of ganja permits a sense of religious communication, marked by meditation and contemplation."
– 1970 Jamaican study conducted by the National Institute of Mental Health's Center for Studies of Narcotic and Drug Abuse. The study also concluded "that there is little correlation between the use of ganja and crime, except insofar as the possession and cultivation of ganja are technically crimes."

Some people believe cannabis allows for the ultimate transfer of intelligence from plants to humans and that the spiritual nature of this is a gift from Divinity. The belief is that the thoughts and feelings a person can experience after smoking or ingesting cannabis is something that should be respected as a communication from the power of Nature, used only under nurturing circumstances in natural surroundings, and used only in a way that will broaden or fine tune talents, skills, and intellect. If used respectfully it can bring about an elevation of consciousness and enlightenment while cultivating wisdom that a person may have been unable or unwilling to explore. But if abused, it can drag a person down, which is why some shamanists frown upon using the substance without intention.

When modern science discovered that the human brain has cannabinoid receptors where the cannabinoid molecules in cannabis can dock, some people began citing this as proof that we humans are physically designed to use cannabis to help our brains function. Maybe this explains why people have been using cannabis for thousands of years, often with the belief that it is a sort of deliverer of messages from the Divine.

325

"Hashish will be, indeed, for the impressions and familiar thoughts of a man, a mirror which magnifies, yet no more than a mirror."
– Charles Baudelaire, *The Poem of Hashish*, 1860

Some people use cannabis for "deep play," which is a combination of mental and physical exercise, such as yoga exercise sessions interspersed with sessions of such things as creative writing, supportive conversation, massage, and/or ecstatic dance. Deep play is done in a positive, uplifting, nurturing, and nonjudgmental atmosphere. It may involve instrumental music listened to while reading from literature that has to do with personal growth and life transformation. Deep play is exploratory, conducted in groups, is often scheduled as a weekend retreat, and is done with the goal of awakening and strengthening intellect and talent. It does not have to involve the use of cannabis or other drugs.

Cannabis is only one of the introspective substances that shamans, medicine men, medicine woman, and other spiritual advisors of primitive cultures used in their rituals. In every part of the world the ancient societies used substances to alter the mind, often in ceremonial settings. The substances have been treated sacredly and include ayahuasca, peyote, mushrooms, tobacco, coca leaves, the extracts of certain vines, flowers, and other plants, and even the body fluids of certain frogs. Even the land where the substances were found were treated with respect as they too were thought to be connected to the Divine. Many people still use these substances in the same way as the ancients. There is a renewed interest in substances traditionally used by shamans, even so much so that annual gatherings are held for people interested in learning about them. Many of the substances have been made illegal. Hallucinogenic mushrooms have been illegal under international law since 1971.

Interestingly, alcohol is considered by many to interfere with or block spiritual revelations. This was something learned by shamanistic cultures as alcohol was introduced to them by European colonists. Some advised their communities that alcohol would bring them down. As the colonists and Christian missionaries established themselves around the world they often worked to eliminate the "pagan rituals" of ancient cultures, including the substances used for spiritual ceremonies. In North America those who wished to continue living the way of their people were killed off, or forced into "reservations," and looked to as burdensome pariahs. Unfortunately alcohol has done much damage to Native American peoples, many of whom are genetically susceptible to alcohol addiction. Shamanistic cultures on other continents have suffered similar consequences as their sacramental substances have been outlawed, religions have been dismissed, lands have been taken over, protesters have been killed, and tax revenue-generating alcohol has been brought in.

Today North America has hundreds of thousands of commercial venues selling alcohol while the substances the ancient cultures used in their spiritual practices throughout history have been outlawed. Even during the Prohibition era, America allowed the Catholic Church to continue using wine in the sacrament. While alcohol causes more problems than any drug ever has, the Indigenous peoples who use peyote as well as other people who wish to use magic mushrooms or other substances for spiritual matters are treated as criminals. The spiritual beliefs of the native cultures are often dismissed as nonsense while a variety of religions that came from Europe and other countries are openly practiced in buildings constructed in ways that destroy land the Natives treated sacredly.

The people living in lands where cannabis is believed to have originated still use cannabis in their religious practices.

The Hindus believe that Shiva brought cannabis from the Himalayas over three thousand years ago. They believe that cannabis helps them commune with Shiva, Lord of Bhang. The Hindu religious festival Kumbh Mela and the devotional practice called puja include the use of cannabis.

Cannabis also has a history within the Buddhist religion, with the story being that Buddha survived for several years by eating hemp seeds while on the path to enlightenment.

The Buddhist Tantra sect has a history of using cannabis to become free of consciousness and heighten spirituality. Today the tantric sex practiced by many different people around the world may or may not involve some use of cannabis along with breathing patterns, massage, and intertwined yoga type practices to heighten spirituality and build respect of the sacredness of the act while healing, awakening, and strengthening the soul union.

It is known that THC increases the effectiveness of morphine taken by patients on that prescription pain killer. THC may also heighten the effects of natural drugs produced by the brain, such as the pleasure sensation-inducing neurotransmitter anandamide, which docks with the same cell receptors in the brain and other areas of the body with which THC has been found to dock. In addition to the receptors that are found on the cells of the brain and spinal chord, some of the receptors that receive both anandamide and THC have been found on the cells of the tissues in the sex organs. THC also increases the sensation of touch, making sex more sensual.

Yoga has been practiced for thousands of years. Breathing techniques that can increase sexual energy between two people have been known forever. THC wasn't identified until the 1960s. The cell receptors weren't identified until the 1980s. And anandamide wasn't identified until the 1990s.

But for thousands of years people didn't need the scientific understanding of all this to have incredible sex combined with the feelings of love for their partner that they considered to be spiritually enlightening.

The medieval Catholic Church considered cannabis to be a tool used by heretics. When Pope Gregory IX began the Inquisition of the Holy Catholic Church in 1231, those who used cannabis were among those hunted for persecution. Unfortunately, the persecution that the Catholic Church doled out during the inquisitions often translated to ruin, imprisonment, torture, maiming, and sometimes death.

In 1484 Pope Innocent VIII banished the use of cannabis because it was thought to be part of witchcraft and used in satanic rituals. The deviant vision people often think up when they hear the word *witch* is commonly greatly exaggerated compared to the reality of who was considered to be a witch. A witch could be anyone, including those who used plants as medicine for others, or they could be crazy lunatics. A person who was considered to be a witch was often a shamanistic type of person who used plant substances in his or her work, which may have included being a sort of caretaker for the local community. The medicines used by the healers of the day included simple herbal teas, or plants that were applied to the skin, or plants that were burned, which sometimes included marijuana. Opium also began to have a European presence during this era. These were the days before an understanding of germs and where anything possible would be used to kill pain. A simple cut could result in an infection that could spread to the brain and leave the person mentally disabled; or could lead to an infected limb, which was then amputated in the most barbaric manner, which also lead to many deaths. Oftentimes, before people understood germs, infections led to death. When healers applied plant remedies that effectively healed someone the healer could be considered magical. If they weren't part of the organized church, they could be considered heretics who were getting their power from the devil. Therefore, they were subject to punishment by the church. The punishment often included prison, torture, and/or death.

Pope Innocent VIII issued a precedent declaring marijuana to be an "unholy sacrament." His view was that Arabic culture and Arabs who smoked hashish were ruining society. Those who used it were to be punished.

All of these actions to demonize cannabis and persecute those who may or may not have used it didn't stop people from partaking of it. The Celts had used it, and made porridge out of its seeds (or, more specifically, they made porridge from what we now call hemp seeds). But their smoking of cannabis became secretive because of medieval Christianity. As I mention, some of those who were considered to be witches used it. Some people in Europe wrote about it, most notably the satirist Francois Rabelais, a French Benedictine monk who was born in 1483. Rabelais's *Gargantua and Pantagruel* was published in 1532.

The use of cannabis for spiritual enlightenment continues today. There have been many people claiming that cannabis has benefits just as there have been those who say cannabis causes problems.

Some say marijuana causes mental health problems. Is that so?

"Armed with sound bites reminiscent of the 1936 propaganda film *Reefer Madness*, the U.S. government recently kicked off yet another smear campaign on the supposed dangers of marijuana. The Fed's latest charge: Pot causes mental illness.

'A growing body of evidence now demonstrates that smoking marijuana can increase the risk of serious mental health problems,' U.S. Drug Czar John Walters announced at a press conference hyping the White House's latest antipot campaign. 'New research being conducted here and abroad illustrates that marijuana use, particularly during teen years, can lead to depression, thoughts of suicide, and schizophrenia.'

Those looking for the science behind the White House's alarm would be hard-pressed to find any. Absent from their campaign was any mention of a recent clinical study published in the April 2005 issue of the journal *Psychiatry Research* refuting a causal link between cannabis use and behavior suggestive of schizophrenia. 'The current study… suggest[s] a temporal precedence of schizotypal traits before cannabis use in most cases,' its authors concluded. 'These findings do not support a causal link between cannabis use and schizotypal traits.'

Survey data published in the journal *Addictive Behavior* also puts a damper on the White House's 'pot leads to depression' claims. After analyzing survey results from 4,400 adults who had completed The Center for Epidemiologic Studies Depression scale (a numerical, self-report scale designed to assess symptoms of depression in the general population), researchers at the University of Southern California found: 'Despite comparable ranges of scores on all depression subscales, those who used [marijuana] once per week or less had less depressed mood, more positive effect, and fewer somatic (physical) complaints than non-users… Daily users [also] reported less depressed mood and more positive effect than non-users.'

Last, there are the results of a recent meta-analysis published in the journal *Current Opinion in Pharmacology*. The study's verdict? Those who use cannabis in moderation, even long-term 'will not suffer any lasting physical or mental harm… Overall, by comparison with other drugs used mainly for 'recreational' purposes, cannabis could be rated to be a relatively safe drug.' "

329

– Cannabis, Mental Health and Context: The Case for Regulation, by Paul Armentano, Senior Policy Analyst, National Organization for the Reform of Marijuana Laws/NORML Foundation; January 27, 2006; NORML.org

What marijuana may do is similar to what alcohol or other drugs may do: help expose a pre-existing problem in a person's life. Who hasn't been around someone who has had too much to drink who then admits to some life issue that needs attention, or who displays a state of mind that is in need of healing?

As is the case with alcohol and other mind-altering substances, what some people are doing when they smoke marijuana is possibly trying to escape their problems, or to deal with an issue that they are not able to handle otherwise and/or they aren't managing in the best way. In other words, what they may be displaying is a call for help. Hopefully they will be able to get the help they need and be able to straighten out their life.

Others may simply be using cannabis in a way that is helping them to explore thoughts that can lead to enlightenment on certain issues, finding ways to attain their goals and practice their talents. Artists are often trying to explore their creativity. Art begins in the mind, and mind-expanding drugs have often been used by artists wanting to get into their own minds.

Mind-assisting substances may help a person to utilize areas of the brain that had not been accessed. This can result in opening a person to his or her potential, intellect, talents, and life. But using mind-altering substances too often or too much may also close off the person from these very same opportunities and attributes – and drag them down to the level of self-destruction.

"Cannabis serves as a guide to psychic areas which can then be re-entered without it."
– William Burroughs, Points of Distinction Between Sedative and Consciousness-Expanding Drugs, *Evergreen Review*, 1964

Cultures throughout the world are known to advance members of their communities by assisting them through a ceremony where substances of some type are taken and the thought processes of the person explored and/or guided. Results of this can be seen in the art, architecture, music, and literature of ancient people. From the intricate patterns on their fabrics to the design of their structures and cities, ancient people expressed what they discovered on substance-assisted adventures of exploratory and/or guided thought. This is why some cultures treat certain plants and mushrooms as sacred substances that should be respected. They understand the potential these substances can aid in releasing. They also understand how misuse and disrespect for certain substances can limit or damage a person. Modern-day partiers could learn a thing or two from studying the way ancient cultures and present-day shamanistic medicine people treat various ceremonial substances.

Great minds throughout history have been known to be under the influence of some sort of substance when they created their landmark works. If you have ever listened to music, enjoyed art, read novels or poetry, observed architecture, and even read religious texts, you have likely observed works that have been created under the influence of something other than pure sobriety.

As the African American culture began to flourish after slavery ended, many African Americans formed social groups, clubs, professional and church organizations, and created their own form of art and music. Jazz and blues and the clubs where they were played helped form the culture. New Orleans was considered the center of these forms of music, and it was also where cannabis not only grew easily, but also was easily available because New Orleans was a port town where cannabis arrived from the islands as well as from Central and South America. While many jazz and blues musicians sang songs about cannabis, others refrained from partaking of the substance and considered it to be something that hampered talent and/or was simply not a good thing.

Jazz and blues aren't the only types of music influenced by cannabis. At the same time that jazz music was developing in the U.S., the Greeks were developing a type of music called *rebetika*, which was influenced by Turkish folk songs that they became familiar with during the Greco-Turkish war.

Jamaica became known for its reggae music, its most famous musician being Bob Marley, who just as famously was known for his use of ganja. Little Richard, Jerry Lee Lewis, and Elvis Presley were obviously influenced by jazz and the blues, which led to rock and roll. While not all rock and roll has been influenced by cannabis, it is no secret that some of it has. As has some American folk music, bluegrass, and other forms of musical expression.

There are a large number of books written by authors known to have experiences with some form of cannabis and/or other drugs, such as opium and an extract first derived from it in 1803, morphine. If you have read a variety of works of the European writers of the 1700s and 1800s, then you have likely read material written under the influence of, or that was influenced by cannabis.

Thomas de Quincey's autobiographical *Confessions of an English Opium Eater* was first published in *London Magazine* in 1821, and the next year in book form. In it he gave a description of what it was like to partake of laudanum, a widely overprescribed medication made of alcohol and opium, and sometimes sugar. "Here was the secret of happiness, about which philosophers had disputed for so many ages, at once discovered; happiness might now be bought for a penny, and carried in the waistcoat pocket; portable ecstacies might be had corked up in a pint bottle; and peace of mind could be sent down by the mail." While he had been prescribed laudanum for "acute neuralgia pains" in 1804, his addiction to it apparently lasted the rest of his life. In the medical world laudanum was losing favor, after the use of highly addictive morphine was isolated in 1804 and became more common as a painkiller after the 1853 invention of the hypodermic needle, but laudanum is still available today as a prescription drug. The descriptions de Quincey gave of his experiences with laudanum influenced other writers to explore drugs. His book became known in literary circles, including his own circle of friends and acquaintances such as Richard Woodhouse, Samuel Taylor Coleridge (also a laudanum addict), Charles Lamb, and William Wordsworth.

Other drugs of the 1800s included heroin, which was synthesized from morphine in 1874, and cocaine, which was first successfully isolated from the leaves of the South American coca plant by German chemist Friedrich Gaedcke in 1855 (*not* cacao, which is a different plant with beans harvested to make chocolate).

For centuries the leaves of the coca plant had been used as a mild stimulant by the South American Andean natives. That all changed when science learned to extract the active ingredient in the leaves that provided the slight energy boost. It was quickly understood that the pure powder was very different from the whole leaf, and that it created health problems never experienced by the natives who chewed the leaves. It has been discovered that coca leaves contain modifying substances that soften the effects of the stimulant.

By 1863 cocaine was being used in Vin Mariani wine in Italy, with Catholic Pope Leo XIII being one of its most outspoken fans.

Cocaine was also used in the original recipe of Coca-Cola™. That "soda drink" also contained caffeine derived from kola nuts, an African rainforest nut that is related to the cacao (chocolate) trees of South America.

Druggist John Pemberton, who invented what became Coca-Cola in the late 1800s, intended the drink to be used as a patent medicine. As his cocaine-laced alcoholic beverage became popular in Atlanta, Pemberton began marketing it in 1885 as Pemberton's French Wine Coca. The Atlanta-based company had been importing what amounted to tons of cocaine to use in its "soft drinks" that they marketed as "brain food." Each serving was estimated to contain as much as nine milligrams of cocaine.

After Atlanta placed prohibition on alcohol in 1886, Pemberton omitted alcohol from the recipe and renamed the cocaine- and caffeine-laced beverage Coca-Cola. It was originally sold from fountains in Atlanta's

Jacob's Pharmacy. Ironically, Pemberton advertised his drink in the Atlanta Journal as a health tonic capable of curing morphine addiction, impotence, and headaches.

By 1887 Coca-Cola was being sold by a number of companies. The first bottled product was sold in the 1890s. In 1899 a bottling factory was opened in Chattanooga, Tennessee. By that time, a whole lot of people had become addicted to the cocaine-laced drink and distribution was expanding throughout the U.S. The mass-produced bottle was mistakenly based on the cacao nut pod (chocolate) when the designer was trying to find out what one of the ingredients, coca, looked like in its natural state. Coca-Cola bottles, cans, and packaging have become some of the most recognizable forms of land and water pollution in the world.

After Atlanta placed cocaine on a list of prescribable medications, in 1903 Coca-Cola omitted the cocaine from the recipe and kept the caffeine, which is also addictive.

In 1911, the U.S. government seized 40 barrels and 20 kegs of Coca-Cola syrup from the Chattanooga bottling company. Trying to prove that caffeine was injurious to children's health, the government took case against the company with United States vs. Forty Barrels and Twenty Kegs of Coca-Cola. The case was dismissed, but the next year the Pure Food and Drug Act was amended to require that the "habit-forming" and "deleterious" substance of caffeine be listed on any substance meant for human consumption.

The Coca-Cola sold in the modern day still contains extract of the coca leaves. Tons of these leaves are legally imported from Peru and Bolivia by Stepan Company of Maywood, New Jersey. The cocaine extracted from the leaves is turned into medical grade cocaine by Mallinckrodt Incorporated of Missouri. Mallinckrodt also imports opium from India, and uses it to make medical grade morphine.

Today, Coca-Cola contains coca-leaf extract, kola nut extract, and caffeine. If that isn't enough unhealthful ingredients, it is also made with high fructose corn syrup and/or artificial sweeteners, dye, and flavorings, and the cans and bottles also contain substances that are not ideal for health. It makes billions of dollars around the planet. Ironically, the Coca-Cola Company is one of the lead sponsors of sporting events, including the Olympics.

Among those who experimented with cocaine was the famous psychoanalyst, Sigmund Freud. He shared cocaine with his wife, and wrote an upbeat essay about it in 1884. Apparently his use of cocaine left Freud with permanent damage to his sinuses. Some say this is why he liked to sit out of view of his patients as they reclined on a sofa.

Warnings of cocaine's addictive qualities began surfacing, and were written about in the November 28, 1885, edition of *Medical Record* journal, which stated, "Continuous indulgence finally creates a craving which must be satisfied; the individual then becomes nervous, tremulous, sleepless, without appetite, and he is at last reduced to a condition of pitiable neurasthenia."

While those other highly addictive drugs made their rounds, cannabis and its extract, hashish, were becoming more common. Cannabis was becoming known as a safe drug because, unlike cocaine, heroin, morphine, and opium, people learned that they could do it without becoming physically addicted. Poets, including Earnest Dowson, Arthur Rimbaud, John Addington Symonds, Baylor Taylor, and Paul Verlaine were known to use hashish.

"External objects acquire, gradually and one after another, strange new appearances; they become distorted or transformed. Next occur mistakes in the identity of objects, and transposals of ideas. Sounds clothe themselves in colours; and colours contain music."
– Charles Baudelaire, describing his experiences on hashish

In the 1840s a group of writers in Paris formed a club they called The Hashish-Eaters Club (Le Club des Hachichins). Among the first members was Theophile Gautier, author of *Mademoiselle de Maupin* and writer of *Art for Art's Sake*. In addition to Gautier, members of the club included the writers Honore de Balzac (*Lost Illusions*), Charles Baudelaire (*The Flowers of Evil*), Alexandre Dumas (*The Count of Monte Cristo*; *The Three Musketeers*), Victor Hugo (*Les Miserables*; *The Hunchback of Notre-Dame*), and Gerard de Nerval (*Journey to the Orient*). The members of the club gathered at the Hotel Pimodan apartment of painter Fernand Boissard de Boisdenier. Some of the writers, including Dumas, mentioned hashish or cannabis in their novels. A French doctor, Jacques-Joseph Moreau, was also associated with the Club des Hachichins and kept records of his meetings with the members, exploring the effects of hashish on their imaginations and minds. Because the writers were eating hashish, which is much stronger than simply smoking a few puffs of it, and because the club members were known to partake of opium and other drugs, Moreau's notes are unreliable as a study on cannabis.

Another person of note in this era was author, playwright, poet, philosopher, and doctor Charles Robert Richet. In 1877 he observed that under the influence of hashish, "in the space of a minute we have fifty different thoughts; since in general it requires several minutes to have fifty different thoughts, it will appear to us that several minutes are passed, and it is only by going to the inflexible clock, which marks for us the regular passage of time, that we perceive our error. With hashish the notion of time is completely overthrown, the moments are years, and the minutes are centuries; but I feel the insufficiency of language to express this illusion, and I believe, that one can only understand it by feeling it for himself." In 1887 Richet was named a professor of physiology at the College de France in Paris. He won the Nobel Prize for Physiology or Medicine in 1913 for his work on anaphylaxis (shock that can result in death when a person is exposed to an antigen).

American novelists, artists, and musicians of all sorts during the Bohemian era were outspoken about their use of cannabis, and/or included some reference to it in their art. Perhaps the most popular was a good friend of Samuel Clemens (Mark Twain), Fritz Hugh Ludlow, whose *The Hasheesh Eater: Being Passages from the Life of a Pythagorean* was published in *Putnam's* magazine in 1850, then as a book in 1857. The book has been read by famous writers, including the Beat Poets, and it is still being published 150 years later.

The British version of *The Hasheesh Eater* was published in 1903 and featured illustrations by Aubrey Beardsley, who famously partook of hashish for the first time before having dinner at a Paris restaurant in 1896 with poet Earnest Dowson, Leonard Smithers, and Henri de Toulouse-Lautrec. Dowson wrote, "Beardsley's laughter was so tumultuous that it infected the rest of us – who had not taken haschish and we all behaved like imbeciles."

Helena Petrovna Blavatsky's 1870s book, *Secret Doctrine*, originally published as *Isis Unveiled*, was strongly influenced by her hashish use.

It is apparent that *Little Women* author Louisa May Alcott was familiar with cannabis. Characters in her short story *Perilous Play* used hashish. She wrote that hashish would give a young bashful man "the courage of a hero, the eloquence of a poet, and the ardor of an Italian."

Anyone who has read Lewis Carroll's *Alice's Adventures in Wonderland* read about the main character eating what are clearly hallucinogenic mushrooms. Afterwards, Alice came across "a large blue caterpillar" "quietly smoking a long hookah" while sitting on a mushroom so large that Alice had to spring up on her tiptoes to peep over the edge of it. It is quite apparent that the author was well aware of not only cannabis, but also the events that can play out in one's mind upon consuming a certain type of mushroom.

Britain had its own group of writers and artists in the late 1800s that were quite familiar with cannabis. They were known as "The Tragic Generation" and as "The Decadents." They included artist Aubrey Beardsley, poet Earnest Dowson, Havelock Ellis (*Psychology of Sex*), Richard Le Gallianne (*My Ladies' Sonnets and Other Vain and Amatorious Verses*), artist Selwyn Image, Arthur Symons (*The Symbolist Movement in Literature*), Oscar Wilde (*Importance of Being Earnest, An Ideal Husband*), and poet and playwright William Butler Yeats.

335

Another group, of whom Yeats was a founding member, was the Rhymers Club. This London group of writers formed in 1890 and included novelist, poet, essayist, and playwright Ernest Rhys, and Yeats' lover, the actress, activist, and writer Maud Gonne (*A Servant of the Queen*). They met at Cheshire Cheese, a tavern near Fleet Street. Yeats' *The Secret Rose* was influenced by his experiences with hashish and opium.

On the American continent, some of the Beat Poets were influenced by books about people or cultures that used cannabis. In addition to Ludlow's *The Hasheesh Eater*, Milton Mezz Mezzrow's autobiography, *Really the Blues*, were books that strongly influenced The Beats.

Jack Kerouac had read *Really the Blues* and went on to write *On The Road*. That book contains a number of references to *tea* (cannabis) and jazz clubs.

Some of the Beats had traveled to visit the Santa Fe and Taos writing communities that had formed in the 1910s-1930s. There they attended lively dinner parties. During their exploration of local culture some of the writers gained first-hand experience with the peyote cactus used in the local Native American ceremonies, and with the hallucinogenic alkaloid extract of peyote, mescaline (which was first isolated and identified by German chemist Arthur Heffter in 1897).

> "I have always loved marijuana. It has been a source of joy and comfort to me for many years. And I still think of it as a basic staple of life, along with beer and ice and grapefruits – and millions of Americans agree with me."
> – Hunter S. Thompson

Some of the Beat Poets and other American writers of the early and mid 1900s traveled to countries where hash was commonly used, such as Morocco. It was there that author and composer Paul Bowles lived as an expatriate with his wife, author and playwright Jane Auer. An outspoken proponent of the influence cannabis could have on creativity, Bowles wrote a book *The Sheltering Sky* that included characters who smoked hashish or ate majoun, which was a type of jam consisting of fruits, honey, nuts, spices, and cannabis. In 1990, Bernardo Bertolucci made *The Sheltering Sky* into a film staring Debra Winger and John Malkovich. Bowles is seen briefly in the film. In his writings Bowles mentioned that some of the local people carried a pouch with different pockets to keep a variety of grades of cannabis that they shared, with the best grade being for those they respected.

Among the writers and other artists who visited Bowles in Tangier were Cecil Beaton, William Burroughs, Truman Capote, Gregory Corso, Allen Ginsberg, Brian Gysin, Jack Kerouac, Timothy Leary, Joe Orton, Gertrude

Stein and Alice B. Toklas, Gore Vidal, Tennessee Williams, and David Herbert, the son of the Earl of Pembroke – who also lived in Tangier.

Within this group of famous American writers it was Alan Ginsberg who was perhaps the most outspoken about cannabis and the laws against it. Or, at least it appears that he received the most media attention.

"I was somewhat disappointed later on, when the counterculture developed the use of grass for party purposes rather than for study purposes. I always thought that was the wrong direction."

– Alan Ginsberg, who thought cannabis was a useful mind tool for "aesthetic study" and "deepened" "aesthetic perception." His famous book *Howl* was published by Lawrence Ferlinghetti's City Lights bookstore in San Francisco. The police charged Ferlinghetti with publishing and selling obscene material. A landmark legal battle ensued. The publicity the case received helped attract attention to the book, the Beats, and the lifestyle they led, which involved jazz clubs, marijuana, and free thought. It also helped to make Jack Kerouac's 1957 book *On the Road* a hit, bringing Beat culture into public consciousness. In 1961 J. Edgar Hoover declared, "The three biggest threats to America are the Communists, the beatniks, and the eggheads."

"Marijuana is a useful catalyst for specific optical and aural aesthetic perceptions."

– Alan Ginsberg, in The Great Marijuana Hoax: First Manifesto to End the Bringdown, *Atlantic Monthly*, November 1966

"I think that marijuana should not only be legal, I think it should be a cottage industry. It would be wonderful for the state of Maine. There's some pretty good homegrown dope. I'm sure it would be even better if you could grow it with fertilizers and have greenhouses."

– Author Stephen King

"I was a heavy drinker, but the alcohol affected my heart rather than my liver. So I stopped. I smoke grass now. I say that to everybody, because marijuana should be legalized. It's ridiculous that it isn't. If at the end of the day I feel like smoking a joint I do it. It changes the perception of what I've been through all day."

– Film director Robert Altman

"I'm not a great pothead or anything like that… but weed is much, much less dangerous than alcohol."

– Actor Johnny Depp, *Film Review Magazine*, June 2001

"I used to smoke marijuana. But I'll tell you something: I would only smoke it in the late evening. Oh, occasionally the early evening, but usually the late evening – or the mid-evening. Just the early evening, midevening, and late evening. Occasionally, early afternoon, early midafternoon, or perhaps the late-midafternoon. Oh, sometimes the early-mid-late-early morning... But never at dusk."
– Comedian and actor Steve Martin

"There's been no top authority saying what marijuana does to you. I tried it once but it didn't do anything to me."
– Actor John Wayne

"I drink moderately, I've tried drugs. I do like weed. I have a different outlook on marijuana than America does. I've never been a major smoker, but I think America's view on weed is ridiculous. I mean – are you kidding me? If everyone smoked weed, the world would be a better place. I'm not talking about being stoned all day, though. I think if it's not used properly, it can hamper your creativity and close you up inside. My best friend Sasha's dad was Carl Sagan, the astronomer. He was the biggest pot smoker in the world and he was a genius."
– Actress Kirsten Dunst, quoted in England's *Live* magazine; April 2007

"Brad (Pitt) and I would stand around in the morning and get stoned out of our minds waiting for the van to come take us to the set."
– Actor Michael Madsen describing the start of his days working on the film *Thelma & Louise*; *Premier* magazine, 2001

"Though the laws regarding the use of alcohol and recreational drugs vary from country to country, we remind you that the policies of Ocean's Twelve, Warner Bros Productions, and Warner Bros Entertainment Italia strictly prohibit the use of these substances during work hours."
– May 8, 2004 memo from the studio to the cast and crew of the film *Oceans Twelve* while they were filming scenes in Amsterdam; May 8, 2004. The cast included George Clooney, who once said he could never run for president because he had done everything that people could pick apart as making him a bad candidate, including drinking the bong water. While appearing on the Howard Stern cable TV show, the film's co-star, Julia Roberts, said she had

smoked weed at one time in her life, but said she didn't need it because she already laughs and has fun without using pot.

A lot of amazing people have been known to partake of cannabis or hashish. Wolfgang Amadeus Mozart is said to have eaten cannabis chocolate with his lovers. If anyone could be considered a great artist it is Mozart. This is not to say that all great works have been influenced this way, nor am I saying that all artists should try some sort of mind-assisting substance. All I am saying is that doing things to assist the mind in exploring may not always be a bad thing. Even many prescription drugs have some influence on the mind, as do coffee and some types of food. Many things can be considered to be drugs when their influence is compared to the definition of the word. Are we going to outlaw chocolate?

Among the popular contemporary authors who apparently have an understanding of marijuana culture is P.T. Boyle. Among his novels that include pot smoking characters are *Budding Prospects: A Pastoral*, and *Drop City*.

"Myth: Marijuana kills brain cells.

Fact: Allegations that marijuana smoking alters brain function or has long-term effects on cognition are reckless and scientifically unfounded. Federally sponsored population studies conducted in Jamaica, Greece, and Costa Rica found no significant differences in brain function between long-term smokers and nonusers. Similarly, a 1999 study of 1,300 volunteers published in *The American Journal of Epidemiology* reported 'no significant differences in cognitive decline between heavy users, light users, and nonusers of cannabis' over a 15-year period. More recently, a meta-analysis of neuropsychological studies of long-term marijuana smokers by the National Institute on Drug Abuse reaffirmed this conclusion."

– Marijuana: Myth vs. Fact, National Organization for the Reform of Marijuana Laws, NORML.org; quoting from Cannabis use and cognitive decline in persons under 65 years of age, *American Journal of Epidemiology* 149: 794-800

Recent studies have shown that cannabinoids not only can protect brain cells, especially from the ravages of alcohol, but also may even spur brain cell growth. (Cannabinoids promote embryonic and adult hippocampus neurogenesis and produce anxiolytic and depressant-like effects; *The Journal of Clinical Investigation*, 2005. Comparison of cannabindiol, antioxidants and diuretics in reversing binge ethanol-induced neurotoxicity, *Journal of Pharmacology and Experimental Therapeutics*, 2005. Cannabidiol prevents cerebral infarction, *Stroke*, 2005. Cannabidiol and Delta9-

tetrahydro-cannabionol are neuroprotective antioxidants, *Proceedings of the National Academy of Sciences*, 1998.) This should be no surprise. The brain wires itself according to what we are thinking and doing. Marijuana often triggers creativity, such as through the realms of music, drawing, painting, sculpture, dance, and writing. It also influences some people to become physically active, including through dance, running, yoga, skateboarding, snowboarding, and more sensual, open, and eager sexual performance.

However, partaking of cannabis, or any other drug, clearly is not necessary to participate in and excel in any art, sport, or other physical, intellectual, and/or professional activity. Clearly, many people who have excelled in a variety of arts, sports, skills, and professions would strongly agree that living a clean life free from drugs is the best route. The brain and body greatly benefit from a regular sleep pattern, daily exercise, intellectual and social stimulation, goal-oriented living, plant-based nutrition, and healthful relationships.

# The Myth of Marijuana and Criminal Violence

What harms marijuana users most are the laws against marijuana and how those laws are being enforced. Many people have been killed in drug raids, or by overzealous law enforcement. Tragically, many law enforcement officers have also been killed while enforcing the marijuana laws. Many of those arrested on marijuana charges have had their lives destroyed by getting arrested, being put on probation, having their belongings seized, losing college funding, losing their jobs, having their children taken away, accumulating legal expenses, and/or being sent to prison for breaking the intrusive marijuana laws, which are clearly based on misinformation, lies, and unrighteous dominion.

"Amnesty International, the UN and Human Rights Watch have all condemned womens' prisons in the U.S. due to the extreme violence and inhumane conditions that women are enduring in American prisons today."
– Renee Boje Legal Defense Fund, ReneeBoje.com, 2006. Renee Boje is living in Canada with her son and husband, but the U.S. government is trying to extradite her to the U.S. to imprison her for up to her entire life on marijuana charges because she lived in a house where marijuana was growing.

"Myth: Marijuana and violence are linked.
Fact: Absolutely not.
No credible research has shown marijuana use to play a causal factor in violence, aggression or delinquent behavior, dating back to former President Richard Nixon's 'First Report of the National Commission on Marihuana and Drug Abuse' in 1972, which concluded, 'In short, marijuana is not generally viewed by participants in the criminal justice community as a major contributing influence in the commission of delinquent or criminal acts.' More recently, the Canadian Senate's 2002 'Discussion Paper on Cannabis' reaffirmed: 'Cannabis use does not induce users to commit other forms of crime. Cannabis use does not increase aggressiveness or anti-social behavior."
– Marijuana: Myth vs. Fact, National Organization for the Reform of Marijuana Laws, NORML.org

"There is no systematic empirical evidence, at least that drawn from the American experience, to support the thesis that the use of marihuana either inevitably or generally causes, leads to or precipitates

341

criminal, violent, aggressive or delinquent behavior of a sexual or nonsexual nature.

Laboratory studies of effects have revealed no evidence to show that marihuana's chemical properties are, by themselves, capable of producing effects which can be interpreted as criminogenic; that is, that marihuana is an independent cause of criminal or aggressive behavior. If anything, the effects observed suggest that marihuana may be more likely to neutralize criminal behavior and to militate against the commission of aggressive acts.

… In other words, the observed relationship between the use of marihuana and criminal, violent, aggressive and delinquent behavior is spurious. It is dependent on such extra-pharmacological factors as the age, race and education of the user; the type of community in which he lives; his past history of psychosocial maladjustment; and his involvement in a criminal or delinquent subculture (use of other drugs; drug buying and selling activities; associations with friends who also use, buy and sell cannabis or other drugs).

… To put it still another way, to believe that marihuana causes criminal, violent, aggressive or delinquent behavior is to confuse the effects of the drug with the people who use it."

– Shafer Commission Report: Marihuana, a Signal of Misunderstanding: The Report of the National Commission on Marihuana and Drug Abuse: Summary and Conclusions: Marihuana and Crime; Commissioned by President Richard M. Nixon; March 1972

"Does it cause violence?

No; if anything, it reduces it. The only crime most cannabis users commit is obtaining and using marijuana. The U.S. Shafer Commission report, one of the most comprehensive studies ever done on drugs, reported that cannabis smokers 'tend to be under-represented' in violent crime, 'especially when compared to users of alcohol, amphetamines and barbiturates.' The California Attorney General's panel wrote in 1989 that 'objective consideration shows that cannabis is responsible for less damage to the individual and society than alcohol and cigarettes.' The federal government reports that 71 million Americans have smoked it… possibly including some of the nicest people you know."

– Family Council on Drug Awareness, 2006; FCDA.org

"There is no evidence that spending billions of dollars over the past 20 years for antidrug messages has diminished young people's

interest in trying marijuana."
– ChangeTheClimate.org

"I think that's long overdue.
I think everybody knows what (U.S. Senator) John McCain said is right: We've pretty well lost the War on Drugs doing it the way we're doing it. Drugs are more available and cheaper than ever before. What we're doing is not working."
– The lead Texas governor candidate Kinky Friedman, running as an independent to unseat Republican Gov. Rick Perry. He was saying he'd make marijuana legal and release all those jailed on marijuana charges to free up prison space and save money. September 2006

"Drug users and police officers are both responding to a larger social policy context that reinforces their mutual roles as victims and aggressors or, viewed from the perspective of the police, law breakers and law enforcers. It is our decision as a society to criminalize drug addiction, rather than understand and treat those behaviors as medical and social issues, that ultimately forces both sides of the equation into an endless dehumanizing cycle of criminalized behavior, arrest, incarceration, release, and further criminalized behavior. And until we change the way we deal with drug use, we will not have a real opportunity to heal this wounding cycle."
– Vancouver's Pivot Legal Society, October 29, 2002

"What we ought to do is try to get at the source of this problem, which is poverty and disillusionment, and put out resources behind that and turn it around. I suggest it is time to abolish the prohibition – to cease treating indulgence in mind-alteration as a crime. The result would be the elimination of the profit motive, the gangs, the drug dealers. Obviously, the model is the repeal of [alcohol] Prohibition and the end of Al Capone and Dutch Schultz."
– U.S. District Judge Robert Sweet, addressing the Drug Policy Foundation, 1991

"If we judge whether the existing drugs policy is working by measurable reductions in the number of people who use drugs, the number who die or suffer harm as a result, the supply of drugs, the amount of crime committed to get money to buy drugs and the organised criminality involved in transporting and supplying drugs, we have to say that the results are not coming through."
– The Association of Chief Police Officers, UK

"I have long believed that the laws regarding marijuana are too harsh. Those who keep pot for their own personal use should not be treated as criminals. Thirty years in prison makes no sense whatsoever. I'm with you."
    – Ann Landers, advice columnist, in her response to a mother whose son was arrested on marijuana charges; January 5, 1999

For more information, access:
**Drug Policy Alliance**, DrugPolicy.org
**Marijuana Policy Project**, MPP.org
**National Organization for the Reform of Marijuana Laws**, NORML.org

# Politicians Using Pot Convicts
# As Political Pawns

At most, the marijuana convictions may satisfy the needs of some politicians and certain law-enforcement workers who seem to feel as if they are engaged in a good cause while they are actively searching for and convicting so-called marijuana offenders. The politicians may think it makes them look tough on crime, but knowing that they are supporting unjust laws and using so-called marijuana offenders as political pawns, the enforcement of marijuana laws makes politicians look like weaklings for not sticking up for what is right: to abolish these insane laws.

"The rate of incarceration in prison and jail was 701 inmates per 100,000 residents in 2002, up from 601 in 1995. At year end 2002, 1 in every 143 U.S. residents were incarcerated in state or federal prison or a local jail."
– Harrison, Paige M. & Allen J. Beck, Ph.D., US Department of Justice, Bureau of Justice Statistics, Prisoners in 2002; Washington, D.C.: U.S. Department of Justice, July 2003; Page 2

According to the International Center for Prison Studies at King's College, London, there are more Americans in jail than in any other country. Every year there are record numbers of people being incarcerated in U.S. prisons. In 2005 there were 2.2 million Americans in prison or jail, a figure that represents a 2.7 percent increase over 2004. China was second with 1.5 million of its citizens in prison, and Russia was third with 870,000. Additionally, there were 737 per 100,000 people, or one in every 32 American adults behind bars, on probation, or on parole in 2006. The 2006 incarceration rate for many other Western industrialized nations was about 100 per 100,000 people. The population of U.S. prisons is larger than the populations of some countries. The U.S. spends more of their budget on prisons than they do on higher education.

"It makes a lot of sense to treat marijuana the same way we treat alcohol. There's no evidence that demand for marijuana will ever go away. Demand for intoxication in one way or another has been around for millennia. It's part of human nature. The heavy-handed, prohibitionist approach is clearly the wrong approach"
– Jeffrey Miron, Harvard University economist who estimated that taxing marijuana sales similar to tobacco would bring in about $6.2

345

billion in revenue, and legalizing it would save $5.3 billion for state and local governments, and $2.4 billion for the federal government.

In 2007, the state of California had an $8 billion prison budget. Since 1980 the state has mandated imprisonment for many crimes and reduced the chances of early release for good behavior while building more than 20 prisons. The prison inmate population in the state increased from 26,000 in 1978 to 170,000 in 2006. Over the same time period the union of prison guards established itself as a major player in state politics. The 2006 overtime pay for more than 6,000 prison guards in California was over $100,000, and one guard made $252,570 in the fiscal year that ended in June 2006. In their "get-tough" stance, the prison system has dropped most of the educational, job training, and counseling opportunities for prisoners, increasing the likelihood that prisoners would fail to improve their lives during or after prison.

About one in forty Americans who are in jail are there because of "marijuana offenses," and about two million of the seven million people in U.S. prisons in 2005 were there for breaking drug laws, and about 800,000 for breaking marijuana laws. According to the Justice Department's Bureau of Justice Statistics, 49 percent of the growth in federal prison population from 1995 to 2003 could be attributed to drug prisoners. According to the U.S. Department of Justice's Bureau of Justice Statistics report, Drug Use and Dependence, State and Federal Prisoners, 2004, about 12.7 percent of state inmates and 12.4 percent of federal inmates who are being held on drug violations in federal prisons were there for breaking marijuana laws (this does not include local or county jail inmate populations). The incarceration and criminal justice costs for arresting, convicting, and imprisoning people who break marijuana laws was estimated to be $8.5 billion in 2005.

"Today's figures fail to capture incarceration's impact on the thousands of children left behind by mothers in prison. Misguided policies that create harsher sentences for nonviolent drug offenses are disproportionately responsible for the increasing rates of women in prisons and jails."
– Marc Mauer, executive director of The Sentencing Project, December 2006; SentencingProject.org

"The United States has 5 percent of the world's population and 25 percent of the world's incarcerated population. We rank first in the world in locking up our fellow citizens. We now imprison more people

for drug law violations than all of Western Europe, with a much larger population, incarcerates for all offenses."
– Ethan Nadelmann of the Drug Policy Alliance, December 2006; DrugPolicy.org

"We send more people to prison, for more different offenses, for longer periods of time than anybody else."
– Ryan King, policy analyst for The Sentencing Project, December 2006; SentencingProject.org

"Why are so many people in prison? Blame mandatory sentencing laws and the record number of nonviolent drug offenders subject to them."
– Julie Stewart, President of Families Against Mandatory Minimums, December 2006; FAMM.org

How did those arrested and charged with marijuana "crimes" become pawns for politicians to show how they are "tough on crime"?

"If I am elected president of the U.S., America will once again set about the business of winning the War on Drugs. I will get the Guard back to where it belongs – in the forefront."
– Bob Dole, speaking before the annual convention of the National Guard Association, September 1, 1996

In September 1996, while criticizing the Clinton administration for the increase in drug use among teens, Republican presidential candidate Bob Dole once again pledged to expand the role of the National Guard in fighting illegal narcotics, including marijuana. Under the Posse Comitatus Act of 1878, the military is supposed to stay out of domestic policy. But, as I mention elsewhere in the book, the Reagan administration had the act amended in 1982 so that the military could be used to enforce drug laws within U.S. borders.

After Dole lost the election he went on to work in drug sales as a spokesmodel for a pharmaceutical company selling erection pills.

The claim by the presidential candidate was somewhat schizophrenic. Record numbers of people were arrested and imprisoned on drug-related charges during the Clinton administration. And here was a candidate saying he wanted to increase the spending on the so-called drug war, and imprison more people. It should have been very clear by then that the War on Drugs was and is a complete failure, a waste of billions of tax dollars every year, and that arresting people on drug charges is not going to prevent people from taking drugs. But perhaps Bob Dole was behaving just like other politicians, completely detached from the true needs of the people, and only interested in those who donate to their campaigns – such as the prison employee unions, the companies that construct and manage prisons under government contract, and pharmaceutical companies.

As I was writing this I heard about a plan being presented by the U.S. Senate Finance Committee to cut down on prostitution and pimpery. They wanted to start requiring pimps to file employment forms and withholding taxes for their prostitutes/employees. As if we haven't already discovered that trying to control the sex lives of humans doesn't work. The politicians should move on to important matters, such as the environment, dramatically reducing fossil fuel use; pollution reduction; eliminating nuclear warheads; shutting down the nuclear energy industry; legalizing industrial hemp farming; species and terrain preservation; forest and wildland restoration and protection; and education.

Many politicians seem clueless as to what would be best for American youth, and society in general. As politicians pledge to increase drug war spending and continue to pass and enforce arcane marijuanaphobic drug laws that also outlaw hemp farming, one has to wonder if they know anything about the condition of the schools and educational system in the U.S. Would it not be better to help improve the U.S. educational system by increasing teacher pay and creating better programs for the children of the country rather than to spend the money arresting the children and young adults who may turn to drugs to stimulate their minds that go wasted sitting in dull classrooms in neglected school systems for twelve years?

If the politicians would stop focusing on useless laws and pandering to corporations, and start using their time for things that would actually help society, such as defending the works of Nature that are the artwork of this God in which so many politicians profess a belief, the people who elected them to their grandstanding pedestals would be served.

One thing politicians can do if they are really interested in improving society and the condition of their fellow citizens is to stop this Drug War, which is a war on its own citizens, and a war on citizens of other countries, and to completely legalize the farming of industrial hemp.

"A majority of the American public opposes sending marijuana smokers to jail, and three out of four support the medical use of marijuana. Yet many elected officials remain fearful that if they support these reform proposals, they will be perceived as 'soft' on crime and drugs and defeated at the next election.

Tell your elected officials that you know the difference between marijuana and more dangerous drugs and between marijuana smoking and violent crime, and that you do not support spending billions of dollars per year incarcerating nonviolent marijuana offenders.

To make that easy, NORML has a program on our Web site that will identify your state and federal elected officials, and provide a sample letter that you can fax to Congress or e-mail to state legislators."
– National Organization for the Reform of Marijuana Laws, NORML.org

"Marijuana prohibition may be defined as the set of laws that establish criminal penalties for all marijuana offenses, including possession and cultivation for personal use. Efforts to change these laws – even if only to remove the prohibition against medical use – have invariably been met with the argument that the prohibition of marijuana is necessary to curtail adolescent drug abuse. This report shows that the prohibition of marijuana in the United States has not curtailed adolescent marijuana use. The Marijuana Policy Project Foundation was unable to find any scientific evidence demonstrating that the marijuana prohibition results in decreased use or that removing criminal penalties would result in increased use of marijuana by adolescents.

Conclusions

• Existing scientific evidence indicates that the prohibition of marijuana does not curtail adolescent marijuana use.
• The prohibition of marijuana has not decreased availability or served as an effective deterrent.
• Marijuana prohibition may actually increase adolescent marijuana use.
• Marijuana prohibition may increase the likelihood that the marijuana users will use hard drugs.
• Existing evidence indicates that removing criminal penalties for the personal use and acquisition of marijuana would not lead to an increase in use among adolescents."
– Marijuana Prohibition has not Curtailed Marijuana Use by Adolescents, Marijuana Policy Project Foundation study, by Chuck Thomas, director of communications; MPP.org/Adolescents.html

"Arresting these otherwise law-abiding citizens serves no legitimate purpose; extends government into inappropriate areas of our private lives; and causes enormous harm to the lives, careers and families of the more than 700,000 cannabis consumers arrested each year in this country.

According to recent statistics provided by the federal government, nearly 80 million Americans admit having smoked marijuana. Of these, twenty million Americans smoked marijuana during the past year.

Cannabis consumers are no different from their nonsmoking peers, except for their cannabis use. Like most Americans, they are responsible citizens who work hard, raise families, contribute to their communities, and want a safe, crime-free neighborhood in which to live. They are certainly not part of the crime problem in this country, and it is terribly unfair to continue to treat them as criminals.

Many successful business and professional leaders, including many state and elected federal officials, admit they have smoked marijuana.

Responsible cannabis use causes no harm to society and should be of no interest to state and federal governments. Today, far more harm is caused by cannabis prohibition than by the use of cannabis itself.

We must reflect this in our state and federal laws, and put to rest the myth that marijuana smoking is a fringe or deviant activity engaged in only by those on the margins of American society."
   – National Organization for the Reform of Marijuana Laws, NORML.org


"It is not too late for the U.S. to move to a more sensible path. We are approaching three quarters of a million marijuana arrests annually. Every year that the U.S. fails to adopt a policy based on research, science and facts we destroy millions of lives and tear apart millions of families.

Where will we be in another thirty years if we don't change course and make peace in the marijuana war? Now that we know the war's roots are rotten – and after we've lived through the decades of damage and failure it has produced – we should face the facts. The thirty-year-old recommendations of the Shafer Commission are a good place to start."
   – Once-secret Nixon Tapes Show Why the U.S. Outlawed Pot, by Kevin Zeese, president of Common Sense for Drug Policy, CSDP.org; Tuesday, July 12, 2005

# Bring Back Hemp
# It's What the World Needs NOW!

"The easiest way to consider the implication of hemp and agriculture on our society is to remember, anything produced from hydro-carbon (fossil fuels) can also be produced from carbohydrate (plant matter)."
– *Practical Guide to Hemp*, HempLobby.org

"With focused and sustained research and development, hemp could spur dramatic change. Renewable, fast-growing hemp could allow major industries to reduce their dependence on nonrenewable, fast-disappearing resources and move toward sustainable production."
– HempIndustries.org

"We are growing, processing and supplying hemp fiber on an increasing basis to replace glass fiber for composites in the automotive sector."
– Geof Kime, Hempline, Delaware, Ontario, Canada; North American Industrial Hemp Council Director who runs a Canadian hemp fiber separation facility that in 1994 brought in the first crop of industrial hemp in North America since the 1950s after being instrumental in persuading the Canadian government to change its policy; quoted in pamphlet *Industrial Hemp*, by the NAIHC; NAIHC.org

"The largest maker of industrial carpet in the world is focused on producing carpet that is biodegradable and results in full life cycle sustainability. Research proves that carpet made from industrial hemp is both biodegradable and recyclable."
– Dr. Raymond A. Berard, Senior VP of Technology, Interface Research Corporation, Kennesaw, Georgia. North American Industrial Hemp Council, NAIHC.org

"Our bill is about letting California farmers grow a crop that's legal worldwide. We can import hemp, we can process it into shampoo, plastics, and food, but we won't let our farmers grow it. AB 1147 is a common sense measure that regulates the industrial farming of hemp to conform with federal law while relieving law enforcement of the

351

burden of having to discern legal hemp from illegal marijuana grown in clandestine groves."
  – California's Republican Assemblyman Chuck DeVore, co-author of the same bill, June 2006. It was later vetoed on September 30, 2006 by Governor Arnold Schwarzenegger (See Appendix 3). It was reintroduced in 2007.

"Once this bill is enacted, it will create a more efficient market, leading to better prices for the consumer, and provide an opportunity to expand the market for the nutritious hemp seed."
  – Hopeful words of David Bronner, head of Dr. Bronner's Soaps, a natural, biodegradable, hemp-based soap company that imports over $125,000 per year to import hemp seed oil from Canada; commenting on AB 1147; 2006

"Many people mistakenly think hemp is no longer an economically viable crop. As you now know, hemp remains the most versatile and profitable crop on Earth. The legal penalties on using hemp now are just a pretext to confuse people and protect oil and timber companies from fair competition. This hurts America both financially and environmentally. Please help to correct this injustice."
  – From the 1980s-era flyer, *Hemp: Friend to People and Ecology*, distributed by the Business Alliance for Commerce in Hemp

"Despite the hurdles in its way the hemp industry is coming together in this country. It's small but it's growing. Here in Bluegrass Country, the Kentucky Hemp Growers Cooperative and the Kentucky Industrial Hemp Association are working to develop it. The hemp movement is exciting; there are untold opportunities just waiting to be tapped. Just think: Paper-free forests and over 20,000 different products to complement them! Hemp can help promote rural economic development by bringing agriculture and industry together, creating jobs and saving family farms. Currently, however, our government won't even allow us to grow research [hemp] crops, so keep an eye on Canada. Canadian farmers harvested their first commercial crop in 1998 and the results are promising. You've got to start somewhere, right? Go Canada!"
  – Kentucky Hemp Museum, KentuckyHemp.com

"It is time to clear up the misunderstanding, change the law, and clear the way for ecologically sustainable, economically viable opportunities for American farmers and businesses."
  – HempIndustries.org

"Industrial hemp is one of the longest and strongest natural fibers in the plant kingdom. It is also one of the most versatile plants, with approximately 25,000 uses – ranging from paper to textiles to cosmetics.

According to the Institute for Local Self-Reliance, in 1999, hemp yields averaged 800 pounds (17 to 22 bushels of grain), grossing $308 to $410 per acre. These figures compare favorably to the $103 to $137 gross made on canola and wheat crops per acre.

… Industrial hemp is not a drug. The DEA's intrusion into the realm of agriculture is preventing American farmers from growing a crop that has the potential to help address the global depletion of forest resources, the harmful effects of petrochemicals, the excessive use of pesticides for fiber crops, and the economic depression of farming communities.

… Concerned citizens should let their House members or Congress know their feelings about this wonder crop."
– Ralph Nader, The DEA should get out of regulating hemp agriculture; *San Francisco Bay Guardian* editorial, April 3, 2000

"Hemp is an agricultural crop presently being grown in Canada, England, France, Germany and China to name only a few hemp-producing countries. If hemp is really a drug, why aren't these countries being denounced as enemies in our war against marijuana? Why is hemp listed as a legitimate commodity in both the NAFTA and GATT agreements?"
– Kentucky Hemp Museum, KentuckyHemp.com

"The fibers from hemp fall into three categories:
• Bast (or 'long') fibers which stretch the length of the stalk and are used for cordage, textiles, building materials, as a forest product extender (involving paper recycling).
• Hurd is the woody core in the center of the stalk which is cellulose-laden, thus ideal for paper, plastics, animal bedding.
• Tow (or 'short') fibers come from the interior of the plant used in nonwoven materials (felts), paper, home and industrial insulation, building materials, etc."
– *Practical Guide to Hemp*, HempLobby.org

It has been only a few hundred years since the world was a pristine wreath of Nature where all who lived on it relied on its abundance, and not on toxic chemicals. Some may argue that the world wasn't that pristine since humans had developed large cities. But at least the humans were using biodegradable and environmentally safe materials, and not toxic chemicals developed from fossil fuels, or developing massive amounts of nuclear weaponry and other nuclear uses that produce radioactive waste that remains dangerous for many thousands of years.

Massive land "development" in the form of the construction of suburbs, highways, and new cities has covered millions of acres of land with homes, buildings, parking lots, roads, and sidewalks. Dam building, coal mining, oil drilling, and the construction of power plants have taken place just to feed the fossil fuel-based lifestyles, turning humans away from their connection to Nature and making them increasingly dependent on multinational corporations to supply their food, shelter, clothing, and entertainment.

"Back in 1935, approximately 58,000 tons of hemp seed was used just to make nontoxic paint and varnish. When hemp was banned, these safe paints were replaced with toxic petro-chemical versions."
– Hemp: A True Gift from God(ess), by Dr. Heather Anne Harder, SeattleHempFest.com/Facts; 2006

The reliance on petroleum has created a toxic, synthetic society. We are now seeing the destruction, death, and long-lasting poisons resulting from over 100 years of a still increasing global dependence on fossil fuels.

Allowing for industrial hemp farming can help us unplug from petroleum and coal, live more in tune with Nature, and help to reverse some of the damage we have done to Earth.

Because the major greenhouse gas that is created by burning fossil fuels, carbon dioxide, stays in the atmosphere for several decades, and because hemp absorbs so much of the greenhouse gasses while emitting oxygen, planting hundreds of thousands of acres of hemp around the world will take carbon dioxide out of the atmosphere and help to slow and reverse global warming. The products made from all that hemp can save trees by providing pulp for paper, and provide food, clothing, building materials, clean burning fuels, and a safer environment. Because we would rely less on trees in a hemp society, the forests could regenerate, which would absorb more pollution, put forth oxygen, improve air and water quality, and provide homes for wildlife.

"I used to be skeptical about hemp until I read about this and realized that this was the way of the future.
Desperate times call for desperate measures. Times have turned away from tobacco. We're losing farmers just like we lost soldiers in WWII.
Farmers are the lifeblood of this state.

354

We can't live in the past; we must look to the future. Kentucky needs to be in the forefront.

Industrial hemp is not legalized marijuana. There is a very definite distinction between the two. And if the state police and Kentucky law enforcement are not able to determine the difference, then I think they can be adequately educated – they're basically intelligent people."

– Former Kentucky Governor Louie Nunn, speaking at the first Southern Kentucky Hemp Expo, April 2000. Nunn, a Republican who is also an attorney, represented actor Woody Harrelson in court when Harrelson was tried for illegally planting four hemp seeds in an attempt to bring hemp farming out of the Dark Ages. The jury agreed that Harrelson didn't break the law.

"I had the opportunity to talk to some of the jurors afterward, and, regardless of what the Supreme Court says and regardless of what the legislators say, those people don't think it's right that someone should go to jail for growing industrial hemp.

To me, they're sending out a very strong message."

– Woody Harrelson, after his acquittal for planting four hemp seeds; August 2000

"We don't think we can turn our backs on the family farm and we ought to look at anything that can give relief to the family farmer. And this is one."

– Former Kentucky Governor Edward "Ned" Breathitt; March 2000

"Major markets have opened up for hemp fiber in the US. We are importing Canadian and European hemp, since it is illegal to grow hemp here in the U.S."

– Hugh S. McKee, president, Flaxcraft, Inc., Cresskill, New Jersey, North American Industrial Hemp Council Director; HAIHC.org; 2006

"Hemp farming in Canada is well regulated by Health Canada ensuring that only legitimate farmers are licensed and that they only grow government approved low-THC hemp. Requirements include applicant background checks, GPS coordinates of hemp fields, the use of varieties of approved low-THC certified hemp seed purchased from licensed seed vendors, and random inspections and testing. This licensing scheme ensures that farmers are only growing nondrug industrial hemp and not marijuana. Even though law enforcement is able to distinguish the difference between hemp and marijuana, the

licensing process eliminates the need for them to visually distinguish between industrial hemp and its drug psychoactive cousin."
– Vote Hemp press release, Vote Hemp Exposes White House Office of National Drug Control Policy and Drug Administration Lies, February 8, 2007

"Why not give back to American agriculture an old crop for which new technologies are creating a large market so that our farmers can take a step towards profitability and sustainability?"
– A. Bud Sholts, chairman, North American Industrial Hemp Council, NAIHC.org

"The U.S. needs to become more sustainable in terms of fibers, fuels, and energy. A strong and viable agriculture is important to the national security. Current trade deficits and near depression conditions in agriculture are not a good recipe for long-term national economic security.
… The widespread use of industrial hemp could result in numerous environmental benefits, including but not limited to:
1) Less reliance on fossil fuels
2) More efficient use of energy
3) Less long-term atmospheric buildup of carbon dioxide
4) Soil redemption
5) Forest conservation
6) Agricultural pesticide use reduction
7) Dioxin and other pollution reduction
8) Landfill use reduction
Hemp is superior to many other plants for a variety of uses."
– North American Industrial Hemp Council, NAIHC.org; 2006

"We can no longer afford to allow the hemp production to remain a matter of ignorance versus politics. This insane prohibition against one of the world's most valuable plants must stop."
– *Hemp: A True Gift from God(ess)*, by Dr. Heather Anne Harder, SeattleHempFest.com/Facts; 2006

Today America could greatly benefit by once again growing hemp and using it for a variety of products.
Millions of trees and varieties of wildlife around the world could be saved if people would rely more on paper made from hemp. With modern machinery it is less expensive to make paper from hemp pulp than from tree pulp.

The harsh sulfuric acids and other chemicals used in the manufacture of tree pulp paper are not needed to process hemp pulp into paper. Tree pulp paper factories are major sources of water pollution that poison drinking water and are toxic to marine life.

Hemp provides more pulp per acre than many types of trees. Wood chips are 30 percent cellulose. Hemp is 70 percent cellulose and is better suited as a paper ingredient. Hemp was once the main source of material for paper in America. When slavery ended, the labor-intensive hemp processing became too expensive with the antiquated machinery, and hemp farming became less popular.

As mentioned elsewhere, hemp had become less and less popular as a material for fabric after the 1793 invention of the Eli Whitney cotton gin, which greatly sped up the processing of cotton, and made the south the king of cotton production, and the slave owners wealthy. While the hemp fabric and textile industry continued in the U.S. into the 1900s, the industry was killed by the U.S. government in the late 1930s. Today we do have technology that processes great quantities of hemp, but the technology is only being used in other countries, where industrial farming is legal, and not in the U.S.

"Cotton is the dominant natural fiber used in textiles worldwide today. It accounts for about 40 percent of textile production, while synthetic fibers (primarily polyester) account for approximately 55 percent of textile production. One study of hemp for the U.S. market suggests that, 'an area of land only 25 miles square (the size of a typical U.S. county) is sufficient to produce enough hemp fiber in one year to manufacture 100 million pair of denim jeans, thus providing an equivalent yield to an area ten times the size planted in cotton, and offering the additional benefit of producing clothing which is 10 times stronger than cotton and that, in contrast to cotton which requires exceptionally high applications of pesticides and enormous quantities of water, requires no pesticides and only minimal quantities of water as well.' In fact, cotton inputs and yields show very large variation throughout the world as well as within the cotton-producing areas of the United States. Based on the best available estimates for domestic cotton and hemp production, the degree of industrial hemp efficiency over cotton appears to be somewhat exaggerated in popular references on the topic, in part due to incomplete life-cycle analyses of each fiber.

The United States grows an average of 14 million acres of cotton each year, with lint (fiber) yield for the past 10 years averaging a little more than 700 pounds per acre. (Cotton fiber, derived from the flower of the plant rather than the stalk as in hemp, is a little more than one-third of the raw cotton yield, after the seed is removed.) By

comparison, industrial hemp fiber production for high quality paper markets in France yields a dry-stem average of 3.1 tons per acre, of which 34 to 39 percent (an average of 2300 pounds per acre) is long fiber suitable for cotton-type textiles. Industrial hemp-fiber yield appears to be roughly three times per acre that of domestic cotton—not 10 times—although, cotton crops take twice as long to mature (180 days instead of 90)."
    – March 2008 Reason Foundation Study on Hemp, Illegally Green: Environmental Costs of Hemp Prohibition. Policy Study 367, by Skaidra Smith-Heisters

The government's ban on hemp and combining it with a ban on marijuana is absurd and deprives us of a useful medicine as well as a plant that can be instrumental in healing both the environment and financial crisis. There are many individuals working for the government who are well aware of this.

Because U.S. drug policy affects other countries, the U.S. laws banning hemp have resulted in massive worldwide environmental damage. The example that many people have cited is that if the oil spills in the oceans consisted of hemp fuel (or other seed fuels) and not of petroleum, the environmental damage would be minimal. As the Organic Consumers Organization explains it, "Hemp fuel is biodegradable; so oil spills become fertilizer, not eco-catastrophes." Cannabis carbohydrates can be used to make the same products made from petroleum hydrocarbons, but without the environmental damage.

"It is unfortunate that the federal government has stood in the way of American farmers, including many who are struggling to make ends meet, competing in the global industrial hemp market. Indeed the founders of our nation, some of whom grew hemp, surely would find that federal restrictions on farmers growing a safe and profitable crop on their own land are inconsistent with the constitutional guarantee of a limited, restrained federal government."
    – Dr. Ron Paul, House of Representatives (R-Texas), when introducing a bill (Industrial Hemp Farming Act: HR3037) to legalize hemp farming in the U.S., June 23, 2005

The 1961 United Nations Single Convention on Narcotic Drugs was amended by the 1972 Protocol Amending the Single Convention on Narcotic Drugs, 1961, to allow an exemption for hemp farming. Article 28 of that amendment states, "This convention shall not apply to the cultivation of the cannabis plant exclusively for industrial purposes (fibre and seed) or horticulture purposes." Thus, changing U.S. law to allow hemp farming would not be in conflict with international law as established by the Single Convention, of which the U.S. is a signatory.

"Perhaps someday Americans will realize what they are missing out on by allowing a few antidrug zealots in the government (along with the lobbying of threatened companies) to continue to ban this remarkable crop, with its enormous potential to produce high-quality products at a low environmental cost. Meanwhile, Canadian farmers are going to cash in on this potential."
– Don Lotter, Ph.D., in Transcontinental Farm Tour: Crossing Canada with Don Lotter: Hemp Heaven... and hell: A story in two parts, The New Farm, newfarm.org/international/canada_don/manitoba/index.shtml; 2007, The Rodale Institute, RodaleInstitute.org. Lotter has worked in sustainable agricultural development in North America, Latin America, and Africa over the past 25 years. DonLotter.com

"Nations that followed the United States in prohibiting hemp cultivation have, for the most part, rescinded these laws—some more than a decade ago. A report by the Congressional Research Service in 2005 noted that, 'the United States is the only developed nation in which industrial hemp is not an established crop.' It seems likely that the United States cannot maintain hemp prohibition indefinitely. Reasons given for hemp prohibition in the United States make little sense today. Drug enforcement officials have argued that hemp shouldn't be grown because it looks like marijuana; in that case, the USDA should stop growing kenaf, which, as its Latin name Hibiscus cannabinus suggests, has a palmate leaf that can be mistaken for marijuana. Others have argued that hemp shouldn't be grown because the market for it is too speculative, and the crop may turn out to be unprofitable; in that case, corn (subsidized by the USDA at $9.4 billion in 2005) should top the list of prohibited crops."
– March 2008 Reason Foundation Study on Hemp, Illegally Green: Environmental Costs of Hemp Prohibition. Policy Study 367, by Skaidra Smith-Heisters

Hemp farming needs to be legalized in the U.S. Not doing so would continue our destructive relationship with Earth, and would be a crime against all life forms on the planet. In WWII the U.S. grew thousands of acres of hemp to save the country. Now we need to grow it to save the world. Hemp is what the world needs NOW.

# Nuclear Power Plants and the Proliferation of Nuclear Weapons

At a time when governments are considering building more nuclear power plants, it is the time to consider safer alternatives.

It is a disappointment to know that, soon after he took office, Obama, who campaigned using the message that he was for "green energy" and sustainability, started promoting the construction of many more nuclear energy plants. That was perhaps my greatest disappointment with that man, with a quick second being his appointment of very many Monsanto-friendly business people and politicians to various offices within the administration, and his alliance with the petroleum industry. Not that I thought the guy going to be to live up to the hype of his campaign, but he certainly disappointed me with his nuclear energy, petroleum, and Monsanto alliances.

It is not quite true that nuclear power plants don't release greenhouse gases. Additionally, all the sweet talk about how nuclear energy is a clean energy ignores the very ugly side of that industry.

Nuclear energy plants require a tremendous amount of resources to construct and maintain, and they produce dangerous spent nuclear fuel that remains tremendously hazardous for at least tens of thousands of years. Currently nuclear power plants around the world are producing waste that is being stockpiled. Almost all of it sits stagnate near the power plants where it was created, unable to be shipped to another location for permanent storage because of ongoing conflicted negotiations on where it would be appropriate to safely store the stuff.

The Yucca Mountain nuclear waste storage site in Nevada was supposed to open in 1989, but various groups successfully have stopped it from opening. Issues arose not only on how to transfer nuclear waste from all over the continent through towns and cities, but also on how it would be stored at the mountain.

"The transportation of this waste would require over 96,000 truck shipments over four decades. Almost every major east-west interstate highway and mainline railroad in the country would experience high-level waste shipments as waste is moved from reactors and other sties in 39 states."
– Congressman Dennis Kucinich, who has spoken out against both nuclear energy and the opening of the Yucca Mountain nuclear waste site.

360

Where do you store something safely for tens of thousands of years with an assurance that it will not be disturbed by geological disturbances, flooding, or other natural disasters (including meteor strikes), and in areas where future generations of humanity will know how to safely deal with it? Why are we allowing more of this waste to be created when we don't know what to do with what has already been made? Why are we binding every future generation with the burden of dealing with this tremendously hazardous nuclear waste?

"A severe nuclear accident has the potential to do catastrophic harm to people and the environment. A combination of human and mechanical error could result in an accident killing several thousand people, injuring several hundred thousand others, contaminating large areas of land, and costing billions of dollars."
– The Union of Concerned Scientists, 2007, UCSUSA.org

At a time when people are feeling threatened by ongoing wars and the unfortunate choices of various warring groups, it should be taken into consideration that nuclear waste can be used to poison communities; spent nuclear fuel can be used to make bombs; plutonium that has been separated from waste materials can be stolen and used to make bombs; and countries that produce enriched uranium for nuclear fuel can also create weapons grade uranium. Plants that reprocess spent nuclear fuel also produce radioactive waste.

Nuclear waste recycling plants in Japan and Britain have reported hundreds of kilograms of missing plutonium. This plutonium has gone unaccounted for, and it is not publicly known how many other plants in other countries have experienced similar losses.

It takes about six kilograms of plutonium to create the kind of bomb that the U.S. dropped on Nagasaki, Japan on August 9, 1945. That bomb turned the city into a hellish nightmare and instantly killed about 40,000 people. Tens of thousands more people died from that same bomb over the following several months. The nuclear bomb that the U.S. dropped on Hiroshima on August 6, 1945 instantly killed about 90,000 people, and tens of thousands more people over the following months. There are now tens of thousands of nuclear bombs in storage and at least a few thousand on continual alert. Countries that are known to have nuclear bombs include Britain, China, France, India, Israel, North Korea, Pakistan, Russia, and the United States. These countries have enough nuclear bombs to obliterate the life of Earth. As of this writing the U.S. has been the only country that has ever used nuclear bombs.

However, plutonium can be found in many of the munitions presently being used by the U.S. military. Tank armor and missiles contain so-called depleted uranium, uranium-238, which makes munitions super hard and able to penetrate secured buildings and bunkers. Areas where these bombs have been exploded will remain toxic for many years, contributing to cancers, birth deformities, and miscarriages among the people exposed to the residues that now cover parts of Afghanistan, Bosnia, Iraq, and Kosovo. An estimated 300 tons of depleted uranium munitions were used in the Gulf War, and more have been used in the ongoing military operations in that region.

While the government continues producing depleted uranium bombs that are used in various parts of the world, the production of the munitions and fuel for military uses is poisoning U.S. citizens at home.

Since the 1960s, the privately owned Nuclear Fuel Services Inc. in Erwin, Tennessee produced fuel for the nuclear submarines of the U.S. Navy. The company also converts weapons-grade uranium into fuel for commercial nuclear reactors. In July 2007 the Nuclear Regulatory Commission revealed that employees at the 65-acre complex mishandled highly enriched uranium, and that on March 6, 2006 nine gallons of uranium spilled from a transfer line of the commercial nuclear fuel department. That spill could have caused a devastating nuclear reaction.

The 570-square-mile Hanford Nuclear Reservation next to the Columbia River in Washington State where the plutonium used in the Nagasaki bomb as well as other nuclear warheads now sits poisoned with a tremendous amount of nuclear waste, industrial chemicals, heavy metals, and asbestos. Closed since 1990, the site was originally called Hanford Engineer Works and was part of the Manhattan Project, a top-secret government program started in the 1940s to develop an atom bomb. Some of the most hazardous substances on the planet were processed there. Now nine nuclear reactors sit shuttered and the site has turned into a multibillion-dollar project for the government to manage the toxic leftovers. Hundreds of billions of gallons of contaminated groundwater pose a continuing threat and the underground "tank farms" hold more than 50 million gallons of radioactive waste. Workers who have been employed in managing the site show signs of radiation poisoning and others show signs of exposure to asbestos and the heavy metal beryllium, which is used in bomb manufacturing and causes incurable lung disease. Since the 1940s residents of nearby farm communities have experienced a rash of cancers. Many believe the illnesses are related to exposure to the toxins that blew from the Hanford Nuclear Reservation and spread as far as Montana and southern Canada. Ways through which people could have been exposed to the toxins include food, water, and air. Fields where fruits and vegetables grow were tainted with the iodine-131 as was grazing land where cattle feed. Iodine-131 is produced when uranium rods are dissolved in nitric acid. It collects in the thyroid gland and causes cells there to grow abnormally.

When citizens groups successfully used the Freedom of Information Act in the 1980s to gain access to 19,000 pages of classified records it was revealed that the Hanford Nuclear Reservation had been dumping radioactive material into the Columbia River for decades.

Numerous toxic sites dot the American landscape, such as the hundreds of uranium mines dug from the 1940s through the 1980s on the Navajo reservation in Arizona, New Mexico, and Utah. The mines destroyed vast parts of the reservations, leaving hazardous dust and poisoned groundwater. Each of these sites carries its own set of what seem to be permanent problems with poisoned land. Wind, drought, and rain have worn down dirt used to cover many of the sites. Other sites are on hillsides where rainwater and rock slides spread the hazards to lowlands and into stream-beds. The residents of nearby communities experience health problems directly related to the hazardous substances, and they live with the looming high risk of lung, bone, liver, breast, and other cancers. Some Navajo unknowingly increased their exposure to the uranium by building their homes using cement made of uranium ore, radioactive sand, and processing mill waste left over from the abandoned uranium mines. Many Navajo children played on and around the abandoned mines. Many Navajos drank and cultivated their crops with water tainted with uranium, arsenic, and heavy metals left over form the mines and processing mills. And some still do. These are the risks more and more people will face as more nuclear power plants are constructed around the world.

As I was writing this book, the George W. Bush administration was pushing for the construction of more nuclear power plants while at the same time pressuring other countries to refrain from developing nuclear energy plants. John McCain was campaigning with the foolish claim that he was going to improve America's energy independence by building up to 100 new nuclear power plants. And, as I am still writing, and as I have mentioned, Obama is advocating the expansion of nuclear energy.

The U.S. should do away with its nuclear programs, and encourage other countries to do the same. Countries that are involved in building additional nuclear power plants include China, Russia, and India. France has 60 nuclear power plants. Russia is building nuclear power plants that float on water and that can be sold to other countries. And Iran now has a nuclear power plant.

Even if the U.S. approves construction of more nuclear power plants, how is the country going to deal with all of the nuclear power plants that need to be closed because they are outdated? One nuclear power plant costs about tens of billions of dollars to build, and more money to run. To replace all of the current nuclear power plants around the world while building more nuclear power plants to increase the amount of electricity produced by nuclear power plants would mean spending in the hundreds of trillions of dollars.

"The NRC (Nuclear Regulatory Commission) must address the vulnerability of spent fuel storage at all U.S. nuclear power plants now. Spent fuel pools contain more highly radioactive fuel than the reactor cores. And the spent fuel pools at all U.S. nuclear plants are located outside the reactor containment structure. When the spent fuel pools fill up, spent fuel is stored in concrete casks outside the plant. Thus, spent fuel is a softer target that could yield graver consequences than an aircraft crashing through the reactor containment structure.
  The spent fuel pool is a 45-feet deep concrete pit that stores highly radioactive fuel assemblies after their removal from the reactor core. Water storage is required because spent fuel assemblies continue to emit considerable amounts of both heat and radiation for many years. The fuel pool water is continuously cooled to remove the heat produced by the spent fuel assemblies. Without cooling, the fuel pool water will heat up and boil. If the water boils or drains away, the spent fuel assemblies will overheat and either melt or catch on fire. NRC studies have estimated that many thousands of people living within 50 miles could die from the radiation released when spent fuel assemblies melt or catch on fire."
  – Union of Concerned Scientists, 2007, UCSUSA.org

Safety issues require that nuclear plants have 24-hour security and the latest technology. If an accident occurs the region must be evacuated within minutes. Like the reactors, evacuation plans are not failsafe. If towns and cities can't be evacuated in days to prepare for a hurricane, how do the authorities expect to evacuate them in minutes in the case of a nuclear accident? Depending on the seriousness of the accident, the residents may not be able to return home for days, weeks, months, years, or ever. What price are people willing to pay for this costly and unsafe form of electricity?
  A 2007 study by the University of Mainz for German's Federal Office of Radiation Protection concluded that children living near nuclear power plants have a much higher rate of leukemia and other forms of cancer.
  More than half of Americans live within 75 miles of a nuclear power plant.
  The world's worst nuclear power plant disaster happened on April 26, 1986. That was when the number 4 reactor at the Chernobyl nuclear power plant in the Ukraine exploded and burned in what is known as a "nuclear meltdown" turning the concrete of the reactor floor into lava. Radiation spewed from the plant and spread across the former Soviet Union and large areas of Europe. Communities and some of the continent's most fertile

farmland in an area the size of Italy were contaminated. Trees in the immediate vicinity turned brown. Rivers and lakes throughout the region were contaminated and the life in and around them was deemed unfit for human consumption. Many forms of wildlife, horses, and farm animals died, miscarried, or stopped producing. Over three hundred thousand people had to be evacuated and resettled outside of the area. Many people were told that they would only have to evacuate for a few days, thus the surrounding community remains as it was abandoned with belongings in the homes, businesses, and schools. In an attempt to cover the reactor, tons of sand was dropped from helicopters. Many fire and rescue workers died from radiation poisoning. Because Soviet authorities did not permit doctors to list "radiation" as a cause of death on death certificates it is not known how many people died immediately from the disaster. It is estimated by the U.N. and Greenpeace that anywhere from ten thousand to one hundred thousand people will have experienced cancer relating to the exposure to the radiation. Decades later, the governments of Europe are still working on ways to encapsulate the reactor to lessen ongoing release of radiation. The hastily erected covering that was put over the reactor is currently falling apart and may collapse, which could cause a release of more radioactive material.

Many nuclear power plants have been built in earthquake zones, hurricane zones, tsunami zones, and in locations that are otherwise unstable, such as on the edges of large rivers – which tend to occasionally broadly change course during large storms, which can undermine and demolish any type of structure. If even one of these nuclear power plants is seriously damaged it can lead to an entire region being unsafe for humans and wildlife for many years. As I was writing this paragraph in the summer of 2007 the largest nuclear power plant in the world had been closed after it was damaged in a magnitude 6.8 earthquake that hit the coast of Japan where the power plant sits. Many other nuclear power plants have been found to be faulty at some level and operate under dangerously weak security. Many are potential Chernobyls.' Considering that the waste each of these plants produces, and the subsequent storage problems, and that the waste remains hazardous for at least tens of thousands of years, and that history reveals that all land undergoes dramatic changes in tens of thousands of years, it should be clear that no land is stable enough to store nuclear waste.

Nuclear power plants operate under secrecy that no other industry is allowed. When nuclear accidents happen the public isn't always permitted to know. Many hazardous situations that have happened at nuclear power plants have remained out of the news because Nuclear Regulatory Commission reports aren't made available to the public. As of July 2007, the Union of Concerned Scientists reported that 41 of the 104 current U.S.

nuclear power plants have been shut down for more than a year after safety was compromised. Many of the plants are so outdated that they will soon be closed.

If you live on the same planet as nuclear power plants, you should be concerned about how the plants operate, what is done with the nuclear waste produced by the plants, and on working to get the plants closed. And on making sure that no more nuclear plants are constructed.

"The amount of electricity that could be generated simply by making existing non-nuclear power plants more efficient is staggering. On average, coal plants operate at 30% efficiency worldwide, but newer plants operate at 46%. If the world average could be raised to 42%, it would save the same amount of carbon as building 800 nuclear power plants.

Nevertheless, the U.S. government spends more on nuclear power than it does on renewables and efficiency. Taxpayer subsidies to the nuclear industry amounted to $9 billion in 2006, according to Doug Koplow, a researcher based in Cambridge, Mass., whose Earth Track consultancy monitors energy spending. Renewable power sources, including hydropower but not ethanol, got $6 billion, and $2 billion went toward conservation."
– *Los Angeles Times,* editorial July 23, 2007

"The most hazardous toxic waste comes from petro-chemicals and nuclear power. Hemp can safely, cleanly, and completely replace them both."
– *Hemp: A True Gift from God(ess)*, by Dr. Heather Anne Harder, SeattleHempFest.com/Facts; 2006

"Uranium, plutonium, and mercury are the most dangerous minerals known. Once uranium is mined and powdered it is, from that point forward due to its extended half-life, forever toxic to the environment (such as rivers, estuaries, surrounding farms, etc.) and carcinogenic to all higher life forms. The destination of all mined uranium is either as fuel for nuclear power plants (this makes the uranium even more toxic than before) and/or nuclear weapons – including depleted uranium nuclear weapons currently being used in Iraq (in blatant violation of the Geneva Convention).

Canadians should consider the karmic implications of Canadian uranium being used by the United States military. Both nuclear bombs dropped on Hiroshima and Nagasaki used uranium mined in Canada.

Uranium mining has no positive benefits for the environment, families, or you. Nuclear power and nuclear weapons are not

sustainable. It is up to us to stop the mining of this dangerous, toxic, deadly substance."
— David Wolfe, founder of The Fruit Tree Planting Foundation, ftpf.org,

The process involved in creating nuclear energy creates radioactive isotopes, including cesium-137, strontium-90s, and plutonium-239. The first two remain radioactive for at least decades. Scientists estimate that Plotunium-239 remains dangerous for more than 24,000 years. Some nuclear energy facilities reprocess nuclear waste into fuel. The reprocessing creates the plutonium used in weaponry. Some of the waste from the facilities, including fuel rod casings, can't be recycled and needs to be permanently stored away. All of the nuclear waste can cause fatalities from direct exposure, and a variety of cancers and life-threatening illnesses from limited exposure.

Some countries have been dumping nuclear waste in the wilds of Russia.

France has mass quantities of spent nuclear fuel that has been vitrified into black glass that will remain radioactive for thousands of years and that are buried in the Cherbourg peninsula of Normandy. The company used to treat the waste and fuel also recycles waste from nuclear plants in Australia, Belgium, Germany, Japan, the Netherlands, and Switzerland.

What can heat the water that works the turbines of electric generators? The most toxic is nuclear energy. The second most toxic is coal. The third most toxic is petroleum. Then there is ethanol made from crops. The safest is perhaps solar energy, but that requires a region with lots of sun. All regions of the U.S. grow hemp and landscape clippings, which can be used to make ethanol, which can fuel electric generators.

Industrial hemp farming needs to be legalized in the U.S. to allow humanity to become less dependant on fossil fuels and other unsafe forms of energy.

# APPENDIX 1

## Products that can be made using hemp

"As an industrial crop, hemp has been grown either for the long fibers located in the outer layer of the plant's stem (called "bast" fiber), for seed, or a combination of both. A secondary product of the high-quality bast fiber crop is the internal core, or "hurd," consisting of short fibers and cellulosic biomass with a variety of industrial applications. Seed is also a valuable commodity derived from multi-purpose hemp crops."
– March 2008 Reason Foundation Study on Hemp, Illegally Green: Environmental Costs of Hemp Prohibition. Policy Study 367, by Skaidra Smith-Heisters

- **Acoustic boards** for sound absorption
- **Air filters.** When made of hemp they are both biodegradable and compostable
- **Animal bedding**
- **Animal feed.** Quality nutrition, as explained below.
- **Artist's canvas and paints.** Rembrandt and Van Gogh painted on hemp canvas. Many oil paintings were created using paints containing hemp oil. Hemp oil paints do not contain the toxins of petroleum oil paints, and are safer for the artist.
- **Bags.** Billions of paper and plastic bags are used every year in America and other countries. Much of these end up in landfills or strewn throughout communities as litter. The oceans and lakes of the world are now dumping zones for billions of plastic bags, which swirl in the water, killing many varieties of marine life. Hemp fabric shopping bags can last many years, eliminating the use of paper and plastic shopping bags, saving trees, and preventing damage to the environment and wildlife. Hemp fabric is biodegradable, compostable, and nontoxic.
- **Bandages and medical tape.** With its natural antimicrobial properties, hemp fabric is naturally resistant to mold and mildew. Its fibers are longer than cotton, making it more ideal than cotton for bandages and medical tape. The glue on the tape can also be made from hemp oil extracts.
- **Book binding and covers.** Many of the first books were made using hemp paper, fabric, and board. In sixteenth-century Europe, hemp paper was common. The King James and Gutenburg Bibles were printed on hemp paper.

Hemp paper is preferred for fine books because it is strong and doesn't yellow.

Today, because of laws that shouldn't exist, it is difficult and expensive to get a book printed on hemp paper in the U.S., even though hemp paper is easier and cheaper to grow and produce, and more environmentally friendly than paper made from tree pulp.

Hemp also makes an excellent form of paper to recycle, and also to add to wood pulp paper. This is because hemp fiber is longer and stronger than wood fiber.

Because it is illegal to grow hemp in the U.S., any hemp paper has to be imported from other countries, or made from imported hemp material. This makes hemp paper expensive. If hemp farming were legal in the U.S., hemp paper would be far cheaper than paper made from tree pulp.

- **Candles.** Hemp wax candles are safer for the environment, and are cleaner to burn than petroleum wax candles.
- **Canvas.** Safer to grow than cotton, hemp fiber is stronger than cotton, and it takes longer to degrade in sunlight. The word "canvas" is a form of the word cannabis.
- **Cardboard.** There is no need to cut down forests to make cardboard when we can be using hemp pulp and hemp fiber instead of trees.
- **Cellophane.** Made from hemp, it is safer than cellophane made from petroleum.
- **Clothing:** In addition to fabric, hemp can be used to make plasticized shoe soles, bands, fasteners, and other clothing features. Calvin Klein, Ralph Lauren, Patagonia, Versace, Converse, and Addidas have all used hemp in their clothing lines.
- **Coal.** Hemp has a heating value of 5,000 to 8,000 BTU per pound and can be used in place of coal for producing electricity, greatly reducing mining, acid rain, mercury pollution, and global warming.
- **Coffee filters.**
- **Compression molding materials.** Car dashboards, kitchen countertops, hangers, storage containers, etc. Many cars in the U.S. already contain hemp material grown in other countries. These include dashboards, seat linings, insulation, mats, and fiberglass panels found in BMW, Ford, Daimler Chrysler, General Motors, Honda, Mitsubishi, Porsche, and Volkswagen vehicles.
- **Concrete.** A form of moldable construction stone that lasts thousands of years can be made out of hemp, and is safer for the environment than traditional concrete. It is also both stronger, more flexible, and lighter in weight than traditional concrete, which means it would be excellent for use in places where there are earthquakes.

We have seen what earthquakes can do to structured built of unreinforced concrete.

The 94 kilns used in the production of concrete in the U.S. emit tons of mercury, a neurotoxin, into the environment annually. In December 2006 the Environmental Protection Agency, under pressure from the Bush administration, refused to set standards on mercury emissions from cement kilns. Coal-fired power plants also emit tons of mercury into the atmosphere. Hemp can also replace coal. Worldwide demand for cement increases every year. (Access: EarthJustice.org)

Hempcrete is made of hemp hurd, lime (calcium hydroxide), sand, and water. It is called by various names, including hempcrete, hampstone, or Agstone. In France there is Isochanvre, which is a patented hemp cement. It demonstrates excellent insulation as well as waterproof and fireproof characteristics. It is also carbon negative because the plant absorbs greenhouse gasses as it grows, then the carbon gets locked into the hempcrete.

"In the UK, the construction and use of buildings accounts for over 50% of the carbon dioxide produced. Studies have shown that up to 200kg of CO2 is emitted in the production of each square metre of walling for houses alone – equating to 40 tonnes for the walls of a typical house.

To significantly reduce this figure, Lime Technology has launched Tradical® Hemcrete®, a new product innovation of cast in situ hemplime walling.

Created in partnership with Lhoist UK Castle Cement and Hemcore, three of the world's leading authorities on lime and hemp based products, Tradical® Hemcrete® can actually reverse the damaging effects of greenhouse gases by locking up harmful CO2 emissions within wall construction."
– Lime Technology of Britain is at the forefront of hempcrete construction; LimeTechnology.co.uk

Steve Allin, author of *Building with Hemp* explains that "Different mixtures are created for using the hempcrete as either attic or cavity insulation. When slightly more lime is added to this mixture, it becomes suitable to cast around a timber frame between shuttering formwork as a nonload-bearing masonry wall. With a further increase in the lime element, it can be used as an insulating floor, and when sufficient binder is incorporated to produce a sticky paste, it can be spread on a wall as a plaster or molded into decorative shapes. The phrase 'heat store' refers to the ability of a material to store heat, i.e., thermatic capacity. It is especially relevant to hempcrete as it is unusual for a material to both insulate and store heat."

Some of the most ancient structures that exist today in the Mediterranean countries and in Asia contain fabricated stone material made with hemp and/or that was made in a manner similar to hempcrete. Roman stone or cement was made with clay and lime and often mixed with plant fiber.

- **Cosmetics**. Hemp extracts can be used in place of the toxic petrochemicals that are now used in many cosmetics and body care products, such as shampoo, balm, salves, lotions, and soaps. Emollients and lubricants made from hemp extracts are safer than those made from petroleum and coal extracts and byproducts. Why would you use cosmetics that contain cancer-causing and hormonal disrupting petroleum chemicals when you could use cosmetics containing safe hemp extracts?
- **Curtains and blinds.**
- **Detergent**. Made with hemp and/or other plant extracts, the detergent is safer than those made using petroleum. Hemp is also an ingredient in natural laundry stain removers.
- **Diapers**. Because hemp fabric is naturally resistant to mold and mildew and more absorbent than cotton, it is a better choice than cotton for cloth diapers. Because it is less susceptible to decomposition from UV rays, it lasts longer than cotton when the diapers hang in the sun to dry.

  Hemp can also be used to make disposable diapers that are 100 percent biodegradable. Currently the manufacture of disposable diapers uses over 250,000 trees per year (for wood pulp fiber). Hemp provides more pulp per acre and is easier to grow. Hemp can also be used to make the plastics that are used in disposable diapers. Unlike plastic made from petroleum, the plastic made from hemp is 100 percent biodegradable.
- **Diesel fuel**. Hemp oil, or any vegetable oil, can be used to run diesel engines in place of the toxic, heavy particulate, cancer-causing petrofuels that are a major cause of global warming. When fossil fuels are burned they release carbon dioxide, contributing to global warming and the poisoning of the oceans, lakes, and rivers. The sulfur released in burning fossil fuels also contributes to acid rain.

  All diesel engines can run on hemp fuel. It is a cleaner burning, nonfossil fuel that is safer for the environment than petroleum diesel fuel. An acre of hemp produces about 300 gallons of oil.

  A variety of plant oils can be used in diesel engines, but hemp oil is the easiest to grow and process. If we used seed oils instead of petroleum oil for diesel engine vehicles, the air would be cleaner, not only from less toxic fuel, but also from thousands of acres of farmed plants that would provide oxygen and absorb the elements that cause global warming. The oceans and lakes would be cleaner, and the world would be a better place if we used seed oil fuel for diesel engines rather than petroleum diesel fuel.

Currently the corn fuel/petro diesel fuel blends create more pollution than what would be caused by hemp fuel/petro diesel blends.

The corn industry is the most subsidized industry in the U.S. The corn industry would lose money and funding if hemp were legalized for bio-methanol production (corporate welfare from the government provides hundreds of millions of dollars in funding for corn-based ethanol companies). Hemp ethanol is more economically feasible, is easier to produce, uses less energy to produce, causes less pollution when produced, is easier on and better for the soil, takes less land to produce, and requires less irrigation to produce than corn ethanol.

Hemp farms also absorb more greenhouse gasses than burning of the fuel releases. Hemp fuel can help governments accomplish their goal of reducing greenhouse gases.

As mentioned elsewhere in the book, hemp diesel and plant diesel fuels of any kind are not without their problems. Soil depletion issues and intensive production matters should be taken into consideration when balancing the environmental safety of any sort of fuel.

"Of all the various uses for Cannabis plants, add another, 'green' one to the mix.

Researchers at UConn have found that the fiber crop Cannabis sativa, known as industrial hemp, has properties that make it viable and even attractive as a raw material, or feedstock, for producing biodiesel - sustainable diesel fuel made from renewable plant sources.

The plant's ability to grow in infertile soils also reduces the need to grow it on primary croplands, which can then be reserved for growing food, says Richard Parnas, a professor of chemical, materials, and biomolecular engineering who led the study.

'For sustainable fuels, often it comes down to a question of food versus fuel,' says Parnas, noting that major current biodiesel plants include food crops such as soybeans, olives, peanuts, and rapeseed. 'It's equally important to make fuel from plants that are not food, but also won't need the high-quality land.'"
– Christine Buckley, UConn Today; October 6, 2010

- **Engine oil and mechanical lubricant.** Again, environmentally safer and more economically feasible than petroleum oil in every way. It works well on bike chains. During World War II the U.S. government used hemp oil as a lubricant on machinery and airplanes.
- **Erosion control blankets** made from hemp rope and netting can be used to prevent soil erosion. In landscaping, an underlying, biodegradable "growth mat" fabric made purely of hemp fiber can be used as a way to hold soil in place while roots of trees, bushes, and plants grow into stabilizing root systems. Eventually the roots of the foliage take over, and the growth mat composts into the soil.
- **Ethanol.** As mentioned above, hemp can be used to make ethanol. Because hemp provides more biomass per acre than other crops, hemp is an excellent crop to grow for ethanol.

  Ethanol is best made using low lignan, high cellulose plants, which makes cellulosic ethanol rather than the starch- or sugar-based ethanol made from corn.

  Cellulosic ethanol produces greatly lower tailpipe emissions than starch ethanol, and is better for the engines. Hemp has the best lignan/cellulose ratio of all plants. Hemp is a better choice than corn, sugar beets, and other plants being used for ethanol production. This is so in relation to the amount of fuel, farming chemicals, soil degradation caused by other crops. Hemp is less intensive, uses fewer resources to grow, and is an excellent producer of fuel in relation to its absorption of greenhouse gasses and sequestering in the parts of the plant not used for fuel.

  Petroleum gasoline is a toxic, cancer-causing "fossil fuel" and is distilled with the toxic, cancer-causing chemicals benzine, hexene, touline, and zylene. Replacing petroleum gasoline with cellulosic ethanol made from hemp would prevent the use of these chemicals that are deadly for all forms of life.

  However, as explained earlier in the book, when certain issues surrounding ethanol are taken into consideration, it should be obvious that it is not the answer to world problems. Ethanol requires an enormous amount of water, and creates water pollution. Removing too much farm waste in the form of plant matter from the land degrades the soil. Building ethanol plants all over the world to serve the combustible engine economies requires enormous resources, including cement, steel, roads, and fuel to produce the ethanol.

  In other words, walk or ride a bike instead of driving.
- **Fabric.** For clothing, shoes, hats, furniture, bags, bedding, towels, tenting, etc. Hemp fabric is safer than cotton, which is grown using toxic chemicals in the form of herbicides and pesticides that lead to

373

poisoned rivers, aquifers, oceans, and lakes and to global warming. Hemp plants also provide more fiber per acre than cotton and are better for the soil than cotton.

Unlike cotton, hemp is naturally resistant to mold and mildew.

Hemp shower curtains also do not emit toxic fumes the way plastic shower curtains do. These are reasons why hemp shower curtains are becoming popular.

Some people use the term, "India hemp" as a name for plants including hemp, jute, and dogbane. However, by most definitions, India hemp only includes true hemp, and no other fiber plants.

Also, "linen" historically was made from hemp. But some people believe linen only describes fabric made from flax. But the "bast fiber" plants, including flax, hemp, kenaf, and nettles, have been used to make linen.

- **Fiberboard.** Made from hemp, it is stronger than fiberboard made from wood because hemp has longer fibers. It is also more resistant to bug infestation. See Plywood below.
- **Fiberglass.** Hemp fiber can be used in fiberglass. Hemp extracts can also be used to make the resin, replacing the toxic resins used in fiberglass materials. Other plants used to make plastics are soy and corn. When the plastics and industrial resins made from hemp are combined with hemp fiber, the product is environmentally safer in a number of areas as compared to petroleum and glass fiberglass. Producing hemp fiberglass uses less energy than petroleum-based fiberglass, and it does not require the drilling and intensive refinement used to create petroleum plastic. The greenhouse gasses sequestered in the hemp plant remain in the fiberglass, which is also biodegradable (unless it contains petroleum byproducts, including polypropylene). Hemp fiberglass is lighter and stronger than traditional fiberglass. This is one reason why car companies are pleased by it. A lighter car means better fuel mileage.
- **Flooring.** Various flooring materials made from hemp include ceramic-like tile, linoleum-like plastics, and compressed planks.
- **Food.** Hemp seed does not contain THC, the psychoactive substance of marijuana that induces pleasurable feelings. There may be very minimal amounts of THC residue on the hull of the hemp seed, but not enough to get someone high. Even consuming a cup of hemp seed will not provide a buzz. You are likely to get more drunk from a teaspoon of beer than high from a bushel of hemp seeds.

The seeds of hemp can be used in cereals, trail mix, and chips. They can be ground into highly nutritious protein powder that can be used as flour, and added to smoothies, meatless burgers, and other foods. Raw hempseed oil is a high-quality dietary oil that can be used in salad dressings, frozen desserts, and other foods.

"Peanut, Almond, Cashew, and Macadamia nut butters, are familiar to most Americans. It is safe to say that Peanut butter is the most favored of these, used in traditional ways handed down by generations of caring parents, who were concerned about their children having good protein in their diet. The problem is that some proteins are potential allergens, which include soy, and dairy, as well as peanut proteins. Peanuts may also carry unacceptable amount of a potent carcinogen found on other field crops as well. They are known as Aflatoxins, and are derived from the presence of mold before they are harvested.

The good news is that hemp butter is made from hemp seeds, and no hemp seed allergies have ever been reported. Although most nut butter users have not heard of Hemp Butter, times are changing, and hemp butter is now available in the marketplace. Not the least important fact about hemp butter is that it is a dark green color due to the rich content of chlorophyll, which is a powerful antioxidant."
– Jacquie Schmall, *Helium*, October 2010

- **Fuel.** Hemp oil and ethanol fuels, along with other sustainable plant fuels, can help replace petroleum gasoline, kerosene, and diesel fuel.
  Hemp fuel burns cleaner than petroleum and doesn't contain sulfur, so it won't cause acid rain, or lead to the acidifying of the world's oceans and lakes, which is leading to global warming and damage to all marine life.
  See Diesel Fuel and Ethanol above.
- **Furniture.** From the fabric to the stuffing, wood and paint hemp can be used to create furniture that is environmentally safe. Many types of furniture manufactured today are made out of chemically treated wood, plasticized fabrics, petroleum-based finishes, and foam rubber made from petrochemicals.
- **Hammocks.** Being naturally resistant to mold and mildew as well as to decomposition from sunlight makes hemp an excellent fiber material for hammocks and outside furniture.
- **Ink.** Common nonpetroleum ink is made from soy. Hemp provides more ink-making substances per acre than soy. Soy is often grown using chemicals made from petroleum and other fossil fuels in the form of pesticides, herbicides, and fertilizers. There is no need for these chemicals on farms, and they are not needed to grow hemp.
- **Insulation.** Fiber from hemp can be used for making. Hemp insulation is safer than fiberglass insulation, which can damage lungs,

and may emit formaldehyde, which can cause cancers of the breathing passageways.

"Insulation made from hemp has definite advantages: its production requires relatively little energy, it's not harmful to health, and it can be disposed of by composting or carbon-neutral incineration. In addition, it is light, has low heat conductivity and meets fire safety regulations. On top of that, it easily absorbs and releases moisture, helping to prevent damage to the building.

Hemp insulation is manufactured by several companies, including the Fraunhofer Institute for Chemical Technology (Germany) which uses a biopolymer extracted from corn instead of polyester to hold the hemp fibers together, creating an insulating material made entirely of natural products that is completely biodegradable."
– VoteHemp.com; March 2007

- **Jobs**. Although not a "product," an industrial hemp industry creates jobs on a local level. From farming to processing the harvested hemp into raw material and into products, the hemp industry creates jobs every step of the way. It can bring the production of fabric, fuel, paper, food, and other products and materials into the local sector in an environmentally sustainable way unlike any other material. It makes communities more self-sufficient, and greatly reduces the dependence on materials having to be brought into a community from distant parts of the planet. Instead of depending on fuel imported from other parts of the world, a community can create its own fuel. Instead of bringing in wood, paper, fabric, paint, oil, and food products from other parts of the planet, the community growing hemp can create its own. Everyone from small farmers to small business owners can benefit from a local hemp industry. Wildlife and the environment will benefit from healthier forests and cleaner air and water. Again, I ask the question: Why is the U.S. importing hemp materials from Australia, Canada, China, England, France, Germany, Holland, Hungary, Poland, Spain, Thailand, and the Ukraine when the U.S. can be growing it locally? Growing it locally would reduce pollution created in transporting the materials from distant lands. It would keep the revenue in the local community. Keeping the farming of industrial hemp illegal in the U.S. is irresponsible and irrational. An active industrial hemp industry in the U.S. would greatly reduce world pollution.
- **Lamp oil**. Hemp is a clean-burning oil that is much safer than petro oils, and it burns brighter. Put hemp oil in your oil lamp and you will

immediately notice the difference in a cleaner-burning oil that smells better and doesn't create black smoke.

Before lamps were known as "kerosene lamps," they were known as oil lamps. The two most common forms of oil used in the lamps were whale fat oil and hemp oil. Kerosene is a petroleum product and didn't come into wide use until the middle of the 1800s. Eventually, the use of kerosene faded as the electric light bulb became popular.

- **Linen.** See: Fabric
- **Lotion.** Hemp-based lotions are safer than lotions made with petroleum extracts.
- **Mulch.** For farming and gardening. The leaves of hemp plants are naturally high in soil nutrients and they work as natural, safe fertilizer as they decompose.
- **Netting.** See Hammocks.
- **Nutritional powders and oils.** Hemp is an excellent source for nutritional oils and powders.
- **Oil.** When hemp is grown for seed, it provides about 1,000 pounds of seed per acre. One acre of hemp produces as much fuel from oil and ethanol as 25 barrels of petroleum oil. With a 35 percent oil content, hemp can provide a lot of oil for many of the uses listed here.

  After the seeds are pressed to extract the oil, the remaining caking can be used for a variety of the other products, including as a nutritional ingredient in food, in nutritional powders, and in pet food.
- **Outdoor fabric uses.** Hemp fabric is less affected by UV rays than cotton, and even more so than some synthetic fiber fabrics. This makes hemp fabric ideal for tarps, tenting, sails, hammocks, and other outdoor uses.
- **Packaging.** Why are we cutting down trees to make disposable packaging when we can save the forests and use fast-growing hemp instead?

  Disposable packaging made from hemp is recyclable, compostable, and biodegradable. Compare that to Styrofoam cups, or to plastic cups and plastic utensils that may be around for thousands of years.

  Food containers made out of tree pulp are made using bleaches that result in poisoned rivers, lakes, and oceans. They are often also coated with petroleum wax, which is another poison, and this wax leaches into the food that is stored in them.

  Along the same lines, why are we cutting down 100 million trees every year to print junk mail? Not that I am for junk mail, but allowing the forests to survive and using hemp to create paper for marketing materials would do several things that would support the environment rather than destroy it. It would keep the forests where they should be, absorbing carbon and air pollution while filtering rainwater and serving as homes to wildlife. Fields of hemp would absorb more pollution while emitting oxygen and reduce the use of chemicals that are used in making paper from tree pulp. The greenhouse gasses absorbed by the fields of hemp would be locked into the paper products, which could be composted, recycled, or used to make building materials, including insulation.

- **Paint.** Safer for both people and the environment than paint made from petroleum extracts. Paint made with hemp oil is less likely to blister under the sun.
- **Paper.** Hemp provides more pulp per acre than many type of trees that are used for paper. Genetically engineered trees can provide more pulp per acre, but genetic engineering is a dangerous practice that has introduced a number of problems for wildlife and the environment.

    We could stop cutting down the forests for paper if we were to legalize industrial hemp farming. This would help save endangered species; protect animal environments; and improve the health of streams, rivers, lakes, and oceans. Allowing the forests to regenerate while also planting millions of acres of hemp around the world would absorb global warming gasses from the atmosphere while putting forth oxygen.
- **Pet food.** Pets can benefit from the excellent quality nutrients in hemp seeds.
- **Phytoremediation.** This is not a "product," but is a process by which growing hemp can be used to clean soil that has been contaminated with industrial pollutants and nuclear waste. In other words, growing hemp can help remove toxins from polluted soil. The Institute of Bast Crops in the Ukraine has been involved in experiments to grow hemp in soil contaminated by the 1986 Chernobyl nuclear power plant disaster.
- **Pillows.**
- **Pipe.** Hemp plastic piping for plumbing needs can be used instead of toxic polyvinyl chloride (PVC) piping.

    Polyvinyl chloride is a known carcinogen that requires large amounts of fossil fuels and chlorine to produce. It leaches dioxin into the environment. PVC is not a good thing.
- **Plastic.** From the raw material to the final product, plastic made from hemp can be environmentally safer than plastics made from petroleum. Hemp plastic can be made to be biodegradable. Even if it isn't made to be biodegradable, hemp plastic is still safer plastic than petroleum plastic because it doesn't require drilling into the ground,

or beneath the bottoms of the seas, such as what has been done in the Gulf of Mexico. Plastic can also be made from such plants as corn, cotton, and sugar beets, but those crops are most often grown using toxic farming chemicals that are harmful to wildlife, to streams, rivers, lakes, and oceans, and cause global warming.

"Terminology-wise, we need to be extremely careful with the word 'bioplastic.' It is a neurolinguistic booby trap. Bioplastics, like regular plastics, are synthetic polymers, it's just that plants are being used instead of oil to obtain the carbon and hydrogen needed for polymerization. Bioplastic may or may not be biodegradable, may or may not be toxic, just like any other plastic. A plastic such as high-density polyethylene HDPE, can be 100 percent bio-based (for instance 100 percent organic hemp), and yet still be non-biodegradable. The public, however, is led to think that any bio-based plastic is biodegradable, which is not at all the case. Dasani (bottled water) and Coke's 'Plant Bottle' is a notorious example of this type of greenwashing."
– The Bioplastic Labyrinth, by Manuel Maqueda; Earth Island Journal, autumn 2010; EarthIslandJournal.org

- **Plywood**. Again, another way we could stop cutting down the forests is to make plywood out of hemp and bamboo instead of trees.
Common plywood emits formaldehyde, which can cause cancers of the breathing passageways. Plywood is also often treated with toxic chemicals. Hemp and bamboo plywood can be made without these toxins and is less susceptible to bug infestation.
Fiberboard made from hemp is two to three times stronger than fiberboard made from wood. One of the reasons for this is that wood fiber is very short, while hemp fiber can be feet long.
- **Rayon**. This popular fabric can be made from hemp hurd.
- **Roofing**. Resins and fibers of the hemp plant are used to create long-lasting roofing materials that are biodegradable and do not contain toxic chemicals that poison the environment. Many roofing materials in use today are made out of tar and other toxic derivatives of petroleum.
- **Resins**. For fiberglass and other structural and industrial uses. Using hemp for these would help reduce the use and dependence on toxic fossil fuels.
- **Rope**. The use of hemp fiber to make rope is one of the most common worldwide uses of the plant. Hemp rope was used during the construction of the Great Pyramids.

- **Rugs**. Many of the most common materials used in rugs are cancer-causing and hormone-disrupting, and emit toxic gasses into homes. Additionally, traditional carpeting isn't biodegradable and it takes up a large amount of space in landfills.

  Hemp fiber is a strong material ideal for rugs, holds up under high foot traffic, and can be cleaned using common carpet cleaning machinery.
- **Sails.** The first triangular sails were made by Arabs. Soon after that they expanded their trade routes. It was only after hemp sails came into use that England established its trade route with the Orient. Hemp sails were used on Columbus's ships, on the *Mayflower*, on the USS *Constitution*, and on other famous ships.
- **Sealants.**
- **Shampoo.**
- **Shoe laces.**
- **Shower curtains.**
- **Soap.**
- **Sporting goods and clothing.** Frisbees, gloves, hackie sacks, protective gear, running shoes, skateboards, snowboards, socks, surfboards, umbrellas, and yoga clothing and mats can all be made from hemp materials.
- **Tea bags.**
- **Towels.**
- **Vacuum cleaner filters.**
- **Varnish.**
- **Wallpaper.**

"Overall, social pressure and government mandates for lower dioxin production, lower greenhouse gas emissions, greater bio-based product procurement, and a number of other environmental regulations, seem to directly contradict the wisdom of prohibiting an evidently useful and unique crop like hemp."
– March 2008 Reason Foundation Study on Hemp, Illegally Green: Environmental Costs of Hemp Prohibition. Policy Study 367, by Skaidra Smith-Heisters

# APPENDIX 2

## Marijuana Tax Act of 1937

THE MARIHUANA TAX ACT OF 1937

U. S. TREASURY DEPARTMENT BUREAU OF NARCOTICS REGU-
LATIONS No. 1 RELATING TO THE IMPORTATION, MANU-
FACTURE, PRODUCTION COMPOUNDING, SALE, DEALING IN,
DISPENSING PRESCRIBING, ADMINISTERING, AND GIVING
AWAY OF MARIHUANA UNDER THE ACT OF AUGUST 2, 1937
PUBLIC, No. 238, 75TH CONGRESS
NARCOTIC-INTERNAL REVENUE REGULATIONS
JOINT MARIHUANA REGULATIONS MADE BY THE COMMISS-
IONER OF NARCOTICS AND THE COMMISSIONER OF INTER-
NAL REVENUE WITH THE APPROVAL OF THE SECRETARY OF
THE TREASURY EFFECTIVE DATE, OCTOBER 1, 1937

LAW AND REGULATIONS RELATING TO THE IMPORTATION,
MANUFACTURE, PRODUCTION, COMPOUNDING, SALE, DEAL-
ING IN, DISPENSING, PRESCRIBING, ADMINISTERING, AND
GIVING AWAY OF MARIHUANA

THE LAW

(Act of Aug. 2, 1937, Public 238, 75th Congress)
Be it enacted by the Senate and House of Representatives of the United
States of America in Congress assembled, That when used in this Act,
(a) The term "person" means an individual, a partnership, trust, association,
company, or corporation and includes an officer or employee of a trust,
association, company, or corporation, or a member or employee of a
partnership, who, as such officer, employee, or member, is under a duty to
perform any act in respect of which any violation of this Act occurs.
(b) The term "marihuana" means all parts of the plant Cannabis sativa L.,
whether growing or not; the seeds thereof; the resin extracted from any part
of such plant; and every compound, manufacture, salt, derivative, mixture,
or preparation of such plant, its seeds, or resin – but shall not include the
mature stalks of such plant, fiber produced from such stalks, oil or cake
made from the seeds of such plant, any other compound, manufacture, salt,
derivative, mixture, or preparation of such mature stalks (except the resin
extracted therefrom), fiber, oil, or cake, or the sterilized seed of such plant
which is incapable of germination.

381

(c) The term "producer" means any person who (1) plants, cultivates, or in any way facilitates the natural growth of marihuana; or (2) harvests and transfers or makes use of marihuana.

(d) The term "Secretary" means the Secretary of the Treasury and the term "collector" means collector of internal revenue.

(e) The term "transfer" or "transferred" means any type of disposition resulting in a change of possession but shall not include a transfer to a common carrier for the purpose of transporting marihuana.

SEC. 2. (a) Every person who imports, manufactures, produces, compounds, sells, deals in, dispenses, prescribes, administers, or gives away marihuana shall ( 1 ) within fifteen days after the effective date of this Act, or (2) before engaging after the expiration of such fifteen-day period in any of the above mentioned activities, and (3) thereafter, on or before July 1 of each year, pay the following special taxes respectively:

(1) Importers, manufacturers, and compounders of marihuana, $24 per year.

(2) Producers of marihuana (except those included within subdivision (4) of this subsection), $1 per year, or fraction thereof, during which they engage in such activity.

(3) Physicians, dentists, veterinary surgeons, and other practitioners who distribute, dispense, give away, administer, or prescribe marihuana to patients upon whom they in the course of their professional practice are in attendance, $1 per year or fraction thereof during which they engage in any of such activities.

(4) Any person not registered as an importer, manufacturer, producer, or compounder who obtains and uses marihuana in a laboratory for the purpose of research, instruction, or analysis, or who produces marihuana for any such purpose, $1 per year, or fraction thereof, during which he engages in such activities.

(5) Any person who is not a physician, dentist, veterinary surgeon, or other practitioner and who deals in, dispenses, or gives away marihuana, $3 per year: Provided, That any person who has registered and paid the special tax as an importer, manufacturer, compounder, or producer, as required by subdivisions (1) and (2) of this subsection, may deal in, dispense, or give away marihuana imported, manufactured, compounded, or produced by him without further payment of the tax imposed by this section.

(b) Where a tax under subdivision (1) or (5) is payable on July 1 of any year it shall be computed for one year; where any such tax is payable on any other day it shall be computed proportionately from the first day of the month in which the liability for the tax accrued to the following July 1.

(c) In the event that any person subject to a tax imposed by this section engages in any of the activities enumerated in subsection (a) of this section at more than one place, such person shall pay the tax with respect to each such place.

(d) Except as otherwise provided, whenever more than one of the activities enumerated in subsection (a) of this section is carried on by the same person at the same time, such person shall pay the tax for each such activity, according to the respective rates prescribed.

(e) Any person subject to the tax imposed by this section shall, upon payment of such tax, register his name or style and his place or places of business with the collector of the district in which such place or places of business are located.

(f) Collectors are authorized to furnish, upon written request, to any person a certified copy of the names of any or all persons who may be listed in their respective collection districts as special taxpayers under this section, upon payment of a fee of $1 for each one hundred of such names or fraction thereof upon such copy so requested.

SEC. 3. (a) No employee of any person who has paid the special tax and registered, as required by section 2 of this Act, acting within the scope of his employment, shall be required to register and pay such special tax.

(b) An officer or employee of the United States, any State, Territory, the District of Columbia, or insular possession, or political subdivision, who, in the exercise of his official duties, engages in any of the activities enumerated in section 2 of this Act, shall not be required to register or pay the special tax, but his right to this exemption shall be evidenced in such manner as the Secretary may by regulations prescribe.

SEC. 4. (a) It shall be unlawful for any person required to register and pay the special tax under the provisions of section 2 to import, manufacture, produce, compound, sell, deal in, dispense, distribute, prescribe, administer, or give away marihuana without having so registered and paid such tax.

(b) In any suit or proceeding to enforce the liability imposed by this section or section 2, if proof is made that marihuana was at any time growing upon land under the control of the defendant, such proof shall be presumptive evidence that at such time the defendant was a producer and liable under this section as well as under section 2.

SEC. 5. It shall be unlawful for any person who shall not have paid the special tax and registered, as required by section 2, to send, ship, carry, transport, or deliver any marihuana within any Territory, the District of Columbia, or any insular possession, or from any State, Territory, the District of Columbia, any insular possession of the United States, or the Canal Zone, into any other State, Territory, the District of Columbia, or insular possession of the United States: Provided, That nothing contained in this section shall apply to any common carrier engaged in transporting marihuana; or to any employee of any person who shall have registered and paid the special tax as required by section 2 while acting within the scope of his employment; or to any person who shall deliver marihuana which has been prescribed or dispensed by a physician, dentist, veterinary surgeon, or other practitioner registered under section 2, who has been employed to prescribe for the particular patient receiving such marihuana; or to any United States, State, county, municipal, District, Territorial, or insular officer or official acting within the scope of his official duties.

SEC. 6. (a) It shall be unlawful for any person, whether or not required to pay a special tax and register under section 2, to transfer marihuana, except in pursuance of a written order of the person to whom such marihuana is transferred, on a form to be issued in blank for that purpose by the Secretary.

(b) Subject to such regulations as the Secretary may prescribe, nothing contained in this section shall apply:

(1) To a transfer of marihuana to a patient by a physician, dentist, veterinary surgeon, or other practitioner registered under section 2, in the course of his professional practice only: Provided, That such physician, dentist, veterinary surgeon, or other practitioner shall keep a record of all such marihuana transferred, showing the amount transferred and the name and address of the patient to whom such marihuana is transferred, and such record shall be kept for a period of two years from the date of the transfer of such marihuana, and subject to inspection as provided in section 11.

(2) To a transfer of marihuana, made in good faith by a dealer to a consumer under and in pursuance of a written prescription issued by a physician, dentist, veterinary surgeon, or other practitioner registered under section 2: Provided, That such prescription shall be dated as of the day on which signed and shall be signed by the physician, dentist, veterinary surgeon, or other practitioner who issues the same; Provided further, That such dealer shall preserve such prescription for a period of two years from the day on which such prescription is filled so as to be readily accessible for inspection by the officers, agents, employees, and officials mentioned in section 11.

(3) To the sale, exportation, shipment, or delivery of marihuana by any person within the United States, any Territory, the District of Columbia, or any of the insular possessions of the United States, to any person in any foreign country regulating the entry of marihuana, if such sale, shipment, or delivery of marihuana is made in accordance with such regulations for importation into such foreign country as are prescribed by such foreign country, such regulations to be promulgated from time to time by the Secretary of State of the United States.

(4) To a transfer of marihuana to any officer or employee of the United States Government or of any State, Territorial, District, county, or municipal or insular government lawfully engaged in making purchases thereof for the various departments of the Army and Navy, the Public

Health Service, and for Government, State, Territorial, District, county, or municipal or insular hospitals or prisons.

(S) To a transfer of any seeds of the plant Cannabis sativa L. to any person registered under section 2.

(c) The Secretary shall cause suitable forms to be prepared for the purposes before mentioned and shall cause them to be distributed to collectors for sale. The price at which such forms shall be sold by said collectors shall be fixed by the Secretary but shall not exceed 2 cents each. Whenever any collector shall sell any of such forms he shall cause the date of sale, the name and address of the proposed vendor, the name and address of the purchaser, and the amount of marihuana ordered to be plainly written or stamped thereon before delivering the same.

(d) Each such order form sold by a collector shall be prepared by him and shall include an original and two copies, any one of which shall be admissible in evidence as an original. The original and one copy shall be given by the collector to the purchaser thereof. The original shall in turn be given by the purchaser thereof to any person who shall, in pursuance thereof, transfer marihuana to him and shall be preserved by such person for a period of two years so as to be readily accessible for inspection by any officer, agent, or employee mentioned in section 11. The copy given to the purchaser by the collector shall be retained by the purchaser and preserved for a period of two years so as to be readily accessible to inspection by any officer, agent, or employee mentioned in section 11. The second copy shall be preserved in the records of the collector.

SEC. 7. (a) There shall be levied, collected, and paid upon all transfers of marihuana which are required by section 6 to be carried out in pursuance of written order forms taxes at the following rates:

(1) Upon each transfer to any person who has paid the special tax and registered under section 2 of this Act, $1 per ounce of marihuana or fraction thereof.

(2) Upon each transfer to any person who has not paid the special tax and registered under section 2 of this Act, $100 per ounce of marihuana or fraction thereof.

(b) Such tax shall be paid by the transferee at the time of securing each order form and shall be in addition to the price of such form. Such transferee shall be liable for the tax imposed by this section but in the event that the transfer is made in violation of section 6 without an order form and without payment of the transfer tax imposed by this section, the transferor shall also be liable for such tax.

(c) Payment of the tax herein provided shall be represented by appropriate stamps to be provided by the Secretary and said stamps shall be affixed by the collector or his representative to the original order form.

(d) All provisions of law relating to the engraving, issuance, sale, accountability, cancellation, and destruction of tax-paid stamps provided for in the internal-revenue laws shall, insofar as applicable and not inconsistent with this Act, be extended and made to apply to stamps provided for in this section.

(e) All provisions of law (including penalties) applicable in respect of the taxes imposed by the Act of December 17, 1914 (38 Stat. 785; U. S. C., 1934 ed., title 26, secs. 1040-1061, 1383-1391), as amended, shall, insofar as not inconsistent with this Act, be applicable in respect of the taxes imposed by this Act.

SEC. 8. (a) It shall be unlawful for any person who is a transferee required to pay the transfer tax imposed by section 7 to acquire or otherwise obtain any marihuana without having paid such tax; and proof that any person shall have had in his possession any marihuana and shall have failed, after reasonable notice and demand by the collector, to produce the order form required by section 6 to be retained by him, shall be presumptive evidence of guilt under this section and of liability for the tax imposed by section 7.

(b) No liability shall be imposed by virtue of this section upon any duly authorized officer of the Treasury Department engaged in the enforcement of this Act or upon any duly authorized officer of any State, or Territory, or of any political subdivision thereof, or the District of Columbia, or of any insular possession of the United States, who shall be engaged in the enforcement of any law or municipal ordinance dealing with the production, sale, prescribing, dispensing, dealing in, or distributing of marihuana.

SEC. 9. (a) Any marihuana which has been imported, manufactured, compounded, transferred, or produced in violation of any of the provisions of this Act shall be subject to seizure and forfeiture and, except as inconsistent with the provisions of this Act, all the provisions of internal-revenue laws relating to searches, seizures, and forfeitures are extended to include marihuana.

(b) Any marihuana which may be seized by the United States Government from any person or persons charged with any violation of this Act shall upon conviction of the person or persons from whom seized be confiscated by and forfeited to the United States.

(c) Any marihuana seized or coming into the possession of the United States in the enforcement of this Act, the owner or owners of which are unknown, shall be confiscated by and forfeited to the United States.

(d) The Secretary is hereby directed to destroy any marihuana confiscated by and forfeited to the United States under this section or to deliver such marihuana to any department, bureau, or other agency of the United States Government, upon proper application therefore under such regulations as may be prescribed by the Secretary.

SEC. 10. (a) Every person liable to any tax imposed by this act shall keep such books and records, render under oath such statements, make such returns, and comply with such rules and regulations as the Secretary may from time to time prescribe.

(b) Any person who shall be registered under the provisions of section 2 in any internal-revenue district shall, whenever required so to do by the collector of the district, render to the collector a true and correct statement or return, verified by affidavits, setting forth the quantity of marihuana received or harvested by him during such period immediately preceding the demand of the collector, not exceeding three months, as the said collector may fix and determine. If such person is not solely a producer, he shall set forth in such statement or return the names of the persons from which said marihuana was received, the quantity in each instance received from such persons, and the date when received.

SEC. 11. The order forms and copies thereof and the prescriptions and records required to be preserved under the provisions of section 6, and the statements or returns filed in the office of the collector of the district under the provisions of section 10 (b) shall be open to inspection by officers, agents, and employees of the Treasury Department duly authorized for that purpose, and such officers of any State, or Territory, or of any political subdivision thereof, or the District of Columbia, or of any insular possession of the United States as shall be charged with the enforcement of any law or municipal ordinance regulating the production, sale, prescribing, dispensing, dealing in, or distributing of marihuana. Each collector shall be authorized to furnish, upon written request, copies of any of the said statements or returns filed in his office to any of such officials of any State or Territory, or political subdivision thereof, or the District of Columbia, or any insular possession of the United States as shall be entitled to inspect the said statements or returns filed in the office of the said collector, upon the payment of a fee of $1 for each 100 words or fraction thereof in the copy or copies so requested.

SEC. 12. Any person who is convicted of a violation of any provision of this Act shall be fined not more than $2,000 or imprisoned not more than five years, or both, in the discretion of the court.

SEC. 13. It shall not be necessary to negate any exemptions set forth in this Act in any complaint, information, indictment, or other writ or proceeding laid or brought under this Act and the burden of proof of any such exemption shall be upon the defendant. In the absence of the production of evidence by the defendant that he has complied with the provisions of section 6 relating to order forms, he shall be presumed not to have complied with such provisions of such sections, as the case may be.

SEC. 14. The Secretary is authorized to make, prescribe, and publish all necessary rules and regulations for carrying out the provisions of this Act

387

and to confer or impose any of the rights, privileges, powers, and duties conferred or imposed upon him by this Act upon such officers or employees of the Treasury Department as he shall designate or appoint.

SEC. 15. The provisions of this Act shall apply to the several States, the District of Columbia, the Territory of Alaska, the Territory of Hawaii, and the insular possessions of the United States, except the Philippine Islands. In Puerto Rico the administration of this Act, the collection of the special taxes and transfer taxes, and the issuance of the order forms provided for in section 6 shall be performed by the appropriate internal revenue officers of that government, and all revenues collected under this Act in Puerto Rico shall accrue intact to the general government thereof. The President is hereby authorized and directed to issue such Executive orders as will carry into effect in the Virgin Islands the intent and purpose of this Act by providing for the registration with appropriate officers and the imposition of the special and transfer taxes upon all persons in the Virgin Islands who import, manufacture, produce, compound, sell, deal in, dispense, prescribe, administer, or give away marihuana.

SEC. 16. If any provision of this Act or the application thereof to any person or circumstances is held invalid, the remainder of the Act and the application of such provision to other persons or circumstances shall not be affected thereby.

SEC. 17. This Act shall take effect on the first day of the second month during which it is enacted.

SEC. 18. This Act may be cited as the "Marihuana Tax Act of 1937."

(T. D. 28)

Order of the Secretary of the Treasury Relating to the Enforcement of the Marihuana Tax Act of 1937

September 1, 1937

Section 14 of the Marihuana Tax Act of 1937 (act of Congress approved August 2, 1937, Public, No. 238), provides as follows:

The Secretary is authorized to make, prescribe, and publish all necessary rules and regulations for carrying out the provisions of this Act and to confer or impose any of the rights, privileges, powers, and duties conferred or imposed upon him by this Act upon such officers or employees of the Treasury Department as he shall designate or appoint.

In pursuance of the authority thus conferred upon the Secretary of the Treasury, it is hereby ordered:

I. Rights, Privileges, Powers, and Duties Conferred and imposed Upon the Commissioner of Narcotics

1. There are hereby conferred and imposed upon the Commissioner of Narcotics, subject to the general supervision and direction of the Secretary of the Treasury, all the rights, privileges, powers, and duties conferred or

imposed upon said Secretary by the Marihuana Tax Act of 1937, so far as such rights privileges, powers, and duties relate to:

(a) Prescribing regulations, with the approval of the Secretary, as to the manner in which the right of public officers to exemption from registration and payment of special tax may be evidenced, in accordance with section 3 (b) of the act.

(b) Prescribing the form of written order required by section 6 (a) of the act, said form to be prepared and issued in blank by the Commissioner of Internal Revenue as hereinafter provided.

(c) Prescribing regulations, with the approval of the Secretary, giving effect to the exceptions, specified in subsection (b), from the operation of subsection (a) of section 6 of the act.

(d) The destruction of marihuana confiscated by and forfeited to the United States, or delivery of such marihuana to any department, bureau, or other agency of the United States Government, and prescribing regulations, with the approval of the Secretary, governing the manner of application for, and delivery of such marihuana.

(e) Prescribing rules and regulations, with the approval of the Secretary, as to books and records to be kept, and statements and information returns to be rendered under oath, as required by section 10 (a) of the act.

(f) The compromise of any criminal liability (except as relates to delinquency in registration and delinquency in payment of tax) arising under the act, in accordance with section 3229 of the Revised Statutes of the United States (U. S. Code (1934 ed.) title 26, sec. 1661), and the recommendation for assessment of civil liability for internal-revenue taxes and ad valorem penalties under the act.

II. Rights, Privileges, Powers, and Duties Conferred and Imposed upon the Commissioner of Internal Revenue

1. There are hereby conferred and imposed upon the Commissioner of Internal Revenue, subject to the general supervision and direction of the Secretary of the Treasury, the rights, privileges, powers, and duties conferred or imposed upon said Secretary of the Marihuana Tax Act of 1937, not otherwise assigned herein, so far as such rights, privileges, powers, and duties relate to

(a) Preparation and issuance in blank to collectors of internal revenue of the written orders, in the form prescribed by the Commissioner of Narcotics, required by section 6 (a) of the act. The price of the order form, as sold by the collector under section 6 (c) of the act shall be two cents for the original and one copy.

(b) Providing appropriate stamps to represent payment of transfer tax levied by section 7, and prescribing and providing appropriate stamps for issuance of special tax payers registering under section 2 of the act.

(c) The compromise of any civil liability involving delinquency in Registration, delinquency in payment of tax, and ad valorem penalties, and of any criminal liability incurred through delinquency in registration and delinquency in payment of tax, in connection with the act and in accordance with Section 3229 of the Revised Statutes of the United States (U. S. Code (1934 ed.), title 26, sec. 1661)- the determination of liability for and the assessment and collection of special and transfer taxes imposed by the act; the determination of liability for and the assessment and collection of the ad valorem penalties imposed by Section 3176 of the Revised Statutes, as modified by Section 406 of the Revenue Act of 1935 (U. S. Code (1934 ed.) title 26, secs. 1512-1525), for delinquency in registration; and the determination of liability for and the assertion of the specific penalty imposed by the act, for delinquency in registration and payment of tax.

General Provisions

The investigation and the detection, and presentation to prosecuting officers of evidence, of violations of the Marihuana Tax Act of 1937, shall be the duty of the Commissioner of Narcotics and the assistants, agents, inspectors, or employees under his direction. Except as specifically inconsistent with the terms of said act and of this order, the Commissioner of Narcotics and the Commissioner of Internal Revenue and the assistants, agents, inspectors, or employees of the Bureau of Narcotics and the Bureau of Internal Revenue, respectively, shall have the same powers and duties in safeguarding the revenue thereunder as they now have with respect to the enforcement of, and collection of the revenue under, the act of December 17, 1914, as amended (U. S. Code (1934 ed.), title 26, sec. 1049).

In any case where a general offer is made in compromise of civil and criminal liability ordinarily compromisable hereunder by the Commissioner of Internal Revenue and of criminal liability ordinarily compromisable hereunder by the Commissioner of Narcotics, the case may be jointly compromisable by those officers, in accordance with Section 3229 of the Revised Statutes of the United States (U. S. Code (1934 ed.), title 26, sec. 1661).

Power is hereby conferred upon the Commissioner of Narcotics to prescribe such regulations as he may deem necessary for the execution of the functions imposed upon him or upon the officers or employees of the Bureau of Narcotics, but all regulations and changes in regulations shall be subject to the approval of the Secretary of the Treasury.

The Commissioner of Internal Revenue and the Commissioner of Narcotics may, if they are of the opinion that the good of the service will be promoted thereby, prescribe regulations relating to internal revenue taxes where no violation of the Marihuana Tax Act of 1937 is involved, jointly, subject to the approval of the Secretary of the Treasury.

The right to amend or supplement this order or any provision thereof from time to time, or to revoke this order or any provision thereof at any time, is hereby reserved.

The effective date of this order shall be October 1, 1937, which is the effective date of the Marihuana Tax Act of 1937.

STEPHEN B. GIBBONS, Acting Secretary of the Treasury.

REGULATIONS Introductory

The Marihuana Tax Act of 1937, imposes special (occupational) taxes upon persons engaging in activities involving articles or material within the definition of "marihuana" contained in the act, and also taxes the transfer of such articles or material.

These regulations deal with details as to tax computation, procedure, the forms of records and returns, and similar matters. These matters in some degree are controlled by certain sections of the United States Revised Statutes and other statutes of general application. Provisions of these statutes, as well as of the Marihuana Tax Act of 1937 are quoted, in whole or in part, as the immediate or general basis for the regulatory provisions set forth. The quoted provisions are from the Marihuana Tax Act of 1937 unless otherwise indicated.

Provisions of the statutes upon which the various articles of the regulations are based generally have not been repeated in the articles. Therefore, the statutory excerpts preceding the several articles should be examined to obtain complete information.

Chapter I Laws Applicable

SEC. 7 (e) All provisions of law (including penalties) applicable in respect of the taxes imposed by the Act of December 17, 1914 (38 Stat. 785; U. S. C., 1934 ed., title 26, secs. 1040- 1061, 1383-1391), as amended, shall, insofar as not inconsistent with this Act, be applicable in respect of the taxes imposed by this Act.

ART. 1. Statutes applicable. All general provisions of the internal revenue laws, not inconsistent with the Marihuana Tax Act, are applicable in the enforcement of the latter.

Chapter II Definitions

SEC. 1. That when used in this Act:

(a) The term "person" means an individual, a partnership, trust, association, company, or corporation and includes an officer or employee of a trust, association, company, or corporation, or a member or employee of a partnership, who as such officer, employee, or member is under a duty to perform any act in respect of which any violation of this Act occurs.

(b) The term "marihuana" means all parts of the plant Cannabis sativa L., whether growing or not; the seeds thereof; the resin extracted from any part of such plant; and every compound, manufacture, salt, derivative, mixture, or preparation of such plant, its seeds, or resins; but shall not include the

391

mature stalks of such plant, fiber produced from such stalks, oil or cake made from the seeds of such plant, any other compound, manufacture, salt, derivative, mixture, or preparation of such mature stalks (except the resin extracted therefrom), fiber, oil, or cake, or the sterilized seed of such plant which is incapable of germination.

(c) The term "producer" means any person who ( 1 ) plants, cultivates, or in any way facilitates the natural growth of marihuana; or (2) harvests and transfers or makes use of marihuana.

(d) The term "Secretary" means the Secretary of the Treasury and the term "collector" means collector of internal revenue.

(e) The term "transfer" or "transferred" means any type of disposition resulting in a change of possession but shall not include a transfer to a common carrier for the purpose of transporting marihuana

ART. 2. As used in these regulations:

(a) The term "act" or "this act" shall mean the Marihuana Tax Act of 1937, unless otherwise indicated.

(b) The term "United States" shall include the several States, the District of Columbia, the Territory of Alaska, the Territory of Hawaii, and the insular possessions of the United States except Puerto Rico and the Virgin Islands. It does not include the Canal Zone or the Philippine Islands.

(c) The terms "manufacturer" and "compounder" shall include any person who subjects marihuana to any process of separation, extraction, mixing, compounding, or other manufacturing operation. They shall not include one who merely gathers and destroys the plant, one who merely threshes out the seeds on the premises where produced, or one who in the conduct of a legitimate business merely subjects seeds to a cleaning process.

(d) The term "producer" means any person who induces in any way the growth of marihuana, and any person who harvests it, either in a cultivated or wild state, from his own or any other land, and transfers or makes use of it, including one who subjects the marihuana which he harvests to any processes rendering him liable also as a manufacturer or compounder. Generally all persons are included who gather marihuana for any purpose other than to destroy it. The term does not include one who merely plows under or otherwise destroys marihuana with or without harvesting. It does not include one who grows marihuana for use in his own laboratory for the purpose of research, instruction, or analysis and who does not use it for any other purpose or transfer it.

(e) The term "special tax" is used to include any of the taxes, pertaining to the several occupations or activities covered by the act, imposed upon persons who import, manufacture, produce, compound, sell, deal in, dispense, prescribe, administer, or give away marihuana.

(f ) The term "person" occurring in these regulations is used to include individual, partnership, trust, association, company, or corporation; also a hospital, college of pharmacy, medical or dental clinic, sanatorium, or other institution or entity.

(g) Words importing the singular may include the plural; words importing the masculine gender may be applied to the feminine or the neuter.

1. The definitions contained herein shall not be deemed exclusive.

# APPENDIX 3

## Press release from VoteHemp.com in response to the end of DEA ban on hemp foods

Following is the press release from VoteHemp.com announcing the ruling against the DEA goal to ban foods containing hemp.

February 12, 2004 FOR IMMEDIATE RELEASE VOTEHEMP.com

**Hemp Industry Demands Apology from DEA After Three Years of Harassment**

Landmark Court Decision Saves Jobs and Nutritious Foods Made with Hemp Seed

WASHINGTON, DC - Manufacturers and consumers of nutritious hemp food products are thrilled about the legal battle they won on February 6 when a three-judge federal panel ruled unanimously that hemp foods are perfectly legal and safe to consume. The Hemp Industries Association (HIA), representing over 200 hemp companies in North America, won their 2 1/2-year-old lawsuit HIA v. DEA (Hemp Industries Association v. Drug Enforcement Administration), invalidating the Drug Enforcement Administration's misguided attempt to rewrite the definition of marijuana to include nutritious and safe hemp seed.

"Health-conscious consumers of hemp waffles, bread, cereal, vegetarian burgers, protein powder, salad dressing and nutrition bars can finally relax that these foods are going to stay on store shelves," David Bronner, Chair of the HIA Food and Oil Committee. "The decision in HIA v. DEA is a huge boost to the hemp food market, and we expect to see many more hemp food products on store shelves. The three-judge panel agreed with our main argument that the DEA's 'Final Rule' ignores Congress's specific exemption in the Controlled Substances Act (CSA) under the definition of marihuana that excludes hemp seed and oil from control along with hemp fiber. Based on the decision, the court reasonably views trace insignificant amounts of THC in hemp seed in the same way as it sees trace amounts of opiates in poppy seeds," says Bronner.

Fighting the DEA ban cost leading hemp companies roughly $200,000 (money that might be recoverable) and resulted in some retailers temporarily pulling hemp products from store shelves. "The public and media should question the motives of the DEA," says Eric Steenstra, president of Vote Hemp. "We have uncovered documents through the Freedom of Information Act that prove the DEA's own attorneys at the Department of Justice as far back as March 2000 knew they lacked the authority to ban hemp food products." (See votehemp.com/PDF/roth_letter.pdf) "The DEA owes over 200 companies and every American an apology for wasting taxpayer money pursuing a ban on hemp foods."

Hemp Food Was Victim of Drug War Hysteria

"The truth is that the DEA, at the direction of the Office of National Drug Control Policy and the urging of the Family Research Council, attempted to kill the legitimate, burgeoning hemp foods industry not because hemp is harmful to the human body, but because they see it as a 'stalking horse' for the marijuana movement," says Patrick Goggin, an attorney for the HIA. "The damages this egregious policy have caused are wide-spread to say the least. The industry is fully considering its options for recovering these damages and the cost of defending against this underhanded governmental action." (See ONDCP memo on Hemp foods, April 2000 VoteHemp.com/PDF/Jurith_Robles.pdf.)

DEA Admitted Hemp Food Does Not Pose Any Harm, Leading Nutritionist Agrees

During final arguments, the DEA acknowledged that hemp foods have no abuse potential, stating "The concern of the Drug Enforcement Administration isn't particularized to the particular products that these Petitioners make. The DEA has never said, has never focused on the particular products and said anyone can get high from them, or that they pose a harm to people." According to nutritionist and best-selling author Dr. Andrew Weil, "There is absolutely no health concern about trace amounts of THC in hemp foods. I think the federal court decision is great."

Public Outrage Against DEA Hemp Food Ban

In regard to widespread outrage over the DEA's "Final Rule" 115,000 public comments, a letter from the Canadian government, and a letter from Congress co-signed by 22 representatives submitted to DEA opposed to the hemp food ban, Ninth Circuit Chief Judge Mary Schroeder asked the DEA: "Did you take into account the objections of people who might say that this doesn't make a lot of sense?" Dormont admitted the rule 'wasn't popular.' Protests were organized by Vote Hemp against [the] DEA's attempts to ban hemp foods. In December 2001 and again in April 2003, at more than 50 DEA offices nationwide, activists gave away hemp foods, poppy seed bagels and orange juice that contain trace THC, opiates and alcohol, respectively, to highlight the absurdity of DEA's rules. These "Hemp Food Taste Tests" generated public outrage and forced former DEA Administrator Asa Hutchinson to debate Vote Hemp Director Eric Steenstra on National Public Radio.

Eating Hemp Food Does Not Cause Failed Drug Tests

U.S. hemp food companies voluntarily observe reasonable THC limits similar to those adopted by European nations as well as Canada and Australia. These limits protect consumers with a wide margin of safety from workplace drug-testing interference (see hemp industry standards regarding trace THC at Testpledge.com). The DEA has hypocritically not targeted food manufacturers for using poppy seeds (in bagels and muffins, for example) even though they contain far higher levels of trace opiates. The recently revived global hemp market is a thriving commercial success. Unfortunately, because the DEA's drug war paranoia has confused nonpsychoactive industrial hemp varieties of cannabis with psychoactive "marihuana" varieties, the U.S. is the only major industrialized nation to prohibit the growing of industrial hemp.

Hemp Companies React to Ninth Circuit Court Ruling

"We are very excited that our best-selling Organic Hemp Plus Granola Cereal® and our LifeStream Natural Hemp Plus Waffles® will continue to be available in thousands of stores nationwide," says Arran Stephens, president and founder of Nature's Path Foods®.

"[The] DEA was foolish to try to ban hemp seed because it is a rich source of protein, dietary fiber, minerals, iron, vitamin E, and a near perfect composition of essential fatty acids – Omega 3 and 6," says Lynn Gordon, president of French Meadow Bakery, which sells Healthy Hemp Bread®. "We expect sales to increase enormously as result of the court ruling."

"Nutiva's organic hemp bars and protein powder can finally be sold without concern over its legality," says John Roulac, president of Nutiva®.

"Vegetarians everywhere should celebrate this court ruling," says Ken Holmes, cofounder of Living Harvest®. "People have a right to eat our nutritious Hemp Power Bar, Hemp Protein, Hemp Oil and Hemp Seed Nut."

"The decision will boost demand for our bulk and private label oil and seed products, as well as retail brand hemp food and body care products," says Shaun Crew, President of Hemp Oil Canada®.

"The court ruling will jumpstart sales of our new meatless Omega Burgers® made from organic hemp seed," says Ruth Shamai, president of Ruth's Foods®.

"This decision now allows consumers to vote with their dollars. Healthy hemp food products like Hemp Seed Oil and Hemp Seed Nut (shelled hemp seed) are available now at major retailers like Whole Foods Market," says Michael Fata, Manitoba Harvest® Hemp Foods & Oils.

Hemp Foods Are Safe and Nutritious – DEA Rules Were Ridiculous!

Hemp seed is one of the most perfect sources for human nutrition in all of nature. In addition to its excellent flavor profile, the seed meat protein supplies all essential amino acids in an easily digestible form and with a high protein efficiency ratio. Hemp oil offers high concentrations of the two essential fatty acids (EFAs) in a perfect ratio of the omega-3/omega-6 acids. EFAs are the "good fats" that doctors recommend as part of a healthy, balanced diet.

This superior nutritional profile makes shelled hempseed and oil ideal for a wide range of functional food applications and an effective fatty acid supplement. Not surprisingly, shelled hempseed and oil are increasingly used in natural food products, such as bread, nutrition bars, hummus, non-dairy milks, meatless burgers, and cereals.

## APPENDIX 4

## Representative Ron Paul's introduction of the Industrial Hemp Farming Act of 2007 to Congress

HON. RON PAUL OF TEXAS
BEFORE THE U.S. HOUSE OF REPRESENTATIVES
February 13, 2007

Madame Speaker, I rise to introduce the Industrial Hemp Farming Act. The Industrial Hemp Farming Act requires the federal government to respect state laws allowing the growing of industrial hemp.

Seven states – Hawaii, Kentucky, Maine, Maryland, Montana, North Dakota, and West Virginia – allow industrial hemp production or research in accord with state laws. However, federal law is standing in the way of farmers in these states growing what may be a very profitable crop. Because of current federal law, all hemp included in products sold in the United States must be imported instead of being grown by American farmers.

Since 1970, the federal Controlled Substances Act's inclusion of industrial hemp in the Schedule I definition of marijuana has prohibited American farmers from growing industrial hemp despite the fact that industrial hemp has such a low content of THC (the psychoactive chemical in the related marijuana plant) that nobody can be psychologically affected by consuming hemp. Federal law concedes the safety of industrial hemp by allowing it to be legally imported for use as food.

The United States is the only industrialized nation that prohibits industrial hemp cultivation. The Congressional Research Service has noted that hemp is grown as an established agricultural commodity in over 30 nations in Europe, Asia, and North America. My Industrial Hemp Framing Act will relieve this unique restriction on American farmers and allow them to grow industrial hemp in accord with state law.

Industrial hemp is a crop that was grown legally throughout the United States for most of our nation's history. In fact, during World War II, the federal government actively encouraged American farmers to grow industrial hemp to help the war effort. The Department of Agriculture even produced a film *Hemp for Victory* encouraging the plant's cultivation.

In recent years, the hemp plant has been put to many popular uses in foods and in industry. Grocery stores sell hemp seeds and oil as well as food products containing oil and seeds from the hemp plant. Industrial hemp is also included in consumer products such as paper, cloths, cosmetics, and carpet. One of the more innovative recent uses of industrial hemp is in the door frames of about 1.5 million cars. Hemp has even been used in alternative automobile fuel.

It is unfortunate that the federal government has stood in the way of American farmers, including many who are struggling to make ends meet, competing in the global industrial hemp market. Indeed, the founders of our nation, some of whom grew hemp, would surely find that federal restrictions on farmers growing a safe and profitable crop on their own land are inconsistent with the constitutional guarantee of a limited, restrained federal government. Therefore, I urge my colleagues to stand up for American farmers and cosponsor the Industrial Hemp Farming Act.

110TH CONGRESS 1ST SESSION
H. R. 1009 To amend the Controlled Substances Act to exclude industrial hemp from the definition of marihuana, and for other purposes. IN THE HOUSE OF REPRESENTATIVES FEBRUARY13, 2007 Mr. PAUL (for himself, Ms. BALDWIN, Mr. FRANK of Massachusetts, Mr. GRIJALVA, Mr. HINCHEY, Mr. KUCINICH, Mr. MCDERMOTT, Mr. GEORGE MILLER of California, Mr. STARK, and Ms. WOOLSEY) introduced the following bill; which was referred to the Committee on Energy and Commerce, and in addition to the Committee on the Judiciary, for a period to be subsequently determined by the Speaker, in each case for consideration of such provisions as fall within the jurisdiction of the committee concerned A BILL to amend the Controlled Substances Act to exclude industrial hemp from the definition of marihuana, and for other purposes. Be it enacted by the Senate and House of Representatives of the United States of America in Congress assembled, SECTION 1. SHORT TITLE. This Act may be cited as the "Industrial Hemp Farming Act of 2007." SEC. 2. EXCLUSION OF INDUSTRIAL HEMP FROM DEFIN-ITION OF MARIHUANA. Paragraph (16) of section 102 of the Controlled Substances Act (21 U.S.C. 802(16)) is amended (1) by striking "(16)" at the beginning and inserting "(16)(A)"; and (2) by adding at the end the following new sub-paragraph: "(B) The term 'marihuana' does not include industrial hemp. As used in the preceding sentence, the term 'industrial hemp' means the plant Cannabis sativa L. and any part of such plant, whether growing or not, with a delta-9 tetrahydrocannabinol concentration that does not exceed 0.3 percent on a dry weight basis." SEC. 3. INDUSTRIAL HEMP DETERMINATION TO BE MADE BY STATES. Section 201 of the Controlled Substances Act (21 U.S.C. 811) is amended by adding at the end the following new subsection: "(i) INDUSTRIAL HEMP DETERMINATION TO BE MADE BY STATES. – In any criminal action, civil action, or administrative proceeding, a State regulating the growing and processing of industrial hemp under State law shall have exclusive authority to determine whether any such plant meets the concentration limitation set forth in HMBILLS

sub-paragraph (B) of paragraph (16) of section 102 and such determination shall be conclusive and binding."

## APPENDIX 5

## North Dakota Department of Agriculture Press Release

For Immediate Release January 12, 2007

Hemp Growers License Applications Available

BISMARCK – Applications for licenses to grow industrial hemp are now available from the North Dakota Department of Agriculture (NDDA). "Prospective growers can write or call the department or go online at agdepartment.com and click on 'Hot Topics' for an application form," Agriculture Commissioner Roger Johnson said Wednesday.

"We urge all producers who intend to raise industrial hemp this year to begin the application process as soon as possible."

The department address is 600 E. Boulevard Ave., Dept. 602, Bismarck, ND 58505-0020; the telephone number is (701) 328-2231, and the e-mail address is ndda@nd.gov.

Johnson said North Dakota is the first state to license industrial hemp growers.

"Our Legislature has passed numerous bills with strong, bipartisan support to make it possible for North Dakota farmers to grow this potentially valuable crop," Johnson said. "Our regulations, which become effective this month, require licensed industrial hemp farmers to submit to criminal background checks and fingerprinting. They must also provide satellite coordinates that identify the locations of industrial hemp fields. These regulations apply to everyone who owns, operates or works at a hemp farm or who grows, handles or processes industrial hemp."

Johnson said that in addition to the application form, prospective growers must also obtain an official fingerprint card from NDDA. The card is not available online.

"The fingerprinting must be administered by local law enforcement officials," Johnson said. "When the application forms and fingerprint cards are completed, they must be returned to NDDA with the required fees."

The state charges two fees: $52 to cover the cost for fingerprinting and criminal background checks, and a $5-per-acre grower's fee (minimum $150). The fees are nonrefundable.

Once approved by North Dakota authorities, the licenses will be forwarded to the U.S. Drug Enforcement Agency (DEA) for final approval.

"It is up to the DEA to register the license holder," Johnson said. "If registration is withheld or denied, the license holder cannot grow the crop."

Johnson has asked the DEA to waive its registration fees for individual

401

growers.

"We still have not heard back from DEA," he said. "But in the meantime, a prospective grower must have a North Dakota license in hand before applying for DEA registration."

# APPENDIX 6

## Letter from the late Jack Herer to California Governor Arnold Schwarzenegger

From Jack Herer: JackHerer.com

September 4, 2006

Governor Arnold Schwarzenegger
State Capitol Building
Sacramento, CA 95814

Dear Governor Schwarzenegger,

I have been writing about industrial hemp and campaigning for the legalization of all forms of cannabis hemp since 1985. Growing hemp as nature designed it is vital to our urgent need to reduce greenhouse gases and ensure the survival of our planet. However, AB1147 in its present form could severely compromise hemp's scarce remaining germplasm and endanger the lives of Californians who legally grow cannabis for medicine.

A provision that seeds originate from native California hemp strains was struck from AB1147 at the last minute, and if you sign it, only cannabis with a minuscule amount of THC (0.3 percent) could be grown in our state. Lower THC strains grown in Canadian studies have resulted in lesser yields and shorter stalks than those with natural amounts of the cannabinoid, which serves as a sunscreen for the plant.(1) Without its natural sunscreen, yields of the crop will be insufficient to justify hemp cultivation in California, and pollen from low-THC hemp could infect native hemp and ruin its seeds.

We cannot let this happen.

A 1916 USDA report found hemp could make four times as much paper per acre as trees, superior paper that does not need chlorine bleach.

Hemp seed oil is the healthful food oil with a better balance of essential fatty acids than even flax.

Hemp is the best plant in the world to make building materials, fabric and fuel, from both its stalk and seed. Currently biodiesel fuel is primarily made of soy, and 81 percent of the U.S. soy crop is genetically modified. Biotechnology forces are mobilizing to cash in on the biodiesel bonanza.

On August 15, Monsanto, which has experimented with hemp, acquired Delta and Pine Land Company, the developer of terminator technology – plants that are genetically modified to produce sterile seeds at harvest. D&PL claims that it is already growing genetically modified cotton and tobacco containing terminator genes. Under the guise of a group called CropLife America, Monsanto, Dow Chemical, Du Pont and other corporations spent $621,000 to oppose Mendocino county's anti-GMO Measure H in 2004. In response, Measure H backers brought in 73-year-old Canadian farmer Percy Schmeiser, whose canola crops were contaminated with Monsanto's patented "Round-up Ready" GMO/GE canola, causing him to be sued by Monsanto for "property theft" and "patent infringement."

Cross-pollination is also an issue for medicinal marijuana growers, who are protected by Proposition 215, made law by California voters in 1996. John LaBoyteaux, an organic farmer, testified before the Senate Agriculture Committee on June 29 saying he and his fellow farmers planned to grow low-THC hemp in a malicious attempt to ruin marijuana gardens in Northern California. Pollen can travel for miles, and large fields of low-THC could well accomplish this mean-spirited goal. It could also drive the crop further indoors, causing environmental problems, overconsumption of electricity, diesel spills, and noise. This is a life or death issue for Californians with AIDS, cancer, and other serious illnesses.

For all of these reasons and more, I ask you to veto AB1147 and instead call for the legalization of cannabis in its natural form.

I know that you have bravely and honestly admitted your own youthful marijuana use, and I see that it hasn't hurt your health or ability to accomplish your goals. We want hemp without harassment and no more marijuana smokers clogging California prisons.

Cannabis industries could be a boon for California like our state has never before seen, enabling us to stop using petrochemicals and felling our forests, while recovering our forested lands and protecting our farmlands. It is in your hands to make this happen and make yourself a hero to the planet and its people.

Sincerely,

Jack Herer

1. A 2003 Hemp Report from the Saskatoon Research Center in Canada by Cecil L. Vera of Agriculture and Agri-Food Canada concludes that of six hemp cultivars grown in Melfort, SK that year, the one with the best yield also had the most THC. A 1999 study from Thunder Bay showed marked differences between 1 percent cultivars vs. 0.3 percent ones. See: AGF.Gov.BC.ca/SpecCrop/Publications/Ind_Hemp.htm

Myspace.com/HempJack

## APPENDIX 7

## Vote Hemp's Response to California Governor Arnold Schwarzenegger's Veto of Hemp Bill

For Immediate Release
Monday, October 2, 2006

CONTACT:
Patrick Goggin 415-312-0084
Adam Eidinger 202-744-2671
Adam@VoteHemp.com

**Governor Schwarzenegger's Veto of Hemp Bill is Bad for the Environment, Farmers and Economy**
**Veto is "Irrational" Agriculture Policy Based on Fear**

**SACRAMENTO, CA** – Waiting until the last possible day to decide, Governor Arnold Schwarzenegger vetoed AB 1147, *The California Industrial Hemp Farming Act*, late in the day on Saturday, September 30. This landmark, bipartisan legislation if enacted would have established clear guidelines for farming of industrial hemp, which is used in a wide variety of everyday consumer products, including food, body care, clothing, paper and auto parts. Demand for hemp products has been growing rapidly in recent years with the U.S. hemp product market now exceeding an estimated $270 million in annual retail sales. The new law would have given farmers the ability to legally supply numerous California manufacturers that currently import hemp seed, oil and fiber.

"Governor Schwarzenegger's veto is a letdown for thousands of farmers, business people and consumers who want to bring back industrial hemp to California to create jobs, new tax income and to benefit the environment," says Eric Steenstra, founder and president of Vote Hemp, the nation's leading industrial hemp farming advocacy group. "The veto was not based on facts but instead on an irrational fear he would look soft on drugs in an election year. His veto message shows he knew industrial hemp is an economic development and agriculture issue, but he instead allowed himself to be cowed by confused Drug War lobbyists. AB 1147 would have reined in the overreach by federal authorities that has prevented nondrug industrial hemp varieties of cannabis from being grown on U.S. soil for fiber and seed. It is disingenuous to cite federal restrictions when Drug War lobbyists refuse to sit down with the large coalition of farmers, business people and environmentalists who crafted the industrial hemp legislation. Industrial hemp will continue to be the only crop in California that is legal to import, sell and consume, but illegal to grow."

AB 1147 clarified that the cultivation of industrial hemp is legal only on the condition it contains no more than three-tenths of one percent (0.3 percent) tetrahydrocannabinol (THC). The legislation was jointly authored by Democratic Assemblyman Mark Leno and Republican Assemblyman Chuck Devore. *The California Industrial Hemp Farming Act* passed its final vote in the Senate on August 16 by a margin of 26-13 and passed in the Assembly on August 21 by a margin of 44-29.

"It's unfortunate that Governor Schwarzenegger vetoed AB 1147. We had looked forward to the hemp oil and seed in our products being grown and produced right here in California," says David Bronner, chair of the Hemp Industries Association's Food and Oil Committee and president of ALPSNACK/Dr. Bronner's Magic Soaps. "Farmers in California, like farmers all across the United States, are always looking for profitable crops like hemp to add to their rotation. This veto clearly points out why HR 3037, the *Industrial Hemp Farming Act of 2005*, needs to be passed on the federal level."

According to USDA researcher Lyster H. Dewey in the 1901 *USDA Yearbook*, hemp was first cultivated in California in the late 1800s in Butte County, near the town of Gridley, between Chico and Yuba City. In the 1913 *USDA Yearbook* Mr. [Lyster H.] Dewey wrote that "In 1912 hemp was first cultivated on a commercial scale under irrigation at Lerdo, near Bakersfield, Cal., and a larger acreage was grown there in 1913." Commercial industrial hemp farming ceased in the state shortly after World War II.

The last commercial hemp crops in the United States were grown in central Wisconsin in 1957, and these crops were purchased and processed by the Rens Hemp Co. in Brandon, about 40 miles northwest of Milwaukee. The primary reason industrial hemp has not been grown in the U.S. since then is because of its misclassification as a Schedule I drug in the Controlled Substances Act (CSA) of 1970. The Marihuana Tax Act of 1937 had provisions for farmers to grow non-psychoactive hemp by paying an annual occupational tax of $1.00. The exemption for hemp products was contained in the definition of marihuana in the Act:

*'The term 'marihuana' means all parts of the plant Cannabis sativa L ... but shall not include the mature stalks of such plant, fiber produced from such stalks, oil or cake made from the seeds of such plant, any other compound, manufacture, salt, derivative, mixture, or preparation of such mature stalks (except the resin extracted therefrom), fiber, oil, or cake, or the sterilized seed of such plant which is incapable of germination."*

The language of the exemption was carried over almost verbatim in the definition of marihuana in the CSA [21 U.S.C. §802(16)] which superseded the 1937 Tax Act, but since there was no active hemp industry at the time the provisions for hemp farming were not part of the new act.

There is also an exemption for hemp farming in the 1961 United Nations Single Convention on Narcotic Drugs, as amended by the 1972 Protocol Amending the 1961 Single Convention on Narcotic Drugs. Article 28 states that:

*"2. This convention shall not apply to the cultivation of the cannabis plant exclusively for industrial purposes (fibre and seed) or horticultural purposes."*

The United States is a signatory of the United Nations Single Convention, and laws allowing the farming of industrial hemp would not be in conflict with the agreement.

The industrial hemp plant's stalk is long and strong, has few branches, has been bred for maximum production of fiber and/or seed, and grows up to 16 feet in height. It is planted in densities of 100 to 300 plants per square yard. On the other hand, drug varieties of cannabis grow up to only six feet or less in height and have been bred to have many branches to maximize flowering and minimize seeds. They are planted with wide spaces between plants to enhance their bushiness. The drug and nondrug varieties are harvested at different times, and the planting densities look very different from the air.

In 1999, California Assemblywoman Virginia Strom-Martin introduced HR 32. The resolution declared, among other findings, that the legislature should consider action to allow industrial hemp production in California as an agricultural and industrial crop. The Assembly passed HR 32 the following month. Then Assemblywoman Strom-Martin introduced AB 448 in 2001 to license industrial hemp for commercial purposes. The bill died in committee. In 2002, Assemblywoman Strom-Martin introduced AB 388, requesting that the University of California conduct an assessment of industrial hemp among other crops. AB 388 ultimately passed the legislature but was vetoed by Governor Gray Davis later that year.

Seven states (Hawaii, Kentucky, Maine, Maryland, Montana, North Dakota and West Virginia) have already changed their laws to give farmers an affirmative right to grow industrial hemp commercially or for research purposes; however, unlike California's AB 1147, all require a license from the Drug Enforcement Administration (DEA) to grow the crop. Only Hawaii has grown hemp in recent years, but the research program ended when the DEA refused to renew the license. California's AB 1147 addressed the DEA's bad faith interference by providing that the federal government has no basis or right to interfere with industrial hemp grown in California pursuant to AB 1147.

Vote Hemp is a nonprofit organization dedicated to the acceptance of

and a free market for industrial hemp and to changes in current law to allow
U.S. farmers to grow low-THC industrial hemp. More information about
hemp legislation and the crop's many uses may be found at VoteHemp.com
and HempIndustries.org. BETA SP or DVD Video News Release featuring
footage of hemp farming in other countries is available upon request by
contacting Adam Eidinger at 202-744-2671.

# APPENDIX 8

## Hemp and Genetically Engineered Organisms

FOR IMMEDIATE RELEASE
Date: August 28, 2006
CONTACT: MIGHTY MOUTH MEDIA mightymouth@asis.com
JACK HERER 707-279-2333

### CONNECTING THE DOTS: BACKGROUND ON HEMP AND GMOs

A 2003 Hemp Report from the Saskatoon Research Center in Canada by Cecil L. Vera of Agriculture and Agri-Food Canada concludes that of six hemp cultivars grown in Melfort, SK, that year, the one with the best yield also had the most THC. A 1999 study from Thunder Bay showed marked differences between 1 percent cultivars vs. 0.3 percent ones. See: AGF.Gov.BC.ca/SpecCrop/Publications/Ind_Hemp.htm

A 1998 Vermont state auditor's report evaluating the DEA's marijuana eradication efforts in the U.S. revealed that over 99 percent of the 422,716,526 total cannabis plants eliminated nationwide by the agency in 1996 were "ditchweed," non-psychoactive hemp. Many of those plants were remnants from government-subsidized plots grown during World War II's "Hemp for Victory" campaign.

See: NORML.org/Index.CFM?Group_ID=4401

Commenting on the study in summer 1998, publisher Mari Kane wrote in *HempWorld* magazine, "That hemp cultivation is not currently legally allowed in the United States has not stopped seed and chemical corporations from developing low-THC hybrids using European seed stock. Once they patent these new strains, I suspect that hemp prohibition will magically become a thing of the past, with the usual players monopolizing the seed supply. The wild hemp growing on the prairies is a threat to these companies' plans to control hempseed, and government-sponsored eradication is the simplest way to eliminate the competition. Perhaps that is what this plan is really about." [Plant breeder Dr. David West says that hemp seed is not hybridized, and that extrapolating from studies is speculative, since factors other than seed type affect yields.]

Of the Monsanto/D&PL merger, Ibrahim Coulibaly, president of the National Coordination of Peasants' Organizations of Mali, said, "This merger guarantees an intensification of the already immense political pressure on West African governments to accept genetically modified seeds." Monsanto and D&PL together account for over 57 percent of the

409

US cotton seed market. See: Banterminator.org/

Under the guise of a group called CropLife America, Monsanto, Dow Chemical, Du Pont and other corporations spent $621,000 to oppose Mendocino county, California's anti-GMO Measure H in 2004. In response, Measure H backers brought in 73-year-old Canadian farmer Percy Schmeiser, whose canola crops were contaminated with Monsanto's patented "Round-up Ready" GMO/GE canola, causing him to be sued by Monsanto for "property theft" and "patent infringement." Measure H passed, but Mendocino and a handful of hamlets across California are fighting off a state bill that would undo the law and preclude other cities and counties from outlawing GMOs. See: GMOFreeMendo.com

The use of seed oils for fuel has been on the international stage as far back as 1992, when George H.W. Bush raised tariffs on seed oils as his first act as president. (In retaliation, France raised their tariff on wine.) At BIO 2006, the annual Convention of the Biotechnology Industry Organization held in mid-April in Chicago, "biofuels" – renewable fuels made from plant materials – were the center of attention, with biodiesel and ethanol as the industry's two leading hopes for spurring renewed interest and investment, wrote Charles Shaw of AlterNet.

On the heels of [George W.] Bush's "addicted to oil" speech, heading into the convention, BIO released a letter to Congress on March 13, 2006, requesting full funding for programs that would support research and development into ethanol production.

At a BIO conference plenary session on biofuels, former CIA head and NAIHC lobbyist R. James Woolsey claimed that "Biotechnology will be for the twenty-first-century what physics was to the 20th," unlocking the secret potential of the planet in ways never before imagined, while at the same time rescuing us from the social and environmental perils of the petrochemical system. "For every billion dollars we shift from foreign oil to domestic biofuels, we can add anywhere from 10-20,000 American jobs," Woolsey said, "and at least half of our gasoline needs can be grown here with cellulose."

Biodiesel fuel is primarily made of soy, grown by farmers in the Midwest. Although there's no sure way to say how much soy-based biodiesel comes from genetically modified stock, as of 2003, 81 percent of the U.S. soy harvest was genetically modified.

See: Alternet.org/EnviroHealth/35243

# APPENDIX 9

# Backgrounder from Canadian Hemp Trade Alliance

## Canadian Hemp Overview: May 2006

Canada developed regulations for the cultivation and processing of industrial hemp in 1998. Alan Rock, health minister at the time (whose ministry remains in charge of licensing hemp), said, "This new crop has a tremendous potential for creating new jobs in agriculture, industry, research and retail."

### Size of Production

At this point, most hemp production in Canada is for seed or grain destined for the North American health food/natural bodycare market. Field production fluctuated in the early years, experiencing a peak of close to 1,400 h. in 1999, and falling to a low of 1,300 h. in 2001. Since 2002, field production has consistently risen, and by 2005, 9,725 h. were licensed. Production trends have followed the growth of the consumer market. Most production is now centered in the prairie provinces: licensed acres in 2005 include Manitoba's 5,000 h, Saskatchewan's 3,400 h. and Alberta's 916 h, 85 percent of Canadian production. Acreage could be over 15,000 h in 2006.

The markets for hemp are growing, driving a steady increase in the cultivation and processing of hemp with the corresponding development of many new businesses, new products and marketing initiatives. The Canadian Hemp Trade Alliance, established in 2003 to better represent the sector, currently represents over 80 businesses in Canada. It is estimated that the hemp sector has directly created 100-150 new jobs in the country, as well as contributing to the profitability and expansion of existing businesses and giving farmers a valuable crop choice.

### Hemp Seed Markets

Hemp seed attracts interest because of high protein and fibre content as well as a strong essential fatty acid profile. Most of the market is in health food, nutraceuticals, supplements and natural bodycare. The expansion of hemp markets has trended with the growth of the global organic and natural foods markets. As a niche product not found in many grocery stores it has been difficult to measure and track hemp sales. However, a recent 2005 SPINS report (SPINS.com) estimated that the U.S. market for hemp foods in select stores had grown 49.9 percent over 2004-2005 to reach (at least) $5.1 U.S. million. Based on voluntary company reporting, this represents about half of the total market. Additionally, the market for

411

natural bodycare products using hemp oil as an ingredient is estimated to be at least $10.9 million, representing a 15 percent growth over 2004-2005.

Currently, much of the hemp marketplace is in the U.S. As the U.S. does not permit hemp farming, there is a large captive market for Canadian production south of the border. Much of the American market is in the large, natural-food conscious California market.

Hemp has been sold into the international birdseed market but faces stiff competition from cheaper overseas sources and other seed crops. The potential for domestic pet/vet markets is very promising; as well, the potential for feed (cattle, fish) is significant. Both remain underdeveloped and hemp seed is not yet approved as an animal feed in Canada.

Any new crop can take between 15-50 years for markets to mature, as seen historically with such crops as canola and buckwheat.

### Hemp Fibre

There is great interest nationally in fibre uses; however fibre production opportunities are closely tied to processing capabilities. These are very limited. Interesting markets under development include nonwovens, composites and animal bedding. Canadian pulped and made hemp-content paper is under research and development. Garment textiles represent a particularly challenging scenario – there is yet no "Dirt to Shirt" production in Canada – though it remains a goal of some companies. Much work is happening on all levels across the country to make the fibre side of the hemp equation work.

A rising demand for alternatives to wood and synthetic fibres in a variety of industries points towards hemp's potential. As well, the rising prices of fossil fuels, used to make synthetic fibres, are helping make hemp fibre much more competitive in the marketplace. In general, fibre processing in Canada faces such hurdles as: technology and infrastructure shortcomings, insufficient financing and unfamiliarity with end markets. Analysts have concluded that the major constraints on the use of natural fibers in Canadian industry is a general lack of knowledge, vision and will on the part of the private sector, farmers, government and researchers to take advantage of the opportunities available.

# APPENDIX 10

## Did Dick Nixon Say He Smoked Weed?

On September 9, 1971, in a lengthy Oval Office conversation that was clearly about marijuana, Nixon said something that is an interesting admission for the king of the "Drug War." Did he or didn't he? He was speaking with Raymond P. Shafer, Jerome H. Jaffe, and Egil G. "Bud" Krogh, Jr.

In the meeting Nixon was informing Shafer that he wanted the Shafer Commission Report conclusion to be against marijuana so that the administration could meet Nixon's goal of permanently classifying marijuana as a Schedule 1 narcotic substance.

For the full transcript, access the Web site of Common Sense for Drug Policy, CSDP.org/News/News/Nixon.htm.

Richard Nixon: "Read an amusing story, [unintelligible] was telling me…"

Raymond P. Shafer: "I have an amusing story too…"

Nixon: "Uh, it is uh, this is a father and son, got, got arrested [unintelligible], his father says, you [unintelligible]. [unintelligible] a couple more weeks you know he says, our, says you know I'm working my garden and everything, father says ok, father says well, uh maybe the kid couldn't [unintelligible] that day, go out and work in the garden. He found out that the little son of a bitch was growing marijuana, had to wait for the crop to come in. It's an absolute true story. But, I, I, I believe having said all I have, I have a tremendous [unintelligible], I see these kids, and we've all, we've all, uh, grown up, and, there was smoking, there was alcohol, there's a lot of other things people do, er, in the old days, etc., etc. I mean, there's a, the uh, maybe, uh, uh, going to see Greta Garbo in the day, etc., etc. Don't call me yellow, is that…"

Unknown person in room: "It was, 'I Am Curious Yellow.'"

Nixon: "But anyway. It's a [unintelligible] what we did, but, by golly, the thing to do now is to alert the country to the problem and say now, this far no farther, and I think that that's what you want to do, is take a strong line."

# APPENDIX 11

## When Elvis Met Dick

For more than a year the American public was denied knowing about a meeting at the White House that took place between Nixon and a well-known barbiturate addict. It was only on January 27, 1972, that *The Washington Post* let America in on the secret.

On December 21, 1970, Elvis Presley went to the offices of the U.S. Bureau of Narcotics and Dangerous Drugs. He wanted to become a "federal agent at large" to help fight the War on Drugs. But Elvis was turned down with the explanation that the only person who could overrule the decision would be Richard Nixon.

Elvis had his limousine driver take him to the White House, where he gave the Secret Service agents at the gates a five-page letter written on American Airlines letterhead. Elvis waited inside his limousine as the letter was delivered to Nixon by an aide named Egil "Bud" Krogh.

Two and a half hours later Elvis entered the Oval Office. He apparently froze and had to be guided over to the presidential desk with the help of Krogh.

Elvis showed pictures of his daughter to Nixon and also flashed a pair of cufflinks he received from vice president Spiro Agnew. He also showed Dick badges he received from various law enforcement departments, and asked if he could receive an official badge of the U.S. Bureau of Narcotics and Dangerous Drugs.

The administration thought it wise for the president to suggest that Elvis should record an album with the theme of "get high on life" to suggest to young people that, "lasting talent is the result of self-motivation and discipline, and not artificial chemical euphoria."

The letter and a photograph of Elvis shaking hands with Dick are now kept by the National Archives. In the photo Elvis is wearing a huge gold belt, gold neck chain dangling with a medallion, a black velvet cape, and black leather boots. Presley gave Dick a World War II .45-caliber Colt revolver. The outfit and the gun are also part of the National Archives and have been displayed at the Nixon library in Yorba Linda, California.

Dear Mr. President.

First, I would like to introduce myself. I am Elvis Presley and admire you and have great respect for your office. I talked to Vice President Agnew in Palm Springs three weeks ago and expressed my concern for our country. The drug culture, the

414

hippie elements, the SDS [Students for a Democratic Society], Black Panthers, etc. do NOT consider me as their enemy or as they call it The Establishment. I call it America and I love it. Sir, I can and will be of any service that I can to help The Country out. I have no concern or Motives other than helping the country out.

So I wish not to be given a title or an appointed position. I can and will do more good if I were made a Federal Agent at Large and I will help out by doing it my way through my communications with people of all ages. First and foremost, I am an entertainer, but all I need is the Federal credentials. I am on this plane with Senator George Murphy and we have been discussing the problems that our country is faced with.

Sir, I am staying at the Washington Hotel, Room 505-506-507. I have two men who work with me by the name of Jerry Schilling and Sonny West. I am registered under the name of Jon Burrows. I will be here for as long as it takes to get the credentials of a Federal Agent. I have done an in-depth study of drug abuse and Communist brainwashing techniques and I am right in the middle of the whole thing where I can and will do the most good.

I am Glad to help just so long as it is kept very Private. You can have your staff or whomever call me anytime today, tonight, or tomorrow. I was nominated this coming year one of America's Ten Most Outstanding Young Men. That will be in January 18 in my home town of Memphis, Tennessee. I am sending you the short autobiography about myself so you can better understand this approach. I would love to meet you just to say hello if you're not too busy.

Respectfully,
Elvis Presley

P. S. I believe that you, Sir, were one of the Top Ten Outstanding Men of America also.
I have a personal gift for you, which I would like to present to you and you can accept it or I will keep it for you until you can take it.

Nixon aide Dwight Chapin sent a memorandum to H. R. Haldeman:

Memorandum
The White House

Washington
December 21, 1970

Memorandum for: Mr. H.R. Haldeman
From: Dwight L. Chapin
Subject: Elvis Presley

Attached you will find a letter to the President from Elvis Presley. As you are aware, Presley showed up here this morning and has requested an appointment with the President. He states that he knows the President is very busy, but he would just like to say hello and present the President with a gift.

As you are well aware, Presley was voted one of the ten outstanding young men for next year and this was based upon his work in the field of drugs. The thrust of Presley's letter is that he wants to become a "Federal agent at large" to work against the drug problem communicating with people of all ages. He says that he is not a member of the establishment and that drug culture types, the hippie elements, the SDS, and the Black Panthers are people with whom he can communicate since he is not part of the establishment.

Chapin request to ask for approval to have Elvis visit Dick:

I have talked to Bud Krogh about this whole matter, and we both think that it would be wrong to push Presley off on the Vice President since it will take very little of the President's time and it can be extremely beneficial for the President to build some rapport with Presley.

In addition, if the President wants to meet with some bright young people outside of the Government, Presley might be a perfect one to start with.

On the note, H.R. Haldeman wrote, "You must be kidding," but he initialed the line, "Approve Presley coming in at the end of "Open Hour."

Nixon aide Egil "Bud" Krogh took notes during the 30-minute meeting:

The White House
Washington
December 21, 1970
Memorandum for: The President's File
Subject: Meeting with Elvis Presley

The meeting opened with pictures taken of the President and Elvis Presley.

Presley immediately began showing the President his law enforcement paraphernalia including badges from police departments in California, Colorado, and Tennessee. Presley indicated that he had been playing Las Vegas and...

Presley indicated that he thought the Beatles had been a real force for anti-American spirit. He said that the Beatles came to this country, made their money, and then returned to England where they promoted an anti-American theme. The President nodded in agreement and expressed some surprise. The President then indicated that those who used drugs are also those in the vanguard of anti-American protest. Violence, drug usage, dissent, protest all seem to merge in generally the same group of young people.

Presley indicated to the President in a very emotional manner that he was "on your side." Presley kept repeating that he wanted to be helpful, that he wanted to restore some respect for the flag which was being lost. He mentioned that he was just a poor boy from Tennessee who had gotten a lot from his country, which in some way he wanted to repay. He also mentioned that he is studying Communist brainwashing and the drug culture for over ten years. He mentioned that he knew a lot about this and was accepted by the hippies. He said he could go right into a group of young people or hippies and be accepted which he felt could be helpful to him in his drug drive. The President indicated again his concern that Presley retain his credibility.

Elvis Presley was addicted to prescription drugs and died of an overdose after falling off his toilet on August 16, 1977. The BioScience Laboratories report listed that fourteen drugs had been detected in his system. The drugs included an assortment of barbiturates, amphetamines, tranquilizers, and sleeping pills prescribed by Dr. George Constantine Nichopoulos.

# Resource Guide

## Biofuels

**Books:**
- *Biodiesel America: How to Achieve Energy Security, Free America from Middle-east Oil Dependence and Make Money Growing Fuel*, by Josh Tickell
- *From the Fryer to the Fuel Tank: The Complete Guide to Using Vegetable Oil As an Alternative Fuel*, by Joshua Tickell
- *Powerdown: Options for a Post-Carbon World*, by Richard Heinberg

**Documentary:**
- *Who Killed the Electric Car?* Watch this documentary.

**Berkeley Biodiesel Collective**, BerkeleyBiodiesel.org

**Better World Club**, BetterWorldClub.com

**BioDieselAmerica.org**

**National BioDiesel Board**, BioDiesel.org

**BioDieselCommunity.org**

**BioDiesel-CoOp.org**

**BiodieselNow.com**

    Site contains a link to locations where biofuel is available.

**BioDiesel.org**

**BioDieselSolutions.com**

**BioFuelOasis.com**

**BioFuels.ca**

**BoulderBioDiesel.org**

**ClimateCrisis.net**

**CoalitionForCleanAir.org**

**EndOfSuburbia.com**

**GoldenFuelSystems.com**

**Grassolean.com**

**GreaseCar.com**

**GreenDepot.org**

**HempCar.org**

**HempOilCanada.com**

**JourneyToForever.org**

**LABioFuel.com**

**LiveGreenGoYellow.com**

**LoveCraftBioFuels.com**

**MakeBioDiesel.com**

**Mayors for Climate Change**, CoolMayors.org

**Piedmont Biofuels**, Pittsboro, NC; Biofuels.coop

**PathToFreedom.com**

**StopGlobalWarming.org**

**SustainableOptions.com**

**SustainableTransportClub.com**

**TerraPass.com**

VieggieAvenger.com
Yokayo Biofuels, YBiofuels.org

## Building Materials and Supplies

**Books:**
- *Building with Hemp*, by Steve Allin
- *Good Green Homes*, by Jennifer Roberts
- *Green Building Products*, edited by Mark Piepkorn
- *Green Remodeling: Changing the World One Room at a Time*, by David Johnston and Kim Master
- *Little House on a Small Planet: Simple Homes, Cozy Retreats, and Energy Efficient Possibilities*, by Shay Salomon; LittleHouseOnASmallPlanet.com
- *The New Ecological Home*, by Dan Chiras
- *Solar Living Source Book: The Complete Guide to Renewable Energy Technologies and Sustainable Living*, edited by John Schaeffer

**Architects, Designers & Planners for Social Responsibility**, ADPSR.org
**BuildingForHealth.com**
**BuildingGreen.com**
**BuildItGreen.org**
**BuildNaturally.com**
**Cape Fear Green Building Alliance**, CFGBA.org
**Chanvre-Info.CH/Info/Fr/Procede-Isochanvre.html**
    The site for the French company that makes patented hemp cement. The site can be read in French or English.
**Colorado Yurt Company**, ColoradoYurt.com
**EarthFriendlyGoods.com**
**EcoBuilderNetwork.org**
**EcoHome.org**
**Environmental Building News**, http//:www.BuildingGreen.com
**Environmental Construction Outfitters**, EnvironProducts.com
**Green Building Council**, USGBC-LA.org
**Green Building Press**, NewBuilder.co.uk
**TheGreenGuide.com**
**HempBuilding.com**
**International Cellulose Corporation**, Spray-On.com
**Jefferson Recycled Woodworks**, EcoWood.com
**Lars' Yurt Page**, RDrop.com/~Glacier/Yurt.htm
**LivingArchitectureCentre.com**
**Living Architecture Centre Dot Com,** Ireland, LivingGreen.com
**NewDream.org**
**Northwest EcoBuilding Guild**, EcoBuilding.org
    Publishes the *EcoBuilding Times*.
**OrganicInteriorDesign.com**
*Permaculture Magazine*, England; PermaCulture.co.uk
**ReBuildingCenter.org**
**SmallHouseSociety.org**

SustainableABC.com
Traditional Lime Company, Ireland, TraditionalLime.com
U.S. Green Building Council, USGBC.org
Yurts.com
YurtWorks.co.uk

# Candles

If you buy candles, avoid those that are made out of petroleum wax (paraffin). Paraffin is one of the leftover byproduct residue extracts of petroleum (crude) oil. Other extracts of crude oil include gasoline, jet fuel, kerosene, diesel fuel, and asphalt.

When you burn paraffin wax candles in your home, you are essentially poisoning your air. The soot given off by a paraffin wax candle is similar to the soot given off by engines that burn fossil fuels.

Contaminates in the smoke of paraffin wax candles include benzene, methyl ethyl keyton, naphthalene, and toluene, which are also found in lacquer, paint, and varnish removers, and are known to cause cancer, birth defects, and learning disabilities.

If you purchase candles, buy those that contain lead-free wicks (nonmetallic cores), and are made out of such things as hemp oil, soy, vegetable glycerin, and beeswax, palm wax, or vegetable wax. If you are a vegan you may want to avoid beeswax candles.

If the candle says it contains scented oils, find out if the oil is petroleum based, or if it is a plant oil. Some scents used in oils are also toxic and contain hormone-disrupting phthalates. Choose plant-based oils and scents.

Be aware that even some soy candles contain such toxic substances. Solvent extraction using petroleum chemicals is often part of the manufacturing process.

In addition, avoid candles that have leaded wicks. Candle companies use leaded wicks because they are easier to keep straight. Candles with leaded wicks emit lead into the atmosphere, creating a health hazard.

# Cars

There are many things you can do to reduce air pollution and dependence on fossil fuels. While plant-based fuels are becoming more popular, it is important to take action in your community to make change. Avoid driving, such as by walking, riding a bike, or taking public transport.

City Car Share, CityCarShare.org
FlexCar, FlexCar.com
CAN Car (Cooperative Auto Network), CoOperativeAuto.net

# Clothing: Natural and Organic Fiber

"Today's hemp-based fabrics are nothing like eighteenth-century canvas sailcloth (canvas derives from the Latin cannabis). Hemp fiber, blended with everything from tencel to organic cotton, can be used to create textiles as different as terrycloth, flannel, and luxurious satin brocades. Hemp fiber offers greater durability than cotton, which accounts for 25 percent of the pesticides sprayed on the world's crops. Hemp-based textile products on the market include apparel and accessories such as T-shirts, pants, dresses, baby clothes, bathrobes, and shoes; housewares such as blankets, shower curtains, and rugs; and sundries such as hammocks and pet supplies."
 – Hemp Industries Association, 2005; HIA.org

One of the best ways to protect the environment is to limit your clothing choices to those that are made of organically grown fiber. It has only been since the drilling of oil began on a major scale in the 1800s that fibers started to be developed from petroleum and coal. And those are the worst fibers of all as they are not sustainable, are not biodegradable, and are often treated with health-damaging chemicals that are absorbed into the skin of the wearer, as well as into the environment. The drilling and processing of petroleum is massively environmentally destructive.

Most cotton grown on the plant is also damaging to health and the environment because it is most often grown using large doses of defoliants, fertilizers, herbicides, insecticides, and pesticides. Most cotton is also bleached during processing, which releases dioxin, a long-lasting toxic chemical. Altogether, the cotton industry releases hundreds of millions of pounds of toxic chemicals into the environment in the form of farming chemicals, chemical dyes, and finishing agents. When buying cotton fabrics, seek those made from cotton grown organically and that are dyed with natural coloring agents.

A safe clothing fiber is hemp. It produces more fiber per acre than cotton and does not require the use of the chemicals used in intensive cotton farming or processing.

Hemp clothing is currently costly in the U.S. because of the ridiculous laws that prevent U.S. farmers from growing hemp, so hemp fabric must be imported from other countries.

Not to be overlooked in the form of natural fabrics that are environmentally safe are those made from bamboo. It is growing in popularity.

AHappyPlanet.com
Conscious Clothing; GetConscious.com
EarthCreations.net
EarthRunnings.com
EarthSpeaks.com
Earth-Wear.com
The Emperor's Clothes, EmperorsHemp.com
Evergreen Hemp Co., EverGreenHemp.com
FaeriesDance.com

GlobalHempStore.com
HempStores.com
Hemp Utopia, Canada-Shops.com/Stores/HempUtopia
Hempys.com
HerbivoreClothing.com
International Hemp Fair, CannaTrade.CH
Kentucky Hemp Outfitters, KentuckyHemp.com
LoomState.org
Maggie's Functional Organics, MaggiesOrganics.com
NaturalHighLifestyle.com
OfTheEarth.com
OrganicClothes.com
OrganicThreads.com
PlanetHemp.net
SweatshopWatch.org
SweetGrassFibers.com
TwoStarDog.com
Vital Hemptations, VitalHemp.com

## Cosmetics

**Books:**
* *Drop Dead Gorgeous: Protecting Yourself from the Hidden Dangers of Cosmetics*, by Kim Erickson
* *Mother Nature's Guide to Vibrant Beauty & Health*, by Myra Cameron
* *The Truth About Beauty: Transform Your Looks and Life from the Inside Out*, by Kat James and Oz Garcia

> "Hemp oil's high and balanced EFA content also makes it an ideal ingredient in body care products. The EFAs soothe and restore skin in salves and creams and give excellent emolliency and smooth after-feel to lotions, lip balms, conditioners, shampoos, soaps, shaving products, and massage oils. Recent Canadian research shows that hemp oil has potential as a broad-spectrum ultraviolet skin protector."
> – Hemp Industries Association, 2005; HIA.org

Did you know that many of the skin, hair, and oral care products sold in stores today contain toxins that can cause cancer and that also poison our lakes, rivers and oceans; and can cause birth deformities, miscarriages, and learning disabilities in both humans and wildlife?

Many of these products contain petroleum-derived parabens. These are known carcinogens and are used as preservatives in the products. Parabens are known to mimic estrogen and disrupt testosterone levels. Many of the same chemicals used on insecticides are often used in body scents and other cosmetics. Other chemicals used on the most popular cosmetic products include coal tar coloring, labeled as D&C and FD&C colors; formaldehyde, a known carcinogen; lead, phthalates; and nonylphenols, chemicals that disrupt hormonal balance and that are contained in many shampoos, shaving creams, and hair dyes.

**AllForAnimals.com**
**The Campaign for Safe Cosmetics**, SafeCosmetics.org
**ChooseCrueltyFree.org.AU**
**The Coalition for Consumer Information on Cosmetics**, LeapingBunny.org
**Dr. Bronner's Magic Soaps**, DrBronner.com
**The Environmental Working Group**, EWG.org
**FlourideAlert.org**
**The Fluoride Education Project**, Bruha.com
**Green Products Alliance**, GreenProductsAlliance.com
**Hemp Organics**, ColOrganics.net

# Drug War

**Books:**
- *Demons, Discriminations & Dollars: A Brief History of the Origins of American Drug Policy,* by David Bearman, M.D.
- *Human Rights and the U.S. Drug War,* by Chris Conrad, Mikki Norris, and Virginia Resner
- *Shattered Lives: Portraits from America's Drug War,* by Mikki Norris, Chris Conrad, and Virginia Resner
- *Smoke and Mirrors: The War on Drugs and the Politics of Failure*, by Dan Baum
- *Why Marijuana Should Be Legal*, by Ed Rosenthal and Steve Kubby with S. Newhart; Green-Aid.com/EdRosenthal.htm

**AddictInTheFamily.org**
**Alternet.org/DrugReporter**
**The American Civil Liberties Union**, ACLU.org
**AngelJustice.org**
**Australian Cannabis Law Reform Movement**, NimbinAustralia.com.Cyber-Pod.com/ACLRM
**Canadian Foundation for Drug Policy**, CFDP.ca
**CannabisConsumers.org**
**ChangeTheClimate.org**
**Common Sense for Drug Policy**, CSDP.org
**Common Sense for Drug Policy**, CommonSenseDrugPolicy.org
**Drug Policy Alliance**, DrugPolicy.org; DPF.org
**The Drug Reform Coordination Network,** DRCNet.org; StopTheDrugWar.org
**DrugScope.org.uk**
**DrugSense.org**
**Drug Truth Network**, DrugTruth.net
**DrugWarDistortions.org**
**DrugWarFacts.org**
**Educators for Sensible Drug Policy**, EFSP.org
**End Prohibition, Canada**; EndProhibition.ca

Families Against Mandatory Minimums, FAMM.org
Family Council on Drug Awareness, FCDA.org
Forfeiture Endangers American Rights, Fear.org
Human Rights and the Drug War, HR95.org
International Harm Reduction Association, IHRA.net
Judges Against the Drug War, JudgesAgainstTheDrugWar.org

"For the past thirty years Judges have looked on as America's War on Drugs has played itself out before their eyes. They have seen the inevitable increase in police powers and erosion of civil rights needed to facilitate the investigation of drug offenses. They have witnessed the widespread, unprecedented use of asset forfeiture. And they have been forced to impose unjust mandatory minimum sentences.

Judges Against the Drug War is the first extensive online database of judicial opinions critical of the government's War on Drugs. Collected from state and federal jurisdictions from 1970 to the present date, these opinions contain the firsthand observations of judges presiding over drug cases and represent a unique historical record of judicial dissent against drug prohibition."

Law Enforcement Against Prohibition, LEAP.CC

LEAP is a 5,000-member organization created to: 1. Give voice to law enforcers who know the U.S. War on Drugs is a failed policy and 2. Support legalized regulation of drugs as an alternative that will lower incidence of death, disease, crime and addiction while saving tax dollars.

LEAP produced a documentary giving voice to those who have worked in the drug war and who are now against the failed policies of the War on Drugs.

"Anyone concerned about the failure of our $69 billion-a-year War on Drugs should watch this 12-minute program. You will meet front-line, ranking police officers who give us a devastating report on why it cannot work. It is a must-see for any journalist or public official dealing with this issue."
– Walter Cronkite

The Media Awareness Project, MAPInc.org
National Organization for the Reform of Marijuana Laws (NORML), NORML.org
National Organization for the Reform of Marijuana Laws, Canada, NORML.ca
The November Coalition, November.org
Online Library of Drug Policy, DrugLibrary.org
Oregon NORML, ORNRML.org
Safer Alternative for Enjoyable Recreation, SaferChoice.org; SaferDenver.com
Schaffer Library of Drug Policy, DrugLibrary.org/Schaffer/Index.htm
Students for Sensible Drug Policy, SSDP.org
Jeffrey Steinborn, attorney, PotBust.com
TaxAndRegulate.org
Veterans for More Effective Drug Strategies, VetsForMeds.org
The Voluntary Committee of Lawyers, VCL.org

# Hemp Companies, Organizations, and Issues

**Books:**
- *Building with Hemp*, by Steve Allin
- *The Emperor Wears No Clothes: The Authoritative Historical Record of Cannabis and the Conspiracy Against Marijuana,* by Jack Herer, JackHerer.com
- *Cannabis: A History*, by Martin Booth
- *The Great Book of Hemp: The Complete Guide to the Environmental, Commercial, and Medicinal Uses of the World's Most Extraordinary Plant,* by Rowan Robinson
- *Hemp for Health: The Medicinal and Nutritional Uses of Cannabis*, by Chris Conrad
- *Hemp Horizons: The Comeback of the World's Most Promising Plant*, by John W. Roulac
- *Hemp: Lifeline to the Future: The Unexpected Answer for Our Environmental and Economic Recovery,* by Chris Conrad
- *Hemp Masters – Getting Knotty: More Ancient Hippie Secrets for Knotting Hip Hemp Jewelry,* by Max Lunger
- *Substituting Agricultural Materials for Petroleum-Based Industrial Products*, Institute for Local Self-Reliance

**Documentary:**
- *The Emperor of Hemp,* directed by Jeff Jones, narrated by Peter Coyote. Tells the story of Jack Herer and the history of hemp. The DVD includes the U.S. Government's 1943 film for farmers, *Hemp for Victory*. JackHerer.com

**Boston Hemp Fest**, BostonHempFest.com

**Business Alliance for Commerce in Hemp**, EqualRights4All.org/BACH/BACHCore.html

**Campaign for the Restoration and Regulation of Hemp**, CRRH.org

**Canadian Hemp Trade Alliance**, HempTrade.ca

**DrBronner.com**

Produces hemp-based soaps and foods. They donate a portion of their profits to work to make hemp farming and hemp products legal. Their site contains interesting information about hemp and the government's unfair and unwise treatment of, and concern about, hemp.

Dr. Bronner's has spent loads of money to fight the U.S. Drug Enforcement Administration, which has foolishly worked to make hemp products illegal, and to keep industrial hemp illegal to grow in the U.S. In February 2005 the U.S. Court of Appeals for the Ninth Circuit ordered the DEA to pay $21,265 to Dr. Bronner's to compensate the company for the money Dr. Bronner's spent on legal fees to fight the DEA's dangerous drug war paranoia activities to outlaw products containing hemp.

**Happy Hippie Hemp Directory**, HappyHippie.com/Directory/HempRet.htm

**Hemp Advocates,** HempAdvocates.or

**HempBuilding.com**

**HempCar.org**

**The Hempen Road**, HempenRoad.com

**HempExpo.com**

**HempForVictory.BlogSpot.com**

**Hemp4Fuel.com**

**HempGuide.com**

**The Hemp Industries Association**, TheHIA.org
**HempIndustries.org**
**Hemp in History**, ArtisticTreasure.com/HempHistory.html
**Hemp in Japan**, Taima.org
**Hemp Lobby,** HempLobby.org
**HempMagazine.com**
**Hemp News**, THC-Foundation.org
**Hemp Oil Canada**, HempOilCan.com
**The Hemp Party**, HempEmbassy.net/HP2/Index.html
**HempReport.com**
**Hemp-Resources.com**
**HempStores.com**
**HempTimes.com**
**HempTraders.com**
**Hemp Wholesale Australia**, HempWa.com
**JackHerer.com**
**The Industrial Hemp Network**, HempTech.com
**International Hemp Association**, HempReport.com/IHA
**International Hemp Fair**, CannaTrade.ch
**Kentucky Hemp Museum**, KentuckyHemp.com
**Kentucky Hemp Outfitters**, KentuckyHemp.com
**Living Harvest Hemp Seed Nutrition**, LivingHarvest.com
**Manitoba Harvest,** ManitobaHarvest.com
**NaturalHighLifestyle.com**
**North American Industrial Hemp Council**, NAIHC.org
**OntarioHempAlliance.org**
**RuthsHempFoods.com**

"Hemp has been eaten for thousands of years in different parts of the world. It's the seed that we eat, and it's beneficial in terms of protein and essential fatty acids. People in Persia used to eat it, and they still do, actually. I know Iranians who grew up eating toasted hemp seeds. There's evidence that goes back thousands of years that it was being eaten in China and in different places around the world for those health benefits. Hemp has kind of had a renaissance starting in the early 90s. I was part of the lobby that helped to legalize or re-legalize hemp in Canada, which we accomplished in 1998 for commercial growth. Since then, I have been producing a line of hemp foods to spread the news and the nourishment of hemp.

... I've personally stood in a burning field of hemp, and if you wanted a buzz, you'd have to drink a beer."

– Ruth Shamai, owner of Ruth's Hemp Foods

**Seattle Hempfest,** HempFest.org, SeattleHempfest.com
**Southern Humboldt Hemp Fest**, 3Americas.org/Hempfest
**VoteHemp.com**

# Marijuana Issues

American Alliance for Medical Cannabis, LetFreedomGrow.com
Americans for Safe Access, SafeAccessNow.org
Artists Helping End Marijuana Prohibition, AHEMP.org
California Cannabis Research Medical Group, CCRMG.org
Californians for Compassionate Use, Marijuana.org
Canadian AIDS Society, CdnAIDS.ca
Canadian Cannabis Coalition, CannabisCoalition.ca/html/Index.php
Canadians for Safe Access, SafeAccess.ca
Cannabis As Living Medicine (CALM), CannabisClub.ca
Cannabis College, CannabisCollege.com
*Cannabis Health* journal, CannabisHealth.com
CompassionateMoms.org
ChrisConrad.com
ConvictionFree.com
DrugWarSurvival.com
End Prohibition, Canada; EndProhibition.ca
GrowingPlantsIsNotACrime.com
International Cannabinoid Research Society, CannabinoidSociety.org
London Cannabis Compassion Center, DrugSense.org/LCCC
Managing Chronic Pain, ManagingPain.org
TheMarijuanaMission.com
MarijuanaNews.com
Marijuana Policy Project, MPP.org
Marijuana the Forbidden Medicine, RxMarijuana.com
Medical Marijuana Mission, TheMarijuanaMission.com
Multidisciplinary Association for Psychedelic Studies, MAPS.org
National Organization for the Reform of Marijuana Laws, NORML.org
NORML.org
QuickTrading.com
The Science of Medical Marijuana, MedMJScience.org
Society of Cannabis Clinicians, CCRMG.org.html
Voter Power, VoterPower.org
WeedTracker.com
Wild Rose Seed Company, VancoverSeedBank.ca
The Wo/Men's Alliance for Medical Marijuana, WAMM.org
Women's Organization for National Prohibition Reform, WONPR.org

# Nuclear Proliferation

Office of Civilian Radioactive Waste Management, OCRWM.DOE.gov
Natural Resources Defense Council, nrdc.org
Nuclear Age Peace Foundation, WagingPeace.org
Nuke Watch, NukeWatch.com
Union of Concerned Scientists, UCSUSA.org

## Paper That Isn't from Trees

"Hemp produces more pulp per acre than timber on a sustainable basis, and can be used for every quality of paper. Hemp paper manufacturing can reduce wastewater contamination. Hemp's low lignin content reduces the need for acids used in pulping, and its creamy color lends itself to environmentally friendly bleaching instead of harsh chlorine compounds. Less bleaching results in less dioxin and fewer chemical byproducts.

Hemp fiber paper resists decomposition, and does not yellow with age when an acid-free process is used. Hemp paper more than 1,500 years old has been found.

The low impact of the farming and processing of hemp stalks and the high strength, length and yield of the bast fibers make hemp, a traditional source of high-strength specialty paper, a favorite in today's ecologically aware market. Pulp made from hemp's bast fiber is superior to short-fiber wood, and is an ideal additive to strengthen recycled post-consumer waste (PCW) pulp, thus expanding PCW's use. Tough and durable, hemp content paper can be finished to a smooth-surfaced sheet with as good as or better print qualities than virgin wood-based paper. The markets for hemp content paper are growing, including not only high-quality PCW printer paper, but also ecological product packaging, brochures and promotional materials for progressive businesses."

– Hemp Industries Association; TheHIA.org; HempIndustries.org

**Chlorine Free Products Association**, ChlorineFreeProductcs.org
**Earth Island Institute**, EarthIsland.org
**Ecosource Paper Inc.**, IslandNet.com/~Ecodette/EcoSource.htm
**Evanescent Press**, Tree.org
**FiberFutures.org**
**Forest Stewardship Council**, FSCOAX.org
**Living Tree Paper,** LivingTreePaper.com
**Old Growth Free**, OldGrowthFree.com
**Rainforest Action Network**, RAN.org
**Recycled Paper Coalition**, PaperCoalition.org
**WoodWise.org**

## Peak Oil

CultureChange.org
EclipseNow.org
EndOfSuburbia.com
FromTheWilderness.com
HubbertPeak.com
LifeAfterTheOilCrash.net
NewUrbanism.org
Odac-Info.com
OilAwareness.Meetup.com

OilCrash.com
PeakOilAction.org
PeakOil.net
Portland City Repair Project, CityRepair.org
PostCarbon.org
PowerFromSun.com
SurvivingPeakOil.com

# Pesticides

Pesticides are toxic chemicals designed to kill living things. They also lead to birth defects, learning disabilities and cancers in humans and animals.

Farmers who work on farms where pesticides are used are at the greatest risk, as are those who live in farm communities where the pesticides lurk in the air, land, and water. Children who live in farm communities where pesticides are used on nearby fields have higher than average rates of asthma and other ailments. People who work in the pesticide factories and those who live near the factories are also at risk.

When you purchase food, cosmetics, and fabrics, seek out those that have been grown without the use of pesticides.

BeyondPesticides.org
FoodNews.org
Mindfully.org/Pesticide
Pesticide Action Network International, PAN-International.org
Pesticide Action Network of North America, PANNA.org

# Prisoner Rights

"The United States has the highest prison population rate in the world, some 686 per 100,000 of the national population, followed by the Cayman Islands (664), Russia (638), Belarus (554), Kazakhstan (522), Turkmenistan (489), Belize (459), Bahamas (447), Suriname (437) and Dominica (420). However, more than three-fifths of countries (62.5 percent) have rates below 150 per 100,000. (The United Kingdom's rate of 139 per 100,000 of the national population places it above the midpoint in the World List; it is now the highest among countries of the European Union.)."
– Walmsley, Roy, *World Prison Population List, Fourth Edition*; London, England, UK: Home Office Research, Development and Statistics Directorate, 2003; page 1; HomeOffice.Gov.UK/RDS/PDFS2/R188.pdf

"Our findings indicate that being a woman prisoner in U.S. state prisons can be a terrifying experience. If you are sexually abused, you cannot escape from your abuser. Grievance or investigatory procedures, where they exist, are often ineffectual, and correctional employees continue to engage in abuse because they believe they will rarely be held accountable, administratively or criminally. Few people outside the prison walls know what is going on or care if they do know. Fewer still do anything to address the problem."

– Human Rights Watch, 2000, HRW.org

**Amnesty International,** AIUSA.org
**Anarchists Prisoner Legal Aid Network,** APLAN@Tao.ca
**Civil Liberties Defense Center,** CLDC.org
**Critical Resistance,** CriticalResistance.org
**Drug Policy Alliance,** DrugPolicy.org
**Earth Liberation Prisoner's Support Network,** SpiritOfFreedom.org.Uk
**Families Against Mandatory Minimums,** FAMM.org
**FlexYourRights.org**
**Human Rights Watch,** HRW.org
**InternationalExtradition.com**
**The Moratorium Campaign,** MoratoriumCampaign.org
**North American Earth Liberation Prisoners Support Network,**
NAELPSN@Tao.ca
**The November Coalition,** November.org
**Prison Activist Resource Center,** PrisonActivist.org
**Prison Dharma Network,** PrisonDharmaNetwork.org
**The Sentencing Project,** SentencingProject.org
**Stop Prisoner Rape,** SPR.org

## Solar Energy

**American Solar Energy Society,** ASES.org
*Home Power* **magazine,** HomePower.com
**International Solar Energy Society,** ISES.org
**Solar Energy Society of Canada,** SolarEnergySociety.ca
**Solar Living Institute,** SolarLiving.org

## Trees and Plants

"Every year an amount of land the size of Greece is logged – some 32 million acres... Deforestation both reduces biodiversity and increases the presence of greenhouse gasses in the atmosphere."
– Reuters, November 15, 2005

"Most of the world's most valuable forests, especially in the tropics, are vanishing as fast as ever."
– Simon Counsell, Rainforest Foundation, 2006

Help plant trees, protect native flora, and reclaim land for the wild that has been damaged by human activities. Help support at least one of the following groups.
**Action for Community and Ecology in the Rainforests of Central America;**
ACERCA.org
**Allegheny Defense Project,** AlleghenyDefense.org/
**American Chestnut Foundation,** ACF.org

**American Forests**, AmFor.org
**Ancient Trees, Citizen's Campaign for Old Growth Preservation**, AncientTrees.org
**Bay Area Coalition for Headwaters Forest**, HeadwatersPreserve.org/
**Botanic Gardens Conservation International**, BGCI.org
**Budongo Forest Project**, Budongo.org
**California Community Forests Foundation**, CalTrees.org
**California Native Plant Society**, CNPS.org
**Cascadia Rising EcoDefense**, CascadiaRising.org
**Cascadia Wild**, CascadiaWild.org
**Center for Native Ecosystems**, NativeEcosystems.org
**Center for Watershed Protection**, Pipeline.com/~mrRunOff/
**ChicagoWilderness.org**
**Children's Eternal Rainforest, Monteverde Conservation League**, ACMCR.org/Rain_Forest.htm
**Circle of Life Foundation**, CircleOfLifeFoundation.org
**Earth First!**, EarthFirstJournal.org
**Earth Watch Institute**, EarthWatch.org
**Eastern North American Native Forest Network**, Forests.org
**Forest Guardians**, FGuardians.org
**Forests Forever**, ForestsForever.org
**Forest Ethics**, ForestEthics.org
**Forest Voice**, ForestCouncil.org
**Fruit Tree Planting Foundation**, FTPF.org
**FutureForests.com**
**Gifford Pinchot Task Force**, GPTaskForce.org
**Granby Wilderness Society**, GrandbyWilderness.org
**Green Anarchy**, GreenAnarchy.org
**Green Korea United**, GreenKorea.org
**Greenpeace.org**
**Heartwood Forest Council**, Heartwood.org/ForestCouncil.htm
**Heritage Forests Campaign**, OurForests.org
**Illegal Logging at Suaq Balimbing**, http://www.Duke.Edu/~MYM1/Suaq.htm
**MangroveRestoration.com**
**Mattole Forest Defenders**, MattoleDefense.org
**Mountain Justice Summer**, MountainJusticeSummer.org
**The National Council for the Conservation of Plants and Gardens**, England, NCCPG.com
**National Forest Protection Alliance**, ForestAdvocate.org
**National Tree Society**, Natural-Connection.com/Institutes/National_Tree.html
**National Tropical Botanical Garden**, NTBG.org
**Native Forest Council**, ForestCouncil.org
**Native Forest Network**, NativeForest.org
**Natural Resources Defense Council, NRDC.org**
**Northern Nut Growers Association**, NorthernNutGrowers.org, or NutGrowing.org

**Pawpaw Foundation,** PawPaw.KYSU.Edu
**Theodore Payne Foundation,** TheodorePayne.org
**Plantlife International: The Wild Plant Conservation Charity,** Plantlife.org.UK
**Rainforest Action Network,** RAN.org
**Rainforest Foundation,** SaveTheRest.org
**Rainforest Alliance,** RA.org; Rainforest-Alliance.org
**RainForestPortal.org**
**Redwood Action Team,** Stanford.Edu/Group/RATS
**Save America's Forests,** SaveAmericasForests.org
**Save the Redwoods League,** SaveTheRedwoods.org
**Swamp Watch Action Team,** SwampWatch.org
**Tree Musketeers,** TreeMusketeers.org
**Tree People,** TreePeople.org
**Trees for Life,** TreesForLife.org
**Trees for the Future,** TreesFTF.org
**Trees Foundation,** TreesFoundation.org
**United Plant Savers,** UnitedPlantSavers.org
**TheWatershedProject.org**
**World Rainforest Information Portal,** RainforestWeb.org

John McCabe

## About the Author

John McCabe's first book was *Surgery Electives: What to Know Before the Doctor Operates*. First published in 1994, and now out-of-print, it was an exposé of the financial ties of the medical school, hospital, pharmaceutical, and health insurance industries whose unethical business practices result in the deaths of tens of thousands of people in the U.S. every year. The book was endorsed by some Congresspersons and by all of the patients' rights groups in North America.

McCabe also wrote a similar book specific for those considering cosmetic surgery. *Plastic Surgery Hopscotch* was published in 1995 and detailed many of the risks involved with the various surgeries, and in dealing with the medical industry in general.

In 2007 McCabe's *Sunfood Living: Resource Guide to Global Health* was published as a companion to David Wolfe's, *The Sunfood Diet Success System*. McCabe did research for and had helped to compose the first edition of *The Sunfood Diet Success System*. He worked as a content and research editor to overhaul the manuscript for the following five revised editions. He did the same on the first two editions of Wolfe's book *Eating for Beauty*. He was also the ghost co-author on Frederic Patenaude's recipe book, *Sunfood Cuisine*.

McCabe is also the author of the 2010 book, *Sunfood Traveler: Guide to Raw Food Culture, Restaurants, Recipes, Nutrition, Sustainable Living, and the Restoration of Nature*.

McCabe has been a content and research editor, and a ghost co-writer on books by other authors. He also has been involved in fostering writers, including screenplay writers. He is a screenplay consultant, polishing scripts in preparation for sale and/or filming.

McCabe is also the author of *Hemp: What the World Needs Now*. It details the history and uses of hemp, including the political and corporate corruption that lead to industrial hemp farming being outlawed in the U.S., which helped lead to the modern-day Drug War. His book explains why industrial hemp farming needs to be legalized freely in the U.S. and other countries to help build a more sustainable and self-sufficient society.

McCabe is the author of the 2010 book *Igniting Your Life*, an inspirational work combining wisdom quotations from throughout history with information on sustainable living, plant-based nutrition, and self-motivation. The foreword was written by Cherie Soria, Founder and Director of Living Light International, and author of *The Raw Food Revolution Diet*.

McCabe is also an artist and an environmental and wildlife activist. He encourages people to plant and protect trees and forests; to protect animals and wildlife habitat; to protect the environment; to walk or to ride a bike

435

instead of driving a car; to use cloth shopping bags instead of "paper or plastic"; to use biodegradable cleaning and otherwise environmentally-safe household products; to work against the genetic engineering of food; to stop the spread of nuclear energy and halt the creation of nuclear weaponry; to work to legalize industrial hemp farming so it can be made into paper, clothing, food, building materials, energy, biodegradable plastics, and other materials while supporting family farmers. (Access: VoteHemp.com)

McCabe advocates disconnecting from the corporate food chain by planting organic food gardens and supporting local organic farmers; and to live close to Nature by following a plant-based diet consisting of organically grown, non-GMO foods free of synthetic food additives, MSG (monosodium glutamate); fried oils; corn syrup and other processed sugars; and low-quality salt. (Access: FoodNotLawns.com)

IgnitingYourLife.com
SunfoodLiving.com
SunfoodTraveler.com
HempNowBook.com

**To contact the author:**
John McCabe
C/O: Carmania Books
POB 1272
Santa Monica, CA 90406-1272, USA

Think globally. Act locally.
Plant an organic food garden.
Compost your food scraps.
Follow a plant-based diet.
Plant massive amounts of trees.
Protect and restore the forests.
Get involved.
Support EarthFirst.org.
Support the Natural Resources Defense Council: Access: NRDC.org.
Get industrial hemp farming legalized in every country. VoteHemp.com.

"When the big trees are gone, the birds have no home and our children will not know the joy of their songs."
– Chief Filipe, Porvenir, Peru

"Don't expect politicians, even good ones, to do the job for you. Politicians are like weather vanes. Our job is to make the wind blow."
– David Brower, founder of Earth Island Institute; EarthIsland.org

Made in the USA
Lexington, KY
01 May 2011